Identity Politics in the Women's Movement

Identity Politics in the Women's Movement

EDITED BY

Barbara Ryan

New York University Press

NEW YORK AND LONDON

NEW YORK UNIVERSITY PRESS
New York and London

Library of Congress Cataloging-in-Publication Data
Identity politics in the women's movement / edited by Barbara Ryan.
p. cm.
Includes bibliographical references and index.
ISBN 0–8147–7478–4 (cloth : alk. paper) — ISBN 0–8147–7479–2 (pbk. : alk. paper)
1. Feminism.   2. Group identity.   3. Women—Identity.   I. Ryan, Barbara, 1942–

HQ1154 .I43 2001
305.42—dc21   2001032636

New York University Press books are printed on acid-free paper,
and their binding materials are chosen for strength and durability.

Manufactured in the United States of America

10 9 8 7 6 5 4 3 2 1

In memory of
Bill Phillips

Who knew a thing or two about identity
and politics

Contents

Acknowledgments

I have many people to thank for the help they provided to this project. Before engaging in this work, I had little to no awareness of the difficulties before me. It had always seemed to me that editing a book was easy: you just take other people's work, put it together in a meaningful collection, and perhaps write an introduction. That was it. Little did I know.

This work came about as the result of an inquiry from Niko Pfund, editor in chief of New York University Press. Niko asked me if I would meet with him during the American Sociological Association meeting in Washington, D.C. in 1996. My paper there was titled "How Much Can I Divide Thee, Let Me Count the Ways: Identity Politics in the Women's Movement." Niko liked the title and idea behind it and wondered if I had any plans for going further with it. I thought the only possible thing would be a collection of readings in which women wrote about their experiences and thoughts on identity politics. He agreed and asked me to put together a proposal for consideration. Some five years later, this book is the result of that initial conversation.

Niko left NYU Press for Oxford University Press a few months before I turned in the final product. After he left, I was introduced to my new editor, Jennifer Hammer. Niko had never rushed me, even as months went by. But Jennifer did. Somehow she must have sensed she was working with a person who required firm deadlines (even though I hate them). One e-mail to me said, "I need the finished product NOW." That weekend I completed the introduction to each section. In spite of my reservations about a new editor and particularly losing Niko, with whom I had developed an easy relationship, I found Jennifer to be a wonderful editor. In none of my previous books had I been given the opportunity to reject two book covers and to have the input she allowed. We are both pleased with the final cover and thank the graphic artists who worked on each cover submitted.

Many thanks go to Widener University, particularly Provost Buck and the Faculty Grants and Awards Committees for the Provost Grants, and Dean Panek for the Faculty Development Awards that allowed me to hire student workers over these years. I have a long list of the many tasks these student workers did for me: photocopying, completing interlibrary loan orders, handling correspondence, filing, reading, writing brief descriptions, conducting Internet searches, and bringing order (or a semblance thereof) to my highly disordered office. Thank you Monica Dickerson, Tom McFarlane, Nancy Lewis, Wendy Shepard, and Jennifer D' Antonio.

To the many editors, permission officers, and other affiliated staff of journals, magazines, and books, I appreciate your efforts. The amount of correspondence and phone calls undertaken for this project were extensive. Some I negotiated fees with, almost all agreed to payment upon publication, there were those whom I contacted but then decided against using the article I was considering, some contacts were quick and easy, most were not. Journals were sometimes no longer in existence or had been taken over by another company. Old publishers did not always have the information to steer me in a new direction. Authors were not always still living where their publishers listed them and locating them was left to me. Here I turned to two list serves where I hoped to gain the information I needed, SWS list (Sociologists for Women in Society) and wmst-l (monitored by Joan Korenman at the University of Maryland). Thanks to the many people who responded to my inquiries on both of those lists.

Thanks most of all to the authors of this collection. Your patience has been gratifying. In the middle of doing this work I went on a Fullbright to India, and upon my return I appreciated the fact that although many contributors had corresponded with me regarding the status of the book, they seemed to accept my perennial delays. Most of the work I edited, both original pieces and those published previously. I thank the authors for the agreements we were able to reach between their thoughts and my needs for space considerations. Some articles I was not able to get because of problems in finding people or negotiating the permission fee. The articles that made it to the final selection stage came from a much larger list of readings. I am satisfied and happy to note that they capture the essence of what identity politics is about, for good and for bad.

And finally to my friends, colleagues, and family: David, Carla, Michael, Ryan, Paul, and Kristen Harris, Jeanne and Scott Smith, Edith Ryan, Mary Ann Randell, Joseph DeMarco, Krystyna Warchol, Janet Rosenberg, Pat Benson, Donna Theis, Geneie Williamson-Dowling, Myra Marx Ferree, John Zipp, Ronnie Steinberg, Joan Spade, Marian Fox, David Ward, Ilene Lieberman, Barbara Norton, Kathy Mason, and the many others who have graced my life. I thank you for sustaining me in all the ways you do.

Introduction

Identity Politics: The Past, the Present, and the Future

Barbara Ryan

What is identity? Is identity recognition of a shared characteristic that enables a solidarity with members of a group? And does it conversely entail distance from those who lack this common feature? Or, is identity a social construction that ebbs and flows, is always in process, multilayered, and fragmented? What is gender? As a defining identity, does it fit the former or the latter conceptualization?

These questions are at the heart of understanding how identity politics affects social movements and, in particular for this book, the women's movement. The women's movement is a gender-focused movement. Yet, within the category of women there are other identities that work to keep women from recognizing gender commonalties. For instance, living in a largely segregated society, women of color feel a bonding with men of color that they do not usually feel with white women (Bell-Scott 1994; Collins 1990; Dill 1983; Fleming 1993; McKay 1993). Likewise, studies of lesbian feminist communities reveal the positive aspects of joining together to find acceptance and emotional support where it is lacking in the straight world (Franzen 1993; Kreiger 1982, 1983; Taylor and Whittier 1992).

Proponents of identity politics believe it important to affiliate with those who confront similar experiences based on social group characteristics. Members of an oppressed group may organize to change their situation, as well as their feelings of self-worth and place in the social structure. Hence, social characteristics that have been used to exclude certain groups have led to social movements organized by those groups to change their condition.

Critics of identity politics assert that it leads to further marginalization and that it prevents uniting with those who are working on similar issues but who differ in physical/social features (Gitlin 1993). Class, too, is left out of this analysis, as are differences within groups, which may have everyday practical consequences (Allison 1993). Indeed, Hall (1996:4–5) argues that unities based on essentialist identities are constructed within the dynamics of power and exclusion, "and thus are more the product of the marking of difference and exclusion, than they are the sign of a naturally constituted unity." And problematically, as Grossberg (1996:88) points out, groups organized around their own model of repression often lack the capability of creating alliances with others.

The selections in this book explore arguments both in favor of and opposed to separate organizing based on identity factors of and beyond gender. These papers look at the role of identity for creating group distinctions, the relationship between identity politics and new social movement theory, the effects of the loss of class analysis, and the overall impact of essentialism on the women's movement.

The articles cover a broad range of identity claims, including gender, race, class, sexual orientation, sexual practice, ethnicity, religion, age, occupation, disability, and politics. They employ a variety of writing styles, ranging from personal narrative to empirical research. The first section lays out the critiques of identity politics, and is followed by two sections discussing why identity claims are necessary. These initial sections lay the groundwork for understanding the debate; subsequent chapters cover types of identity claims, successful attempts to work with diverse interests, and a look to the future.

Critiques

Postmodern thought sees identity as a process rather than a fact or deterministic force. Yet, recognizable identity traits continue to draw people together and to provide them with support for attempting social change. This means identity and identity politics are serious contenders in the political process and social movement arenas.

Eric Hobsbawm (1996) points out that in the late 1960s the *International Encyclopedia of the Social Sciences* had no entry under identity. Thus, Hobsbawm sees identity politics as a recent phenomenon. He also sees it as a problematic category. First, he argues that a collective identity is defined against others and is based not on what their members have in common but, rather, on differences between them when, in fact, "we" may have little in common except not being the "others." Second, no one has only a single identity; yet, identity politics leads one to disclaim other identities. And finally, identities are not fixed—they depend on contexts, which can change.

Hobsbawm places his discussion of identity politics within a claim of universalism of the Left. He is particularly partisan to the Labour Party in Britain, the party of class, of "equality and social justice" (1996:42). In applying Hobsbawm's work to the women's movement, it is striking to note that he does not consider gender (or race and sexual orientation) as legitimate identities separate from class. Nevertheless, he presents a critique of identity politics that raises important points.

Todd Gitlin (1995), like Hobsbawm, calls for a Left politics based on class position. However, his analysis is somewhat different, fashioned on a contemporary and North American model. According to Gitlin, the most serious and negative identity politics is white men who fear identity gains will come at their expense. But he is also opposed to identity politics in general because he feels it cultivates unity only within special groups, and there is an obsession with difference leading to the "borders identity politics draws" (severson and stanhope 1998).

Rather than organizing to reduce inequalities between rich and poor, Gitlin argues that identity politics struggles to change the color of inequality. And, what we need to be doing, instead, is to tend mutualities. Identity politics, according to Gitlin, (1995:236) has failed to tend and, even worse, has left the centers of power uncontested.

Gitlin calls for a Left politics that includes everyone, a common—a cause of all. Although his argument is compelling in many ways, he barely mentions gender. Socialist feminists in the 1960s and 1970s explicitly pointed out how the inclusion of "all" in the Left of their day did not include them. When leftist writers in the late 1990s have little to say specifically to gender, are we to believe them? Does commonality leave women's "difference" out? Is leftist universalism like postmodern and deconstructionist analysis, wiping away all difference, even denying there is difference because there is no reality? Does identity politics as we know it in the women's movement leave the centers of power uncontested? These questions raised by leftist scholars present serious critiques of identity politics.

Feminist analysis also contains critiques of identity politics. Daphne Patai (1992), for instance, discusses the zealousness of feminist adherents to control thought and appearance, what she calls "ideological policing." Patai objects to the assumption that one's racial/ethnic identity is the same as one's views. Even more, she believes there has been a reversal of privilege, now residing with women of color, in which no white person can challenge their version of reality. These inclinations have led to concern for the "dogmatic turn" identity politics has presented to women's studies. In her experience, *Eurocentric* became a slur and teaching courses on other racial/ethnic groups was not accepted of a North American white.

Further, Patai (1992:B3) questions the ways identity politics gets used in a scarce job market, calling it "the fraud that accompanies familiar old ambitions dressed up in appropriate ideology." Patai feels distress that these tendencies have arisen and, even more, that they are not discussed. Instead, identity politics has led to silencing. She considers her writing on these issues to be a defense of feminism.

Others also point to problems within feminism, particularly the focus on personal experience, which may have isolated the women's movement from more general social change struggles. Often, rather than oppression's being fought in the wider society, struggles are being fought on local levels (Adams 1989). L. A. Kauffman (1990) takes a more nuanced look at identity politics, dividing it into political and nonpolitical frameworks. Kauffman dates the beginning of identity politics not with black women's challenge to sisterhood but to the civil rights movement of Martin Luther King and the Black Power movement, where activists called for a new collective identity to offset white imperialism. In turning to the women's movement, Kauffman credits Kate Millett's *Sexual Politics* (1970) with defining gendered power as politics—structured relationships whereby one group controls another. In the 1980s and 1990s, though, she fears identity politics has evolved into fragments where "the notion of solidarity, so central to any progressive politics" is lost (Kauffman 1990:76).

Kauffman (1990:78) makes the point that the increasing movement of self-transformation (as political change) leads to thinking that problems are attitudes rather than power differentials and vested interests. Like Patai, she sees this leading to an emphasis on lifestyle (who one reads, what one eats or wears) rather than on the actions one takes. Still, Kauffman calls for using identity as entry to challenging institutions of power, and as politics intent upon both social and individual transformation.

A central issue of importance is whether difference has displaced inequality as a central concern of social movements. As Anne Phillips (1997) points out, an *injustice* perspective seeks to eliminate differentiation used against powerless groups, and *difference* perspectives are intent on highlighting these identities. She cites the dilemma between strategies that are meant to diminish the significance of gender and strategies that focus on the intrinsic worth of one's sex.

Hazel Carby (1990) adds another perspective when she questions whether the emphasis on diversity in feminist thought and practices is a way to avoid the politics of race, even as it appears that race is being confronted. Similarly, the disjunction between inclusive feminism and the reality of the organizations that make up the women's movement raises the crucial point "on whose behalf" inclusive ideologies are meant (Leidner 2001).

Identity Claims

In spite of critical questions associated with identity politics, there are important rationales for the development of a politics of identity, beginning with *The Second Sex,* Simone de Beauvoir's (1953) classic work. Her introduction sets the tone, unveiling a gendered identity politics by calling women "the other." By this, she means that women have failed to identify themselves as a group because they are considered a part of man (the subject) and, thus, are not segregated into their own group, as are some racial and ethnic groups. They have no history or religion that is particularly their own. She calls for women to see themselves as a group in order to change their situation.

De Beauvoir's writings inspired a collective conscience of women, which laid the foundation for the reemergence in the 1960s of women's activism in their own behalf. Yet, by the early 1980s, writings by women of color spoke to the need to claim an identity of their own. They formulated a base for organizing around that identity, even if it separated women from one another. The Combahee River Collective, a group of black feminists and forerunner to this claim, began meeting in 1974. They issued the first statement on black feminism, twelve years after the contemporary women's movement emerged and many more years after the U.S. publication of *The Second Sex*. The statement combined gender and race identity. Black women proclaimed the task of combating simultaneous oppressions as theirs because other movements failed to acknowledge their specific oppression. They named what they were doing "identity politics" based on their conclusion that "the only people who care enough about us to work consistently for our liberation are us" (Combahee River Collective 1978:275).

How did white feminists react to this challenge? Some were angry or dismissive. Some had already reached this awareness. Others welcomed it. Still others struggled with their past and worked to become multicultural in their feminist thought and actions, even as this became a painful process of stripping away their own identity, deciding what to keep, what to eliminate, what to change (Pratt 1984). This difficult process involved the acknowledgment of another's existence while not denying one's own. For instance, Minnie Bruce Pratt (1984:73) describes her fears as she tries to understand herself in "relation to folks different from me, when there are discussions, conflicts about anti-Semitism and racism among women, criticisms, criticisms of me; when, for instance in a group discussion about race and class, I say I feel we have talked too much about race, not enough about class, and a woman of color asks me in anger and pain if I don't think her skin has something to do with class."

Part of the problem in understanding "other worlds" is that women grow up learning different gender roles. For example, in many Native American groups women are strong and valued (Allen 1995), whereas other women have had to work at developing that consciousness. And having acquired an ideology of strength and independence, what happens if you become disabled or when you grow old (Kline 1992)?

Multiple Identities and Changing Identities

An obvious complexity within the field of identity politics is the reality of multiple identities, including those we are in the process of becoming or losing. Audre Lorde, (1984a:41) who called upon women to speak—"your silence will not protect you"—used her life as an example of how we can rid ourselves of others' distortions by reclaiming all our identities so we can define them for ourselves.

As a forty-nine-year-old black lesbian socialist feminist, who was also a mother of two and part of an interracial couple, Lorde discussed her many group identities, including acquired identities that did not fit into acceptable society. This makes life difficult, and yet, she notes it is oppressed people who are expected to bridge the gap between their differences with more privileged groups. Lorde asserted that it is not the differences among us that separate us; it is the refusal to recognize the differences. An example she cites is the idea of "sisterhood." In a famous quote, she tells us: "Some problems we share as women, some we do not. You fear your children will grow up to join the patriarchy and testify against you, we fear our children will be dragged from a car and shot down in the street, and you will turn your backs upon the reasons they are dying" (Lorde 1984b:119).

In applying a wide lens, Lorde also talked about differences within black communities. Where racism is a living reality, differences within groups seem dangerous and suspect. The need for unity is often misnamed as a need for homogeneity, and a black feminist vision mistaken for betrayal. There is a refusal of some black women to recognize and protest against their oppression as women within the black community and of heterosexual women against lesbians, particularly among black women. She urged women to identify with one another and develop new ways of being in this world and new ways for this world to be. For, as she tells us, "the master's tools will never dismantle the master's house" (Lorde 1984b:123). In line with Lorde's analysis of divisions within groups, Marilyn Frye (1992) makes clear that even in what appears to be a cohesive commonality (in this case a lesbian community) there are substantial differences that must be acknowledged and worked through.

The necessity for claiming more than one identity is also true for Chicanas (Nieto 1997), Asians (Shah 1994), and women in developing countries. Like African American women, members of these racial/cultural groups often find U.S. feminism's focus on male/female relations alienating because they, too, are working against multiple oppressions of gender, class, race, and nationalism. But they add a difference to the experiences of African American women, where much of identity politics has been focused, and that is invisibility, which, for them, is another form of oppression (Friedman 1995). Moreover, not all Third World women are women of color and not all women of color are Third World or poor. Hispanic women have reported experiencing racism through the rejection of black sisters because of being light skinned (Quintanales 1983), and class is a dividing agent among women of all nationalities and races.

Regardless of the identity issues that may divide them, feminists are concerned that in the rush to acknowledge and celebrate difference, the relations of power that create that difference are often ignored. Women of color, in particular, find the current popularity of diversity rhetoric all too often offers a decontextualized politics of difference, which turns out to be another way of preserving stratified social arrangements (Aguilar 1995).

In another vein, Carol Queen (1997) voices an unwelcome (at least for some) claim to feminist identity. Queen finds that sex radicals (regardless of race, class, ethnicity, or sexual orientation) have been silenced in the women's movement. She questions what it is that separates women who are opposed to sex work from those who do it, and why feminism does not take a more thoughtful look at this divide. She asks feminists to confront their "whorephobia" and agree to a dialogue, for she believes women have much to learn from sex workers.

The complexity of multiple identities is poignantly voiced by June Jordan (1985). From a vacation experience in the Bahamas she finds that, compared to the Bahamian people, she is a rich American woman. She is dismayed to find herself, as well as other black Americans (and whites), arguing prices on handmade items. Jordan uses this story to raise awareness of the complex interplay of race, class, and gender identity. She notes that she and the women workers are engaged in interactions that preclude seeing themselves as a united group of women. Jordan wonders how women are to connect with such different life circumstances, particularly when many women do not feel poor women's issues of poverty and crime are theirs. She asks, "Why aren't they everyone's?"

Jordan's story shows that race, class, and gender are not automatic paths of connection; there are differences within identities that have been imposed.

Voices of African American Women

It was African American women in the early 1980s, more than any other group, who confronted the women's movement on identity politics issues. There was a desire for a more pluralistic approach to "sisterhood" that recognized similarities and differences among women (Dill 1983). Bernice McNair Barnett (1995:207) makes the interesting and telling remark that the barring of black women from the League of Women Voters in Montgomery, Alabama, showed that "it was white women, rather than black women, who placed their primary emphasis on race over gender." She also points out that the 1940s and 1950s were not a period of "doldrums" for women activists, as has been claimed for the women's movement (see Rupp and Taylor 1987). These were years of activism for black women in the civil rights movement, a movement dedicated to issues of freedom and equality.

Taking a different approach, Barbara Smith (1983) succinctly discusses the reasons feminism frightens black and Third World men and why they resist it. In her introduction to *Home Girls,* an early contribution to writings by black women, Smith shows why black women need a movement of their own. Revealing another perspective some ten years later, Ann duCille (1994) wonders if the effort to promote black women's lives has not gone too far. As a black woman who has long studied black women, she acknowledges having mixed feelings about this rise of "the occult of black womanhood." For instance, she questions the career-enhancing path women academics, white and black, have gained by claiming a "new" specialness for women of color and those who focus on them.

New questions are raised, such as looking at white middle-class women who are "housewives" to their husbands and the black working-class domestics they employ (Kaplan 1995). Both groups of women are in roles of serving others, but the white women exist with race and class privilege by means of their domestics. One conclusion, which can be drawn from this relationship, is that white women collude with the patriarchal/capitalist system that oppresses women. Another conclusion is that domestic workers enable white middle-class women to avoid confronting their spouses about sharing household duties (Kaplan 1995:81). Moreover, household help releases the middle-class woman to become a woman of leisure or to have a career. The ways that women treat other women (using domestics as an example) may help explain why many black women stay away from the (white) feminist movement.

Sexuality and Sexualities

A second area of identity contestation centers on questions of sexual orientation and preference. One of the onerous aspects of heterosexual society is the normative expectation of appropriate sexual behavior that excludes homosexuality, bisexuality, sadomasochism, or transsexuality. Dichotomous thinking, rather than a continuum model of sexual identity, had long been critiqued within the feminist movement, yet it arose in the 1980s among lesbian feminists. These divisions revealed that there are exclusions and antagonisms among gays that differ from the full acceptance of sexual expression found in queer theory or, in the past, in the lesbian concept of the "woman-identified woman" (Radicalesbians 1970).

One challenge to agreed-upon thought was the deconstruction of commonly held views of sex workers, that is, to see them as workers deserving of workers' rights. Women in unions, armed with feminist ideologies, concretely address many of the issues of the women's movement—sexual harassment, maternity benefits, parental leave, and comparable worth (Chernow and Moir 1995). Yet, in the debates over prostitution and pornography, feminists who have argued for other women workers have not taken up these workers' cause (Alexander 1997).

There are differences within lesbianism, within feminism, and even within radical feminism. Eileen Bresnahan (2001) humorously relates an incident where the "original" radical feminists (with roots in the Left) collided with newer radical feminists, who were called cultural feminists. She laments the shift away from political process to lifestyle affirmation that she saw occurring in the mid-1970s. For her, this shift left an ambiguous meaning of radical feminism and was also a departure from the past, when being a radical feminist meant that one accepted definite agreed-upon principles of radical politics. Bresnahan explains her distrust of cultural feminism as the end product of her seriousness about feminist identity. She states that because "I'm a working-class woman who grew up in the 1950s and 1960s, the women's movement was the first time I took myself seriously and the first time I was taken seriously by others whom I could also respect." Thus, the challenge to agreed-upon thought was unwelcome in her mind and in her radical feminist circle.

What is a lesbian—who counts—is a continuing theme of sexuality inquiry. Divisions are found among lesbian feminists based on bisexuality, dress, associations, s/m practices, gender roles, and transgendered people. The 1970s woman-identified women represented a sisterhood against the patriarchy; 1990s lesbians aligned with gay men. Young lesbians have focused more on sex than political theory and often call themselves queer or "bad girls" rather than lesbians. These generational differences have led to clashes between lesbian feminism and queer ideologies. Problematically, these clashes have also raised charges of who is a real or fake lesbian, for example, what if you have a heterosexual past? The essentialism (true lesbian) of the 1970s is now confronted with more than one model for lesbian behavior. And even though this may seem confusing, as Vera Whisman (1993:58) says, "[T]he truth is, most of us sometimes feel incredibly queer, at other times indelibly female."

One highly contested issue that has created division among lesbian feminists is sadomasochism. Shane Phelan considers it a mistake for activists to get involved in arguments of this kind, an issue that is rooted in the identity politics of what feminism is. By this, she does not mean that identity politics should be abandoned; rather, she asks that we be more careful in distinguishing "the sorts of identity issues that are vital to our growth and freedom from those that are not" (Phelan 1989:133).

Other, more "acceptable" divisions among lesbians have been identified as class, age, and ideology. Trisha Franzen discovered that lesbian-feminist university students considered the butch/fem roles played by many working-class-bar lesbians to be tainted with heterosexuality. Thus, she argues that "sexuality is a problematic basis for political solidarity among women" (Franzen 1993:903). A similar dispute occurred at the Michigan Womyn's Music Festival over the admittance of transsexuals. In researching this issue, Joshua Gamson (1997:183) argues that identity requires difference and that building collective identities requires not simply pointing out commonalties but also marking off "who we are not." He finds these acts to be the boundary patrol of identity politics.

From these examples we can see that sexual identities and political affiliations often shift and are always contingent (Whisman 1993:58). Hence, we can no longer assume what the foundation of identical politics presumes; that is, the idea that identity groups, in this case lesbians, share an identity and therefore a politics. Even more pointed at the turn of the twenty-first century is to recognize that sexual identity, indeed all identities, are more provisional than most people realize. As Arlene Stein (1997) discussed in her research on ex-lesbians, there was a restructuring of the identity process based on situational factors that some feminists went through as they moved into lesbianism in the 1970s and out of it by the 1980s.

More Diversities — More Identities

While major divisions have arisen over issues of race and sexual diversity, there are other gender-plus identities that confront the women's movement. There is the issue of Jewish feminists and their place in the movement (Beck 1988), of age from the older woman's perspective (Macdonald 1995), as well as of the younger feminist viewpoint (Dietzel 1999; Heywood and Drake 1997; Looser and Kaplan 1997; Walker 1992). Inclusion itself has been questioned. For instance, Rosa María Pegueros (2001) reports on her own experience as a Latina activist in the National Organization for Women (NOW). Achieving a high, visible position, she questions what that means for her. Is she a token, a traitor to her group, or an accepted member of a feminist elite (and does she want this)? What she has to say raises questions about the sincerity of inclusion some groups are promoting.

And, what of men? How does being a male feminist affect one's identity? There is the possibility that male feminism may be seen as a traitorous identity, indeed, traitorous perhaps to both men and women (Bettie 2001). Although it is self-evident that not all men are powerful, there is a danger in pointing out how men, too, are oppressed. This can be seen as a denial of the history and meaning of gender power relations. De-essentializing identity categories may be a necessary corrective to the conventional application of identity politics, but we must be careful not to become, then, an identity skeptic, refusing to recognize gender, race, and other identities (Bettie 2001).

Cutting across identity concerns is always the issue of class and class transformation. Moving from the working class to the middle class does not mean one has left all vestiges of one's background behind. Class has not been adequately explored in identity politics, perhaps because of the simultaneous desire to both reject and to retain this cultural identity. The challenge is to maintain a vigilant awareness of the inherent power these relations present while guarding against incorrect parallelisms, which can erase the political histories of difference (Bettie 2001).

The history of division within women's studies is legendary. Indeed, one could say that women's studies is itself identity politics (Perry 1995). Yet, in spite of the contentious debates over the category of women in the academy, the term *woman* has not been so starkly problematized in the larger society. Women of all races, ethnicity, sexual orientation (and preferences) are disadvantaged in a society that does not value women.

There are other divisions among women that are not covered in these readings. Women in revolutions, prisons, and armed services, and those living in rural areas are not found in this book. What is their relationship to other women and to feminism? What about differences between single and married women? Or those with or without children?

Divisions are often magnified when we begin to talk of global feminism and organizing transnationally to unite women from around the world. In Yemen in 2000, the Women's Studies Program at San'a University was closed down and the director fled the country because of the use of the word *gender* (Abu-nasr 2000). In Kuwait, women continue to be told they are not to be allowed the vote. How can women join together in India, where women are divided by caste? In what ways can Muslim women organize when ideas of a constructed gender identity are considered a Western concept? There is fear that a transnational unity of women might raise a counterargument, and perhaps repression, from conservative and religious forces that have used biological determinism in order to maintain gender segregation.

At the same time, within countries, it must be recognized that the ideological and political realities women face limits the kinds of issues that can be raised. For instance, Raka Ray (1999) studied women's activism in Bombay and Calcutta, two cities that are similar in many ways. Both have colonial histories where British influence was substantial. The legacy of colonialism is a distinct class of Western-educated citizenry, along with the more common profile of the deep poverty experienced by most of the population. Although Bombay is more prosperous than Calcutta, in general the socioeconomic conditions are more alike than different. The demographic characteristics of sex ratio, marriage age, household size, female literacy, marital status, slum population, and religious affiliation are nearly the same. There is a female labor force difference, although not a consequential one. In Calcutta the official rate is 7 percent; in Bombay, 11 percent. In other words, in neither location does one find high rates of women's labor force participation outside the informal sector, where pay is low and workers are undercounted in official statistics.

Why, then, does the women's movement in these cities differ to such a great extent? Ray's cogent analysis points to differences in political fields. Calcutta is ruled by the Communist Party of India (Marxist), and the government is marked by a centralized dominant power structure. To wit, Calcutta, through the CPI (M) has a hegemonic political field. The largest and most viable women's organization is the women's wing of the party; and "women's issues" such as dowry and kitchen fires are not raised because they do not affect "human" problems, class relations, or the economy. Approved issues are jobs, clean water, poverty, or literacy. Feminist (a maligned term) concerns that address women's subordination or appear to challenge patriarchal power are not legitimate political issues. An autonomous women's organization was able to be feminist but lacked the ability to be heard. In Calcutta's homogenous political culture, there is constraint from above.

With a dispersed political field and heterogeneous political culture in Bombay, the most powerful women's organization, Forum for the Oppression of Women (the Forum), is politically autonomous. The women's wing of the CPI(M) is in a much weaker position. Rather than one dominant political party, there are three main contenders for rule: the Congress, a nationalist right-wing Hindu party, and various coalitions on the Left. In Bombay, there is little to be gained by joining with a political party. Feminist groups raise their own issues; they are free to push for change on the personal, economic, and social levels. Strong social movement activism has been generated around issues of sex-selection abortions (Ray [1999] cites one report of 7,999 out of 8,000 abortions occurring after amniocentesis determined female fetuses), violence against women, and gender equality.

A telling difference in activists' descriptions of rape are the Calcutta feminists' causal explanation of poverty or abnormality compared to the Forum's analysis of rape as "an instrument of power used by all men to keep all women in their place" (Ray 1999:127).

Overcoming Identity Divisions

As difficult as identity politics can be, there are many stories of confronting, and sometimes overcoming, divisions among women activists, particularly if we are drawn back to the highly Eurocentric ways of early international women's groups. Leadership came solely from Western Europe and North America, and attitudes expressed Western societies as "the pinnacle of progress for women in contrast to backward 'Eastern' ways" (Rupp 1996:10). Leaders believed that the women's cause was the same everywhere; they were, in essence, promoting the first ideals of a flawed "sisterhood." Decisions to hold conferences were always considered within the leaders' own boundaries in order to realize a smaller burden in terms of travel, time, and money even as they maintained that they were interested in recruiting women from less advanced nations in order to make their organization truly international.

After many such oversights, they did try to recruit autonomous groups from other countries; however, in bringing in women from around the world they also brought in nationalistic disputes, such as that between Palestinian and Israeli women. Women from developing countries, once they did participate, began to challenge imperialism. In these ways, these activists began the dialogue of difference and identity among women early this century.

Successes have been obtained in small countries with limited resources, which require coalition work and the necessity of crossing class and racial divides, which exist in every country. These efforts have worked across geographical and nationalistic barriers in Latin America, in spite of nationalistic conflicts, on the basis of the common oppression of women in these countries (Carillo 1990). In Latin America, it was necessary for women to form an independent women's movement, separate from the Left, which had always considered women's role in social change efforts to be secondary; it was also necessary to organize separately from European and North American women in order to form a movement on their own terms. Clearly, building alliances with Third World and industrialized countries must be premised on maintaining respect for others' insights and perceptions (Carillo 1990).

Awareness and inclusion means more than opening one's doors; there is the necessity for people to represent themselves. How can we know about people different from ourselves unless we make it possible for them to speak (and us to listen)? Do we need to experience their lives to understand them or to care? International activists and organizations for cross-cultural exchanges promote understanding and empathy. The motto of the 1995 NGO Forum on Women, "Look at the World Through Women's Eyes," captures this necessity, as did the 30,000 women from 180 countries who traveled to Beijing because they believed in a basic commonality among women (Grandia 2001).

On a more local and temporal level, the same dynamic of mutual respect applies, for, in spite of the difficulty of working for diversity in planning an annual event, such inclusion serves as a vehicle for bringing together representation of many groups (Corman 2001). In dealing with inclusion issues, Diane Fowlkes (2001) has found that one way to work through each issue as it arrives anew, is to think of yourself as a spider, entrapping knowledge from others and remaking your web of life over and over again.

By linking the philosophical notions of individualism and privacy with the tension that ideology creates for communitarian ideals, Shane Phelan (1989) finds that adherence to rigid ideologies creates strains and limitations on people's lives. This, then, is a warning that the failure to deal with difference leads to the loss of individuality and even the notion of community. Feminists from many different identity locations call for women to accept their differences and identify with one another to make the changes they each desire (see Bunch 1995; Davis 1995; Lorde 1984c; Phelan 1989).

Maintaining both identity and community is a quest for each person to address herself or himself. After all, who is to tell someone else what her or his identity is or should be, or where individual activism should be placed? Identity does not prevent unity around issues of common concern. Nor does identity prevent activism on issues that do not affect one personally. Coalition work, joining together while maintaining separate identities, can work, has worked, and in the wave of the future, must work. No one has real community when others are shut out or their related issues are ignored (Ryan 2001). This same theme is emphasized by Adrienne Rich (1986) when she asks the next generation of women activists a simple but crucial question: If not with others, how?

The United Nations Conference on Women reveals the vitality and unity that can and did occur among nongovernmental organizations (NGOs) at the Beijing Conference in 1995. This conference demonstrated that women from all over the world could share their experiences and work for change in their own countries and on a worldwide scale (Sears 1996). The same interactive spirit was shown at the 1993 Vienna Tribunal, where women from diverse countries gave similar accounts, with differing particulars, to show United Nations judges that women's rights are human rights (Bunch 1995). Violence against women was a continuing theme that brought home the connection between kitchen fires in India and wife battering in Venezuela, clitoridectomy in Africa and anorexia in the United States. Suffrage struggles of the past show the same demand for citizenship in countries from every continent.

These stories and contributions to this book celebrate how much was accomplished in the twentieth century, even as there is still much to do. Yet, even as the current inclination is to talk of globalization, let us not forget that it is at the local level that the global has effects, and "if we do not closely understand the dynamics of the local, we fall once again into the trap of universalizing and homogenizing" (Ray 1999:166).

The readings in the last section are hopeful accounts, offering the promise of a new century in which women act together to create a better life for women of every nationality, social characteristic, and sociocultural persuasion. Their activism is for themselves, as well as for men, children, the earth, and the creatures in it—this world we all share. And, it is quite certain they will do this without compromising their sense of knowing who they are.

REFERENCES

Abu-nasr, Donna. 2000. "Gender Controversy Shuts Down Women's Studies Program in Yemen." *Philadelphia Inquirer,* May 21, p. A14.

Adams, Mary Louise. 1989. "There's No Place Like Home: On the Place of Identity in Feminist Politics." *Feminist Review* 31 (Spring):22–33.

Aguilar, Delia D. 1995. "What's Wrong with the 'F' Word?" In *Frontline Feminism,* edited by Karen Kahn. San Francisco: Aunt Lute Books.

Alexander, Priscilla. 1997. "Feminism, Sex Workers, and Human Rights." In *Whores and Other Feminists,* edited by Jill Nagle. New York: Routledge.

Allen, Paula Gunn. 1995. "Where I Come From God Is a Grandmother." In *Frontline Feminism,* edited by Karen Kahn. San Francisco: Aunt Lute Books.

Allison, Dorothy. 1993. "A Question of Class." Pp. 46–60 in *Sisters, Sexperts, Queers: Beyond the Lesbian Nation,* edited by Arlene Stein. New York: Plume Books.

Barnett, Bernice McNair. 1995. "Black Women's Collectivist Movement Organizations: Their Struggles during the 'Doldrums.'" In *Feminist Organizations: Harvest of the New Women's Movement,* edited by Myra Marx Ferree and Patricia Yancey Martin. Philadelphia: Temple University Press. Also, chap. 17 in this volume.

Beck, Evelyn Torton. 1988. "The Politics of Jewish Invisibility." *NWSA Journal* 1:93–102.

Bell-Scott, Patricia, ed. 1994. *Life Notes: Personal Writings by Contemporary Black Women.* New York: Norton.

Bettie, Julie. 2001. "Changing the Subject: Male Feminism, Class Identity, and the Politics of Location." Chap. 15 in this volume.

Bresnahan, Eileen. 2001. "The Strange Case of Jackie East: When Identities Collide." Chap. 21 in this volume.

Bunch, Charlotte. 1995. "Global Feminism: Going Beyond Boundaries." In *Frontline Feminism,* edited by Karen Kahn. San Francisco: Aunt Lute Books.

Carby, Hazel. 1990. "The Politics of Difference." *Ms.* 1 (September): 84–85. Also, chap. 1 in this volume.

Carillo, Roxanna. 1990. "Feminist Alliances: A View from Peru." In *Bridges of Power: Women's Multicultural Alliances,* edited by Lisa Albrecht and Rose M. Brewer. Philadelphia: New Society Publishers.

Chernow, Harneen, and Susan Moir. 1995. "Feminism and Labor: Building Alliances." In *Frontline Feminism,* edited by Karen Kahn. San Francisco: Aunt Lute Books.

Collins, Patricia Hill. 1990. *Black Feminist Thought: Knowledge, Consciousness, and the Politics of Empowerment.* Boston: Unwin Hyman.

Combahee River Collective. 1978. "A Black Feminist Statement." In *Capitalist Patriarchy and the Case for Socialist Feminist,* edited by Zillah R. Eisenstein. New York: Monthly Review Press. Also, chap. 7 in this volume.

Corman, June. 2001. "Organizing International Women's Day in the Niagara Peninsula." Chap. 27 in this volume.

Davis, Angela. 1995. "Lifting as We Climb." In *Frontline Feminism,* edited by Karen Kahn. San Francisco: Aunt Lute Books.

de Beauvoir, Simone. 1953. *The Second Sex.* New York: Alfred A. Knopf.

Dietzel, Susanne. 1999. "Talking about My Generation." Unpublished paper.

Dill, Bonnie Thornton. 1983. "Race, Class and Gender: Prospects for an All-Inclusive Sisterhood." *Feminist Studies* 9:131–150.

duCille, Ann. 1994. "The Occult of True Black Womanhood: Critical Demeanor and Black Feminist Studies." *Signs: Journal of Women in Culture and Society* 19 (3):591–621. Also, chap. 19 in this volume.

Fleming, Cynthia Griggs. 1993. "Black Women Activists and the Student Nonviolent Coordinating Committee: The Case of Ruby Doris Smith Robinson." *Journal of Women's History* 4:64–82.

Fowlkes, Diane L. 2001. "A Writing Spider Tries Again: From Separatist to Coalitional Identity Politics." Chap. 29 in this volume.

Franzen, Trisha. 1993. "Differences and Identities: Feminism and the Albuquerque Lesbian Community." *Signs: Journal of Women in Culture and Society* 18 (4):891–906. Also, chap. 22 in this volume.

Friedman, Susan Stanford. 1995. "Beyond White and Other: Relationality and Narratives of Race in Feminist Discourse." *Signs: Journal of Women in Culture and Society* 21 (1):112–149.

Frye, Marilyn. 1992. "Lesbian Community: Heterodox Congregation." In *Willful Virgin: Essays in Feminism, 1976–1992,* by Marilyn Frye. Freedom, CA: Crossing Press. Also, chap. 23 in this volume.

Gamson, Joshua. 1997. "Messages of Exclusion: Gender, Movements, and Symbolic Boundaries." *Gender & Society* 11 (April):178–199. Also, chap. 24 in this volume.

Gitlin, Todd. 1993. The Rise of 'Identity Politics': An Examination and a Critique." *Dissent* (Spring):172–177.

Gitlin, Todd. 1995. *The Twilight of Common Dreams: Why America Is Wracked by Culture Wars.* New York: Henry Holt & Co.

Grandia, Liza. 2001. "Look at the World through Women's Eyes: On Empathy and International Civil Society." Chap. 30 in this volume.

Grossberg, Lawrence. 1996. "Identity and Cultural Studies: Is That All There Is?" Pp. 87–107 in *Questions of Cultural Identity,* edited by Stuart Hall and Paul du Gay. Thousand Oaks, CA: Sage.

Hall, Stuart. 1996. "Introduction: Who Needs 'Identity'?" Pp. 1–17 in *Questions of Cultural Identity,* edited by Stuart Hall and Paul du Gay. Thousand Oaks, CA: Sage.

Heywood, Leslie, and Jennifer Drake, eds. 1997. *Third Wave Agenda: Being Feminist, Doing Feminism.* Minneapolis: University of Minnesota Press.

Hobsbawm, Eric. 1996. "Identity Politics and the Left." *New Left Review* 217:38–47.

Jordan, June. 1985. "Report from the Bahamas." In *On Call: Political Essays,* by June Jordan. Boston: South End Press. Also, chap. 16 in this volume.

Kaplan, Elaine Bell. 1995. "I Don't Do No Windows." In *Frontline Feminism,* edited by Karen Kahn. San Francisco: Aunt Lute Books.

Kauffman, L. A. 1990. "The Anti-Politics of Identity." *Socialist Review* 90:67–80. Also, chap. 2 in this volume.

Klein, Bonnie Sherr. 1992. "We Are Who You Are: Feminism and Disability." *Ms.* 3 (Nov/Dec):70–74. Also, chap. 9 in this volume.

Kreiger, Susan. 1982. "Lesbian Identity and Community: Recent Social Science Literature." *Signs: Journal of Women in Culture and Society* 8:91–108.

Kreiger, Susan. 1983. *The Mirror Dance: Identity in a Women's Community.* Philadelphia: Temple University Press.

Leidner, Robin. 2001. "On Whose Behalf? Feminist Ideology and Dilemmas of Constituency." Chap. 6 in this volume.

Looser, Devoney, and E. Ann Kaplan, eds. 1997. *Generations: Academic Feminists in Dialogue.* Minneapolis: University of Minnesota Press.

Lorde, Audre. 1984a. "The Transformation of Silence into Language and Action." In *Sister Outsider: Essays and Speeches,* by Audre Lorde. Trumansburg, NY: Crossing Press. Also, chap. 11 in this volume.

Lorde, Audre. 1984b. "Age, Race, Class, and Sex: Women Redefining Difference." In *Sister Outsider: Essays and Speeches,* by Audre Lorde. Trumansburg, NY: Crossing Press.

Lorde, Audre. 1984c. "Our Difference Is Our Strength." In *Sister Outsider: Essays and Speeches,* by Audre Lorde. Trumansburg, NY: Crossing Press. Also, chap. 32 in this volume.

Macdonald, Barbara. 1995. "An Open Letter to the Women's Movement." In *Frontline Feminism,* edited by Karen Kahn. San Francisco: Aunt Lute Press.

McKay, Nellie Y. 1993. "Acknowledging Differences: Can Women Find Unity Through Diversity?" Pp. 267–282 in *Theorizing Black Feminisms: The Visionary Pragmatism of Black Women,* edited by S. James and A. Busia. New York: Routledge.

Millett, Kate. 1970. *Sexual Politics.* New York: Doubleday.

Nieto, Consuelo. 1997. "The Chicana and the Woman's Rights Movement." In *Chicana Feminist Thought: The Basic Historical Writings,* edited by Alma M. Garcia. New York: Routledge.

Patai, Daphne. 1992. "The Struggle for Feminist Purity Threatens the Goals of Feminism." *Chronicle of Higher Education* (February 5):B1. Also, chap. 4 in this volume.

Pegueros, Rosa María. 2001. "Sharing Power: A Latina in NOW." Chap. 28 in this volume.

Perry, Ruth. 1995. "I Brake for Feminists: Debates and Divisions within Women's Studies." *Transformations* 17 (Spring):1–13. Also, chap. 14 in this volume.

Phelan, Shane. 1989. *Identity Politics: Lesbian Feminism and the Limits of Community.* Philadelphia: Temple University Press.

Phillips, Anne. 1997. "From Inequality to Difference: A Severe Case of Displacement." *New Left Review* 224 (July/Aug):143–153.

Pratt, Minnie Bruce. 1984. "Who Am I If I'm Not My Father's Daughter?" Earlier version of "Identity: Skin Blood Heart," in *Rebellion Essays, 1980–1991,* by Bruce Pratt. Ithaca: Firebrand Books. Also, chap. 8 in this volume.

Queen, Carol. 1997. "Sex Radical Politics, Sex-Positive Feminist Thought, and Whore Stigma." In *Whores and Other Feminists,* edited by Jill Nagle. New York: Routledge. Also, chap. 13 in this volume.

Quintanales, Mirtha. 1983. "I Paid Very Hard for My Immigrant Ignorance." In *This Bridge Called My Back: Writings by Radical Women of Color,* edited by Cherríe Moraga and Gloria Anzaldúa. New York: Kitchen Table: Women of Color Press.

Radicalesbians. 1970. "The Woman Identified Woman." In *Out of the Closets: Voice of Gay Liberation,* edited by Karla Jay and Alan Young. New York: Douglas Links.

Ray, Raka. 1999. *Fields of Protest: Women's Movements in India.* Minneapolis: University of Minnesota Press.

Rich, Adrienne. 1986. "If Not with Others, How?" In *Blood, Bread, Poetry,* by Adrienne Rich. New York: Norton. Also, chap. 34 in this volume.

Rupp, Leila J. 1996. "Challenging Imperialism in International Women's Organizations, 1888–1945." *NWSA Journal* 8 (Spring):8–27. Also, chap. 26 in this volume.

Rupp, Leila J., and Verta Taylor. 1987. *Survival in the Doldrums: The American Women's Rights Movement, 1945 to the 1960s.* New York: Oxford University Press.

Ryan, Barbara. 2001. "Having It All: The Search for Identity and Community." Chap. 33 in this volume.

Sears, Priscilla. 1996. "What Is Difficult Can Be Done at Once. What Is Impossible Takes a Little Longer: The Beijing Conference." *NWSA Journal* 8 (Spring):179–185. Also, chap. 35 in this volume.

severson, kristin, and victoria stanhope. 1998. "Identity Politics and Progress: Don't Fence Me In (or Out)." *off our backs* 18 (4):12–13. Also, chap. 5 in this volume.

Shah, Sonia. 1994. "Presenting the Blue Goddess: Toward a Bicultural Asian-American Feminist Agenda." In *The State of Asian America: Activism and Resistance in the 1990s,* edited by Karin Aguilar-San Juan. Boston: South End Press. Also, chap. 12 in this volume.

Smith, Barbara. 1983. "Introduction to *Home Girls.*" In *Home Girls,* edited by Barbara Smith. New York: Kitchen Table: Women of Color Press. Also, chap. 18 in this volume.

Stein, Arlene. 1997. *Sex and Sensibility: Stories of a Lesbian Generation.* Berkeley: University of California Press.

Taylor, Verta, and Nancy Whittier. 1992. "Collective Identity in Social Movement Communities: Lesbian Feminist Mobilization." Pp. 104–129 in *Frontiers in Social Movement Theory,* edited by Aldon Morris and Carol McClurg Mueller. New Haven: Yale University Press.

Walker, Rebecca. 1992. "Becoming the Third Wave." *Ms.* (Jan/Feb):39–41. Also, chap. 10 in this volume.

Whisman, Vera. 1993. "Identity Crisis: Who Is a Lesbian, Anyway?" In *Sisters, Sexperts, Queers: Beyond the Lesbian Nation,* edited by Arlene Stein. New York: Plume Books.

Part I

The Problem
Questions and Challenges

This volume includes writings on divisions among feminist activists based upon social-group characteristics of sexual orientation, sexual practice, race, ethnicity, religion, age, nationality, and physical abilities. Some selections are empirical, some theoretical, and some experiential. The first chapter begins with those who present a critique of identity politics; the following chapters contain claims to identity politics along a wide array of categories.

The position one takes concerning identity politics tends to be closely related to the social position one holds. That each individual has more than one status (social position) only deepens the complexity of identity; it does not make it go away. Nor does wishing "Why can't we all just be human?" make different realities disappear. Yet, the critiques are real, and they are important. They are important because people everywhere, including the contributors to this work, are looking for ways to live together with respect and dignity.

Those who are critical of what identity politics has wrought (or might bring to pass in the future) open this discussion. This section's authors are cognizant of the dilemma identity politics creates for resolving divisions among social groups. They are not opposed to such recognition per se; rather, they question the extent that it is needed. They are not alone in this; indeed, in later chapters some of those who are deeply involved in promoting identity recognition also voice concern (although of a different nature) of excess in practice.

The readings are sometimes contentious, but most reveal thoughtful reflections. Many adopt a postmodern emphasis on identity as process rather than genes, place, or social practices. In chapter 1 questions are raised by those who are less likely to experience the social distance of "difference," or to know what it is to be the stranger within. They question the outcome of the response to "otherness," which may have led to further isolation and antagonisms rather than to healing and progressive change. And, as Hazel Carby points out in the first selection, identity politics is the politics of difference that may not turn out the way you want. She is particularly concerned that racism is being avoided in contemporary feminism although it appears as if it is being addressed.

Some critiques come from a Left perspective that still speaks of the "universalism" of a class message (Hobsbawm 1996). Leftists in this volume offer a more nuanced look. For instance, L. A. Kauffman considers the collective identity of the early black movement to be an important challenge to white cultural imperialism.

But in the 1980s and 1990s, Kauffman believes, identity politics evolved into a fragmented mosaic rather than a progressive political movement built on the solidarity of all groups experiencing domination and exclusion.

Todd Gitlin's piece reminds us that the gender gap is not just that women vote in higher numbers for Democrats but also that the Republican tilt of white men is a potent form of identity politics that reflects a reaction (or, as he calls it, a panic) against the relative gains of women and minorities. He warns that increasing friction toward white men can lead only to disastrous political results for multicultural groups.

Stepping back from the political arena, Daphne Patai discusses the errors of identity politics for women's studies, particularly the zealousness she finds among feminist students, whom she accuses of policing thought and appearance. For her, identity politics has fallen into the feminist purity realm and, thus, has created rigid factionalism. Through her own experience she has concluded that there has been a reversal of privilege. She cites as an example those instances when someone of a minority group says she or he is experiencing racism as a time when that belief cannot be challenged, most especially not by a white person, who, by virtue of her or his whiteness, must be guilty of racism. She asks how can we criticize negative tendencies in feminism without being viewed as part of the enemy camp?

kristen severson and victoria stanhope make the argument that identity and political beliefs do not necessarily coincide. They cite the incongruous state of gay Republicans or the antifeminist woman. Failing to find a reasonable explanation for such inconsistencies, they argue that a movement should be about what one believes—one's values and ideologies—rather than who one is or does. Likewise, sexual behaviors should be judged according to concepts such as respect, mutuality, and caring rather than a particular aspect such as gender or sexual orientation. Within women's communities, they reject any category or expectation that calls for conformity, a conformity they hoped to escape in the larger society.

Who, then, is identity politics for and what are the benefits from it? Is it for all women or only some? What about those who want equality but do not want to work for it? What of those who reject it or actively work against feminist goals? Robin Leidner addresses these questions while laying out the complexities of addressing diversity issues. Her work is a good introduction to the sections that follow, where specific identity claims are made.

REFERENCE

Hobsbawm, Eric. 1996. "Identity Politics and the Left." *New Left Review* 217:38–47.

Chapter One

The Politics of Difference

Hazel V. Carby

It is possible now to see that feminist debate has become more concerned with focusing on a pluralist rather than a unitary notion of women, using concepts of difference and otherness. Of course, we are still, all too frequently, confronted by colleagues who assume that the subjects of feminist work are the minority of women in the world who are white, European or North American, and middle- or upper-middle-class, but perhaps now their assumptions do not easily pass unchallenged. I want to use what I am calling "the politics of difference," which could also be described as the politics of diversity, within contemporary feminist critical thinking and practice as an example of the ways in which the politics of race is actually being avoided, displaced, and even abandoned, while it appears as if racism is being directly confronted.

As a black intellectual I am both intrigued and horrified by the contradictory nature of the black presence in the academy. We are, as people and as cultural producers, simultaneously visibly present in, and starkly absent from, university life. Of course, the academy is not a subject of much popular concern, being marginal to the lives of most people. I cannot resist, therefore, making a comment about the unusual event of the presence of a professor, let alone a black professor, on the cover of the *New York Times Magazine*. The main subject of the story was Henry Louis Gates, Jr., but the secondary subject was African American studies. Both the man and his field were repeatedly referred to as "controversial."

On the surface we appear to have "made it"; some would say that we appear to be gaining a voice, that there is at least debate about what should be taught. My response would be to dive beneath this surface and to question on whose terms are these changes happening? As black people, we clearly have to temper any enthusiasm about being taken seriously, at long last, with the recognition that we are being paid attention to for what we have long considered to be good at. We are being seriously considered as higher educational entertainment. Lest we start believing, as black professors, that we have been allowed to evacuate our place on the outside of the real work of academia, the words of Stanley Fish, chair of the Department of English at Duke University, are at the center of the *Times* article, characterizing

Reprinted by permission of the author from *Ms.,* September/October 1990.

Henry Louis Gates as P. T. Barnum of African American studies. If Gates is Barnum, presumably African American studies is a circus and as practitioners in that field, I guess we are the performing animals and trapeze artists. Allowing black folks to play the sideshow is not threatening to the main event.

There is a very important distinction that needs to be made between an apparent black cultural presence in the academy and the presence of black people. If there seems to be a vocal commitment to diversifying university campuses, I would like to remind you that more than 90 percent of all faculty members across the nation are white. The percentage of black students in college populations has also steadily decreased. In graduate schools the proportion of American students who are black is decreasing and the proportion of doctorates awarded to black people is in steady decline. At the professional level, while the number of tenured black faculty members has increased slightly, the number of black people holding untenured appointments has declined. What should be the subject of "controversy," then, is not our presence but our increasing disappearance. An African American intellectual presence in the academy is not being reproduced. It is clearly easier to integrate a syllabus in a course than to recruit black faculty to teach it or black students to engage with it.

It is paradoxical that so much energy is being directed toward a black presence in the curriculum and so little to our material conditions. We now have a white population that has been raised on the celebration of the theme of diversity in *Sesame Street* but refuses to integrate its public school systems, condemns apartheid in South Africa but supports apartheid in the neighborhoods and schools of Hartford and New Haven, Connecticut. High school dropout rates for blacks and Hispanic schoolchildren are significantly higher than those for whites. In 1988 in the U.S., 19 percent of children under 18 were being raised in families with incomes below the poverty line; 44 percent of all black children and 38 percent of all Hispanic children live and will remain living in poverty.

We live, then, in a society in which the practice of apartheid is pervasive and to which a commitment to the language of diversity and difference is a totally inadequate response. What, for example, does the debate about the opening up of the canon mean in relation to the material condition of existence of most black people? And what has been the role of most black people? And what has been the role of feminist theory as it has attempted to diversify the concept of women?

The politics of difference is, perhaps, the most usual way now that feminists try to signal their concern to develop concepts of woman and womanhood that are plural rather than unitary in their effects. I wonder if theories of difference, as they are currently being formulated, are leading to a further ghettoization of our cultural and political presence within academic work? In practice, the category of difference is often used as if it were an absolute social, cultural, and political division, which denies the complexity of a black cultural presence and also censors political response. If ethic differences are absolute, then the response from many liberal, white students is, for example, a refusal to speak because they are of the dominant group. The effect is indistinguishable from not having to take any political position whatsoever in relation to the culture of the other. If one does not take a position; then difference does not actually have to be confronted. Indeed, difference has been preserved as absolute and so has the dominant social order.

On the other hand, if we try to recognize that we live in a social formation that is structured in dominance by the politics of race, then, theoretically, we can argue that everyone has been constructed as a radicalized subject. It is important to recognize the invention of the category of whiteness as well as blackness and, consequently, to reveal what is usually rendered invisible because it is viewed as a normative state of existence. The political practice that should come from this theoretical position would argue that race should be a central conceptual category in all our work. But, because the politics of difference works with concepts of diversity rather than structures of dominance, race is a marginalized concept that is wheeled out only when the subject is black. I am not arguing for pluralism, the results of much work on ethnicity, but for revealing the structures of power that are at work in the radicalization of a social order.

The concept of race is further marginalized in the current use of the phrase "women of color." This phrase has been lifted from its origin in the need to find a common ground among nondominant groups of women and reinserted into the language of difference in feminist theory. In practice we are all familiar with the use of the term as a referent, but do some people lack color? Do white women have no color? What does it mean not to have color? Does it mean somehow those without color are not implicated in a society structured in dominance by race? Are only the "colored" to be the subjects of this specialized discourse and therefore effectively marginalized yet again? Do existing power relations remain intact? Are the politics of difference effective in making visible women of color while rendering invisible the politics of exploitation?

This is how we can start to think about disparity between the fascination for black women as subjects on a syllabus and the total disregard for the material conditions of most black people. Often it seems that black women appear as romantic anthropological subjects or a primitive presence in the university curriculum. Feminism in the university has created an essential black female subject for its own consumption; it is a figure that can be used as an example of the most victimized of the victims of patriarchal oppression or as an example of the most noble of noble womanhood that endured; Faulkner's Dilsey reborn. Certainly, this black female subject seems to be needed to embody an essential black female experience, whatever that may be. But, above all, this new black woman subject, of women's studies in particular, acts to berate the white woman for her racism, acts as a mechanism to cleanse her soul, becomes the hair shirt with which she can beat herself over the head and can then feel self-satisfied and politically correct. Does this fantasized black female subject exist, primarily, to make the white middle class feel better about itself?

What we need to do is to teach ourselves to recognize the existence of historically specific forms of racism: to think in terms of racism instead of an idea of racism that doesn't change through history; to think in terms of racial formation rather than eternal or essential "races." Then, perhaps, we can begin to see how an apparent commitment to diversity in a university can be engaged very intimately in a new form of racism. The important thing to remember about racism is that it promotes a transformation of the whole ideological field in which it operates and this is what I would argue has happened in relation to changes in the curriculum.

Theories of difference and diversity in practice leave us fragmented and divided but equal in an inability to conceive of radical social change. I agree with Barbara Harlow that today we hear a lot about oppression but nothing at all about systems of exploitation; that the concept of resistance is frequently used but the concept of revolution has disappeared. *Oppression* and *resistance* are terms more easily applied to individualists and pluralist ideals of political change. Of course, we are not supposed to use revolutionary theories of history, the "master narratives," because they are the master's tools. It is my contention that the master appropriated those tools along with the labor of those he exploited and that it is high time that they be reclaimed.

Chapter Two

The Anti-Politics of Identity

L. A. Kauffman

Nothing distinguishes contemporary social movement politics from those of the nineteenth and early twentieth centuries more than the politics of identity that have developed over the last twenty or so years. Identity politics express the principle that identity—be it individual or collective—should be central to both the vision and practice of radical politics. It implies not only organizing around shared identity, as for example classic nationalist movements have done. Identity politics also express the belief that identity itself—its elaboration, expression, or affirmation— is and should be a fundamental focus of political work. In this way, the politics of identity have led to an unprecedented politicization of previously nonpolitical terrains; sexuality, interpersonal relations, lifestyle, and culture. Theorists and practitioners of identity politics see these realms, which directly engage the self, subjective experience, and daily life, as crucial sites of political contestation. Taking different forms and intensities in different contexts, this new approach to politics has come to pervade the political practice of an extraordinarily wide range of progressive movements, becoming the most distinctive and truly novel feature of the new social movements.

Advocates and analysts of identity politics have viewed them in widely diverging ways. To some, they represent a liberating new synthesis of the personal and the political. The politicization of matters previously viewed as external to politics, according to this view, opens up the possibility for a more radical challenge to such forms of domination and exclusion as racism, sexism, and homophobia than had been possible with more traditional concepts of the political. Others argue that the attention to identity and hence to difference that this political vision has inspired is a crucial advance toward the development of a truly inclusive and pluralist political culture.[1]

There is substantial evidence to support these claims; one can easily point to any number of movements that have successfully organized around such visions of identity politics. But especially in recent years, a variety of permutations of identity politics have appeared—call them anti-politics of identity—which take the original concerns of identity politics in a number of disturbing directions: away from engagement with institutionalized structures of power, toward a kind of apolitical introspection, and into a cycle of fragmentation and diffusion of political energies. These tendencies, which can be found in more or less hybrid forms in many different movements, arguably form one of the greatest internal barriers to the development of contemporary progressive politics in the United States. This piece will trace the historical development of both the politics and anti-politics of identity in order to suggest some of the pitfalls of the focus on identity as a political model for the left.

From Public Sphere to Collective Identity

Many of those who have written about contemporary or "new" social movements have pointed to continuities between these movements and other social movements of the past. The new social movements of recent decades, it is true, owe much to the social movements of the nineteenth and early twentieth centuries: an impulse to transform not just the state, but also extra-statal social institutions and relations; an emphasis (though far from exclusive) on non-electoral strategies for change; a tendency to develop independent institutions and a distinctive movement culture. All of these elements are legacies of the nineteenth-century social movements, the first organized extra-statal political groupings in Western history.

An emphasis on continuity, however, can mask important changes. Pre-World War II social movements tended to share what might be called a public sphere conception of politics. This understanding of the limits and the nature of the political was derived from the political conjuncture of the late eighteenth-century democratic revolutions, in which a vision and practice of politics as the public activity of citizens replaced the privatized political world of absolutist monarchies. Political life spilled out from the state into the newly created public sphere, a realm of debate and persuasion located outside of the state but oriented around it, in Habermas' famous formulation.[2]

The social and radical movements that developed over the following century and a half expanded this tradition in crucial ways, by directing attention to institutionalized structures of power located outside of the traditional political arena of the state. Their vision and practice of politics addressed a wide range of institutionalized forms of power, such as exploitation and domination in the economic realm and exclusion and discrimination in the institutions of social life. They also became the first movements to institutionalize themselves, through the creation of semipermanent organizations, formalized internal decision-making procedures, and defined strategic objectives.[3] But their fundamental conception of politics remained firmly rooted in the public sphere tradition of emphasizing public institutions as the crucial loci of political contestation.

In the United States, the development of the civil rights movement of the 1950s and 1960s marked the beginnings of a radical departure from this tradition and the emergence of a markedly distinct way of thinking about the nature and purpose of politics. Much of the strategy followed by the civil rights movement was inspired by earlier traditions of social movement politics and aimed at eradicating formal barriers to the full economic, political, and social equality of blacks in the United States. But in the most innovative and daring of the civil rights organizations, the Student Nonviolent Coordinating Committee (SNCC), new concerns gave a changed tone and shape to this political organizing: a focus on the connections between personal and social change.

Within movement circles, an eclectic mix of ideas and influences joined to form a potent mix: Gandhian principles of civil disobedience; spiritual aspirations for personal and collective redemption drawn from the Southern black church; ethical visions of moral responsibility and the possibilities of individual action inspired by European existentialism.[4] For many black SNCC activists, this atmosphere translated into a heightened emphasis on developing black leadership and improving blacks' self-conceptions, for example through the black history curriculum developed for the 1964 Freedom Schools in Mississippi.[5] Many white activists, in a somewhat analogous fashion, "came to believe it was just as important to free *themselves* from the constraints of their racial or class backgrounds as it was to register black voters."[6]

The Black Power Movement—created in large part as a response to frustration over the resilience of barriers to black equality—drew upon this new vision to produce a new understanding of the nature of black identity and a new conception of the place of identity in politics. The movement encompassed many strands, and the phrase "Black Power" itself had multiple interpretations, among them a call for black economic power. However, Black Power's primary thrust was to place the redefinition and affirmation of the black self at the core of its politics. Comparing the words of Marcus Garvey with those of Stokely Carmichael and Charles V. Hamilton, leading exponents of the tenets of the Black Power movement, conveys a sense of the magnitude of the departure this new emphasis entailed from the politics of earlier social movements:

> Prejudice of the white race against the black race is not so much because of color as of condition; because as a race, to them, we have accomplished nothing; we have built no nation, no government; because we are dependent for our economic and political existence.[7]

> Our basic need is to reclaim our history and our identity from what must be called cultural terrorism, from the depredation of self-justifying white guilt. We shall have to struggle for the right to create our own terms through which to define ourselves and our relationship to the society, and to have these terms recognized. This is the first necessity of a free people, and the first right that any oppressor must suspend.[8]

Garvey's nationalism was firmly inscribed within the public sphere tradition shared by the social movements of the early twentieth century. Thus "the true solution of the Negro problem," as he wrote in a 1922 article of that name, was black institution-building and, even more importantly, black state-building.[9] For Carmichael and Hamilton, by contrast, the key site of political activity had shifted to the terrain of a collective identity fashioned through discourse, as part of what

Carmichael elsewhere called the struggle for "psychological equality."[10] Nothing analogous to this new politics of identity can be found in earlier African-American thought and political practice. Even W. E. B. Du Bois, in his nuanced study of the psychological effects of "the Veil," envisioned a political strategy based not on the transformation of representations, but on campaigns for the vote, civic equality, education, and economic and governmental power.[11]

The Black Power project of reclaiming collective identity and developing "black consciousness" was inspired in many ways by anti-colonial movements throughout the Third World, particularly in Africa. Many African-American radicals studied the writings of Frantz Fanon, Aimé Césaire, and Kwame Nkrumah, who explored the psychological ramifications of colonial domination. Groups like the Nation of Islam advocated the study of African and black history as a means of struggling against the effects of white cultural imperialism.

This strategy was widely viewed as a radicalizing complement to more traditional strategies of African-American politics. Harold Cruse wrote,

> In the same way that the Nation of Islam used religion to bind Negroes together into a social and economic movement (without politics), the secular black radical movement must use the cultural ingredient in black reality to bind Negroes into a mass movement *with economics and politics*. This has to be done through a cultural program that makes demands for cultural equality on American society. Without cultural equality there can be no economic and political equality.[12]

The overall effect of the rise of this new identity politics was a major shift in political thinking, deemphasizing the role of institutions in perpetuating discrimination and exploitation and highlighting the role of extra-institutional culture.

The Personal Is Political

The women's liberation movement of the late 1960s, which grew out of the experiences of women organizers in the civil rights movement and the New Left, drew heavily on these new conceptions.[13] In 1964, two white SNCC organizers, Mary King and Casey Hayden, wrote a memo on sexism in the organization that came to be the first manifesto for a new generation of feminists:

> The average white person finds it difficult to understand why the Negro resents being called "boy," or being thought of as "musical" and "athletic," because the average white person doesn't realize that *he assumes he is superior*. . . . So too the average SNCC worker finds it difficult to discuss the woman problem because of the assumption of male superiority. Assumptions of male superiority are as widespread and deep-rooted and every [bit] as crippling to the woman as the assumptions of white supremacy are to the Negro.[14]

Drawing on the new vision of politics developed by African-American radicals, early feminists like King and Hayden focused less on structural inequalities than on psychological ones.

The hallmark of the new feminism was its argument that changing institutionalized structures of domination, though key, was insufficient. To eradicate patriarchy, it was equally necessary to transform ways of thinking, self-conceptions, and cultural categories. One of the early documents of the movement, a manifesto by the New York Radical Feminists, framed the question in the following way:

> We believe that the purpose of male chauvinism is primarily to obtain psychological ego satisfaction, and that only secondarily does this manifest itself in economic relationships. For this reason we do not believe that capitalism, or any other economic system, is the cause of female oppression, nor do we believe that female oppression will disappear as a result of a purely economic revolution. The political oppression of women has its own class dynamic; and that dynamic must be understood in terms previously called "non-political"—namely the politics of the ego.[15]

Other feminist groups of the time defined different mainsprings of oppression but shared this impulse to politicize the previously non-political as a means of organizing against male domination.

Kate Millett's *Sexual Politics,* a landmark work in the development of both the feminist movement and identity politics as a whole, delineated the main elements of the new conception of politics.

> In introducing the term "sexual politics," one must first answer the inevitable question "Can the relationship between the sexes be viewed in a political light at all?" The answer depends on how one defines politics. This essay does not define the political as that relatively narrow and exclusive world of meetings, chairmen, and parties. The term "politics" shall refer to power-structured relationships, arrangements whereby one group of persons is controlled by another.[16]

In a footnote to this text, Millett elaborated on the conceptual underpinnings of this redefinition:

> The American Heritage Dictionary's fourth definition [of politics] is fairly approximate: "methods or tactics involved in managing a state or government." . . . One might expand this to a set of stratagems designed to maintain a system. If one understands patriarchy to be an institution perpetuated by such techniques of control, one has a working definition of how politics is conceived of in this essay.[17]

Millett's equation of politics with power or "power-structured relationships" expressed a new conception: that the domain of politics need not be confined to the realm of institutions, but could be seen as pervading virtually every aspect of individual and social life—a kind of proto-Foucaultianism. This vision of a correspondence between power and politics lay at the core of the new feminism, setting it apart from (though later influencing) the black nationalism by which it was inspired.

But Millett tempered this radical view with the analysis—shared by most radical and socialist feminists of the time—that patriarchy was *itself* an institution. Her identity politics, and to a large extent those of the early second wave feminist movement, thus synthesized two distinct strains of thinking about the nature of politics: one inherited from nineteenth- and twentieth-century radicalism, rooted in the public sphere and based on an understanding of politics as grounded within institutions; and a newly emerging tendency to view the political primarily in terms of power and domination, exponentially increasing the possible sites of both political control and political struggle.

This early, heterogeneous feminist identity politics translated into a correspondingly multilayered political practice, but one that placed significant emphasis on the public sphere tradition's concerns with the institutional underpinnings of power. Radical and socialist feminists brought powerful challenges to state-supported forms of discrimination, as in the case of the 1969 speak-outs on abortion rights. At the same time, they began to develop a political practice oriented to the social, the cultural, and the interpersonal, stressing the role of these realms in perpetuating sexual oppression. Much feminist strategy centered on what one might now call the subversive appropriation and recodification of signs. In the famous 1968 Atlantic City protest against the Miss America pageant, women threw "bras, girdles, curlers, false eyelashes, wigs, and representative issues of *Cosmopolitan, Ladies' Home Journal, Family Circle*," into a "Freedom Trash Can" to represent the liberation of feminist women from the gender roles of the past.[18] In 1970, other groups occupied strategically placed media institutions to protest conservative portrayals of women's vocation, in the case of the *Ladies' Home Journal* sit-in, or the exploitation of women through pornography, in the case of the occupation of Grove Press. These actions not only challenged dominant representations of women; more importantly, they challenged the institutions that produced and disseminated those representations.

The new feminist analysis also led activists to explore a related politics of individual identity. The premise of consciousness-raising, a key element of the new political strategies, was that through discussion women would "begin to see that what they had once been convinced were personal problems are actually political problems."[19] Like the closely related feminist principle that "the personal is the political," consciousness-raising stressed the shared and thus social nature of individual experience. It was because women's individual experiences in relationships, friendships, schools, and work revealed a *systematic* pattern of male domination that second wave feminists labelled them political. Their understanding of the pervasiveness of male power led feminists to reject the older equation of politics and the public sphere in order to actively question the assumptions underlying the very categories of public and private.

These politics of the collective and individual self developed by the Black Power and feminist movements had widespread influence, particularly on the New Left. Certain of these concerns had been shared by New Left activists from the movement's inception; for example, the call for participatory democracy made by SDS activists in Port Huron in 1962 rested upon a vision of self-transformation, of political life as a means to "finding a meaning in life that is personally authentic."[20] Subsequent New Left experience—as variegated and heterogeneous as it was—was in many ways an experiment with the possibilities of politicizing the self, an experiment with politicizing culture and everyday life. At the same time as New Left activists redefined democracy in new and radical ways and mounted highly effective challenges to US military intervention in Vietnam, a thoroughgoing cultural politics developed around the movement. Young radicals came to attribute politically subversive effects to everything from rock music to long hair to the use of marijuana and other drugs.

This politicization of daily life extended beyond the black and feminist movements' concerns with self-conception and representation and gave political content to choices about lifestyle. Quite a few of these choices indeed shocked the middle class and flouted social conventions; however, many New Leftists went much further, claiming that they posed fundamental challenges to "the system." Where Marx in *The German Ideology* had talked about revolution's transformative effects on the self, New Leftists spoke of the revolutionary effects of transforming the self. A writer for a male liberation paper wrote in 1971, "Anything we do, anything which moves us toward becoming better human beings, is revolutionary."[21] "Liberation" became the codeword for the era, shorthand for this complex of ideas about the political implications of culture, the power of individual revolt, the role of subcultures, and the radical potential of fashioning and affirming identities. The new model of political activity—with its "ability to confront . . . oppression simultaneously as an individually experienced and as a collectively organized phenomenon"[22]—spread to a wide range of progressive movements, becoming an implicit common currency of much of the Left.

The Depoliticization of Identity

The early identity politics developed by the civil rights and Black Power movements and the second wave feminist movement inspired a lot of original, daring, and effective political action. It also served as inspiration for a number of key progressive movements, most notably those of gays and lesbians and of other people of color. It led activists to develop new tools and strategies and provided a context within which many previously apolitical people found political voice.

But over the course of the late 1970s and the 1980s, as identity politics proliferated, they became at once more diffuse and more purified, losing much of their connection with earlier traditions of politics. A permutation of identity politics, heavily tinged with the lifestyle concerns of the New Left, came to permeate the discourse and practice of much of the Left. Its influence, though uneven, seems to be growing, which makes it all the more important to identify and analyze.

The focus on identity has been effective and empowering when identity politics has been construed as the active affirmation of the experiences, dignity, and rights of historically marginalized or excluded people, most notably people of color, gays and lesbians, and disabled people. To borrow the words of Michelle Cliff, this kind of politics involves not only "claiming an identity they taught me to despise,"[23] through education and affirmation within communities; it also necessitates a direct engagement with the groups and institutions that have organized, supported, or tolerated these forms of discrimination, hatred, and exclusion.

But when the emphasis on identity has been given a more introspective cast, the search for an identity politics true to the complexities of identity has led not only to a tendency to view self-exploration as a political process in itself, but also to a balkanization and fragmentation of the Left.[24] The ethos it has inspired—that the truest and most radical form of political work consists in "organizing around your own oppression"—has all too frequently worked to reinforce barriers to communication and coalition among diverse groups. Groups have invested their energies in building and sustaining institutions that promote alternative views of history, culture, and identity, sometimes with very positive results; but in the midst of this intense pursuit and perfection of visions and expressions of identity, the notion of solidarity, so central to any progressive politics, has frequently been lost.* Identity politics has done much to pluralize conceptions of radical agency; but the only basis for a radically pluralist politics, as opposed to a fragmented mosaic of political groups, is the principle of solidarity, which exhorts progressives to organize against oppression, exploitation, domination, and exclusion—irrespective of whom they affect.

At another level, there has been a widespread slippage between identity politics' equation of politics with power and the view that all forms of power have equal political significance.† This slippage has contributed to a crisis of strategic thinking and action on the left. When everything is seen as political, it becomes virtually impossible to formulate effective political strategies, for there is no language or theoretical perspective available that might make it possible to distinguish among forms and levels of power and politics. Yet these are some of the most important questions that the project of identity politics initially raised: What are the relations between institutional structures and structures of thought and behavior? What are the mechanisms by which forms of domination such as racism, sexism, and homophobia are reproduced? How it is possible to distinguish between different levels of the political and different operations of power in nonreductionist ways? How can the concept of the political be expanded to incorporate—and help combat—the historical domination and exclusion of women, people of color, and gays and lesbians?

In a similar fashion, identity politics' emphasis on self-transformation as a prelude to political change has frequently been replaced by a vision of self-transformation

---

*One of the great ironies of the evolution of identity politics, of course, has been that those who have the least claim to organizing around their own identity have been those most likely to abandon the principle of solidarity. "It's only when we start talking about our lives and what's missing in them that we can begin to develop a politics that makes the world a better place," wrote a reader of *Mother Jones* recently. "I often get the feeling that the difficulties of life for people in Nicaragua, Argentina, or the barrio, or for a woman anywhere, are real, but my difficulties as a middle-class white American man aren't. . . . You can't have a politics that's totally based on saving the world for everybody else." (*Mother Jones,* November 1989, p. 4). This kind of inverted identity politics—organizing around the identity of the non-oppressed—has taken more sinister form in the discourse of the reinvigorated "white rights" movement, and has found a troubling corollary in the recent proliferation of a politics of non-human (fetal or animal) identities.

†This dissolving of the political into a formless field of operations of power parallels the trend in certain strains of poststructuralist and post-Marxist theory to dissolve the world into a web of undifferentiated and undifferentiable discourses.

as political change. One particularly striking and poignant example of this trend is the widespread degeneration of the feminist practice of consciousness-raising over the course of the 1970s from a radical tactic to a form of group therapy. Consciousness-raising had originally been based, in words of the radical feminist group Redstockings,

> on the premise that personal liberation was impossible. The concept of the "liberated woman" or the "liberated lifestyle" was disproved by the radical feminist analysis of the common oppression of women as a class. The locus of women's oppression, therefore, is not culture but power, men's class power.[25]

That political conception of consciousness-raising was increasingly abandoned in favor of the view that increasing individual women's sense of self-esteem and autonomy itself amounted to a form of political change. In the words of Naomi Braun Rosenthal, an astute critic of this shift, "the message is that women [as individuals] must change and that political action is either unnecessary or futile."[26]

This equation of self-transformation with social transformation underlies the widespread contemporary emphasis among progressives on a politics of lifestyle. Sometimes this emphasis takes the more collective form of building an alternative community, in an echo of the utopian experiments of the nineteenth century. But whether individual or collective, the tendency to claim political content for changes in lifestyle encourages the view that politics need not necessarily involve engagement with external structures of power. A large enough number of individual efforts at self-transformation, in this view, can lead to radical change, as if attitudes rather than vested interests were the primary obstacle to the creation of an ideal society. This kind of reasoning has become very widespread within some strains of the environmental movement, where the pursuit of an "ecologically correct lifestyle" has been promoted as a politically viable solution to environmental destruction, sidestepping the question of its underlying causes.[27]

The wide diffusion of the notion of "political correctness" in progressive circles over the last decade testifies to the pervasiveness of this politics of lifestyle. Even when used jokingly, as it most frequently is, the phrase reveals the impulses and anxieties that underlie contemporary conceptions of the political. The "correctness" in the phrase is not about having "correct" political views or strategies or even about doing "correct" political actions; it refers above all to personal conduct in everyday life. A political life, as viewed through the lens of identity politics, seems to be defined much more by conformity to certain implicit codes of self-fashioning (what one eats, wears, listens to, reads, purchases, etc.) than it is by what one does to change existing structures of domination, exploitation, and exclusion.

Perhaps the wide appeal of this strain of identity politics lies in the convincing solution it appears to give to the problem of leading a political existence in a profoundly depoliticized society. For it holds out the promise of politicizing *oneself,* one's choices about self-presentation, self-conception, and lifestyle, projecting a sense of "being" political at a time when the options for *doing* politics may seem limited. After a decade of apathy and reaction, it is perhaps not surprising that so many have been drawn by this existentialist core, this conscious pursuit and politicization of what Sartre called the process of "*choosing* ourselves."[28]

Yet perhaps the most striking aspect of this broad transformation of identity politics into an introspective, fragmented antipolitics of lifestyle is the extent to which the values it promotes—individual solutions to social problems, attention to lifestyle, choice—mirror the ideology of the marketplace. These parallels point not only to some of the likely causes of the depoliticization of identity politics over the last decade or so, but also to the very real pitfalls that an overemphasis on identity can bring.

That is not to say, however, that the identity politics model should be scrapped. On the contrary, it should be salvaged from the depoliticized rendering it has been given in recent years. A pluralistic radical politics requires balancing concerns with identity with an emphasis on solidarity, as well as with attention to other key categories like interests and needs. It requires careful thinking about both the nature of the political and the relation of politics to institutionalized structures of power. That is the kind of vision that informed the civil rights, Black Power, and second wave feminist movements. And it is the kind of vision that inspires the most innovative movements today, like the AIDS activist group ACT-UP, which has used identity as a point of departure rather than an final destination, working effectively to challenge strategically placed institutions like the Catholic Church and the pharmaceutical industry. Such a radical synthesis between the identity politics of the new social movements and the public sphere tradition of the socialist and earlier social movements can lead beyond contemporary visions of self-transformation to a politics once again based upon transforming the world.

NOTES

1. For a sampling of these arguments, see Jeffrey Escoffier, "Sexual Revolution and the Politics of Gay Identity," *Socialist Review* 82/83, pp. 119–153; Cherrfe Moraga and Gloria Anzaldúa, eds., *This Bridge Called My Back: Writings by Radical Women of Color* (New York: Kitchen Table Women of Color Press, 1983); and Denise Riley, *"Am I That Name?": Feminism and the Category of "Women" in History* (Minneapolis: University of Minnesota Press, 1988).

2. Jürgen Habermas, "The Public Sphere: An Encyclopedia Article (1964)," *New German Critique* 3 (1974), pp. 45–55; Jürgen Habermas, *The Structural Transformation of the Public Sphere: An Inquiry into a Category of Bourgeois Society* (Cambridge: The MIT Press, 1989).

3. For a thoughtful reflection on the implications of this innovation, see Giovanni Arrighi, Terence K. Hopkins, and Immanuel Wallerstein, *Antisystemic Movements* (London and New York: Verso, 1989), especially pp. 29–51.

4. A good account of this atmosphere can be found in Mary King, *Freedom Song: A Personal Story of the 1960s Civil Rights Movement* (New York: William Morrow and Company, 1987), pp. 162–172, 277–288.

5. On the Freedom Schools, see Doug McAdam, *Freedom Summer* (New York and Oxford: Oxford University Press, 1988), pp. 83–86.

6. McAdam, *Freedom Summer,* p. 139.

7. Marcus Garvey, "The Philosophy and Opinions," in Amy Jacques Garvey, ed., *The Philosophy and Opinions of Marcus Garvey,* vol. I (Dover, MA: The Majority Press, 1986), p. 18.

8. Stokely Carmichael and Charles V. Hamilton, *Black Power: The Politics of Liberation in America* (New York: Random House, 1967), pp. 34–35.

9. Garvey, "The Philosophy and Opinions," pp. 52–53.

10. Stokely Carmichael, "Power and Racism," in Floyd Barbour, ed., *The Black Power Revolt* (Boston: Extending Horizons Books, 1968), pp. 61–71.

11. See W. E. B. Du Bois, *The Souls of Black Folk* (New York: New American Library, 1982), as well as his 1915 article, "The Immediate Program of the American Negro," reprinted in August Meier, Elliott Rudwick, and Francis L. Broderick, eds., *Black Protest Thought in the Twentieth Century,* 2nd edition (New York: Macmillan Publishing Co., 1985), pp. 67–72.

12. Harold Cruse, *Rebellion or Revolution?* (New York: William Morrow and Company, 1968), p. 247.

13. For the classic history of this process, see Sara Evans, *Personal Politics: The Roots of Women's Liberation in the Civil Rights Movement and the New Left* (New York: Vintage, 1979).

14. This document is reprinted as an appendix to King, *Freedom Song,* pp. 567–569.

15. "Politics of the Ego: A Manifesto for N.Y. Radical Feminists," in Shulamith Firestone, ed., *Notes from the Second Year: Women's Liberation, Writings of the Radical Feminists* (New York: 1970), p. 124.

16. Kate Millett, *Sexual Politics* (New York: Avon, 1970), p. 23.

17. Millett, *Sexual Politics,* p. 23.

18. See "No More Miss America!" in Robin Morgan, ed., *Sisterhood Is Powerful: An Anthology of Writings from the Women's Liberation Movement* (New York: Viking Books, 1970), pp. 584–586.

19. Sookie Stambler, "Introduction," to Sookie Stambler, ed., *Women's Liberation: Blueprint for the Future* (New York: Ace Books, 1970), p. 11.

20. "The Port Huron Statement," reprinted in James Miller, *"Democracy Is in the Streets": From Port Huron to the Siege of Chicago* (New York: Simon and Schuster, 1987), p. 332.

21. Quoted in John Judis, "The Personal and the Political," *Socialist Revolution* 7 (January-February 1972), p. 27.

22. Michael Omi and Howard Winant, *Racial Formation in the United States from the 1960s to the 1980s* (New York: Routledge & Kegan Paul, 1986), p. 146.

23. Michelle Cliff, *Claiming an Identity They Taught Me to Despise* (Watertown, MA: Persephone Press, 1980).

24. For two very thoughtful treatments of these problems, see Jenny Bourne, "Homelands of the Mind: Jewish Feminism and Identity-Politics," *Race and Class* vol. XXIX, no. 1 (Summer 1987), pp. 1–24; Mary Louise Adams, "There's No Place Like Home: On the Place of Identity in Feminist Politics," *Feminist Review* 31 (Spring 1989), pp. 22–33.

25. Quoted in Naomi Braun Rosenthal, "Consciousness Raising: From Revolution to Reevaluation," *Psychology of Women Quarterly,* vol. 8, no. 4 (Summer 1984), p. 321. I am grateful to Larry Casalino for this reference.

26. Rosenthal, "Consciousness Raising," p. 324.

27. For a critique of this view, see the interview of James O'Connor by Alexander Cockburn in *Zeta,* February 1989, pp. 15–21.

28. Jean-Paul Sartre, *Being and Nothingness* (New York: Philosophical Library, 1956), pp. 597–598.

Chapter Three

The Fate of the Commons

Todd Gitlin

. . . The Republican tilt of white men is the most potent form of identity politics in our time: a huddling of men who resent (and exaggerate) their relative decline not only in parts of the labor market but at home, in the bedroom and the kitchen, and in the culture. Their fear and loathing is, in part, a panic against the relative gains of women and minorities in an economy that people experience as a zero-sum game, in which the benefits accruing to one group seem to amount to subtractions from another. Talk about identity politics! These white men, claiming they deserve color-blind treatment, identify with their brethren more than their wives or sisters, or minorities. But economic jitters are only one force behind the conspicuous loathing of Bill Clinton and Democrats of all factions. Symbols are fuel. The rage of dispossession has been at work, seething, for example, in the savage assaults on Hillary Rodham Clinton and the frenzy directed against Clinton's partial acceptance of gays in the military.

Then, too, victories are won not by census figures and questionnaires but by turnout. It was the Clinton-haters who came out to vote, while an extraordinary number of Democrats voted their alienation and disgruntlement, and stayed home. The white men most fundamentalist in their Protestantism and most dedicated to the National Rifle Association came out to vote because their antagonism to illegal immigrants, welfare mothers, and beneficiaries of affirmative action outweighed anything Democrats offered. In general, those who benefit most from government-sponsored privileges—the old, the cattle-grazers, and the house-rich—vote most, while the unemployed, the poor, the young, minorities, and industrial workers vote least. (The proportion of blue-collar workers who vote in presidential elections declined by one-third between 1960 and 1988.) Those who most resent taxes vote to punish those beneath them. Suburban homeowners refuse to pay taxes for the urban schools from which they have withdrawn their children. The groups who need government most have seceded from politics, feeling that politics has seceded from them.

A Left that was serious about winning political power and reducing the inequal-

Reprinted by permission from *The Twilight of Common Dreams: Why America Is Wracked on Culture Wars* by Todd Gitlin. New York: Henry Holt, 1995.

ity of wealth and income would stop lambasting all white men, and would take it as elementary to reduce frictions among white men, blacks, white women, and Hispanics. Could it be more obvious that the Left and the Democrats alike are helpless unless they offer all these constituencies something they benefit from in common? At the same time, a Left is not a Left unless it defends the scapegoated poor, tries to deliver them (along with the not-so-poor) training, decent jobs, and provision for children, acknowledging that the present welfare state is not kind to the poor. But multiculturalism by itself does not contribute to that political revival. The most insistent multiculturalists do not seem to recognize that there is no Left, there is only more panic, unless a plausible hope emerges for a greater equality of means. The right to a job, education, medical care, housing, retraining over the course of a lifetime—these are the bare elements of an economic citizenship that ought to be universal.

Yet today, virtually unopposed, the market is trumpeted as the sole source of economic growth and the undisputed marker of social health. No one proclaims the virtues of the unbridled market more strenuously than those who benefit from tax breaks and acceptable subsidies. Utopian capitalists, the most potent purists left in the world, proclaim that the market delivers precisely the goods that need delivery and rewards the right winners; as for the rest—well, too bad for the losers. But the market is compatible with immense inequality and social chaos. Corporate secession across borders bleeds away the nation's capacity to bring its citizens together. An unbridled market generates mass panic and beckons gangsterism, theocracy, and authoritarian crackdowns. It fuels fantasies of a "moral community" surrounded by fortifications, of a smug "West" permanently embattled, closed, and unreconstructed.

Of popular movements that actually exist, the ecology movement alone on the Left has serious potential for crossing the identity trenches. Freedom needs a commons that remains green. Most Americans understand that the so-called conservatives have no interest in conserving the earth. But even here, commonality politics does not emerge automatically. Environmentalists who enjoy professional life cannot afford to forget that the dangers to public health from headlong industrial development fall disproportionately on the working classes, whose factories are frequently vile, whose neighborhoods are more likely to be the sites of toxic dumps and poisoned air than the neighborhoods of the better-off, and whose jobs may be at risk if logging is stopped or automakers are ever forced to shift from gasoline to energy sources that would not further heat up the atmosphere.

But let there be no illusions. All left-of-center forces in the world today are chastened if not demoralized, and for good reason. For a generation, throughout the industrial world, most socialist and social democratic parties, and the groupings of intellectuals around them, have lost ground. This is not only, perhaps not even mainly, because of the shadow of the Gulag and the sordid record of the former command economies of the East. It is largely because the various Lefts start with a built-in disadvantage. They operate on a national scale while corporations and capital flows are transnational. The Left wants to mobilize in behalf of democracy and equality, while capital, the least democratic institution of all, slips through the mesh. In power, social democracies end up presiding over mass unemployment.

It is this mobilization for equality and against arbitrary power that is the Left's main business—if there is to be a Left. Just how can a democratic society regulate the demons of technology and the strains of competition? How can multinational corporations be brought under democratic control without resorting to the heavy hand of the state? In the United States, though, the mind-set of identity politics—including the panic against political correctness—aborts the necessary discussion. Cultivating unity within minority groups, the obsession with difference stands in the way of asking the right questions.

To recognize diversity, more than diversity is needed. The commons is needed. To affirm the rights of minorities, majorities must be formed. Democracy is more than a license to celebrate (and exaggerate) differences. It cannot afford to live in the past—anyone's past. It is a political system of mutual reliance and common moral obligations. Mutuality needs tending. If multiculturalism is not tempered by a stake in the commons, then centrifugal energy overwhelms any commitment to a larger good. This is where multiculturalism as a faith has proved a trap even—or especially—for people in the name of whom the partisans of identity politics purport to speak. Affirming the virtues of the margins, identity politics has left the centers of power uncontested. No wonder the threatened partisans of "normality" have seized the offensive.

The dialogue today is inflamed and incoherent in part because the symbolic stakes are overloaded on every side. There is a lot of fantasy in circulation. The melting pot never melted as thoroughly as Henry Ford would have liked; the golden years were mighty white. And the monocultures of Afrocentrists and goddess-worshippers, however foolish, are far less prevalent than their advocates wish or their antagonists fear. But if the Right magnifies the multiculturalist menace, identity partisans inflate the claims they make for multiculturalism. All suffer from a severe lack of proportion. Most of all, while critics of identity politics are looting society, the politics of identity is silent on the deepest sources of social misery: the devastation of cities, the draining of resources away from the public and into the private hands of the few. It does not organize to reduce the sickening inequality between rich and poor. Instead, in effect, it struggles to change the color of inequality. In this setting, the obsession with cultural identity at the expense of political citizenship distracts what must be the natural constituencies of a Left if there is to be one: the poor, those fearful of being poor, intellectuals with sympathies for the excluded.

Make no mistake—the path of commonality offers no utopian destination. It offers, in fact, difficulties galore. Majorities come and go; they are not easy to stitch together under the best of circumstances. A diversity of customs and rages is here to stay—and nowhere more than in amazingly profuse, polychrome, polyglot America. Plainly people are motivated by loyalties to clan, religion, race. Meanwhile, capital moves across frontiers at the speed of light as labor lumbers along at a human pace. Capital can always threaten to take off for lower-wage pastures and bring national reformers to their knees. At the same time, the nation-states that people expect to protect them against the flux may be obsolescent in an age of global markets, but they haven't gotten the news. They exist. They have weight. They wave flags; they recruit armies; they build monuments; people are willing to kill and die for their symbols. By contrast, commonality offers—what? The discredited red flag? The blue banner of UN bureaucracy? The green flag is fine, as far as it goes, and so is the flag of human rights, but neither stirs enough human hearts.

Still, we will not see what lies on the other side of the politics of identity unless, unflinchingly, without illusions, we look, look again, and are willing to go on looking. For too long, too many Americans have busied themselves digging trenches to fortify their cultural borders, lining their trenches with insulation. Enough bunkers! Enough of the perfection of differences! We ought to be building bridges.

Chapter Four

The Struggle for Feminist Purity Threatens the Goals of Feminism

Daphne Patai

A number of years ago I got the idea of putting together a volume with the title "Ideological Policing in Contemporary Feminism." The episodes leading to this intention are by now a bit vague in my mind, but they included stories told to me by feminist colleagues, for example about being criticized by other feminists for wearing makeup, for being heterosexual, for wanting a door put on an office and thus gaining some unsisterly privacy from the feminist staff members in the adjoining office.

In my own courses in women's studies, I have seen similar examples of intolerance among my students—eyes rolled to ceiling in exaggerated disapproval of a classmate's reference to her "boyfriend"; heated criticisms by young women in sturdy boots and pants of the "conventional" apparel of other women in the class; an urgent need to ferret out examples of latent unfeminist tendencies; a certain aggressiveness in displaying one's ideological credentials. Of course, there was surely just as much intolerance elsewhere in the university—antagonism, say, to lesbian students—but at least in my own women's studies courses, I did not see that kind of hostility emerge. It was obvious that women's studies classrooms provided a safe arena in which interesting reversals of prevailing reality could take place. It didn't surprise me that, among young students at least, this might lead to excessive zeal.

All this, of course, was before the burning intellectual question of the day revolved around "political correctness."

I never wrote that book—and a major reason I didn't was that I couldn't decide how to write a critique of feminism that would not in some way hurt feminism and that would not automatically place me in the enemy camp. Despite opponents' assertions, feminist concerns had not had such resounding success in the world that I wanted to hazard a public critique. And the ease with which the charges of PC have been catching on shows that I was right to be wary of writing something that could be taken to support such charges.

But everything one tolerates, that one shouldn't, inevitably returns.

So, today, I am once again exercised over ideological policing within feminism. I

Reprinted by permission from *Chronicle of Higher Education*, February 5, 1992, p. B1.

am still worried about the best way to write about this subject without making my views useful to the opposition—the very real opposition that exists to feminism and to women's studies programs. Indeed, the difficulty in making up my mind about this dilemma is part of what motivates this essay. But its context is provided by the following concatenation of events:

On October 30, 1991, I published a commentary in these pages on "surplus visibility" and the stigma of minority status. In November, as responses to the article came in, I discovered that my argument apparently had led some people to assume that I must be black. Thus, I received a letter requesting that I contribute a brief life story to a book on blacks who had "made it" in academe. At the same time, in my own Women's Studies Program at the University of Massachusetts, I found myself called a racist because, as acting director, I had been unable to come up with extra money for an elective course on indigenous women proposed by two Native American graduate students. Simultaneously, I had used the last bit of money in our budget to finance a required course on the intellectual foundations of feminism, to be taught by a teaching assistant who happened to be white.

The same error was being made in both cases: identity politics—the assumption that a person's racial or ethnic identity and views are one and the same. If people found what I said sympathetic or useful to blacks, I must be black. If minority women were frustrated or disappointed by an administrative decision, I, in my white skin, must be racist.

The consequences of these two cases of mistaken identity were, however, vastly different. In the first case, I merely wrote to explain that I was white and hence not an appropriate candidate for a book on black academics. In the latter case, I tried to explain that "racism" had nothing to do with the events in question. This simple denial brought a storm down upon my head. I was told by a young black colleague that when a woman of color says she has experienced racism, she is the authority on that experience and cannot be challenged. More protests on my part—that this made any kind of discussion impossible—only made the situation worse, as memos and charges came from every direction. Every direction but one: not one of my colleagues who clearly believed that the charges were absurd (and told me so privately) was willing to say so publicly.

I began to realize that we were confronting a new dogma sanctifying a reversal of privilege: instead of the old privileges accompanying the status of "white," truth, righteousness, and automatic justification in the world of women's studies now reside with "women of color." As if in compensation for past oppression, no one now can challenge or gainsay their version of reality. What can be said for such a turnabout, of course, is that it spreads racial misery around, and this may serve some larger plan of justice, sub specie aeternitatis.

But this is hardly adequate for those who believe earthly justice must be pursued case by case, and cannot be won by means that are themselves unjust. In this instance, however, the facts of the case were of no importance: only identity counted. This, let me emphasize, was no misinterpretation on my part, for some memos actually did state that it was absurd for a white, tenured professor to claim she was being unjustly accused. By virtue of having a certain identity (white) and occupying a certain position (tenured), an individual would necessarily be guilty of whatever accusations a woman of color (or an untenured individual) might make against her.

Among my other offenses was an expression of concern at the way some of our students were using the term "Eurocentric" as a new slur: by dismissing an entire culture as "racist," they relieved themselves of the burden of learning anything about it. An administrator at my university told me of a student activist who heatedly said: "Do you know who's teaching Spanish in the Spanish Department? Spaniards!" Nor do I take this merely as a joke; I have often wondered how soon it will be before someone suggests that my "identity" (North American) should cause me to cease teaching classes in one of my areas of research, Brazilian women.

The situation that I describe is, alas, hardly unique. What adds to my distress is that it is not usually discussed. For another dogma of women's studies seems to be that our problems must not be aired. There are some good reasons for this reluctance, of course, given the eagerness with which opponents of women's studies might seize on any disagreements. But the consequences are nonetheless dreadful: a kind of siege mentality, in which demands for loyalty thrive and very little fresh air gets in. What does flourish in this confined atmosphere is a flaunting of correct postures, which everyone rushes to embrace, perhaps in an effort to compensate for sexual, racial, or other identities that have been called into question.

Thus, students in my course on utopian fiction by women wrote papers this past semester displaying attitudes that they apparently had learned were the appropriate ones in their women's studies classes. A young white woman too shy to speak in class wrote repeatedly of having to come to terms with her status as a "white oppressor." A young man wrote that a novel we had read taught him that his relationship with Mother Earth was one of rape and pillage; he now saw his rock collection in a new light. I wondered whether he had intended this as parody—which would have been a more original response.

An extremely articulate student wrote eloquently (and without any apparent irony) about how, as a woman, she was silenced and lacked a language. And a white student who criticized a black writer's metaphorical use of the word "slavery" to describe a casual labor exchange was coldly told by another white student that it was not appropriate for a white person to criticize a black writer's metaphors. It is true, of course, that white society has historically oppressed black people, men have damaged the environment, and women indeed have been silenced, but these facts do not mean that everyone today inherits a simple identity or is personally guilty of everything her or his predecessors did.

Identity politics is a dead end. We are neither right nor wrong because of "who we are," but only, as the feminist scholar Jenny Bourne wrote in an essay several years ago, because of what we do.

But why should identity politics not serve as another weapon for faculty members in a scarce job market and poor economy? Why not use this, too, in the scramble for the goodies of our profession—jobs, tenure, legitimacy? What is distressing is that this tactic is no feminist departure from the bad old ways of "white patriarchal hegemony," but a replication of those ways, pure and simple. Old forms, new contents. What feminism adds to it, however, is its own tone of moral superiority. Part of what makes conflicts within feminist groups so unpleasant is surely the sense of fraud that accompanies familiar old ambitions dressed up in appropriate ideology.

Feminism has played a major role in questioning canonical knowledge and standards. Should we be surprised, then, when, on a women's studies search committee, one group's view that a particular candidate is poorly qualified is met by attacks on the very concepts of "qualifications," "standards," and "knowledge"? Feminism itself has provided the weapons to unleash this sort of self-destructive attack, which can be pursued ad infinitum. While particular criteria have been used in academe in the past to exclude certain groups, you cannot have a university without making judgments about people's expertise. The intellectual and political questions posed by feminism were developed to challenge unfair stereotyping and exclusion of women, not to exempt them from evaluation.

Perhaps "identity" must fill all the gaps left if such attacks prevail, however. For, as I have written previously, feminists today often engage in rhetorical maneuvers that are rapidly acquiring the status of incantations: "As a white working-class heterosexual" or "As a black feminist activist." Such tropes, which do nothing to change the world, carry their own aura of self-righteousness, whether offered as an apology or (as is more often the case) deployed as a badge. In their worst form, they lead to a veritable oppression sweepstakes. And it is not uncommon, in women's studies programs, to hear someone's claim to identity in one category negated by a slur in another—as when a colleague commented to me disparagingly that a student in our program, although she was Latin American, was "upper class."

Where will it end? My fear is that the search—and demand—for feminist purity (of both attitudes and identity) will eventually result in a massive rejection of the very important things that feminism, broadly speaking, aims to achieve. Today, feminists who have the temerity to criticize negative tendencies within feminism risk being automatically placed in the enemy camp, thus seeming to swell the ranks of opponents of progressive scholarship, a conservative group that may actually represent only a small number of people. Marginalizing friendly critics will not advance the credibility of women's studies or other revisionist scholarship.

Unfortunately, the situation I've described is not the first time that rigid factionalism has splintered leftist politics. The entire history of the left is replete with purges and divisions. What is more banal than that the powerless should turn against one another? Whom else can they effectively trounce?

Feminism is hurting itself with identity politics. Those of us who are feminists but who do not accept this simplistic stereotyping and ideological policing must speak up—in defense of feminism.

Chapter Five

Identity Politics and Progress
Don't Fence Me In (or Out)

kristin severson and victoria stanhope

There is no doubt that identity politics has led us into a new awareness of marginalization, discrimination, and equity. Before the suffrage movement, the civil rights movement, the feminist movement, the American Indian movement, and the gay rights movement, to name a few, this country was under the impression that "all men are born equal." By becoming aware that they, as a group, were being denied legal rights, these movements gathered around these "identities" and used them to mobilize against discrimination, create "safe" communities, garner political power, and generate social and economical influence. Today, institutions are more inclusive, minorities are better represented and served, and gradually people are becoming aware of lives beyond the white privileged male. But the struggle is far from over and more awareness and more legal gains clearly are needed as debates continue to swirl around women's roles, race issues, and gay rights. So, given the success of identity politics and the distance yet to go, what could possibly inspire talk about the limitations of identity politics and the emergence of post-liberation movements such as post-feminism?

Identity politics basically uses the "Master's Tools" by adopting the same model dominant groups used to single out minority groups for discrimination. The identities of "gay" or "black" or "woman" have little meaning except in how they relate to what they are not—straight, white, male. Therefore, once upon a time, it would have been possible that these identities would have had no more value than other descriptives or informatives such as red hair, long legs, grandmother, runner. But within our present reality, it matters very much if you are white or Native American, male or female, straight or queer. Identity as a political maneuver is also based off the idea that the given identity does matter—but here is where we must remind ourselves why it matters. It matters because and only because a long time ago someone in power said so and a world was created in which it came to matter.

This article is trying to figure whether the concepts involved in identity politics can ever be long-term tools of change. Is identity politics merely a strategy and compensatory technique to draw attention to the needs of our own political groups?

Reprinted by permission from *Off Our Backs* 18, no. 4, April 1998.

How does it further our thinking? A by-product of identity politics has been fragmentation, divisiveness, and a general lack of unity both within movements and across movements. Political correctness has led us into a First Amendment nightmare and allowed the right-wing to think we are as closed minded as they. We are now faced with the challenge of applying our movements to society as a whole. We can no longer just claim our piece of the pie for equity's sake, we have to show how everyone can participate and more importantly gain from a world free of discrimination.

Perhaps some of the arcane world of postmodernism can in fact help us think through identity politics and even figure out what is right and wrong rather than leaving us in an "anything goes" moral vacuum as is sometimes suggested. Deconstruction helps us get beyond the "red herrings," the things that get cracked up to be significant and in fact are not, they are just made to seem like that because somebody is gaining by it.

Maybe, in response we are creating some red herrings of our own. There has been a lot of nonsense in the past that somehow white straight abled males should have more rights and are more esteemed just because of who they are. Just because that is not true, does not mean that it is true for marginalized identities. However, the experience of oppression can give these groups a depth of insight that is invaluable to any discussion on how we want society to be. Identity politics at its most militant can block the way to genuine social, moral, political process. Shouldn't a movement be essentially about what you believe, your values and ideology rather than who you are or what you do? How many of us have been disappointed by the anti-feminist woman, or the Republican gay person? Political beliefs and identity do not necessarily coincide. But identity is often a tricky concept upon which to base a long term political movement.

In the case of the gay movement, Colin Powell may be right that sexuality is less about what you are and more about what you do, but of course, we would differ profoundly with Powell about his judgment on gay sex. Gay behavior is just one in a huge spectrum of complex, varying, back and forth, imaginative and unimaginative ways that human beings are sexual. But the premise that is prevalent in the gay rights movement is that when it comes to sexual behavior we are born a certain way; the bio-deterministic either you are or you aren't is generally replicating much of oppressive heterosexual culture even if it is in a new proud homosexual face.

Thus, many gays want to get married, fight in the army, and have access to the capitalist structure. In the face of the gay rights mantra of "please give us a piece of the pie, we can't help being like this, we were born like this," human beings are often acting out a much more complex set of behaviors that do not fit into these binary concepts. And maybe more would if there was not so much propaganda that you have to be one or the other. Bisexual people have a hard time feeling part of the gay rights movement and it's because they don't fit the rhetoric. Perhaps we get more short term sympathy if we plead lack of agency in the whole thing and say it is discrimination based on a biological basis, but it takes us no further in creating a truly ethical and inclusive view of sexuality. Until we say yes, I made a genuine choice and it's OK because this is just one of many sexual behaviors that should be judged according to concepts such as respect, mutuality, and caring, and not the particularity of gender, we are not making any real progress. It just takes us further down a road of "them and us." So where does that leave us in the wonderful world of gay pride marches, rainbow calling cards and lesbian cruises? Gay culture has all the wonders of subverting shame to pride and all the energy of the maverick alternative, but at times seems as shuttered as the straight world. If gay culture is to truly rebel against the elitism of this heterosexist world in which we live, it must become more expansive in its views of sexuality and more cognizant of its connections with other identity based liberation movements.

The queer youth movement may be showing the way with the prevalence of bisexuality as a choice on campuses and the inclusiveness of the queer youth movement to transsexuals and transgendered people. There is evidence that shows, despite ourselves, the reality of our behavior is winning through. Even on the Jerry Springer Show, which frequently uses the same-sex relationship as the big shocker, there are few reactions from the audience such as "but you aren't gay" or "what are you really?" And in a weird way it is kind of heartening to see how upset the boyfriends get about their girlfriends having an affair with the girl next door; they approach it as a legitimate act of infidelity—all demonstrating that queer sexual behavior is accepted as a part of the whole morass of human sexual behavior albeit in a very sensationalistic way. There is no longer the incredulity or amazement that people express when you are bisexual or have slept with people of both sexes and both experiences have been authentic. The movement could then become composed of people who believe that sexuality can be a variety of sexual and emotional behaviors all of which are valid if based upon an ethic of caring or respect or whatever we want to agree on. It then has little or nothing to do with what we, ourselves, do.

And what about the women's movement? Clearly, women-only space and women's culture serves us well by giving us a "safe" haven. But it still can prevent us from actually engaging in the way gender has been created to divvy up power and wrestling with what specific qualities we want all human beings to have. The current debates taking place now about whether we should have single-sex schooling and single-sex military training highlight this struggle. Like the gay movement, the separation and celebration of our "female identity" has been profoundly valuable for many in the face of devastating oppression. But again, we have to deal with the question "Do we think gender is biologically based?" If the answer is no, then where are we going? If we say we want men to be more like women, what does that mean? Does it mean there are certain values and behaviors that we esteem over others, including equality? Does that belief create a culture and a movement based on identity or rather on the desired characteristics?

The whole "Men are from Mars, Women are from Venus dialogue," the giving-in to gendered characteristics by offering up complex ways to negotiate this communicative nightmare seems in the end to be self-defeating. An enduring political and ethical approach to a sexist society cannot be based upon these same divisive gender lines, but rather must figure out which behaviors help society and which do not, and work to give all human beings the experiences which will promote these characteristics, not restricting people according to their biology.

Academic or personal movements which resemble a "post-liberation" politics, such as post-feminism, happen when this model of "divisive identities" actually becomes a core political pillar of the identity politics. This model is inherently exclusionary and fosters "Otherness," not only the minority group from the majority group, but within the minority group itself. With such a model, identity politics gets hindered unnecessarily on definitions. For example, what exactly qualifies one to be part of the lesbian community? Is there a checklist? Must one sleep exclusively with women, be a woman-born, double X-chromosome who has not engaged in any transgendering herself? These points have created "Others" within the lesbian community—the discriminatory act which we politically and ethically mobilized against happening to ourselves.

Likewise, stressing one identity to be the basis of a liberation politics ignores the fact that people often have more than one primary identity. The gay movement has members who are women, black, working class, etc. These identities heavily influence the experiences of certain members within the gay movement. Women within the black community experience a sexist reality as much as they do a racist reality. Likewise, queer members of the black community are victims of homophobia as much as they are of racism. And clearly, as the feminist movement has been learning the hard way, women's issues include homophobia, racism, classism, xenophobia, etc., because a feminist movement MUST include ALL women. It is when identity politics sells out "Others" by not being inclusive that we realize our political movements are more like that which we are fighting against than we wish to realize. But to be truly progressive, it seems we must go one step further than including all the diversity within our own identity movement, we must create a belief system that everyone can adopt as their own whatever their identity.

What are the long term goals of the gay rights movement? The black civil rights movement? The feminist movement? These movements are different in that they have very different histories and are advocating for different groups but are the same in that they have all suffered from the straight white abled males creating "Others." Clearly we do not want to just advocate for us to be included, maybe we have far more to gain by denying the notion that any of us are "Other" rather than reflecting and perpetuating it even in a prideful way. Instead of simply homogenizing ourselves, losing the richness of diversity that exists among us, or just asking the straight white abled men to include us, we actually want to engage them in a discussion about how all humanity should behave, including them. Politics would then become more about values and beliefs than identity; what would divide and unite people would be the real issue of their ideologies not their very complex and constructed social identities.

Chapter Six

On Whose Behalf?
Feminist Ideology and Dilemmas of Constituency

Robin Leidner

Feminist ideology defines the constituency of the contemporary women's movement extremely broadly—all women should benefit from the struggle, all could contribute to it, none should feel excluded. The reality has been somewhat disappointing, and the difference between feminist organizations' desired constituencies and their actual participants is the subject of this paper.

Diversity is one of the most widely addressed themes in feminist theory and feminist politics in recent years. In the first giddy throes of sisterhood, contemporary feminists, who were predominantly white and middle-class, often assumed that they could speak for women as a whole (e.g., Friedan 1963; Daly 1978; for discussion, see Buechler 1990; Echols 1989). Within a short time, the error of this stance was made abundantly clear, as lesbians, women of color, women from around the world, and others who were not white, middle-class, heterosexual, U.S. women, spoke up. They were angry at having been rendered invisible, and they argued that a true sisterhood could not emerge until their views of the world were valued and their concerns included on the feminist agenda (see, e.g., Collins 1990; Combahee River Collective 1979; Dill 1983; hooks 1981, 1984; Moraga and Anzaldúa 1981).

At the level of theory and rhetoric, these arguments have been extremely successful (see, e.g., Harding 1987; Ramazanoglu 1989; Jones 1993).[1] While claims about women that overgeneralize from the perspective of the most privileged women have not disappeared entirely, they are no longer likely to go unchallenged. The cogent critiques of women of color, and also the influence of postmodernist theories suspicious of unitary stories have sensitized feminists to the importance of diversity in theorizing and in politics. Unfortunately, however, awareness of the hazards of exclusivity has not meant that solutions have been easy to implement (see Buechler 1990). Despite broader agendas and more diversified curricula, the tension between unity and diversity in feminism is still quite problematic.

In addressing the somewhat sore subject of the constituencies of the women's movement, one should not accept too hastily the familiar dismissive verdict that feminism is simply a middle-class white women's movement. As Barbara Ryan points out (1992: 125), that conclusion suggests that organizations devoted to improving the lives of women of color and of working-class women are not part of the women's movement, and downplays the strong support for feminist goals among those who are not themselves activists (see, e.g., hooks 1981: 148; Mansbridge 1986: 15). It also ignores the contributions of many women of color and working-class women to feminist organizations whose memberships are predominantly white and middle-class, and dismisses the efforts these organizations have made to expand their agendas to reflect the concerns of a wide range of women (see also Buechler 1990: 150–51). In fairness, we should note, as Buechler does (1990: 169), that while "women's movements have always had difficulty transcending their white, middle-class roots . . . few movements have been better and many have been much worse at transcending (or even recognizing) such barriers."

Still, it is true that feminist aspirations to create organizations that reflect and respect the diversity of women have often fallen short, as both protestations from those excluded or treated badly and the mea culpas of other feminists testify (Davis 1990 [1988]; Jones 1993; Leidner 1993; Matthews 1989; Moraga and Anzaldúa 1981). Moreover, their efforts to overcome exclusionary practices have frequently been exceedingly painful, leaving legacies of mistrust, anger, and guilt. Mansbridge and Yeatman (1991: 6) note:

> Many Black feminists have written of their despair in trying to find a welcome place in existing feminist organizations with a predominantly white membership. Almost every major Black feminist writer has some such story to tell, including bell hooks, Audre Lorde, Michelle Wallace, Alice Walker, Barbara Smith, and many whose works are less well known.[2]

For many organizations and social movements, speaking for a narrowly defined constituency is unproblematic. Feminists, however, hope to address the concerns of women of many backgrounds and perspectives. In fact, organizational legitimacy in the eyes of members and external audiences may well depend in part on making sure that feminism does not speak, and does not appear to speak, only for the parochial interests of a subgroup of women.

It is certainly common enough for ideologues to assert that they are speaking for a large mass of people, whether or not those people have indicated their support for the positions espoused. Movements have ideological ways of reconciling their broadly defined constituencies and their frequently meager numbers. For example, socialists in the United States have routinely had to explain why the working classes are overwhelmingly absent from their movement. The standard explanation, of course, is the hegemony of the dominant classes, which causes workers to suffer from "false consciousness."

Feminists early on adopted a similar rationale for the embarrassing reality of huge numbers of women who did not accept a feminist analysis of social life. "Their consciousnesses haven't been raised yet" was an appealing explanation for feminists who had themselves recently experienced a radical transformation in worldview. This interpretation has given way as feminists have come to understand some of the many ways that what they had understood as the feminist agenda, as the perspective of women, as a thorough critique of oppression, were in fact partial visions reflecting the life experiences and concerns of only some women, relatively privileged ones at that (Echols 1989; Ferree and Hess 1985; Harding 1987; Jaggar 1983).

Feminist thought and politics often began from the premise that control of knowledge by men had produced limited and distorted understandings of the world, and control of resources by men had benefited men disproportionately. When women who felt that they were not being represented by the feminist movement used arguments that were identical in form to these (e.g., Moraga and Anzaldúa 1981), principled feminists could not deny their validity.

For many feminists, moreover, breadth of participation is not merely desirable but also essential to both accurate understanding and successful politics. Much feminist ideology has been underpinned by some version of epistemology that rejects the possibility of detached perception. Influential feminist theorists developed various kinds of arguments that women have, or potentially can achieve, a distinctive perspective on reality (see Longino 1993). Some versions (e.g., Flax 1983; Gilligan 1982) suggest that this woman's perspective is rooted in biology, in psychological development, or in widely shared experiences of caregiving.

If a distinct women's perspective arises from biology, near-universal female experience, or a form of oppression common to all women, then presumably there is a coherent woman's standpoint, which any woman either already has or could achieve (Hartsock 1987 [1983]; Jaggar 1983; D. Smith 1987). Such an epistemology supports feminists who claim to speak for women as a whole. Versions of standpoint theory that stress the importance of social location and personal experience, however, suggest that there is no single women's standpoint (e.g., Collins 1990; Stanley and Wise 1990), as does postmodern theory (Flax 1987; Weedon 1987). Assuming that is correct, a number of different conclusions may be drawn. Some have been concerned that standpoint theory could lay the ground for a complete relativism that makes any truth claims problematic (Hawkesworth 1989; Longino 1993). The argument that privilege blinds people to reality could be taken to suggest that those who are most oppressed are in the best position to perceive reality in an unbiased way, that they can achieve the greatest access to truth (see Collins 1990: 207 for comment). Still others conclude that while some standpoints are less distorted than others, any individual's standpoint provides only partial truth, giving her or him insight into some aspects of reality while obscuring others (Albrecht and Brewer 1990: 19). In that case, reality could presumably be best approximated by weighing knowledge drawn from many standpoints (Harding 1991; Stanley and Wise 1990). Postmodernism, with its distrust of essentialism and unitary thought, dampens the hope for any stable, all-encompassing vision but strongly supports the impulse toward multivocality (Hekman 1990).

These epistemological concerns clarify why claims of exclusion must be taken so seriously by feminists. If we accept that people who are white, are middle-class or better-off, have benefited from colonialism, or otherwise are privileged have some stake in the mystifications that allow for oppression to continue, then the grounds for resisting criticisms from those less privileged are severely undercut. The insights of the most oppressed are those that are most crucial to arriving at an adequate understanding of reality, so one could argue that their priorities should guide the feminist agenda.[3] Alternatively, the position that social locations provide only partial insights similarly undercuts the possibility that a group of privileged women could speak for all women, and provides strong motivation to develop a movement in which no women are rendered invisible and no voices are excluded.

But how? Simply reaching out to members of underrepresented groups and encouraging them to join existing feminist organizations has not solved the problem (cf. Davis 1990 [1988]), for several reasons. First, women of color in particular assert that when they have tried to become participants they have frequently been treated disrespectfully or otherwise marginalized by white feminists (Davenport 1981; McKay 1993; Moraga and Anzaldúa 1981; Yamada 1981). Second, the organizations created by white middle-class feminists involved shared cultures that are likely to be unfamiliar, baffling, or sometimes offensive to other kinds of women (e.g., Matthews 1989). Most important, though, is the ongoing reality of divergent priorities. If white middle-class feminists took for granted that the feminist agenda they devised would reflect the concerns of other women and would attract them to feminist activism, that expectation was unrealistic, indeed arrogant and condescending (Spelman 1988). Middle-class white feminists might well perceive that oppression based on gender is the fundamental problem facing them, and that all women would benefit from its elimination. Those less privileged, however, see that eliminating the forms of sexism targeted by these feminists would not in itself bring about their own empowerment or the empowerment of their communities. They have other concerns that are at least as pressing, and unless the agendas of feminist organizations change, they have limited incentive to join (see, e.g., Buechler 1990; Christensen 1997; Dill 1983; Garcia 1989; Giddings 1984; Joseph and Lewis 1981; King 1988; Lorde 1984). Moreover, many women (including Latina, Asian-American, African-American, and white working-class women) perceive mainstream feminists as harshly critical of their cultures without thoroughly understanding them, and as promoting a divisiveness between men and women that would undermine class-based, racial, or ethnic struggles (e.g., Chow 1984; Collins 1990; Garcia 1989). Even when such women support the goals of mainstream feminist organizations, they are unlikely to join if the costs include distancing themselves from their own communities and having their concerns treated as peripheral.

Feminist commitment to participatory democracy would seem to provide some answers to these problems. The desire to empower all women has led feminists to develop organizational practices that do not silence anyone and that enhance the power of those who are in the minority. One hopes that such practices would give women from underrepresented groups the opportunity to gain real power to shape the organizational agenda and culture. But these approaches have been problematic as well.

First, participatory democracy puts higher demands on participants' time, energy, and commitment than other governance forms. Those with multiple responsibilities, multiple political commitments, and little ability to save time by paying for services face barriers to joining such demanding organizations, and could be disadvantaged in gaining influence if they do join because of the limits to their involvement (Mansbridge 1973; Sirianni 1993b).

Small feminist organizations have often used consensus decision making to mandate participation and ensure that minority opinions are fully aired and taken into account. However, unless groups are relatively homogeneous, consensus is likely to be extraordinarily inefficient and frustrating (Mansbridge 1980; Rothschild and Whitt 1986), and the process itself can create pressure to conform. This form of participatory democracy is unlikely to be suitable for diverse groups, and certainly not for large ones.

For larger organizations and polities, some form of special representation may be necessary if those in underrepresented groups are to gain more than token influence. Iris Young (1989) makes the theoretical case for creating forms of "differential citizenship" that acknowledge that the costs of participation disproportionately burden oppressed groups and that equalizing the voices of all participants does not ensure that the interests of disadvantaged minorities will be taken seriously. She recommends that polities provide support for the self-organization of such groups; ensure that their policy proposals are fully considered; and grant veto power over specific policies to groups who are uniquely affected by them. Her bold proposals would help oppressed minorities to exercise real power, but, as Sirianni (1993a) and Phillips (1993) each outline, they pose their own dangers. The experience of the National Women's Studies Association, which moved in the direction of differential citizenship, illustrates some of the problems with this version of participatory democracy (Leidner 1991, 1993). The designation of groups deserving of special representation is bound to be problematic, as new groups seek recognition and as the legitimacy of existing groups' claims of oppression changes over time. Moreover, basing political representations on identities reintroduces the problems of essentialism, creating a false appearance of unanimity within subgroups, undermining accountability, and predetermining which aspects of identity are politically pertinent. The most serious problem with the "strong" version of differential citizenship Young proposes is that it encourages what Phillips (1993: 136) calls a "politics of the enclave," locking people into narrow, specific concerns. Increasing balkanization can generate conflict and resentment, blocking rather than facilitating the development of a wider sense of solidarity (Sirianni 1993a: 375; Phillips 1993: 150).[4]

Thus despite feminist intentions and efforts to empower minorities, forms of participatory democracy have not yet been developed that overcome the difficulties of building unity among diverse women, and some existing or suggested forms themselves present barriers to the effective functioning of diverse organizations.

So far, then, we don't have a solution to the dilemma of predominantly white feminist organizations' actual membership being far less diverse than their ideal constituencies. Democratic theory does not provide much guidance for dealing with this problem, since theorists typically either take the membership of a polity as a given and concern themselves with how best to represent those members or assume that inclusion is eagerly sought (cf. Dahl 1990 [1970]; Walzer 1983). The situation here is that the polity wants to include people who do not choose to join. Like political parties and firms, feminist organizations and other social movement organizations must concern themselves with attracting participants (i.e., members or consumers) and dissuading them from leaving.

Albert Hirschman's ideas (1970, 1993) about voice, exit, and loyalty are helpful here. He analyzes voice and exit as two mechanisms that can allow organizations to recover from problems. When members voice their dissatisfactions, management is given an opportunity to mend its ways and make changes that will satisfy these constituents. If voice is not available or proves unsuccessful, members can choose to leave the organization, and the pattern of exit provides the impetus and necessity for management to make changes to prevent organizational disaster. Why haven't these mechanisms worked to overcome whatever problems have kept many feminist organizations from realizing their aspirations?

One immediate problem, of course, is that exit is available only to those who are already participants, and voice is most effective for them, too. The absence of desired members is the problem here, and efforts by privileged women to figure out for themselves what the concerns and priorities of women unlike themselves are have been subjected to scathing criticism, as have earnest requests for less privileged women to provide education to help others overcome racism or ignorance (Anzaldúa 1990, cited in Jones 1993: 227; McKay 1993; Spelman 1988; Yamada 1981).

However, women other than white middle-class ones are present in many predominantly white organizations, sometimes even in leadership positions. They have made vigorous efforts to exercise voice, yet, for a variety of reasons, organizations have frequently been unable to respond well enough to their dissatisfactions to keep them from choosing to exit (see Mansbridge and Yeatman 1991: 6). The choice to exit, rather than to stay and continue to try to change the faulty organization, is eased by the existence of alternative organizations that can contribute to the empowerment of women of color and working-class women. In fact, feminists would be hard-pressed to dispute the legitimacy of the choice to work in an organization of women from one's own community or in a mixed-gender group (provided that one struggles with sexism there).[5]

If exit can be a signal that prompts positive organizational change under some circumstances, that is unfortunately not typically the case here. For despite recognition of the problems of exclusivity, predominantly white organizations are not likely to be able to solve those problems by themselves. Exit can promote recovery only when the organization is able to figure out how to make the necessary changes and has the means to make them. In some situations, however, exit leads to further deterioration (see Hirschman 1970: 99–104), unless voice can be effectively exercised from outside the organization. In the case of feminist organizations, the exit (or failure to join) of important constituents diminishes the possibilities that predominantly white organizations will be able to redefine their structures and agendas so as to attract a diverse membership.

These rather depressing conclusions suggest that while we should continue to try to diversify predominantly white women's organizations, we will need to pursue other routes to building a diverse women's movement as well. Many writers have suggested that coalitions and alliances are the most promising avenues for working toward unity while allowing diversity to flourish (Albrecht and Brewer 1990; Alperin 1990; Collins 1990; Fraser and Nicolson 1990; Joseph and Lewis 1981; Kaye/Kantrowitz 1986; Reagon 1983). Coalitions and alliances present us with new problems of representation, accountability, and leadership. Creating forms of participatory democracy that cross organizational boundaries is a challenge facing feminists. Indeed, unity among diverse women, we have learned, cannot be an a priori basis for organization; it will have to be a hard-won accomplishment.

NOTES

1. Spelman (1988), however, shows how racism is reproduced within the rhetoric of inclusion and difference.

2. See hooks 1981; Lorde 1984; Walker 1983; B. Smith 1983; Wallace 1990.

3. Davis (1990 [1984]) makes a similar argument on different grounds.

4. Schmitter (1992) proposes a flexible system of public funding that deals with some of these problems.

5. It is possible that lesbians have proved more successful in forcing changes to the feminist agenda than heterosexual women of color and working-class women have because, at least until the development of broad-based queer politics, the choice to exit was less attractive than voice because of the paucity of other bases for political action.

REFERENCES

Albrecht, Lisa, and Rose M. Brewer. 1990. "Bridges of Power: Women's Multicultural Alliances." Pp. 2–22 in Lisa Albrecht and Rose M. Brewer, eds., *Bridges of Power: Women's Multicultural Alliances*. Philadelphia: New Society Publishers, in cooperation with the National Women's Studies Association.

Alperin, Davida J. 1990. "Social Diversity and the Necessity of Alliances: A Developing Feminist Perspective." Pp. 23–33 in Lisa Albrecht and Rose M. Brewer, eds., *Bridges of Power: Women's Multicultural Alliances*. Philadelphia: New Society Publishers, in cooperation with the National Women's Studies Association.

Anzaldúa, Gloria. 1990. *"En Rapport,* in Opposition: *Cobrano Cuentas a las Nuestras."* In Gloria Anzaldúa, ed., *Making Face, Making Soul-Haciendo Caras: Creative and Critical Perspectives by Women of Color.* San Francisco: Aunt Lute Foundation Books.

Buechler, Steven M. 1990. *Women's Movements in the United States: Woman Suffrage, Equal Rights, and Beyond.* New Brunswick: Rutgers University Press.

Christensen, Kimberly. 1997. " 'With Whom Do You Believe Your Lot Is Cast?' White Feminists and Racism." *Signs* 22, 3: 617–648.

Chow, Esther Ngan-Ling. 1984. "The Development of Feminist Consciousness among Asian American Women." *Gender & Society* 1.3: 284–299.

Collins, Patricia Hill. 1990. *Black Feminist Thought: Knowledge, Consciousness, and the Politics of Empowerment.* Boston: Unwin Hyman.

Combahee River Collective. 1979. "A Black Feminist Statement." Pp. 362–372 in Zillah

Eisenstein, ed., *Capitalist Patriarchy and the Case for Socialist Feminism*. New York: Monthly Review Press.

Dahl, Robert A. 1990 [1970]. *After the Revolution? Authority in a Good Society*. Rev. New Haven: Yale University Press.

Daly, Mary. 1978. *Gyn/Ecology: The Metaethics of Radical Feminism*. Boston: Beacon Press.

Davenport, Doris. 1981. "The Pathology of Racism: A Conversation with Third World Wimmin." Pp. 85–90 in Moraga and Anzaldúa.

Davis, Angela. 1990 [1984]. "Facing Our Common Foe: Women and the Struggle against Racism." Pp. 16–34 in *Women, Culture, and Politics*. New York: Vintage Books.

———. 1990 [1988]. "Let Us All Rise Together: Radical Perspectives on Empowerment for Afro-American Women." Pp. 3–15 in *Women, Culture, and Politics*. New York: Vintage Books.

Dill, Bonnie. 1983. "Race, Class, and Gender: Prospects for an All-Inclusive Sisterhood." *Feminist Studies* 9: 131–150.

Echols, Alice. 1989. *Daring to Be Bad: Radical Feminism in America, 1967–1975*. Minneapolis: University of Minnesota Press.

Ferree, Myra Marx, and Beth Hess. 1985. *Controversy and Coalition: The New Feminist Movement*. Boston: Hall/Twayne.

Flax, Jane. 1983. "Political Philosophy and the Patriarchal Unconscious: A Psychoanalytic Perspective on Epistemology and Metaphysics." In Sandra Harding and Merrill B. Hintikka, eds., *Discovering Reality: Feminist Perspectives on Epistemology, Metaphysics, Methodology and Philosophy of Science*. Dordrecht, the Netherlands: D. Reidel Publishing Co.

———. 1987. "Postmodernism and Gender Relations in Feminist Theory." *Signs* 12.4: 621–43.

Fraser, Nancy, and Linda Nicholson. 1990. "Social Criticism without Philosophy: An Encounter between Feminism and Postmodernism." Pp. 19–38 in Linda Nicolson, ed., *Feminism/Postmodernism*. New York: Routledge.

Friedan, Betty. 1963. *The Feminine Mystique*. New York: Dell.

Garcia, Alma. 1989. "The Development of Chicana Feminist Discourse, 1970–1980." *Gender & Society* 3.2: 217–38.

Giddings, Paula. 1984. *When and Where I Enter*. New York: Morrow.

Gilligan, Carol. 1982. *In a Different Voice*. Cambridge: Harvard University Press.

Harding, Sandra, 1987. "Introduction: Is There a Feminist Method?" Pp. 1–14 in Sandra Harding, ed., *Feminism and Methodology*. Bloomington: Indiana University Press.

———. 1991. *Whose Science? Whose Knowledge? Thinking from Women's Lives*. Ithaca: Cornell University Press.

Hartsock, Nancy C. M. 1987 [1983]. "The Feminist Standpoint: Developing the Ground for a Specifically Feminist Historical Materialism." Pp. 157–180 in Sandra Harding, ed., *Feminism and Methodology*. Bloomington: Indiana University Press.

Hawkesworth, Mary E. 1989. "Knowers, Knowing, Known: Feminist Theory and Claims of Truth." *Signs* 14: 533–557.

Hekman, Susan. 1990. *Gender and Knowledge: Elements of a Postmodern Feminism*. Boston: Northeastern University Press.

Hirschman, Albert O. 1970. *Exit, Voice, and Loyalty*. Cambridge: Harvard University Press.

———. 1993. "Exit, Voice, and the Fate of the German Democratic Republic: An Essay in Conceptual History." *World Politics* 45: 173–202.

hooks, bell. 1981. *Ain't I a Woman: Black Women and Feminism*. Boston: South End Press.

————. 1984. *Feminist Theory: From Margin to Center.* Boston: South End Press.

Jaggar, Alison M. 1983. *Feminist Politics and Human Nature.* Totowa, NJ: Rowman & Allanheld.

Jones, Kathleen. 1993. *Compassionate Authority: Democracy and the Representation of Women.* New York: Routledge.

Joseph, Gloria, and Jill Lewis. 1981. *Common Differences: Conflicts in Black and White Feminism.* Garden City, NY: Doubleday.

Kaye/Kantrowitz, Melanie. 1986. "To Be a Radical Jew in the Late 20th Century." Pp. 264–287 in Melanie Kaye/Kantrowitz and Irena Klepfisz, eds., *The Tribe of Dina: A Jewish Women's Anthology.* Montpelier, VT: Sinister Wisdom Books.

King, Deborah H. 1988. "Multiple Jeopardy, Multiple Consciousness: The Context of a Black Feminist Ideology. *Signs* 14.1: 42–72.

Leidner, Robin. 1991. "Stretching the Boundaries of Liberalism: Democratic Innovation in a Feminist Organization." *Signs* 16.2: 263–289.

————. 1993. "Constituency, Accountability, and Deliberation: Democratic Innovation in a Feminist Organization." *NWSA Journal* 5.1: 263–289.

Longino, Helen G. 1993. "Feminist Standpoint Theory and the Problems of Knowledge." *Signs* 19.1: 201–212.

Lorde, Audre. 1984. *Sister Outsider.* Trumansburg, NY: The Crossing Press.

Mansbridge, Jane. J. 1973. "Time, Emotion, and Inequality: Three Problems of Participatory Groups." *The Journal of Applied Behavioral Science* 9: 351–368.

————. 1980. *Beyond Adversary Democracy.* Chicago: University of Chicago Press.

————. 1986. *Why We Lost the ERA.* Chicago: University of Chicago Press.

Mansbridge, Jane, and Gayle Yeatman. 1991. "Becoming a Feminist: African-American and White Experiences." Paper presented at the annual meeting of the Midwest Sociological Association, Des Moines, Iowa.

Matthews, Nancy. 1989. "Surmounting a Legacy: The Expansion of Racial Diversity in a Local Anti-Rape Movement." *Gender & Society* 3.4: 518–532.

McKay, Nellie Y. 1993. "Acknowledging Differences: Can Women Find Unity through Diversity?" Pp. 267–282 in Stanlie M. James and Abena P. A. Busia, eds., *Theorizing Black Feminisms: The Visionary Pragmatism of Black Women.* London: Routledge.

Moraga, Cherríe, and Gloria Anzaldúa, eds. 1981. *This Bridge Called My Back: Writings by Radical Women of Color.* Watertown, MA: Persephone Press.

Phillips, Anne. 1993. *Democracy and Difference.* University Park: Pennsylvania State University Press.

Ramazanoglu, Caroline. 1989. *Feminism and the Contradictions of Oppression.* London: Routledge.

Reagon, Bernice Johnson. 1983. "Coalition Politics: Turning the Century." Pp. 356–368 in Barbara Smith, ed., *Home Girls — A Black Feminist Anthology.* New York: Kitchen Table Press.

Rothschild, Joyce, and J. Allen Whitt. 1986. *The Cooperative Workplace: Potentials and Dilemmas of Organizational Democracy and Participation.* Cambridge: Cambridge University Press.

Ryan, Barbara. 1992. *Feminism and the Women's Movement: Dynamics of Change in Social Movement Ideology and Activism.* New York: Routledge.

Schmitter, Philippe. 1992. "The Irony of Modern Democracy and Efforts to Improve its Practice." *Politics and Society* 20: 507–512.

Sirianni, Carmen. 1993a. "Feminist Pluralism and Democratic Learning: The Politics of

Citizenship in the National Women's Studies Association." *NWSA Journal* 5.3: 367–384.

———. 1993b. "Learning Pluralism: Democracy and Diversity in Feminist Organizations." Pp. 283–312 in John Chapman and Ian Shapiro, eds., *Nomos XXXV: Democratic Community*. New York: New York University Press.

Smith, Barbara. 1983. "Introduction." Pp. xix-xlviii in Barbara Smith, ed., *Home Girls — A Black Feminist Anthology*. New York: Kitchen Table Press.

Smith, Dorothy. 1987. *The Everyday World as Problematic*. Boston: Northeastern University Press.

Spelman, Elizabeth V. 1988. *Inessential Woman: Problems of Exclusion in Feminist Thought*. Boston: Beacon Press.

Stanley, Liz, and Sue Wise. 1990. "Method, Methodology and Epistemology in Feminist Research Processes." Pp. 20–60 in Liz Stanley, ed., *Feminist Praxis: Research, Theory and Epistemology in Feminist Sociology*. London: Routledge.

Walker, Alice. 1983. *In Search of Our Mother's Gardens*. New York: Harcourt Brace Jovanovich.

Wallace, Michelle. 1990. "A Black Feminist's Search for Sisterhood." Pp. 18–25 in *Invisibility Blues*. New York: Verso.

Walzer, Michael. 1983. *Spheres of Justice: A Defense of Pluralism and Equality*. New York: Basic Books.

Weedon, Chris. 1987. *Feminist Practice and Postmodernist Theory*. Oxford: Basil Blackwell.

Yamada, Mitsuye. 1981. "Asian Pacific American Women and Feminism." Pp. 71–75 in Moraga and Anzaldúa.

Young, Iris. 1989. "Polity and Group Difference: A Critique of the Ideal of Universal Citizenship." *Ethics* 99.2: 250–274.

Part II

Claiming an Identity

The stranger can never be a real insider because s/he lives in a borderland, and it is otherness that sets apart her or his difference. "This difference is not merely experienced; it is lived, it becomes the stuff of which a life is thus composed, and it is central to identity and feeling, and thinking" (Stanley 1997:6).

When the contemporary women's movement began organizing in the late 1960s, activists set about raising the consciousness of women to their social condition, and then to changing the barriers that limited them to a gender stratified system. Many of the early organizers had been involved in the New Left, antiwar protests, and civil rights activism. They had the lived experience of working for others but not being recognized as worthy of concern when they raised women's issues. They were intent upon making women's lives the forefront of a new movement for change.

However, in short time there were murmurs within women's groups of differences among women and the impediments those differences made for women working together to enact a feminist vision they could share. In 1974 the Combahee River Collective set itself apart from mainstream feminism by defining its politics as "actively committed to struggling against racial, sexual, heterosexual, and class oppression." It saw its particular task as the need to develop thought on the interlocking nature of major systems of oppression. Its paper in this section is an introduction to how contemporary black feminism began, what this particular collective believed, the problems it encountered in organizing black feminists, and feminist issues and practices particularly relevant to black feminists.

The issues the Combahee River Collective raised led to a broader view of feminism and women as a group. If feminism is to be for all women, then it must be about all women. But this is easier to speak of than to do. Minnie Bruce Pratt shows how difficult this task can be. She claims an identity too, that of a white southern woman. Then she takes a critical look at her life and what she was taught to believe, how she was taught to see the world. She rejects those teachings, realizing that what she thought was an accurate view is actually a lie. Pratt allows herself to feel the fear of thinking outside the worldview she was raised with, to begin to see how her place in the world has not taken into account other people's racial, ethnic, economic, and spiritual places in that same world.

Bonnie Sherr Klein was proud to claim her identity as a feminist and to see herself in that light. But that early exhilaration was shaken when she became the victim of a stroke at an early age. Klein explores her transition from an able-bodied feminist filmmaker to the world of disability. She experiences the invisibility of being a disabled woman, even though she was once highly respected by the same people to whom she is now invisible. She struggles to continue defining herself as a feminist, realizing that as a prestroke feminist she was in relentless pursuit of strength, competence, and independence. Now, poststroke, she is increasingly dependent on her husband, unable to negotiate the physical world as she once did. In solidarity with other disabled and aging women, Klein finds herself redefining what it means to be a woman and a feminist.

Rebecca Walker, daughter of novelist Alice Walker, places feminism in front of her skin color as the place where her activism resides. She uses the public incident of Anita Hill's testimony at the Clarence Thomas confirmation hearings for a seat on the U.S. Supreme Court and a private experience on a train to show why women must join in sisterhood to fight the power structures that divide us all. She protests the claims of a postfeminist era and proudly proclaims that she, and others like her, are the Third Wave in the fight for women's dignity and lives.

Audre Lorde closes this section with a similar call: the call for voice and action. Faced with a life-threatening and life-altering condition, Lorde was forced to reexamine her own mortality. She explores women's invisibility as people and includes all women—black, white, lesbian, straight—in her reflections. Whether we speak or not, she believes others will attempt to divide and, thereby, dismiss us. Through language and action is survival, growth. Lorde challenges the notion that because someone is different from us we cannot learn from his or her teachings. As she reminds us, it is not our difference that keeps us apart but, rather, our silence.

REFERENCE

Stanley, Liz. 1997. "Introduction." Pp. 1–17 in *Knowing Feminisms: On Academic Borders, Territories, and Tribes,* edited by Liz Stanley. London: Sage Publications.

Chapter Seven

A Black Feminist Statement

The Combahee River Collective

We are a collective of black feminists who have been meeting together since 1974.[1] During that time we have been involved in the process of defining and clarifying our politics, while at the same time doing political work within our own group and in coalition with other progressive organizations and movements. The most general statement of our politics at the present time would be that we are actively committed to struggling against racial, sexual, heterosexual, and class oppression and see as our particular task the development of integrated analysis and practice based upon the fact that the major systems of oppression are interlocking. The synthesis of these oppressions creates the conditions of our lives. As black women we see black feminism as the logical political movement to combat the manifold and simultaneous oppressions that all women of color face.

We will discuss four major topics in the paper that follows: (1) The genesis of contemporary black feminism; (2) what we believe, i.e., the specific province of our politics; (3) the problems in organizing black feminists, including a brief herstory of our collective; and (4) black feminist issues and practice.

1. The Genesis of Contemporary Black Feminism

Before looking at the recent development of black feminism, we would like to affirm that we find our origins in the historical reality of Afro-American women's continuous life-and-death struggle for survival and liberation. Black women's extremely negative relationship to the American political system (a system of white male rule) has always been determined by our membership in two oppressed racial and sexual castes. As Angela Davis points out in "Reflections on the Black Woman's Role in the Community of Slaves," black women have always embodied, if only in their physical manifestation, an adversary stance to white male rule and have actively resisted its inroads upon them and their communities in both dramatic and subtle ways. There have always been black women activists—some known, like Sojourner Truth, Harriet Tubman, Frances E. W. Harper, Ida B. Wells Barnett, and Mary

Church Terrell, and thousands upon thousands unknown—who had a shared awareness of how their sexual identity combined with their racial identity to make their whole life situation and the focus of their political struggles unique. Contemporary black feminism is the outgrowth of countless generations of personal sacrifice, militancy, and work by our mothers and sisters.

A black feminist presence has evolved most obviously in connection with the second wave of the American women's movement beginning in the late 1960s. Black, other Third World, and working women have been involved in the feminist movement from its start, but both outside reactionary forces and racism and elitism within the movement itself have served to obscure our participation. In 1973 black feminists, primarily located in New York, felt the necessity of forming a separate black feminist group. This became the National Black Feminist Organization (NBFO).

Black feminist politics also have an obvious connection to movements for black liberation, particularly those of the 1960s and 1970s. Many of us were active in those movements (civil rights, black nationalism, the Black Panthers), and all of our lives were greatly affected and changed by their ideology, their goals, and the tactics used to achieve their goals. It was our experience and disillusionment within these liberation movements, as well as experience on the periphery of the white male left, that led to the need to develop a politics that was antiracist, unlike those of white women, and antisexist, unlike those of black and white men.

There is also undeniably a personal genesis for black feminism, that is, the political realization that comes from the seemingly personal experiences of individual black women's lives. Black feminists and many more black women who do not define themselves as feminists have all experienced sexual oppression as a constant factor in our day-to-day existence.

Black feminists often talk about their feelings of craziness before becoming conscious of the concepts of sexual politics, patriarchal rule, and, most importantly, feminism, the political analysis and practice that we women use to struggle against our oppression. The fact that racial politics and indeed racism are pervasive factors in our lives did not allow us, and still does not allow most black women, to look more deeply into our own experiences and define those things that make our lives what they are and our oppression specific to us. In the process of consciousness-raising, actually life-sharing, we began to recognize the commonality of our experiences and, from that sharing and growing consciousness, to build a politics that will change our lives and inevitably end our oppression.

Our development also must be tied to the contemporary economic and political position of black people. The post–World War II generation of black youth was the first to be able to minimally partake of certain educational and employment options, previously closed completely to black people. Although our economic position is still at the very bottom of the American capitalist economy, a handful of us have been able to gain certain tools as a result of tokenism in education and employment which potentially enable us to more effectively fight our oppression.

A combined antiracist and antisexist position drew us together initially, and as we developed politically we addressed ourselves to heterosexism and economic oppression under capitalism.

2. What We Believe

Above all else, our politics initially sprang from the shared belief that black women are inherently valuable, that our liberation is a necessity not as an adjunct to somebody else's but because of our need as human persons for autonomy. This may seem so obvious as to sound simplistic, but it is apparent that no other ostensibly progressive movement has ever considered our specific oppression a priority or worked seriously for the ending of that oppression. Merely naming the pejorative stereotypes attributed to black women (e.g., mammy, matriarch, Sapphire, whore, bulldagger), let alone cataloguing the cruel, often murderous, treatment we receive, indicates how little value has been placed upon our lives during four centuries of bondage in the Western hemisphere. We realize that the only people who care enough about us to work consistently for our liberation is us. Our politics evolve from a healthy love for ourselves, our sisters, and our community which allows us to continue our struggle and work.

This focusing upon our own oppression is embodied in the concept of identity politics. We believe that the most profound and potentially the most radical politics come directly out of our own identity, as opposed to working to end somebody else's oppression. In the case of black women this is a particularly repugnant, dangerous, threatening, and therefore revolutionary concept because it is obvious from looking at all the political movements that have preceded us that anyone is more worthy of liberation than ourselves. We reject pedestals, queenhood, and walking ten paces behind. To be recognized as human, levelly human, is enough.

We believe that sexual politics under patriarchy is as pervasive in black women's lives as are the politics of class and race. We also often find it difficult to separate race from class from sex oppression because in our lives they are most often experienced simultaneously. We know that there is such a thing as racial-sexual oppression which is neither solely racial nor solely sexual, e.g., the history of rape of black women by white men as a weapon of political repression.

Although we are feminists and lesbians, we feel solidarity with progressive black men and do not advocate the fractionalization that white women who are separatists demand. Our situation as black people necessitates that we have solidarity around the fact of race, which white women of course do not need to have with white men, unless it is their negative solidarity as racial oppressors. We struggle together with black men against racism, while we also struggle with black men about sexism.

We realize that the liberation of all oppressed peoples necessitates the destruction of the political-economic systems of capitalism and imperialism as well as patriarchy. We are socialists because we believe the work must be organized for the collective benefit of those who do the work and create the products and not for the profit of the bosses. Material resources must be equally distributed among those who create these resources. We are not convinced, however, that a socialist revolution that is not also a feminist and antiracist revolution will guarantee our liberation. We have arrived at the necessity for developing an understanding of class relationships that takes into account the specific class position of black women who are generally marginal in the labor force, while at this particular time some of us are temporarily viewed as doubly desirable tokens at white-collar and professional levels. We need to articulate the real class situation of persons who are not merely raceless, sexless workers, but for whom racial and sexual oppression are significant determinants in their working/economic lives. Although we are in essential agreement with Marx's theory as it applied to the very specific economic relationships he analyzed, we know that this analysis must be extended further in order for us to understand our specific economic situation as black women.

A political contribution which we feel we have already made is the expansion of the feminist principle that the personal is political. In our consciousness-raising sessions, for example, we have in many ways gone beyond white women's revelations because we are dealing with the implications of race and class as well as sex. Even our black women's style of talking/testifying in black language about what we have experienced has a resonance that is both cultural and political. We have spent a great deal of energy delving into the cultural and experiential nature of our oppression out of necessity because none of these matters have ever been looked at before. No one before has ever examined the multilayered texture of black women's lives.

As we have already stated, we reject the stance of lesbian separatism because it is not a viable political analysis or strategy for us. It leaves out far too much and far too many people, particularly black men, women, and children. We have a great deal of criticism and loathing for what men have been socialized to be in this society: what they support, how they act, and how they oppress. But we do not have the misguided notion that it is their maleness, per se—i.e., their biological maleness—that makes them what they are. As black women we find any type of biological determinism a particularly dangerous and reactionary basis upon which to build a politic. We must also question whether lesbian separatism is an adequate and progressive political analysis and strategy, even for those who practice it, since it so completely denies any but the sexual sources of women's oppression, negating the facts of class and race.

3. Problems in Organizing Black Feminists

During our years together as a black feminist collective we have experienced success and defeat, joy and pain, victory and failure. We have found that it is very difficult to organize around black feminist issues, difficult even to announce in certain contexts that we are black feminists. We have tried to think about the reasons for our difficulties, particularly since the white women's movement continues to be strong and to grow in many directions. In this section we will discuss some of the general reasons for the organizing problems we face and also talk specifically about the stages in organizing our own collective.

The major source of difficulty in our political work is that we are not just trying to fight oppression on one front or even two, but instead to address a whole range of oppressions. We do not have racial, sexual, heterosexual, or class privilege to rely upon, nor do we have even the minimal access to resources and power that groups who possess any one of these types of privilege have.

The psychological toll of being a black woman and the difficulties this presents in reaching political consciousness and doing political work can never be underestimated. There is a very low value placed upon black women's psyches in this society, which is both racist and sexist. As an early group member once said, "We are all damaged people merely by virtue of being black women." We are dispossessed psychologically and on every other level, and yet we feel the necessity to struggle to change our condition and the condition of all black women. In "A Black Feminist's Search for Sisterhood," Michelle Wallace arrives at this conclusion:

> We exist as women who are black who are feminists, each stranded for the moment, working independently because there is not yet an environment in this society remotely congenial to our struggle—because, being on the bottom, we would have to do what no one else has done: we would have to fight the world.[2]

Wallace is not pessimistic but realistic in her assessment of black feminists' position, particularly in her allusion to the nearly classic isolation most of us face. We might use our position at the bottom, however, to make a clear leap into revolutionary action. If black women were free, it would mean that everyone else would have to be free since our freedom would necessitate the destruction of all the systems of oppression.

Feminism is, nevertheless, very threatening to the majority of black people because it calls into question some of the most basic assumptions about our existence, i.e., that gender should be a determinant of power relationships. Here is the way male and female roles were defined in a black nationalist pamphlet from the early 1970s.

> We understand that it is and has been traditional that the man is the head of the house. He is the leader of the house/nation because his knowledge of the world is broader, his awareness is greater, his understanding is fuller and his application of this information is wise. . . . After all, it is only reasonable that the man be the head of the house because he is able to defend and protect the development of his home. . . . Women cannot do the same things as men—they are made by nature to function differently. Equality of men and women is something that cannot happen even in the abstract world. Men are not equal to other men, i.e., ability, experience, or even understanding. The value of men and women can be seen as in the value of gold and silver—they are not equal but both have great value. We must realize that men and women are a complement to each other because there is no house/family without a man and his wife. Both are essential to the development of any life.[3]

The material conditions of most black women would hardly lead them to upset both economic and sexual arrangements that seem to represent some stability in their lives. Many black women have a good understanding of both sexism and racism, but because of the everyday constrictions of their lives cannot risk struggling against them both.

The reaction of black men to feminism has been notoriously negative. They are, of course, even more threatened than black women by the possibility that black feminists might organize around our own needs. They realize that they might not only lose valuable and hard-working allies in their struggles but that they might also be forced to change their habitually sexist ways of interacting with and oppressing black women. Accusations that black feminism divides the black struggle are powerful deterrents to the growth of an autonomous black women's movement.

Still, hundreds of women have been active at different times during the three-year existence of our group. And every black woman who came, came out of a strongly felt need for some level of possibility that did not previously exist in her life.

When we first started meeting early in 1974 after the NBFO first eastern regional conference, we did not have a strategy for organizing, or even a focus. We just wanted to see what we had. After a period of months of not meeting, we began to meet again late in the year and started doing an intense variety of consciousness-raising. The overwhelming feeling that we had is that after years and years we had finally found each other. Although we were not doing political work as a group, individuals continued their involvement in lesbian politics, sterilization abuse and abortion rights work, Third World Women's International Women's Day activities, and support activity for the trials of Dr. Kenneth Edelin, Joan Little, and Inez Garcia. During our first summer, when membership had dropped off considerably, those of us remaining devoted serious discussion to the possibility of opening a refuge for battered women in a black community. (There was no refuge in Boston at that time.) We also decided around that time to become an independent collective since we had serious disagreements with NBFOs bourgeois-feminist stance and their lack of a clear political focus.

We also were contacted at that time by socialist feminists, with whom we had worked on abortion rights activities, who wanted to encourage us to attend the National Socialist Feminist Conference in Yellow Springs. One of our members did attend and despite the narrowness of the ideology that was promoted at that particular conference, we became more aware of the need for us to understand our own economic situation and to make our own economic analysis.

In the fall, when some members returned, we experienced several months of comparative inactivity and internal disagreements which were first conceptualized as a lesbian-straight split but which were also the result of class and political differences. During the summer those of us who were still meeting had determined the need to do political work and to move beyond consciousness-raising and serving exclusively as an emotional support group. At the beginning of 1976, when some of the women who had not wanted to do political work and who also had voiced disagreements stopped attending of their own accord, we again looked for a focus. We decided at that time, with the addition of new members, to become a study group. We had always shared our reading with each other, and some of us had written papers on black feminism for group discussion a few months before this decision was made. We began functioning as a study group and also began discussing the possibility of starting a black feminist publication. We had a retreat in the late spring which provided a time for both political discussion and working out interpersonal issues. Currently we are planning to gather together a collection of black feminist writing. We feel that it is absolutely essential to demonstrate the reality of our politics to other black women and believe that we can do this through writing and distributing our work. The fact that individual black feminists are living in isolation all over the country, that our own numbers are small, and that we have some skills in writing, printing, and publishing makes us want to carry out these kinds of projects as a means of organizing black feminists as we continue to do political work in coalition with other groups.

4. Black Feminist Issues and Practice

During our time together we have identified and worked on many issues of particular relevance to black women. The inclusiveness of our politics makes us concerned with any situation that impinges upon the lives of women, Third World, and working people. We are of course particularly committed to working on those struggles in which race, sex, and class are simultaneous factors in oppression. We might, for example, become involved in workplace organizing at a factory that employs Third World women or picket a hospital that is cutting back on already inadequate health care to a Third World community, or set up a rape crisis center in a black neighborhood. Organizing around welfare or daycare concerns might also be a focus. The work to be done and the countless issues that this work represents merely reflect the pervasiveness of our oppression.

Issues and projects that collective members have actually worked on are sterilization abuse, abortion rights, battered women, rape, and health care. We have also done many workshops and educationals on black feminism on college campuses, at women's conferences, and most recently for high school women.

One issue that is of major concern to us and that we have begun to publicly address is racism in the white women's movement. As black feminists we are made constantly and painfully aware of how little effort white women have made to understand and combat their racism, which requires among other things that they have a more than superficial comprehension of race, color, and black history and culture. Eliminating racism in the white women's movement is by definition work for white women to do, but we will continue to speak to and demand accountability on this issue.

In the practice of our politics we do not believe that the end always justifies the means. Many reactionary and destructive acts have been done in the name of achieving "correct" political goals. As feminists we do not want to mess over people in the name of politics. We believe in collective process and a nonhierarchical distribution of power within our own group and in our vision of a revolutionary society. We are committed to a continual examination of our politics as they develop through criticism and self-criticism as an essential aspect of our practice. As black feminists and lesbians we know that we have a very definite revolutionary task to perform and we are ready for the lifetime of work and struggle before us.

NOTES

1. This statement is dated April 1977.

2. Michele Wallace, "A Black Feminist's Search for Sisterhood," The Village Voice, 28 July 1975, pp. 6–7.

3. Mumininas of Committee for Unified Newark, *Mwanamke Mwananchi* (The nationalist woman); Newark, N.J., c. 1971, pp. 4–5.

Chapter Eight

Who Am I If I'm Not My Father's Daughter?
A Southerner Confronts Racism and Anti-Semitism

Minnie Bruce Pratt

As a white woman raised small town middle-class, Christian, in the Deep South, I was taught to be a *judge,* of moral responsibility and punishment only in relation to *my* ethical system; was taught to be a *preacher,* to point out wrongs and tell others what to do; was taught to be a *martyr,* to take all the responsibility for change and the glory, to expect others to do nothing; was taught to be a *peace-maker,* to mediate, negotiate between opposing sides because I knew the right way. When I speak, or speak up, about Anti-Semitism and racism, I struggle not to speak with intonations, the gestures, the assumption of these roles, and not to speak out of any role of ought-to; I ask that you try not to place me in that role, I am trying to speak today to women like myself, out of need: as a woman who loves other women passionately and wants us to be able to be together as friends in this unjust world.

But where does the need come from, if by skin color, ethnicity, birth culture, we are women who are in a position of material advantage, where we gain at the expense of others, of other women? A place where *we* can have a degree of safety, comfort, familiarity, just by staying put. Where is our *need* to change what we were born into? What do we have to gain?

When I try to think of this, I think of my father, of how, when I was about eight years old, he took me up the front marble steps of the courthouse in my town. He took me inside, up the worn wooden steps, stooped under the feet of the folks who had gone up and down to be judged, or to gawk at the others being judged, up past the courtroom where my grandfather had leaned back his chair and judged for more than 40 years, up to the attic, to some narrow steps that went to the roof, to the clock tower with a walled ledge.

What I would have seen at the top: on the streets around the courthouse square; the Methodist church, the limestone building with the county health department, board of education, welfare department (my mother worked there), the yellow brick Baptist church, the Gulf station, the pool hall (no women allowed), Cleveland's grocery, Ward's shoe store; then all in a line, connected: the bank, the post office, Dr. Nicholson's office, one door for whites, one for blacks, then separate: the Presbyterian church, the newspaper office, the yellow brick jail, same brick as the Baptist church, and as the courthouse.

What I could not have seen from the top: the sawmill, or Four Points where the white mill folks lived, or the houses of blacks in Veneer Mill quarters.

This is what I would and would not have seen, or so I think, for I never got to the top: When he told me to go up the steps in front of him, I tried to, crawling on hands and knees, but I was terribly afraid. I couldn't—or wouldn't—do it. He let me crawl down: he was disgusted with me, I thought. I think now that he wanted to show me a place he had climbed to as a boy, a view that had been his father's, and his, and would be mine. But I was *not* him. I had not learned to take the height, that being set apart as my own: a white girl not a boy.

And yet I know I have been shaped by my relation to those buildings, and to the people in the buildings, by the ideas of who should be working in the board of education, of who should be in the bank handling money, of who should have the guns and the keys to the jail, of who should be *in* the jail; I have been shaped by what I didn't see, or didn't notice, on those streets.

Each of us carries around with us those growing up places, the institutions, a sort of backdrop, a stage-set. So often we act out the present against a backdrop of the past, within a frame of perception that is so familiar, so safe that it is terrifying to risk changing it even when we know our perceptions are distorted, limited, constricted by that old view.

So this one gain for me as I change: I learn a way of looking at the world that is more accurate, complex, multilayered, multidimensioned, more truthful; to see the world of overlapping circles, like movement on the millpond after a fish had jumped, instead of the courthouse square with me in the middle. I feel the *need* to look differently because I've learned that what is presented to me as an accurate view of the world is frequently a lie: so that to look through an anthology of women's studies that has little or no work by women of color is to be up on the ledge above the town and be thinking that I see the town, without realizing how many lives have been pushed out of sight, beside unpaved roads. I'm learning that what I think that I *know* is an accurate view of the world is frequently a lie: as when I was in a discussion about the Women's Pentagon Action with several women, four of us Christian-raised, one Jewish. In describing the march through Arlington Cemetery, one of the four mentioned the rows of crosses. I had marched for a long time through that cemetery; I nodded to myself, visualized rows of crosses. No, said the Jewish women, they were head stones, with crosses or Stars of David engraved above the names. We four objected; we had all seen crosses. The Jewish women had some photographs of the march through the cemetery, laid them on the table. We saw rows and rows of rectangular gravestones and in the foreground, clearly visible, one inscribed with a name and a Star of David.

So I gain truth, when I expand my constricted eye, an eye that has only let in what I have been taught to see. But there have been other constrictions: the fear around my heart when I must deal with the *fact* of folk who exist, with their own lives, in other places besides the narrow circle I was raised in. I have learned that my fear of these folks is kin to a terror that has been in my birth culture for years, for centuries, the terror of people who have set themselves apart and *above*, who have wronged others, and feel that they are about to be found out and punished. It is the terror that in my culture has been expressed in lies about dirty Jews who kill for blood, sly Arab hordes who murder, brutal Indians who massacre, animal blacks who rise in rebellion in the middle of the night and slaughter. It is the terror that has *caused* the slaughter of all these peoples. It is the terror that was my father with his stack of John Birch newspapers, his belief in a Communist-Jewish-Black conspiracy. It is the desperate terror, the knowledge that something is *wrong*, and tries to end fear by attack.

I get afraid when I am trying to understand myself in relation to folks different from me, when there are discussions, conflicts about anti-Semitism and racism among women, criticisms, criticisms of *me*; when, for instance, in a group discussion about race and class, I say I feel we have talked too much about race, not enough about class and a woman of color asks me in anger and pain if I don't think her skin has something to do with class; when for instance, I say carelessly to a Jewish friend that there were no Jews where I grew up, she begins to ask me: How do I know? Do I hear what I'm saying?, and I get afraid; when I feel my racing heart, breath, the tightening of my skin around me, literally defenses to protect my narrow circle, I try to say to myself: yes, that fear is there, but I will try to be at the edge between my fear and the outside, on the edge at my skin, listening, asking what new things I will hear, will I see, will I let myself feel, beyond the fear. I try to say to myself: that to acknowledge the complexity of another's existence is not to deny my own. I try to say: when I acknowledge what my people, what those who are like me, have done to people with less power and less safety in the world, I can make a place for things to be different, a place where I can feel grief, sorrow, not to be sorry *for* the others, but to mourn, to expand my circle of self, follow my need to loosen the constrictions of fear, be a break in the cycle of fear and attack.

To be caught within the narrow circle of the self is not just a fearful thing, it is a lonely thing. When I could not climb the steps that day with my father, maybe I knew on some level that my place was with women, not with men, that I did not want this view of the world. Certainly, I have felt this more and more strongly since my coming out as a lesbian. Yet so much has separated me from other women, ways in which my culture set me apart by race, by ethnicity, by class. I understood abruptly one day how lonely this made me when a friend, a black woman, spoke to me casually in our shared office: and I heard how she said my name: the lingering accent, so much like how my name is said at home. Yet I knew enough of her history and mine to know how much separated us: the chasm of murders, rapes, lynching, the years of daily humiliation done by my people to hers. I went and stood in the hallway and cried, thinking of how she said my name like home, and how divided our lives were.

It is a pain I come over and over again when for instance, I realize how *habitually* I think of my culture, my ethics, my morality, as the culmination of history, as the logical extension of what has gone before; the kind of thinking represented by my use, in the past, of the word *Judeo-Christian,* as if Jewish history and lives have existed only to culminate in Christian culture, the kind of thinking that the US government is using to promote Armageddon in the Middle East; the kind of thinking that I did until recently about Indian lives and the culture in my region, as if Indian peoples have existed only in museums since the white folks came in the 1500's; the kind of thinking that separates me from other women in cultures different from mine, makes their experience less central, less important than mine. It is painful to keep understanding this separation, within myself and in the world. Yet I have felt that the need to be with other women can be the breaking through the shell around me, painful, but coming through into a new place, where with understanding and change, the loneliness won't be necessary.

If we have these things to gain, and more, by struggling against racism and anti-Semitism in ourselves, what keeps us from doing so, at any one moment, what keeps us from action? In part, I know I hesitate because I have struggled painfully, for years, to make this new place for myself with other women, and I hesitate to disrupt it.

In part I hesitate because the process of uncovering my complicity is so painful: it is the stripping down, layer after layer, of my identity: skin, blood, heart: to find out how much of what I am has been shaped by my skin and family, to find out which of my thoughts and actions I need to change, which I should keep as my own. Sometimes I fear that stripping away the layers will bring me to nothing, that the only values that I and my culture have are based on negativity, exclusion, fear.

Often I have thought: *what* of who I am is worth saving? worth taking into the future? But I have learned that as the process of shaping identity was long, so the process of change is long. I know that change speeds up the more able I am to put into material shape what I have learned from struggling with anti-Semitism and racism, to begin to act for change can widen perception, loosen fear, ease loneliness. I know that we can choose to act in ways that get us closer to the longed-for but unrealized world, a world where we each are able to live, but not by trying to make someone less than us, not by someone else's blood or pain.

Chapter Nine

"We Are Who You Are"
Feminism and Disability

Bonnie Sherr Klein

It all begins in 1987. I am 46 years old, and enjoying an athletic and sexy vacation with my husband, Michael. On a hot day, we bicycle ten miles to the town tennis courts. I feel weak and nauseated, and play badly. We think it must be junk-food poisoning.

Within several hours, I am staggering and slurring my speech. I have double vision. Michael, a family physician, recognizes the signs of central nervous system damage. At midnight, he speeds me home to Montreal, to the emergency room of the hospital where he works.

Diagnostic tests are inconclusive. We are shocked and scared, but I begin to stabilize. Within a few days, I am released from the intensive care unit, and take a few steps with a walker. After two weeks, we celebrate our twentieth anniversary in the hospital with our children. I feel blessed and happy to be alive.

The next day I become totally paralyzed. Semiconscious, I am "locked in" and unable to speak. A respirator breathes for me. A magnetic resonance test (MRI) reveals that a congenital malformation at the base of my brain stem has bled, resulting in several strokes. It is like a time bomb waiting to explode again. Local specialists declare it inoperable because of its inaccessible location. Close family and friends come to say goodbye.

Michael refuses to accept this fatal verdict. He locates a surgeon who is prepared to remove the malformation.

I am jet-ambulanced on a respirator to London, Ontario. By my bed, the surgeon posts a newspaper clipping: a picture of me with Kate Millett from my documentary *Not a Love Story*. I overhear a staff remark: "She used to be a filmmaker." I remain in intensive care for several months. Michael stays with me, acting as husband, family doctor, nurse, and advocate. He will not resume work for several months.

As I come back to life but cannot move, speak, or breathe, I have frequent panic attacks. Only Michael can talk me down. He breathes with me until I fall asleep. The literal meaning of "conspire" is to breathe together. We are in a conspiracy for my life. This becomes the metaphor of our partnership. This is a love story.

Reprinted by permission of *Ms.,* November/December 1992.

Recovery

Back in Montreal, I spend more months in the hospital, and then in a rehabilitation institute. Like a helpless baby, I learn how to swallow, speak, sit upright, use the toilet, stand.

(Memory Journal: When I am sufficiently recovered, I get bathing privileges twice a week. A male orderly transfers me to a gurney and wheels me down the hall. I am "wrapped" diaper-fashion in a rubber sling, and with a horrible-sounding grind, winched into a tub where a nurse bathes and shampoos me. The soothing warm water is one of the few nice body sensations I have. But it is frightening to be winched. I can hear older women screaming and moaning, and all I can think of — as in my nightmares — is a concentration camp.)

But I am never abandoned to institutional care. I am supported and nursed every day by Michael and our daughter, Naomi—then 17. Our son, Seth, 19, begins attending the University of Toronto shortly after my surgery. He studies on the five-hour train commute each way; his enthusiastic comments about my dramatic changes since the previous weekend are like a transfusion. Naomi is just emerging from a difficult adolescence. Conflicted by her mother's highly visible feminism, she has asserted her individuality by learning the skills of femininity. Now she does the intimate niceties for me—shaving the underarms; bleaching the facial hairs darkened by steroids mistakenly prescribed. My skin is blotched, my features lopsided, but my daughter makes me feel pretty. Not surprisingly, Naomi also fails her semester at school.

Several months after the stroke, as soon as I can use a pencil, the occupational therapist helps me to copy circles and squares like a schoolgirl. My first communication is an illegible letter to Naomi, in which I share my fear about how slow recovery may be, an admission I make to no one else. Once I can write, I begin my journal, which becomes a tool for my survival. I use it to process the strange and troubling events happening in my body, to record thoughts I cannot trust my damaged mind to remember, to remind myself how far I have come.

The Long Haul: Rehabilitation

After seven months in the hospital, I am at home over the next two and a half years, in the long process of rehabilitation. I have conventional physical, occupational, and speech therapy. As I gradually improve, I remember my old feminist wisdom that I know my body better than anyone else. I take control. I experiment with so-called alternative approaches like acupuncture. Michael and I dance and play, in whatever motivating ways we can invent to push my physical limits. And I learn to rest. In my prestroke life, this was never easy for me, juggling the three F's: family, filmmaking, and feminism. Now I have no choice. My body's messages are nonnegotiable.

The anguish is profound when I let it emerge, and it comes out at the slightest invitation.

(Journal, March 1, 1989: This evening, when Michael and I dance, I am weepy. Because he's been outside playing basketball, my girlhood sport, while I am curled up inside in bed. And because I can hardly dance, and dancing was one of the things we did together, starting the day we met 22 years ago. I want to kick up my heels, and they won't go, dammit! But strange as it may sound, I also experience the euphoria of just being alive. It is not a cover-up, it is real. I laugh out loud when the leaves riot with autumn colors. I am living on the edge, with no script guides or maps, inventing every moment as I live it.)

The stroke hit me in the middle of editing a film. The producer and editor bring the film to the hospital and my home so we can work on it together. *Mile Zero* is the story of four teenagers—one of whom is Seth—who are organizing against nuclear arms. The premiere, 16 months after my stroke, is the most triumphant moment in my rehabilitation. I have reclaimed the important piece of myself that was a filmmaker.

Yet I still do not accept myself as disabled; disability is "a stage I am just passing through." For the premiere, I reject a fully accessible educational institution and choose a glamorous cinema with inaccessible bathrooms—even though I am in a wheelchair.

I long to hold on to the acute appreciation of life engendered by survival and rebirth, but euphoria does not last indefinitely. My mother dies after a long struggle with Alzheimer's disease. This loss is compounded by Naomi's departure for the University of Toronto. I want to be generous about letting her go, but losses are interconnected: I mourn my mother, my daughter, myself.

In June 1989, almost two years poststroke, I receive a last-minute invitation to participate in a festival of Canadian women's films abroad. Two of my films are featured. My immediate response is "Impossible! I can't travel without personal assistance." The travel money is quickly offered to another filmmaker. When Naomi discovers me crying, she offers to quit work to accompany me. We go off together at great personal expense, and greater trepidation.

The women who had organized the festival—also Canadian filmmakers—had promised to "accommodate" me, but they make no provision for my needs. I am expected to fit in and keep up. They schedule my films late at night when I am too tired; they do not include me in panel discussions or press conferences; they arrange social events in inaccessible places. I miss the informal personal exchanges catalyzed by the shared film experience.

I can no longer move in what had been my world. I feel I have been used for my films, but neglected and made invisible as a person. I feel as if my colleagues are ashamed of me because I am no longer the image of strength, competence, and independence that feminists, including myself, are so eager to project. There is clearly a conflict between feminism's rhetoric of inclusion and failure to include disability. My journals reveal that this is the only moment in which I think of suicide.

I am coming up against multiple barriers, personal and social. I cannot return to my former life, and I do not know what my life will be now. Even feminism has betrayed me. It seems too narrow a lens for the new realities of my life. I also feel an unresolved conflict between feminism and my increased dependence on—and appreciation for—Michael.

About two and a half years poststroke, I have an experience that begins to clarify my thinking about feminism. We spend the winter in Beersheba, Israel, where Michael is working to help me escape Montreal's ice and snow. A woman from the local chapter of the Israel Women's Network phones: as a visiting feminist, would I speak on any "women's issue" of my choosing at their next meeting? Again my first reaction is negative: "I am no longer engaged with women's issues; I have been so self-obsessed with my stroke that's all I could possibly talk about." Her response is quick: "That's exactly what we want to hear about, but were too shy to ask!"

I have forgotten how wonderful it is to share intimately with a group of women! I read bits from my journal, and my story prompts theirs. One woman says, "My relationship with my husband is fine as long as I'm healthy, capable, and available sexually, but I don't know what would happen if I were incapacitated." She hadn't read the United Nations statistic that disabled women are twice as likely to get divorced or separated as disabled men. We realize that we rarely talk about illness, disability, and dying, though we will all confront these realities.

Every issue is a woman's issue; relationships, dependence, and autonomy are as much a part of feminism as day care and violence. I have undersold feminism. I slowly recognize that the way I am living my stroke has everything to do with myself as a feminist—as well as with implications for feminism itself.

"Coming Out" Disabled

I feel comfortable and stimulated in this group of Israeli women; they are middle-class, middle-aged, married Jewish women like me. But no one else there is disabled. I am "other." I desperately need company.

I had first heard of DAWN (the DisAbled Women's Network, Canada) years earlier when it approached Studio D to make our screenings more accessible. We appreciated being sensitized, favored wheelchair-accessible venues, and enjoyed the aesthetics of sign language interpretation with our movies. But sometimes DAWN's demands seemed "excessive"; our meager resources were already exhausted by items on our agenda that seemed to affect *most* women. But in retrospect, I know that as a not-yet-disabled woman I was afraid of disability.

As soon as I return to Canada, I dig DAWN's phone number out of a feminist newsletter. I realize that its agenda is identical to mine (and feminism's): dependence and autonomy, image and self-esteem, powerlessness, isolation, violence, and vulnerability; equality and access; sexuality. Three years after my stroke, I go to my first DAWN meeting at the local YWCA.

I feel apologetic, illegitimate, because I was not born disabled, and am not as severely disabled as many other people. I feel guilty about my privileges of class, profession (including my disability pension), and family. I am a newcomer to the disability movement; I have not paid my dues. (Doesn't this litany sound "just like a woman"?)

Our talk keeps moving between the personal and the political, because disability—like gender, race, age, and sexuality—is a social as well as a biological construct. The DAWN members, typical of disabled women, are mostly unemployed, poor, and living alone. It is like the early days of consciousness-raising in the women's movement: sharing painful (and funny) experiences, "clicks!" of recognition; swapping tips for coping with social service bureaucracies and choosing the least uncomfortable tampons for prolonged sitting. It is exhilarating to cry and laugh with other women again.

Here I am not other, because everyone is other. It is the sisterhood of disability. The stroke has connected me with women who were not part of my world before—working-class women with little education, women with intellectual and psychiatric disabilities, women with physical "abnormalities" from whom I would have averted my eyes in polite embarrassment. All women like me.

"We are women. We are women with disabilities. We are women who are abused. We are your sisters. . . . Your issues are our issues, and each of our issues is also your issue. We are who you are." (From "Meeting Our Needs: An Access Manual for Transition Houses," DAWN, June 1991.)

I discover it is easier for me to be a disabled feminist than a disabled person. Feminism means loving myself as I am. After three long years, I am finally ready to accept myself as permanently, irrevocably disabled: acceptance is not an event but an ongoing process. I learn more about the disability rights movement. I meet other women with disabilities, who become my buddies, sisters, teachers, and "rolling" models. I learn, not surprisingly, that women are leaders in the disability movement.

(Journal, October 1990: Boston's first Disability Pride Day. I usually dislike the rhetoric of rallies, the solicited mass response. But today I want my tape recorder. A gutsy, nervous young woman with the thick drawl of cerebral palsy is emcee. Not only is her speech different, but there is a new language being spoken here. I feel like a privileged eavesdropper at first, but she is speaking for me and about me. Or is she? She cues us for a chant: "Disabled and . . . " The crowd responds: PROUD! My throat jams on the word mid-chant. Is this honest? Who am I trying to fool? It's one thing to accept, but another to be proud. I'm proud of surviving and adapting maybe, but am I proud of being disabled? But it feels good to be shouting with hundreds of other bodies, looking happy despite — because of? — their "deformities." Or is the word "differences"? Or is it "our"?)

Happily, the timing of my personal journey is synchronous with the women's movement. The Canadian Research Institute for the Advancement of Women (CRIAW) announces the theme for its 1990 national conference: "The More We Get Together . . . " on women and disability. I decide to go, alone, to Prince Edward Island. Thanks to the joint efforts of CRIAW and DAWN, this historic event is not only totally accessible but empowering—for both the women with disabilities and those without. Every woman with disability is paired with a "sister" who gives us whatever assistance we need—and who learns firsthand about disability.

It is a coming-out experience for many of us. For me, it is the first time I identify myself publicly as a woman with disability, and revel in the company of so many others. Because women with disabilities are often isolated, for many this is their first conference. They learn from the experience of longtime feminists.

Many of the so-called nondisabled women come out as well. Kay Macpherson, 79, and Muriel Duckworth, 83, are well-known Canadian peace activists and feminists. But we have never considered them "disabled." Now, for the first time, Kay talks about what it means to be losing her sight. She talks loudly because her close friend Muriel has learned to be assertive about her increasing deafness. Muriel and Kay describe their support networks of friends who look after each other by sharing meals, and house keys in case of falls. Our stories lead us to discover the continuum from "ability" to "disability." My stroke has given me a telescope on aging. We are all disabled under the skin—each of us has vulnerabilities, visible or not, and they are part of us. We are interdependent. Feminism is strongest when it includes its "weakest."

I leave CRIAW with a new sense of purpose and continuity. No longer illegitimate among either feminists or people with disabilities, I feel I have a particular contribution to make: perhaps I can help to bridge the gap between our two cultures. After all, my life's work has been about telling each other our stories.

Where Am I Now?

After five years, my physical condition is still evolving—but almost imperceptibly. I feel constantly imbalanced. I stand and walk with two canes, slowly and unsteadily. For longer distances, I drive my electric three-wheeled scooter, Gladys, but she can only be transported in a lift-equipped van, and furthermore is stopped by the smallest step. I am often dependent on someone to push Manny, my portable manual wheelchair. I do not drive a car alone—yet.

I need to exercise and nap every day, and I get weekly massages, acupuncture, and chiropractic to maximize my fluidity and minimize my pain. With only one functioning vocal chord, I choke frequently, but my speech is intelligible (and my voice as breathlessly sexy as I always wanted). I tire easily and tolerate stress badly.

Being forced to slow down is not all negative. The rhythm of my life has changed dramatically. Before, it was governed by the calendar and the clock. Now I follow the natural pace of my body. The tasks of everyday living take me much longer. I have become patient, as have those around me. I have to ration my limited energy and choose carefully who I see and what I do. I have no time to waste on bullshit, but I do have time to smell the flowers. I cherish my solitude, and enjoy the fullness of the company of intimate friends and family.

But I need to be useful and connected, to feel once again that I am contributing to making this a better world. I don't know if I will ever make films again, but I am writing a book about my experience, and spending time with other people with disabilities. As with my walking, it all comes to balance. Some people look at me suspiciously when I hint at the gifts of the stroke. I would never deny the pain of dependence, the grieving for lost freedoms, the fear for the future. Would I take an immediate cure if offered? Probably. But would I want to undo it, as if it never happened? Absolutely not. It has become part of my identity. It is who I am now.

In retrospect, the "clicks!" in my consciousness about disability paralleled my coming to feminist consciousness two decades earlier. For a long time, I denied I was disabled, and kept my distance from other "cripples" in the hospital gym because I was an exception to the rule. Later, I was sure I could "overcome" it; I would be supercrip (superwoman); I would support the rights of other people with disabilities, but *I* was not oppressed. As time passed, I experienced with great pain the ways in which other people's attitudes and societal barriers disempowered me. At first, I internalized the oppression and lost all self-esteem. Then, as I reconnected with feminism and discovered my commonality with other women (and men) with disabilities, I began to see more clearly. With solidarity came strength.

Between writing this piece and correcting the galleys, I have taken a giant step in my journey. I went to Independence 92 in Vancouver, an international conference on disability—more than 2,000 of us from more than 100 countries! For one week, I had the heady feeling that we were taking over the world. Even better—we were remaking it, creating a world in which difference is not the problem but part of the solution.

It is a feast for this disabled filmmaker's eyes: a gridlock of wheelchairs on a freight elevator, a shoulder chain of the blind leading the blind, signing, singing, nursing babies in wheelchairs—images we have not seen because we disabled are invisible, even to each other; images so rare and precious they have not yet been coopted or trivialized.

Somehow, I think I will be making films again.

Chapter Ten

Becoming the Third Wave

Rebecca Walker

I am not one of the people who sat transfixed before the television, watching the Senate hearings. I had classes to go to, papers to write, and frankly, the whole thing was too painful. A black man grilled by a panel of white men about his sexual deviance. A black woman claiming harrassment and being discredited by other women. . . . I could not bring myself to watch that sensationalized assault of the human spirit.

To me, the hearings were not about determining whether or not Clarence Thomas did in fact harass Anita Hill. They were about checking and redefining the extent of women's credibility and power.

Can a woman's experience undermine a man's career? Can a woman's voice, a woman's sense of self-worth and injustice, challenge a structure predicated upon the subjugation of our gender? Anita Hill's testimony threatened to do that and more. If Thomas had not been confirmed, every man in the United States would be at risk. For how many senators never told a sexist joke? How many men have not used their protected male privilege to thwart in some way the influence or ideas of a woman colleague, friend, or relative?

For those whose sense of power is so obviously connected to the health and vigor of the penis, it would have been a metaphoric castration. Of course this is too great a threat.

While some may laud the whole spectacle for the consciousness it raised around sexual harrassment, its very real outcome is more informative. He was promoted. She was repudiated. Men were assured of the inviolability of their penis/power. Women were admonished to keep their experiences to themselves.

The backlash against U.S. women is real. As the misconception of equality between the sexes becomes more ubiquitous, so does the attempt to restrict the boundaries of women's personal and political power. Thomas' confirmation, the ultimate rally of support for the male paradigm of harrassment, sends a clear message to women: "Shut up! Even if you speak, we will not listen."

I will not be silenced.

I acknowledge the fact that we live under siege. I intend to fight back. I have uncovered and unleashed more repressed anger than I thought possible. For the umpteenth time in my 22 years, I have been radicalized, politicized, shaken awake. I have come to voice again, and this time my voice is not conciliatory.

The night after Thomas' confirmation I ask the man I am intimate with what he thinks of the whole mess. His concern is primarily with Thomas' propensity to demolish civil rights and opportunities for people of color. I launch into a tirade. "When will progressive black men prioritize my rights and well-being? When will they stop talking so damn much about 'the race' as if it revolved exclusively around them?" He tells me I wear my emotions on my sleeve. I scream "I need to know, are you with me or are you going to help them try to destroy me?"

A week later I am on a train to New York. A beautiful mother and daughter, both wearing green outfits, sit across the aisle from me. The little girl has tightly plaited braids. Her brown skin is glowing and smooth, her eyes bright as she chatters happily while looking out the window. Two men get on the train and sit directly behind me, shaking my seat as they thud into place. I bury myself in *The Sound and the Fury*. Loudly they begin to talk about women. "Man, I fucked that bitch all night and then I never called her again." "Man, there's lots of girlies over there, you know that ho, live over there by Tyrone? Well, I snatched that shit up."

The mother moves closer to her now quiet daughter. Looking at her small back I can see that she is listening to the men. I am thinking of how I can transform the situation, of all the people in the car whose silence makes us complicit.

Another large man gets on the train. After exchanging loud greetings with the two men, he sits next to me. He tells them he is going to Philadelphia to visit his wife and child. I am suckered into thinking that he is different. Then, "Man, there's a ton of females in Philly, just waitin' for you to give 'em some." I turn my head and allow the fire in my eyes to burn into him. He takes up two seats and has hands with huge swollen knuckles. I imagine the gold rings on his fingers slamming into my face. He senses something, "What's your name, sweetheart?" The other men lean forward over the seat.

A torrent explodes: "I ain't your sweetheart, I ain't your bitch, I ain't your baby. How dare you have the nerve to sit up here and talk about women that way, and then try to speak to me." The woman/mother chimes in to the beat with claps of sisterhood. The men are momentarily stunned. Then the comeback: "Aw, bitch, don't play that woman shit over here 'cause that's bullshit." He slaps the back of one hand against the palm of the other. I refuse to back down. Words fly.

My instinct kicks in, telling me to get out. "Since I see you all are not going to move, I will." I move to the first car. I am so angry that thoughts of murder, of physically retaliating against them, of separatism, engulf me. I am almost out of body, just shy of being pure force. I am sick of the way women are negated, violated, devalued, ignored. I am livid, unrelenting in my anger at those who invade my space, who wish to take away my rights, who refuse to hear my voice. As the days pass, I push myself to figure out what it means to be a part of the Third Wave of feminism. I begin to realize that I owe it to myself, to my little sister on the train, to all of the daughters yet to be born, to push beyond my rage and articulate an agenda. After battling with ideas of separatism and militancy, I connect with my own feelings of powerlessness. I realize that I must undergo a transformation if I am truly committed to women's empowerment. My involvement must reach beyond my own voice in discussion, beyond voting, beyond reading feminist theory. My anger and awareness must translate into tangible action.

I am ready to decide, as my mother decided before me, to devote much of my energy to the history, health, and healing of women. Each of my choices will have to hold to my feminist standard of justice.

To be a feminist is to integrate an ideology of equality and female empowerment into the very fiber of my life. It is to search for personal clarity in the midst of systemic destruction, to join in sisterhood with women when often we are divided, to understand power structures with the intention of challenging them.

While this may sound simple, it is exactly the kind of stand that many of my peers are unwilling to take. So I write this as a plea to all women, especially the women of my generation: Let Thomas' confirmation serve to remind you, as it did me, that the fight is far from over. Let this dismissal of a woman's experience move you to anger. Turn that outrage into political power. Do not vote for them unless they work for us. Do not have sex with them, do not break bread with them, do not nurture them if they don't prioritize our freedom to control our bodies and our lives.

I am not a postfeminism feminist. I am the Third Wave.

Chapter Eleven

The Transformation of Silence into Language and Action

Audre Lorde

I have come to believe over and over again that what is most important to me must be spoken, made verbal and shared, even at the risk of having it bruised or misunderstood. That the speaking profits me, beyond any other effect. I am standing here as a Black lesbian poet, and the meaning of all that waits upon the fact that I am still alive, and might not have been. Less than two months ago I was told by two doctors, one female and one male, that I would have to have breast surgery, and that there was a 60 to 80 percent chance that the tumor was malignant. Between that telling and the actual surgery, there was a three-week period of the agony of an involuntary reorganization of my entire life. The surgery was completed, and the growth was benign.

But within those three weeks, I was forced to look upon myself and my living with a harsh and urgent clarity that has left me still shaken but much stronger. This is a situation faced by many women, by some of you here today. Some of what I experienced during that time has helped elucidate for me much of what I feel concerning the transformation of silence into language and action.

In becoming forcibly and essentially aware of my mortality, and of what I wished and wanted for my life, however short it might be, priorities and omissions became strongly etched in a merciless light, and what I most regretted were my silences. Of what had I *ever* been afraid? To question or to speak as I believed could have meant pain, or death. But we all hurt in so many different ways, all the time, and pain will either change or end. Death, on the other hand, is the final silence. And that might be coming quickly, now, without regard for whether I had ever spoken what needed to be said, or had only betrayed myself into small silences, while I planned someday to speak, or waited for someone else's words. And I began to recognize a source of power within myself that comes from the knowledge that while it is most desirable not to be afraid, learning to put fear into perspective gave me great strength.

I was going to die, if not sooner then later, whether or not I had ever spoken myself. My silences had not protected me. Your silence will not protect you. But for every real word spoken, for every attempt I had ever made to speak those truths for which I am still seeking, I had made contact with other women while we examined the words to fit a world in which we all believed, bridging our differences. And it was the concern and caring of all those women which gave me strength and enabled me to scrutinize the essentials of my living.

The women who sustained me through that period were Black and white, old and young, lesbian, bisexual, and heterosexual, and we all shared a war against the tyrannies of silence. They all gave me a strength and concern without which I could not have survived intact. Within those weeks of acute fear came the knowledge—within the war we are all waging with the forces of death, subtle and otherwise, conscious or not—I am not only a casualty, I am also a warrior.

What are the words you do not yet have? What do you need to say? What are the tyrannies you swallow day by day and attempt to make your own, until you will sicken and die of them, still in silence? Perhaps for some of you here today, I am the face of one of your fears. Because I am woman, because I am Black, because I am lesbian, because I am myself—a Black woman warrior poet doing my work—come to ask you, are you doing yours?

And of course I am afraid, because the transformation of silence into language and action is an act of self-revelation, and that always seems fraught with danger. But my daughter, when I told her of our topic and my difficulty with it, said, "Tell them about how you're never really a whole person if you remain silent, because there's always that one little piece inside you that wants to be spoken out, and if you keep ignoring it, it gets madder and madder and hotter and hotter, and if you don't speak it out one day it will just up and punch you in the mouth from the inside."

In the cause of silence, each of us draws the face of her own fear—fear of contempt, of censure, or some judgment, or recognition, of challenge, of annihilation. But most of all, I think, we fear the visibility without which we cannot truly live. Within this country where racial difference creates a constant, if unspoken, distortion of vision, Black women have on one hand always been highly visible, and so, on the other hand, have been rendered invisible through the depersonalization of racism. Even within the women's movement, we have had to fight, and still do, for that very visibility which also renders us most vulnerable, our Blackness. For to survive in the mouth of this dragon we call america, we have had to learn this first and most vital lesson—that we were never meant to survive. Not as human beings. And neither were most of you here today, Black or not. And that visibility which makes us most vulnerable is that which also is the source of our greatest strength. Because the machine will try to grind you into dust anyway, whether or not we speak. We can sit in our corners mute forever while our sisters and our selves are wasted, while our children are distorted and destroyed, while our earth is poisoned; we can sit in our safe corners mute as bottles, and we will still be no less afraid.

In my house this year we are celebrating the feast of Kwanza, the African-american festival of harvest which begins the day after Christmas and lasts for seven days. There are seven principles of Kwanza, one for each day. The first principle is Umoja, which means unity, the decision to strive for and maintain unity in self and community. The principle for yesterday, the second day, was Kujichagulia—self-determination—the decision to define ourselves, name ourselves, and speak for ourselves, instead of being defined and spoken for by others. Today is the third day of Kwanza, and the principle for today is Ujima—collective work and responsibility—the decision to build and maintain ourselves and our communities together and to recognize and solve our problems together.

Each of us is here now because in one way or another we share a commitment to language and to the power of language, and to the reclaiming of that language which has been made to work against us. In the transformation of silence into language and action, it is vitally necessary for each one of us to establish or examine her function in that transformation and to recognize her role as vital within that transformation.

For those of us who write, it is necessary to scrutinize not only the truth of what we speak, but the truth of that language by which we speak it. For others, it is to share and spread also those words that are meaningful to us. But primarily for us all, it is necessary to teach by living and speaking those truths which we believe and know beyond understanding. Because in this way alone we can survive, by taking part in a process of life that is creative and continuing, that is growth.

And it is never without fear—of visibility, of the harsh light of scrutiny and perhaps judgment, of pain, of death. But we have lived through all of those already, in silence, except death. And I remind myself all the time now that if I were to have been born mute, or had maintained an oath of silence my whole life long for safety, I would still have suffered, and I would still die. It is very good for establishing perspective.

And where the words of women are crying to be heard, we must each of us recognize our responsibility to seek those words out, to read them and share them and examine them in their pertinence to our lives. That we not hide behind the mockeries of separations that have been imposed upon us and which so often we accept as our own. For instance, "I can't possibly teach Black women's writing—their experience is so different from mine." Yet how many years have you spent teaching Plato and Shakespeare and Proust? Or another, "She's a white woman and what could she possibly have to say to me?" Or, "She's a lesbian, what would my husband say, or my chairman?" Or again, "This woman writes of her sons and I have no children." And all the other endless ways in which we rob ourselves of ourselves and each other.

We can learn to work and speak when we are afraid in the same way we have learned to work and speak when we are tired. For we have been socialized to respect fear more than our own needs for language and definition, and while we wait in silence for that final luxury of fearlessness, the weight of that silence will choke us.

The fact that we are here and that I speak these words is an attempt to break that silence and bridge some of those differences between us, for it is not difference which immobilizes us, but silence. And there are so many silences to be broken.

Part III

Multiple Identities

When members of the Combahee River Collective claimed the right to name their identity, the task of recognizing the import of multiple identities began. In this chapter, authors address this issue from a variety of perspectives, most based on their own experiences. Sonia Shaw is an Asian American who learned from black feminists that feminism could have a race analysis. Still, she feels that the discourse on race has been too narrowly defined in black and white terms. Racial discrimination does not capture the experience of many Asian women, particularly those, like her, from South Asia. The "otherness" they experience, based on cultural differences, is largely unnoticed because of the black/white dichotomy that has dominated the attention of feminists and other progressives. She describes a cultural schizophrenia, the feeling of not belonging to either the black or the white culture and proposes that Asian American women re-create themselves. For the women's movement, she calls for a bicultural feminism that recognizes difference along a broader spectrum than has been addressed by the limitation of skin color.

Sex radicalism, as an identity, has had a hard time gaining recognition among feminists. Yet, Carol Queen (1997:125) tells us in her article that it is "both deeply feminist and also profoundly challenging to many attitudes and assumptions promoted by contemporary mainstream feminism." Why the discrepancy and "outlaw" characterization for someone who identifies as a sex-positive feminist? Restrictive expectations do not fit her feminist understanding of women's right to explore and define their own sexuality. She deplores the social conviction that there is only one kind of appropriate sex and that all others are sinful or abusive, just as feminism does in the case of compulsory heterosexuality and nonconsensual sex. Sex-positive "whores" and Queen argues that the only difference between their practices and socially accepted sex is that they have sex with men they are not married to, get paid for it, and enjoy it. If feminists care about the lives of all women and believe they can learn from women different from themselves, Queen believes the time is right for them to hear from the sexual fringe.

The charge Carol Queen makes of the feminist rejection of sex workers does not take serious note of the divisions within feminism on this issue and many others. Ruth Perry considers contrariety the central point of feminist discourse; indeed, she asserts that this is the crucial ingredient of feminism itself. She applauds the diversity in thought that exists among feminist women in all sorts of bodies, and considers the history of women's studies to be the history of debate. Perry takes issue with "pod" feminists who misname the mission and meaning of women's studies courses.

Instead, she tells us what she values in this work and the people who do it. As her title suggests, she "brakes" for feminists because she thinks they are an endangered species in our society.

The concept of identity, either through essentialism or deconstruction raises important questions linked to how one might operate within it, while not of it. Perhaps as Perry suggests, one chooses an identity based on one's beliefs and that becomes the essential component of one's identity politics. But what happens to those other identities that share residence with one's thoughts? Julie Bettie takes us through the poststructuralist and deconstructionist tunnels of postmodernism to examine class as a less easily essentialized category where whites can pass, that is, the origin of class location can be made invisible. She considers how people experience and perform "traitorous identities" such as male feminism, and how parallelisms are sometimes misapplied. In so doing, she questions the import of men's experience of a subordinate identity and, at the same time, reveals a renewed interest in class as a cultural identity. Her paper speaks to the kind of thinking necessary for coalition building and political activism across social identities and political projects.

How many identities do we have and how much does each of them matter? This is a question June Jordan ponders on a trip to the Bahamas, where she confronts the history of white colonialism from the past and the race/class relations of being a tourist in the Bahamas today. She wonders whose issues are poverty, police violence, and exploitation beyond the people living that life? Where is sisterhood among women, between Jordan as a black woman deserving of a break from her academic pressures and the poor black woman waiting on her at her hotel, or among her white middle-class students who are trapped in boxes of privilege? All identities are called into question because the usual concepts of connection do not apply very well once we leave our own back yards. Jordan is talking about the recognition of difference within a common identity and of unity across identity lines.

REFERENCE

Queen, Carol. 1997. "Sex Radical Politics, Sex-Positive Feminist Thought, and Whore Stigma." Pp. 125–135 in *Whores and Other Feminists,* edited by Jill Nagle. New York: Routledge.

Chapter Twelve

Presenting the Blue Goddess
Toward a Bicultural Asian-American Feminist Agenda

Sonia Shah

We all laughed sheepishly about how we used to dismiss the South Asian women in our lives as doormats irrelevant to our cultural location. For most of us in that fledgling South Asian-American women's group in Boston, either white feminists or Black feminists had inspired us to try to find our feminist heritage. Yet neither movement had really prepared us for actually finding anything. The way feminism was defined by either group did not, could not, define our South Asian feminist heritages, which for most of us consisted of stuff like feisty immigrant mothers, ball-breaking grandmothers, Kali-worship (Kali is the blue goddess who sprung whole from another woman and who symbolizes "shakti"—Hindi for woman-power), social activist aunts, and freedom-fighting/Gandhian great-aunts. In many ways, white feminism, with its "personal is political" maxim and its emphasis on building sisterhood and consciousness raising, had brought us together. Black feminism, on the other hand, had taught us that we could expect more—that a feminism incorporating a race analysis was possible. Yet, while both movements spurred us to organize, neither included our culturally specific agendas—about the battering of immigrant women, the ghettoization of the South Asian community, cultural discrimination, bicultural history and identity, and other issues specific to our lives.

Today, our numbers are exploding in our immigrant communities and the communities of their progeny, and subsequently, in our activist communities. Our writers, poets, artists, and filmmakers are coming of age. Our activism, against anti-Asian violence, battery, and racism, is becoming more and more inspired and entrenched. Yet our movement for Asian-American feminism faces crucial internal challenges. Longtime Asian-American feminist activists such as Helen Zia, a contributing editor to *Ms.* magazine, wonder, "What makes us different from white feminists or Black feminists? What can we bring to the table?" And they complain that "these questions haven't really been developed yet."

Our needs, our liberation, and our pan-Asian feminist agenda have been obscured by a Black/white dichotomy that permeates both activist movements and the

Reprinted by permission of South End Press from *The State of Asian America: Activism and Resistance in the 1990s*, edited by Karin Aguilar-San Juan, pp. 147–157. Boston: 1994.

mainstream. This racialist essentialism has divided us, stripping us of the tools we need to articulate an Asian-American feminism. Our movement, in all of its different forms, has been forced to smash itself into definitions, assumptions, and activist protocols that simply don't work for us. So, while we have been able to get a lot of good work done, and will continue to do so, we haven't been able to show each other, tell each other, or teach each other, about what Asian-American feminism really means.

The movements of the '60s, out of which the first wave of Asian women's organizing sprung, collided with the mainstream in defining racism in Black and white terms; racism is still defined as discrimination based on skin color. These earlier activists also, to some extent, elevated discrimination based on skin color to the top layer of oppression. According to these assumptions, an assault on an Indian because she "dresses weird" is not racist; the harassment of a Chinese shopkeeper because she has a "funny accent" is not racist. Neither are as disturbing, unacceptable, or even downright "evil" as, for example, an attack on a Black person because of her skin color. Racism is seen as a problem between people of different skin colors, between Black people and white people, and one must be in either the Black or the white camp to even speak about it. Those of us who are neither Black nor white are expected to forget ourselves. Whites try to convince us we are really *more like them;* depending upon our degree of sensitivity toward racist injustice, we try to persuade Blacks that we are similar to them. This narrow definition has distorted mainstream perceptions of anti-Asian racism and has distorted even our perception of ourselves—we either don't see ourselves as victims of racism or we see ourselves as victims of racism based on skin color.

For example, many Asian-American women have described Asian women's experience of racism as a result of stereotypes about "exotica" and "china dolls," two stereotypes based on the fact that we look different from white people. Of course, we do encounter racism that emanates from these stereotypes. But there are many more layers of oppression just as unacceptable and pernicious as this discrimination based on skin color. By focusing solely on "racial" differences, however, we fail to see them for what they are, and we fail to name the reality of our experiences.

For our experiences of oppression are in *many ways* qualitatively different from those of Black and white people. For me, the experience of "otherness," the formative discrimination in my life, has been a result of culturally different (not necessarily racially different) people thinking they were culturally central: thinking that *my* house smelled funny, that *my* mother talked weird, that *my* habits were strange. They were normal; I wasn't.

The Black/white paradigms of both feminist and civil rights struggles create false divisions and false choices for Asian-American women. Not long ago, a group of South Asian women organizing against battery held a conference on South Asian women. Recent emigrees, the conference organizers tended to hail from greater class privilege than the parents of second-generation South Asian Americans. This difference led second-generation South Asian American activists, born and bred in the United States, to boycott the conference, charging that the organizers, because of their class privilege and because of their relative newness to the Asian-American community, sidelined issues of U.S.-based racism and discrimination.

This is a false division, especially dangerous in such a relatively small activist community. When first faced with U.S. racism and its Black/white constructs, immigrants with class privilege, even activist ones, are apt to dismiss racism as "not their problem." (As it has been defined by the mainstream, strictly speaking, it isn't.) Efforts by second-generation (and beyond) activists, to convince our sisters at other locations on the culture/class continuum that what we suffer is similar to what the Black community suffers are fraught with difficulty precisely because we have been confined to the Black/white paradigm. We need to use an accurate portrayal of our own experiences of racism, defined on *our* terms, to create alliances with our sisters across generation, class, and culture gaps. As long as we don't, false dichotomies will continue to divide us.

As Asian-American women, Asian women in America, American women of Asian descent, or however we choose to think of ourselves, we all grapple with conflicting signals and oppressions in our lives because we are all situated, to differing degrees, in both Asian and American cultural milieus. We suffer not only cultural discrimination (as men do as well) but our own form of cultural schizophrenia, as we receive mixed and often contradictory signals about priorities, values, duty, and meaning from our families and greater communities. We encounter sexist Asian tradition; racist and sexist white culture; antiracist nonfeminist women heroes; racist feminist heroes; strong proud Asian women who told us not to make waves; strong proud non-Asian women who told us to make waves, and on and on.

We all reconcile these tensions and oppressions in different ways: by acting out a model minority myth, for some; by suffering silently, for others; by being activist, for still others. These conflicts, born of cultural duality, along with the experience of cultural discrimination, are what unite us as Asian-American women across our differences. But this commonality has been obscured; there is no room for cultural duality in a world where one is automatically relegated to one racial camp or the other based on biological fact. But as we grapple with conflicting signals and oppressions in our lives, we can reimagine and reinvent ourselves and our priorities. The cultural schizophrenia, the feeling of not belonging to either or any culture, is not necessarily a burden; it is also an opportunity for us to re-create ourselves. We do it every time we encounter a conflict anyway; why not politicize this process of cultural reconciliation, and tag it for feminism and liberation?

We need to reclaim our cultural duality as our commonality and, also, as our greatest strength: for the good of our movement and to save ourselves. When the poor immigrant Asian woman who follows an abusive husband to the United States, who doesn't speak English and is cut off from the women who supported her in her home country, is beaten nearly to death by her one contact to the outside world, she needs a bicultural feminism. Not one that helps her go back to Asia, nor one that suggests she become a typical liberated "American" woman. She needs an activism that recognizes the cultural discrimination she will encounter in this society, while still empowering her to liberate herself in this country (with money, legal services, shelter, and support). She needs a bicultural feminism that will recognize and politicize the cultural reconciliation she must undergo to liberate herself: for example, by reimagining her duty as an Asian wife as a duty to herself.

When my little sister, who is just beginning to see herself as a sexual person, thinks she is a "slut" for wearing tight jeans, she needs this bicultural feminism. Not a mainstream white feminism, which might suggest she throw away her tight jeans because she is objectifying herself, nor one that simply suggests she revert to the dress of her "homeland" and wear a revealing sari—but one that would affirm that she doesn't have to abandon Indian values of filial respect or whatever it is that makes her fear appearing "slutty." It is possible that my parents, first-generation Indian immigrants, reject the trappings of American sexuality, such as tight jeans, as culturally alien. My sister's subsequent interpretation, however, that Indians are antisexual stems from her assumption—promulgated by mainstream society—that there is but one culture, not many. If you don't appreciate the trappings of sexuality, you don't appreciate sexuality. The fact that tight jeans are a particular, cultural expression of sexuality is obscured. An Asian-American feminism that emphasized cultural duality and reconciliation would subvert such narrow-mindedness. There are many cultures, many sexualities. My sister needs to name the cultural conflicts she is involved in for what they are and to reconcile her visions of sexuality and empowerment within the cultural confines of white patriarchy and Indian patriarchy. A bicultural feminism would ensure that she does this in a feminist, liberatory way.

As bicultural feminists with multiple identities, we are empowered to enter the broader discussion and struggles around us with something more substantial than identity politics and a slightly different take on the Black/white dichotomy. The concept and practice of the extended family, for example, might lead us to apply our critical reinventions to the struggle for accessible child care, where we can shift the turgid debate away from paid care to building cooperative care centers and encouraging work-sharing. Understanding social and linguistic difference within Asian-American families, we can apply our insights to the current debates about gay parents raising potentially straight children, or to white families raising children of color, by advocating for the fitness of the child's cultural community rather than for the fitness of the parent. Remembering our histories as Asian women, we can apply our sense of outrage over issues such as the Japanese internment during World War II, "brain drain" immigration to the United States that has robbed the Third World of its professional class, and past and present treatment of refugees to the struggle for just immigration policies. We can reinterpret Asian paradigms of filial and familial duty as social responsibility. We can use antimaterialism as a basis for building an ecological society.

I remember, in that South Asian American women's group, we were all looking forward to Mira Nair's film, *Mississippi Masala*. We took Nair as a kind of model—a seemingly progressive Indian woman filmmaker who had gained the financial backing necessary for reaching wide sectors of the South Asian community. *Masala* was the first film we knew of that would portray an Indian-American woman in her cultural milieu as the protagonist.

I don't know what Nair's intentions were, but her Indian-American protagonist was little more than a standard Western-defined beauty, her biculturalism little more than occasional bare feet and a chureedar thrown over her shoulder. Although a refugee from Uganda living in Mississippi with Indian parents, she was phenomenally unconcerned with issues of race, history, culture, and gender. Given the dearth of accessible activist commentary on biculturalism and feminism beyond the Black/white divide, even a sympathetic "opinion maker" like Nair can hurt our movement, by portraying us as little more than exotic, browner versions of white women who by virtue of a little color can bridge the gap between Black and white (not through activism, of course, just romantic love). If Asian-American women's movements can effectively unite within bicultural feminist agendas, we can snatch that power away from those willing to trivialize us, and Masala and our less sympathetic foes beware.

Chapter Thirteen

Sex Radical Politics, Sex-Positive Feminist Thought, and Whore Stigma

Carol Queen

I grow more disaffected from politics—both traditional and progressive—with every passing year. Only one sort of politics keeps my attention, feels relevant, stays vital: the politics of sex. I don't mean primarily feminism, the politics of gender, but rather what some people call sex radicalism. Sex radical thought departs from both right- and most left-wing ideologies by honoring sex and desire and by positing as important the power relations of sexual orientation and behavior vis-à-vis the culture's traditional sexual mores. What is illegal? What is despised and why? What is transgressive, and what systems are shored up by the boundaries we transgress?

Sex Radicalism and Feminism: Not Always in Bed Together

As we will see, sex radical thought is both deeply feminist and also profoundly challenging to many attitudes and assumptions promoted by contemporary mainstream feminism. While I continue to identify with feminism, I also regard it with some disappointment; though I feel that most of its core principles go without saying, I certainly do not feel their unmodified relevance to all areas of my life, particularly to sex.

Feminism has greatly influenced the intellectual development of sex radicalism, many of whose earliest theorists—Gayle Rubin, Pat Califia, and Carole Vance, to name just a few—were (and are) outspokenly feminist women. Feminism itself, however, does not embrace sex radicalism completely, nor is a feminist political analysis that is untouched by sex radicalism enough to unravel the various sources of sexual, not just gender, oppression. Gayle Rubin notes in her influential essay "Thinking Sex"[1] that sex radicalism's analysis focuses on oppression sourced in "the stigma of erotic dissidence"; feminism, by contrast, is a theoretical attempt to analyze and act against gender oppression, having no position on sex except where sexual issues are seen as devolving from gender inequality. Feminism finds no shortage of gender-linked problems with sex—rape, spousal abuse and abortion rights are three examples that have spurred much feminist organizing and action—though I will argue that it is possible to cast this net too widely, seeing gender as the primary or sole issue where matters are more complex, as in lesbian oppression, S/M, pornography, and prostitution (just a few issues that have challenged mainstream feminism).

I myself grew up into feminist thought when it was fresh from its dalliance with '60s-style sexual liberation ideology. A woman ought to be able to do what she wants with her body and her sexuality, I read in books like *Sisterhood Is Powerful* and *Our Bodies, Ourselves*. In my wholehearted agreement these became my feminist foundation. I was treading water in a sea of hormones, beginning to experiment with partner sex, learning to masturbate, slyly managing to access forbidden books. I wanted to know about sex, I wanted to feel powerful in it, I wanted to experiment, have lots of lovers, love both men and women, be sexually free and sophisticated in a way I knew most women of my mother's generation—and certainly my mother herself—were not.

For a time it seemed—at least, I believed—that feminism was my straightforward ally in these desires. But mainstream feminism, as it turned out, had never been entirely comfortable with sex. While I was happily devouring *Sisterhood Is Powerful* at the age of thirteen, the National Organization for Women was trying to purge lesbians from its membership; not long after, Betty Dodson caused a heated stir—accompanied by walkouts—at one of NOW's national meetings when she showed slides of vulvas. Sexual representation, even that produced by women, was controversial within orthodox feminism long before the mainstream media discovered Andrea Dworkin and Catharine MacKinnon.

The trail of my sexual fascinations, no less than my sexual politics, led me into the lesbian and gay community, and I stayed there from late adolescence through my twenties. There I learned a lot about sexual freedom and living as an outlaw; I was out as a lesbian in a small city, where I got my share of hate mail and death threats. I learned that many people are profoundly unwilling to let others live their own (especially sexual) lives. I saw the politics not only in gender but also in sexual behavior and sexual identity. Within a culture, power accrues not only according to class, race, and gender but also by virtue of sexual orientation and behavior, actual and presumed. Uneven access to power formed the very basis of the way my generation learned to understand politics, even though within feminism the phrase "sexual politics" meant something quite different from the politicized sexual dramas I saw playing out all around me.

The next fork in the road came when I explored S/M with a lover. She was too nervous about other people's opinions to let anyone know about our experiments in power-erotics, although I had heard rumors that in fact there was a small lesbian S/M support group within our community. I learned from this how fearful of discovery over a sexual "kink" even someone who was sexually well-adjusted—and already living counter to social norms—could be. Not long after, I began reading in the lesbian press that many women all across the country were conducting similar explorations, and that my lover had in fact been right to be worried about our community's response. The lesbian/feminist community nationwide was being torn apart by heated disagreements about what constituted appropriate lesbian sex. In this context, more than from the Maoism that had also influenced early radical feminism, I became familiar with the term "politically incorrect." (That this term has been co-opted and used against feminists and progressives is only one of the bizarre political reversals faced by those of us whose politics were forged in '60s-era notions of liberation.)

I had now learned that a key point in my understanding of feminism—that it is my and all women's right to explore and define our own sexuality—was not universally accepted in the community of women who called themselves feminist. Arguments raged about sex and about sexual representation, that is, porn. Increasingly I found myself on the side that was being termed politically incorrect. So when I heard the term "sex radical" for the first time, I knew before I even heard the definition that it applied to me.

Sex Radical, Sex-Positive

Sex radicalism means to me that I am automatically on the side of the minority sexual viewpoint or behavior; because our culture carefully and narrowly *circumscribes* what is acceptable, much of the sexual world gets left on the wrong side of the fence. Sex radicalism also means that when I hear the voices of those who have been left out of the discussion, I choose to believe what they tell me about their own lives, even if it contradicts some "expert's" opinion; it also means that I maintain my own sexual integrity, if not cultural popularity, when I follow my own desires and trust where they lead.

Sex radicalism is also profoundly feminist, and with good reason. While many men are oppressed (in reality or potentially) for their sexual desires and practices, women are encouraged never to explore or experience our alternative sexual feelings in the first place. We are supposed to exist sexually within a (married, monogamous) relationship with a man, or else not at all. When we do step across the boundaries of compulsory heterosexuality and "good girl" propriety, we are often treated viciously. Women need each other's support (although we do not always get it) to navigate the rough waters of living non-traditional sexual lives. Mainstream feminism learned this lesson from lesbians, who would not withdraw their demand for support from feminist organizations and institutions; it has not, however, extrapolated what it learned to women elsewhere on the sexual fringe.

Upon further exploring sex radical thought, I learned the concept of "sex-negativity," which most of us in this erotically benighted culture drink in along with our mothers' milk. I learned that there is indeed a community of people who are sex-positive, who don't denigrate, medicalize, or demonize any form of sexual expression except that which is not consensual. In our general society—where sex is sniggered at, commodified, and guiltily, surreptitiously engaged in—being outspokenly sex-positive is sex radical indeed, for even those of us who love sex are usually encouraged to find someone else's preferred sexual expression abhorrent.

I discovered sex-positive community in various places: through my study of sexology; through my friendships with sexually adventurous others, especially gay men; in the leather community; and, perhaps most importantly, through meeting women who were both outspokenly sexual and feminist and who refused to let one quality cancel out the other. These "sex-positive feminists," as many of us have taken to calling ourselves, embrace the feminist analysis of gender inequality, but challenge the silence or conservative positions of Dworkin- and MacKinnon-influenced feminism on sexual issues. Many sex-positive feminists are veterans of the feminist sex wars over pornography and S/M, and many are current or former sex workers. Coming to a radical sexual world view, especially through my contacts and friendships with women I could relate to and who were willing to mentor me through my confusion about sex and feminism, actually proved to be excellent preparation for becoming a whore. When I did so, I discovered a world very different from the one for which the vague warnings of mainstream feminists had prepared me. My comments are sourced in the whores' world I have known; I do not intend to encompass the experience of those whores who do not work voluntarily, who are underage, who are not sex-positive, and who act out the negative expectations imposed on them by a sexist and sex-negative culture.

Why Whores Need Sex-Positive Thought

Sources as disparate and discordant as Hollywood movies, right-wing Christians, and prominent feminists tell us that women in the sex industry make a career of pandering to men's desires because, as victims of histories of abuse, we have no boundaries and sometimes no choices. For some of us there is some truth to this; there are certainly people whose mental and spiritual health would benefit from getting out of the business, and they are well served by support in doing so. But we learn next to nothing about those women for whom sex work is an excellent occupational choice and nothing at all about male sex workers—isn't it a bit ironic that men are present in the sex industry in every capacity that women are, yet their lives, failing to fit neatly into theory, are simply ignored?

One orthodox feminist argument against whoring is that it gives men further sexual access to women; leaving aside whether reality is so simplifiable, how might they choose to argue against men having access to men? And why aren't more of them clamoring for women to have equal access to sexual entertainment and service? These questions point to more fruitful areas of exploration about the nature of female and male sexual socialization, the reasons males patronize prostitutes (of whatever gender), and the place of sexual pleasure in male and female lives. Sex-positive feminists find these questions compelling; mainstream feminists often do not even ask them.

As an activist in the sex-work community, I have met well over a hundred prostitutes, as many exotic dancers, a few dozen dominatrices, and a number of models and porn actresses—far more than have most anti-sex work activists and even most sex researchers. Just one factor stands out to distinguish those who live well, with no loss of self-esteem, from those who may find sex work a difficult or even damaging career choice. Most of the former have sufficient sex information and are sex-positive. Most, too, are staunchly feminist, even though some of them refuse to embrace that term, associating it with women who do not understand their circumstances and who do not support their right to work and to control their own bodies. Most of the latter have internalized negative attitudes about sex, especially divergent sexual behavior, and certainly about sex work itself.

In this respect, the latter are no different from those who have devoted their lives to agitating against sex work. None of these crusaders, whether they emerge from the religious Right or the feminist Left, voices respect for sexuality. (Rubin, in fact, calls mainstream feminism a "system of sexual judgment"[2]—an accusation its adherents have not yet managed to disprove.)

If these activists truly wanted to improve the lot of sex workers (which, of course, they don't; they merely want to do away with the sex industry) they would insist upon thorough and nonjudgmental sex information for clients as well as whores. One basic piece of information would be that women—and whores—do not exist to be sexually used by men, but that any sexual interaction, including a paid one, benefits from *negotiation*. This would facilitate the climate of respect that anti-sex-work demagogues claim is absent in a paid act of sexual entertainment or gratification. The paucity of sex-positive discussion about what is possible in a commodified context often negatively affects sex workers themselves.

In fact, when we whores see a client or when a peepshow worker or stripper interacts with a customer, the presence or absence of respect has much to do with how sex-positive the client or customer is—and something to do with our own sex-positivity. It also depends upon each person's degree of self-respect and presence or absence of sexual shame. Men who have taken (and internalized) the most damaging blows around their right to sexual pleasure are among the most unpleasant clients to deal with. Unfortunately, the well-publicized opinions of the anti-sex-work crowd are highly judgmental about the motives of those who pay for sexual pleasure and entertainment. I have encountered many men whose self-acceptance—and social skills—have been impaired by hearing too much media credence given to the opinions of people who are in no position to make even an educated guess about what friendly relations between whores and their clients could be like. Sex-positive feminists are only now beginning to get enough media attention that their message can trickle down to these men and to other women.

Combined with our treatment by a sex-negative law enforcement and legal system and the notorious tendency of the police to think of aggressions against us as something other than crimes, many of us are routinely victimized—by police if not by our clients and customers. Meanwhile, most of society looks the other way, including many feminists who are quick to point out how egregiously our clients are "abusing" us simply by giving us money for sex or erotic entertainment. Feminists should be among the first to clamor for decriminalized prostitution, yet many remain silent and even vigilant in the fight to further criminalize prostitution. Feminists should raise their voices in protest when police abuse whores or ignore our need for police protection. Yet too often these voices are silent, even though these socially sanctioned abuses fall disproportionately on those most lacking feminist and other support: women of color, poor women, transgendered women.

Even when a supportive hand is extended, it often comes with a stipulation: get out of the business or do without help. The not-so-silent message is, if you elect to stay in the sex industry you can expect abuse, and we can (will) do nothing to help you. Parallel this to the deep (and deeply legitimate) concern feminists have shown to women in battered and abusive relationships; current thinking in the battered women's movement emphasizes that women be supported where they are, not offered conditional assistance.

Some of us want out of the business, but many of us simply want to see conditions improve, with everybody else out of the way. All of us would be served by a dose of sex-positive thought, which might allow us—many for the first time—to think of what we do as a worthy professional service, not demeaning, on-the-fringe behavior. An ever-increasing number of us want our sexually schizophrenic culture to look at the realities, not the lurid myths, of what we do, and to see that when sexual pleasure is seen as a positive and honorable goal, much of the negative fruit of the sex industry is deprived of soil in which to grow.

Why Johns Need Sex-Positive Prostitutes

One stereotype has it that sex workers provide sexual relief to society's "wretched": the old, the unattractive, the unpartnered. This myth can fetch us a certain amount of grudging respect even as it lets others (who can't imagine having sex with such people) distance themselves from us—as if only the young and the firm are allowed to have a sexuality in the first place, and as if whores render a service by keeping unacceptable sexualities out of the public eye. Certainly we count among our clients those who fall outside the rather narrow limits of the erotically entitled. We also count among our customers the married, the well-off, the conventionally attractive, the famous, the socially skilled: the inheritors of patriarchy. Whores know, if no one else in society is willing to admit, that outside their relations with us, these men often have as little luck getting their erotic needs met as their "less fortunate" brothers.

One also frequently hears that whores are sought out by kinky clients whose desires are unacceptable to other people. This, I think, is the source of part of the contention that clients want to abuse us: in spite of the fact that all over the country women are slurping on their partners' cocks for free, experimenting with bondage, and arranging or at least fantasizing about threesomes. A large percentage of the U.S. population still considers activities like these beyond the pale, degrading, and abusive, even when consensually performed. In fact, many clients bring socially unacceptable desires to sex workers—or at least desires that are unacceptable in their own bedrooms. And until the climates in their bedrooms change, sex professionals will be among their only outlets. The anti-whore sentiment that grows out of the conviction that there is only one kind of appropriate sex and that all others are sinful and/or abusive (depending on the sort of morality embraced by the critic) is precisely the cultural norm in opposition to which sex radical politics grew.

Sex radicals see a problem—and a source of potential oppression—in anyone's conviction that their own sexual patterns and desires are right while someone else's are wrong. Getting between the lines of the anti-sex-work ideologues' reasoning, we find various concerns embedded but often not articulated: a married man is wrong to take his sexual desires to anyone but his wife; a married man is wrong to have sexual desires if his wife isn't comfortable with them; oral sex is depraved; giving men an outlet for getting blowjobs will just make the man want them at home, and blowjobs are demeaning to women; sex is demeaning unless a romantic bond (or a Christian bond) exists between a couple; giving men an outlet for any kind of sex, including sexual looking, will make him want more sex/kinkier sex; if a prostitute isn't immediately available he will harass/rape other women; getting sex from a professional is the same as infidelity; men should not have access to sexual variety; prostitutes spread HIV (to "innocent victims"). (This says nothing of the numerous heterosexually married men who actually patronize male whores; but again, this common situation is scarcely ever recognized and commented on by sex-work abolitionists, especially feminist ones.)

It is as though sex, especially male sex, is a bubbling cauldron of trouble, and if we don't keep a lid on it, awful things will result.

In fact, this is precisely the lesson my mother tried to teach me. Her example, however, was not inspiring; and if all the women who rail against the sex industry have sexualities as miserably closed down as hers, the culture is in a painful, festering state indeed. "Do you know," she whispered to me wide-eyed some months after my father's death, "your father tried to convince me to perform oral sex on him *six times* during our marriage!"

"Dad," I thought, "you animal! Once every five years! Have you no self-control?" More than once I've wished my distressingly buttoned-down dad—whose sexual unhappiness rubbed off on everyone in my family—had turned to a whore to let off some steam.

Like my parents, a majority of our clients have marriages marked by desire discrepancies and difficult communication about sex. Many women have grown up fearful of sex, either because of unpleasant experiences or because these feelings were inculcated in them at (sometimes literally) their mothers' knees. Others have grown up believing that sexual experimentation is wrong. Feminism, when it successfully reaches to these women at all, rarely contradicts the deep sexual antipathy they carry.

The availability of paid sexual gratification and entertainment does nothing to improve these partners' sexual relationships except, perhaps, to take the pressure off; it has been argued that having a valve on the pressure cooker actually preserves marriages like this by minimizing the impact of their sexual contradictions. I'm inclined to believe this is true, but it still doesn't cast a very rosy light on the situation; for one thing, are the women's sexual desires being met in relationships such as these? Not very likely! My answer to the problem—universal sex-positive education and sexual empowerment of women—lies far away on the horizon.

Wives Need (and Can Learn From) Whores, Too

In the meantime, I think the unequal lot of these couples could be balanced somewhat by a growing availability of sexual entertainment for the women whose partners are going out and getting theirs by hiring professionals. Of course, this scenario would involve that our culture take a whole new look at women and sex. The gander may not be ready to share the playground with the goose; but, just as importantly, women may not be prepared to take into the marketplace desires they've been trained to romanticize. Much feminist theory has spotlit the ill effects on women's self-esteem and autonomy of channeling sexuality into a relationship, but few feminists have suggested women could learn something by having more options for sexual fulfillment in the marketplace. As with the question of pornography and its appeal/availability to women, many sex-positive feminists support more female-centered choices in sexual service and entertainment, the proliferation of which might well affect the entire sex industry for the better. And if conflating sex and romance keeps women available for marriage (usually implying their acceptance of male control over their sexuality), how might detaching sex from romance serve to change what women desire from sex?

Viewed through a sex radical lens, whore stigma derives from whores' sexual availability and presumed copious sexual activity. From a sex-positive feminist perspective, most whores are available and sexually active *on their own terms*. It's no wonder that whore stigma attaches itself more viciously to women than to men, for in this society a sexually emancipated woman is threatening and despised; neither "slut" nor "whore" is a name most women want to wear. Sex workers cross this line, either proudly or not, for money, adventure, or rebellion. Would our clients' wives—or even many mainstream feminists—be willing to brave that stigma for a chance at sexual agency? What about for the promise of greater solidarity among all women? Early feminism tried to erase the whore stigma for just that reason; today's feminist orthodoxy would often rather do away with whores. Any issue that divides women—and this is one of the most potent divisions of all—is crucial for feminists to consider and resolve.

Other whores won't necessarily agree with me, but I'd be glad to see sex work wither away because everyone became so sex-positive that a market for our services no longer existed. Perhaps then we could become the sexual healers and sex educators so many of us believe we (potentially or already) are. Of course, we're nowhere close to that utopia; in the meantime sex workers can help facilitate gratification for those who wouldn't ordinarily get it, and we can all—whores, sex radicals, sex-positive feminists, and critics alike—continue to ask questions whose answers point to an increasing level of comfort and safety for sex workers (as well as, incidentally, for our clients).

A Sex Radical, Sex-Positive Feminist, Whore's-Eye View

The stereotype about sex workers that says we are driven to this demeaning lifestyle by a damaged history must be exposed as the sex-negative and, yes, sexist crap it so often is. (How eerily this parallels what used to be said about lesbians!) This image is neither universally truthful nor even helpful for analyzing the situations of those whores whom it describes, unless the question is also asked: What separates those sex workers who experience their lives negatively from those who do not? Abolitionists won't ask this question, because it implies that there might be a strategy for creating a positive sex industry, but we whores and all of our supporters, including sex-positive feminists, must ask it continually. Abundant and accurate sex information, as I noted above, is a key determinant.

And while I maintain that it should be everyone's right to do sex work, I hope people will consider their motives for it whether they are thinking about entering the sex industry or are already a veteran. It is never too late for anyone to begin to root out his or her own sex-negativity, and the whores who haven't done so—those whose damaged lives and horror stories are so eagerly pointed to by the anti-sex-work activists, and even those who disrespect their clients' desires—may lack the most important qualifications for the job. It is the responsibility of the culture to work on its negative attitudes about sex and about us and our work; but it is whores' responsibility to work on our negative attitudes about ourselves.

The movement for sex workers' rights should acknowledge that we have professional responsibilities and should assist every whore in meeting them. Giving sexuality, the basis of our trade, the respect it deserves must be foremost among these. In fact, as of this writing the North American Task Force on Prostitution has a subcommittee that is developing a code of ethics for whores.

Women and men who do sex and sexual entertainment for a living are targeted by laws as well as social opprobrium, and so are our clients and customers—though the latter form a shadowy, hard-to-recognize army. We are regarded more as outlaws than they are, and this can be one of our strengths: seeing, often with the support of other sex workers, that we constitute a group with different sexual norms, oppressed because of these differences, is the first step toward embracing sex radical politics and understanding that we are only one group out of many that has been culturally labeled and mistreated. A feminist analysis, too, helps us see ourselves as a group with shared circumstances, one for whom gender is by no means irrelevant. Certainly we should have pride in ourselves and hopefully in what we do, and sex radical politics, along with a sex-positive belief system and a sex-positive feminist analysis, can go a long way toward ensuring that we develop that pride.

There *is* no sexual majority, although the whole society conspires to behave as though there were. Our clients—mostly married heterosexual men who show an illusory exterior of "normalcy" (whatever that useless concept means)—are also cross-dressers, submissives, anally erotic, bisexual, fetishistic, wrapped up in wild fantasies no traditional heterosexual marriage could ever contain. And what the "poor abused whores" lobby will never tell you is that many sex workers, too, are fetishistic, sexually curious, nonmonogamous by nature, and exhibitionistic, delighting in the secret proof our profession provides us that restrictive sexual mores are rupturing everywhere.

No one should ever, by economic constraint or any kind of interpersonal force, have to do sex work who does not like sex, who is not cut out for a life of sexual generosity (however attractively high the fee charged for it). Wanting to make a lot of money should not be the only qualification for becoming a whore. We in this profession swim against the tide of our culture's inability to come to terms with human sexual variety and desire, its very fear of communicating about sex in an honest and nonjudgmental way. We need special qualifications, or at the very least we need access to a way of thinking that lets us retain our self-esteem when everyone else, especially do-gooders, would like to undermine it.

Activist whores teach, among other things, a view of our culture's sexual profile that differs from traditional normative sexuality. Every whore embodies this difference each time s/he works. It is time for all whores to embrace this difference, to become ambassadors for sex and gratification. The politics of being a whore do not differ markedly from the politics of any other sexually despised group. We must include radical sexual politics in our agenda, becoming defenders of sex itself. Our well-being and our own defense depend on it.

Inviting Feminism into Bed with Us

And in the end, what does this have to do with feminism?

Today, mainstream feminism is a site for anti-whore activism, a locus for demagogues like Andrea Dworkin, Catharine MacKinnon, and Kathleen Barry to agitate for the abolition of our livelihoods and to lobby for our silencing. Ordinary feminist women are often swayed by their rhetoric and may have no opportunity to hear our side of the story. (Certainly every letter I've ever sent to Ms. has gone unpublished.) We have learned to our dismay that a woman's feminism is no guarantee she'll be open to sex radical thought; sometimes, sad to say, the very opposite seems true. Whores make other more traditional feminists defensive around issues of sexual stigma, boundaries, and the nature of women's sexual relationships with men. However, we could equally powerfully raise consciousness around these issues, since sex-positive whores have learned to sexually negotiate at the intersection of our clients' desires, our limits and boundaries, and with regard to issues of safety and emotional well being. Were we to be acknowledged by orthodox feminists as the experts we are, our voices could help push the feminist analysis of sex in positive, productive directions. This could only strengthen feminism's appeal, since sexuality is such a powerful, and often problematic, issue in so many women's—and men's—lives. If feminism were to take seriously my question about what separates the experiences of women who hate sex work from those who thrive doing it, would that not have profound implications for the lives and sexual strategies of ordinary women?

Further, taking whores—whores, not just "degraded" ex-whores—seriously would support a feminist claim that is at the moment fatuous: that feminists care about the experience of all women and are open to learning from the experience of all women. Whores are only one of a multitude of groups who do not get an open-minded hearing in mainstream feminism today.

It can be argued that whores labor on the front lines of patriarchy. Feminists really ought to be more interested in the things we see, hear, and experience there. Sex-positive feminists are, of course, and support the issues we consider important, including improved working conditions, safety, and freedom from harassment. They, unlike so many orthodox feminists, understand that we do not consider our work itself a form of sexual harassment; that many of the abuses committed within the sex industry have little to do, in fact, with sexuality; that we are not *selling* ourselves or our bodies (a reprehensible turn of phrase repeated, often as not, by feminists, who ought to have more concern for the power of language to shape reality) any more than does any worker under capitalism; sex-positive feminists remember that any worker under capitalism is subject to mistreatment.

They also understand that we value our work when it allows us autonomy, free time, and a comfortable income; we often like living outside the narrow circle society circumscribes of ladylike behavior; we are not "good girls," nor do we aspire to be; and we often relish the opportunity our work provides us to learn secrets, to support our clients' forays away from traditional masculine sexuality, to transgress restrictive boundaries and rebel against the rigid limitations created by our own fear of sex.

To what degree is the failure of mainstream feminists to educate themselves about us and support us a result of their fear of sex and/or of being labeled a whore? Like many feminists' antipathy toward lesbianism, this is a feminist issue with implications far beyond the politics of sex work.

Sex-positive feminist whores invite all women to consider these issues, confront their own whorephobia and learn from us.

NOTES

1. Rubin, Gayle. "Thinking Sex: Notes for a Radical Theory of the Politics of Sexuality," in *Pleasure and Danger: Exploring Female Sexuality*, Carole Vance, ed. Boston: Routledge & Kegan Paul, 1984, p. 293.

2. Rubin, p. 282.

Chapter Fourteen

I Brake for Feminists
Debates and Divisions within Women's Studies

Ruth Perry

Needless to say, Women's Studies has had its share of debates and divisions. To begin with, there is the debate about whether Women's Studies is a corrective lens through which to view traditional disciplines or whether by asking our epistemological and ontological questions about the nature of knowledge, we have created a new subject matter. Does sensitivity to the pervasive gender coding of most discourses constitute a new kind of reading or is it simply a refinement of an old kind of reading? Is Virginia Woolf's *A Room of One's Own* a founding text in a new discipline inaugurating a kind of reading that is always contextual, that weaves back and forth between life and art, walking first on the pavement and then the turf—or is it a book about the distortions with which women's writing has been viewed historically and the material differences underlying men's and women's literary production?

Another debate within Women's Studies has been the extent to which generalizations about "women" are possible at all. How are readings of gender problematized by racial, ethnic, and class differences? Just how essential are any of those categories? Are the writing strategies of a French aristocratic woman of the seventeenth century, say Mme. de LaFayette, relevant to the way women writers today negotiate literary conventions? Are there any constants that correlate with gender across cultures and historical periods? What is the difference between Northern urban Black women's literary production and Southern rural Black women's literary production, and how does class further complicate those categories?

The British, who have always had a Labour Party, theorize that identity is created by the work a person does. British feminists have frequently criticized American feminists for paying too little attention to the material conditions of women's labor. From the other side, French feminists, championed by Toril Moi,[1] have attacked U.S. feminists as being too empiricist and positivist in assessing women's place in society.

And then there's the debate about theory and practice—about whether or not there is any value in theorizing about merely discursive phenomena without recon-

Abridged from *Transformations* 7, no. 1 (Spring 1996):1–13.

necting those phenomena usefully to the lived experience of real women. Did post-structuralists merely replace "material determinism" with "linguistic determinism"? On the other hand, aren't those who defend experience as opposed to theory (as in "the personal is political") open to criticism as individualist and privatizing, indulging in the luxury of personalist criticism while evading the necessary work of theorizing the unequal access of post-colonial subjects to the means of literary production—not to mention their unequally alienated conditions of labor?

And of course, in any movement that is 25 years old, generational differences emerge in the natural order of things. "Younger" critics today seem to have moved beyond the study of "woman" and are more interested in differences within that category and in blurring gender boundaries altogether. This interest in sexualities and performative gender definition—rather than in body types—rests on an assumption that liberation lies in de-stabilizing the gender system, that repressive social systems are based on a foundation of binary classification that can be undermined by gender-bending. They argue that the study of women is just a subset (as we say at MIT) of a more general study of gender, and that feminist scholars can use (for example) queer theory, studying gay male writers in order to investigate the social category of gender, how it has changed over time, and how assumptions about it saturate the rest of what we know.

Again, I am sure that most of this is familiar to many of you and I rehearse these developments at the risk of boring you in order to put them on the table. I want to show you, among other things, how irrelevant to our real discourse and debates are the recent attacks on Women's Studies in the popular press and in highly publicized books by gynophobic feminists.

The most common mischaracterization in the media at present is the charge that Women's Studies is devoted to male-bashing and man-hating. I don't have to tell you how absurd that is—how more and more feminist men are taking Women's Studies classes, teaching in Women's Studies programs, and publishing feminist scholarship. Indeed, the latest hot topic in eighteenth-century studies is "historicizing masculinity." Women's Studies examines those cultural structures that devalue women and whatever is associated with women and overvalue what is associated with men and masculinity; Women's Studies is not about how individual men or women feel about the other sex. Women's Studies is analysis, not soap opera—although the latter makes better newsprint.

Critics of Women's Studies—in their willful ignorance—also claim that Women's Studies represents women as victims, denying that women are the free individuals that they, in fact, are. This, despite the fact that feminist scholarship has focused for at least the last dozen years on women's agency and subversion in the context of a culture that marginalizes their experiences, perceptions, contributions. Are we imagining women's poverty? Did feminists invent the fact that although women make up 45% of the work force they only earn $.72 to every dollar that men earn, that 1 out of every 3 single mothers and 1 out of every 4 children live below the poverty line? Is it merely coincidence that only 10% of the Congress is female? Pretending that women have the same life chances as men won't change the fact that 1 woman out of every 9 in the U.S. will be raped—at a conservative estimate.

Surely these facts constitute part of the context in which women operate. Nor is identifying and naming a threat the same as succumbing to it. . . .

Obviously, there are reductive and dogmatic people everywhere in university life. Since I am not an essentialist, I do not think that these traits belong exclusively to male—or female—academics. They have even been detected, sorry to say, in Women's Studies faculty as well as in the usual range of historians, physicists, and philosophers. But no one proposes that history, physics, and philosophy have "gone wrong" or that we do away with them because of some substandard practitioners. So why is anyone willing to buy *ad feminam* arguments about Women's Studies? Those who claim that Women's Studies is political rather than scholarly, focused on male-bashing and promoting feelings of victimization, cannot have read any of the scholarship of the last 20 years, or if they have, cannot have understood it. We analyze the construction of knowledge: in the case of literary critics that means the construction of the canon and the categories of literary analysis (that is, period, genre, voice, narrative stance, diction, pace, figurative language, etc.) to see how gender (or class or race or global location) weighs in the construction of literary value. These are very sophisticated analytic moves, when done well, and are hardly reducible to male-bashing or victimization.

Other false charges made by the pod feminists, and amplified eagerly by the sensation-seeking media, are that Women's Studies scholars and teachers are a touchy-feely lot, intolerant of dissent, who dominate the university. "Pod feminists" is Susan Faludi's name[2] for the likes of Christina Sommers, Karen Lehrman, Cathy Young, Katie Roiphe, and Camille Paglia. It is a name she borrows from an old sci-fi movie, *The Invasion of the Body Snatchers* in which the pod people—instrumental automata without real feelings, and distinguishable by a faint hum, from the human bodies they come to inhabit—slowly infiltrate human society. These "pod feminists," gynophobic popularizers allege psychobabble in the classroom and unprofessional behavior on the part of Women's Studies faculty. They condemn paying attention to individual lives as trivial and unscholarly. For twenty years and more feminists have been writing articles on feminist pedagogy, experiments with authority in the classroom and the inadequacy of the male professional idiom in constituting knowledge about women. But the pod feminists never cite that literature, never grant pedagogy as a contested issue within the community of Women's Studies scholars. Journalists looking for a story would rather expose "shocking unprofessionalism" than write about educational experiments fitting form to content, teaching process in addition to transmitting information, taking seriously nondiscursive sources of knowledge, or challenging the extent to which the personal should be bracketed in education.

It must also be noted that students react differently to their Women's Studies classes than to their other classes, disturbed by what they learn about the dynamics of gender in the culture. It makes them anxious–both men and women—because the implications of what they are learning are closer to the bone, more disturbing, than, say, the structure of DNA. They often react peculiarly to their teachers as the bearers of these tidings. Indeed, a recent study of student reactions to required courses on the twenty-campus California State University system showed that while subjects in Women's Studies and Ethnic Studies courses—organized centrally around race and gender—received the highest overall ratings of the six curriculum areas surveyed, the negative descriptors of instructors in these courses—and particularly Women's Studies courses—were overwhelmingly more personal, virulent, and crude.[3] It was an extreme case of "shoot the messenger." So it appears that classroom dynamics are different in Women's Studies subjects independent of teacherly style.

Pod feminists also claim that Women's Studies faculty are femi-nazis who tolerate no dissent. Yet as I tried to indicate earlier, the history of Women's Studies is the history of debate: whether feminism means sharing the privileges of ruling-class men or dismantling the system of privilege; whether the values and roles traditionally associated with women are to be valorized or eschewed; whether Women's Studies is a lens through which to examine traditional disciplines or whether it is a subject unto itself; whether race and class scramble gender difference or whether there is an essential female nature; theory and praxis; the sex wars; mainstreaming, and so on. You cannot pick up a feminist book or journal without encountering strongly-felt debates on every page. Indeed, as a field, Women's Studies is committed to political and ideological multiplicity from its French metaphor of orgasmic *jouissance* vs. the unitary law of the father, to its experiments with pedagogy. . . .

If by "intolerant of dissent" our critics mean that we ask our students to suspend their disbelief that gender makes a difference until they have considered some of the assigned reading, that's true enough. No one expects the biology faculty to offer the creationist thesis as a serious alternative or physicists to teach the Ptolemaic system for anything other than its importance in the history of the field.

As for the claim that feminists dominate the university, that could only be believed by those who have no experience of Women's Studies teaching or administration. At my institution, as at many other high-prestige institutions, feminist scholarship has been so undervalued that tenure has been almost impossible to get on the basis of feminist publications alone. Women's Studies programs at most institutions have been staffed and administered by part-time, untenured faculty on revolving appointments with a high burnout rate. Senior feminist scholars, grateful for long overdue recognition from their home departments, are often tapped for administrative duties, leaving Women's Studies understaffed.

The pod feminists, always growing tropistically towards the limelight, ignore the enormous intellectual contribution made by feminist scholarship to modern thought; they pretend that no ideas are developed, debated, refined in Women's Studies programs. No one acting in good faith would condemn an entire field for the excesses of individuals in it—anymore than anyone would seriously call a halt to the scholarly investigation of the African diaspora because of the rantings of an extremist one disagrees with.

That is not to say that we are not facing a real crisis in feminist literary studies, because we are. On the negative side, the crisis has to do with the failure of identity politics, insofar as multiple identities dilute our collective identity and fragment our movement—as in "Black heterosexual" or "Jewish lesbian." We have also learned to our cost that asserting the rights of one sociological group seems inevitably to entail suppressing the rights of another. Focus on Black women's problems can erase the gender terms of Korean culture; queer theory marginalizes straight women's desire. Yet Women's Studies has been built on identity politics, broadly speaking, and although the term "Woman" has been problematized in the academy, it has not been problematized in the larger society. Women of all ethnicities, sexual preferences, and even classes, will be disadvantaged by proposed changes in welfare regulation, means-tested custody, and the rolling back of abortion rights and affirmative action guidelines.

On the positive side, the crisis in Women's Studies is a kind of growth pain, due to the enormous success of our enterprise, the institutionalization of feminist criticism, and our inexperience as a movement with generational transfers of power. In 25 years, feminist literary criticism has not only changed the way literary criticism is practiced, but has seeded many new areas of study. Recognizing that Women's Studies was patterned on the Black Studies programs of the '60s, I think we should take credit in turn for gay and lesbian studies, queer theory, cultural studies and post-colonial studies. There are many places in the academy in the '90s where one can "do" feminist scholarship. Where once there was only one hospitable intellectual home for feminist critics, there are now several. But these new arenas drain the intellectual energy and collective commitment of Women's Studies faculty. Trendy and glamorous, they leave Women's Studies looking like a dumpy holdover from another era. Although programmatically concerned with race, class, and global location, Women's Studies is sometimes assumed to be the domain of white middle-class Anglo-American women while area studies and cultural studies skim off queer theorists, marxists, and post-colonial theorists. Meanwhile, after perfunctory gestures in the direction of gender, most cultural studies courses/programs/articles evacuate their feminist content as fast as they can, relegating work on women once again to the least prestigious rung of the academic ladder thus making feminism safe for the academy. . . .

Senior scholars must not let themselves be used by institutions to police other women. We must not prove our own quality by setting the unrealistic standards for women's work and letting men take care of their own. Where women's position is debased we must improve it, not escape it. We need to stop competing primarily with other women. Where we disagree, let it be with respect for one another as feminist intellectuals and explicitly within the same movement. . . .

Which brings me to my title, intended as a tag to encapsulate some of what I have been saying. The pun calls attention to the breaking apart, the disassembling of old habits of thought as well as referring to my own personal breaking point, where I draw the line. In the language of bumper stickers, those mass-produced assertions of individual identity, my slogan most closely resembles "I brake for whales" or "I brake for wildflowers," both parodies of the original warning "I brake for animals." If you are willing to slam on the brakes for something, it means that you are willing to make an intervention that defends life against technology. For what are you willing to interrupt the flow of traffic, stop the machines, bring business as usual to a screeching halt, so that, as in the children's book set here in Boston, a line of ducklings can waddle leisurely across the street?

"I brake for animals" was originally intended as a warning to the cars driving behind: This car is skittish; it responds to life's chaotic imperatives and not just to traffic signals. "I brake for whales," on the other hand, calls attention to an embarrassed idealism, mocking those who announce their beliefs while recognizing the cachet of caring for something. A sad commentary on progressive attitudes towards idealism these days.

Finally, "I brake for feminists" because I think that, like whales and wildflowers, women are an endangered species in our society. By "women" I mean that bundle of roles and expectations constructed as the province of females in eighteenth-century England to hedge the cost-accounting instrumentality of capitalism. Nurturance, empathy, kindness, the capacity for contactful intimacy—what Gilligan calls "the ethic of care"[4] and what Ruddick calls "maternal thinking"[5]—those qualities and capacities associated with women since about 1740, highly contested by feminists who find such interpersonal conscientiousness claustrophobic and demeaning—and valued even less by our system of commodity capitalism and the professionalization of all human activity. These virtues are fast disappearing into the maw of the ever-expanding work week and the demands of an international 24-hour production schedule. Most feminists value the labor of social reproduction although few think that women should have sole responsibility for it. But because we were socialized to do it, or because we want to valorize our mothers' lives, most feminists do not demean or take for granted the effort that creates comfort and beauty in daily life. I brake for feminists because they value this non-productive work that creates no commodity, but that reproduces the conditions for living. I brake for feminists because we're going to need everyone we've got in the coming years. I brake for feminists because they have revolutionized knowledge. I brake for feminists because they fill an irreplaceable niche in the ecosystem of the academy. I brake for feminists as our best beginning for nonauthoritarian coalition politics. I brake for feminists because they are precious and overworked and deserve protection. I'm even thinking of printing up a bumper sticker.

NOTES

1. Toril Moi, *Sexual/Textual Politics: Feminist Literary Theory* (London and New York: Methuen, 1985).

2. *Ms.*, March/April 1995.

3. Beth Hartung, "Selective Rejection: How Students Perceive Women's Studies Teachers," *NWSA Journal* 2 (Spring 1990): 254–262.

4. Carol Gilligan, *In a Different Voice* (Cambridge: Harvard University Press, 1982), passim.

5. Sarah Ruddick, "Maternal Thinking," *Feminist Studies* 6.2 (Summer 1980).

Chapter Fifteen

Changing the Subject
Male Feminism, Class Identity, and the Politics of Location

Julie Bettie

As one man recently confessed, "it's easier to be damned if you don't."
—Newton and Stacey 1997: 441

An instructive dialogue in the literature on male feminism is the one between Elaine Showalter and Terry Eagleton published in *Men in Feminism* (Jardine and Smith 1987).[1] In her essay "Critical Cross-Dressing: Male Feminists and the Woman of the Year," Showalter criticizes attempts at feminist writing by both Jonathan Culler and Terry Eagleton. I will briefly summarize and examine the conversation between Showalter and Eagleton as a way of exploring the problems of identity politics as it is often put into practice and how it might better be reformulated and practiced as a politics of location. Contemporary discussions about the relationship between identity and politics raise challenging questions about "traitorous" (Moraga 1986; Harding 1991) political practices such as "white antiracism" and "male feminism." References are often made to the need for broad alliances, but little concrete thinking about what facilitates and what hinders us in actually constructing them exists.

While Showalter claims to welcome the idea of male feminist criticism, she is critical of the manifestation it takes in the work of some male scholars, and remains suspicious of their motives. She queries whether male feminism is "a genuine shift in critical, cultural and sexual paradigms, a break out of the labyrinth of critical theory," or "a form of critical cross-dressing, a fashion risk . . . that is both radical chic and power play?" (p. 120). In Showalter's analysis, Eagleton's "phallic feminism" is deemed appropriative and "insensitive to the politics of acknowledgment" (p. 128). Its effect is to "silence or marginalize feminist criticism by speaking for it, and to use feminist language to reinforce the continued domination of a male literary canon" (p. 129). Showalter asserts that "sexual difference begins with a 'fact that few male theorists have ever had to confront: the possibility of never having been empowered to speak' " (p. 129).[2] In short, Showalter argues that, taken to an extreme, the "decentered subject" and the "death of the author" make the question of who wrote a text irrelevant. Thus, men performing feminist criticism can too easily displace real women writers.

Showalter does not, however, leave us to believe that men cannot do feminist criticism altogether. Men can read as feminists but this requires stating the relationship between their reading and their own cultural position, which she tells us Eagleton fails to do. As she puts it, male feminist criticism must avoid "female impersonation." It must "involve a confrontation with what might be implied by reading as a man and with a questioning or surrender of paternal privileges" (pp. 126–127).

Eagleton responds to Showalter's essay by telling a story about his experience of going to Cambridge as a working-class kid. He describes the self-righteous attitude he and his small cohort of proletarian friends maintained toward the privileged, but socialist-speaking, students who were simultaneously "other/ally." "We . . . scrutinized their socialist credentials for the least flicker of ideological impurity. We made them feel bungling, inept, wet behind the ears, second-class socialists" (pp. 133–134). Eagleton goes on to describe the history of the Labour Party in Britain as one "littered with smooth-talking ambitious men who climbed to power on the backs of working men and women, took over their language, claimed empathy with their sufferings, and then proceeded to sell them out" (p. 134). And the mistake of the working people was to "trust these opportunists" (p. 134). In conclusion he states, "I still think that we were wrong to have been so self-righteous. Yet of course we were not" (p. 135).

Showalter's cutting, witty reply to this narrative simply cites research that shows that men dominate in conversation with women by "ignoring topics introduced by the women, and by developing topics that they had initiated themselves" (p. 136). Women's topics fail in conversation because "men don't work interactionally to develop them" (p. 136). She states that Eagleton has "chang[ed] the grounds of discussion by initiating a narrative of his own," and she refuses to engage in "a one-sided dialog" leaving the story "for others to consider" (p. 136). I would like to respond to this invitation.

From Impersonation to Traitorous Identities

Discussions of male feminist criticism have revolved around the tension expressed in the Showalter/Eagleton exchange: on the one hand exists the desire for men to ally with feminism; on the other, feminists often criticize male feminist criticism for appropriating feminist discourse and displacing women. While conventional notions of identity politics risk conflating political positionality with an essentialized identity (as in the formulation, feminist equals woman and therefore feminist does not equal man), newer articulations of the relationship between identity and politics, which include a radical critique of the "subject," pose their own set of problems for alliance.[3] If we refuse to conflate feminist and woman, we see that reading as a feminist requires "impersonation" whether one is a woman or a man (Fuss 1989).[4]

To say that doing feminist criticism means to impersonate *feminists* not *women* is to point out the slippage often made between those identities easily thought of in an essentialist way, such as gender in this case, and those more readily acknowledged as chosen political positions, such as feminism.

But Modleski (1991) has argued that a too radical antiessentialist critique of identity categories can risk "feminism without women." This "can mean the triumph either of a male feminist perspective that excludes women or of a feminist antiessentialism so radical that every use of the term 'woman,' however 'provisionally' it is adopted, is disallowed" (p. 14). Modleski queries whether a theoretical position that posits a radically decentered subject is suspect politics if the implication is that men can situate themselves as women, thereby displacing women. Morris echoes this concern when she worries that the "female speaking position" might come to be seen only as a "genre" (1988: 7). Likewise, hooks (1990), among others (Alarcon 1990; Chabram and Fregoso 1990; Rosaldo 1994), has pointed out how race and ethnic "difference" as a subject of study or of theory (in feminism and in cultural studies) can work to justify the exclusion of people of color from the discussion itself and from institutionalized positions of power.

It is difficult at times not to see the radical decentering and displacement practiced in some poststructuralist and deconstructionist enterprises as a process of absorption and co-optation. While this problem is not necessarily *inherent* in antiessentialist discourse, it can easily be put into practice in this fashion. Bordo (1990) describes this most effectively when she tells us that the objectivist epistemology, or "The View from Nowhere," has been replaced with "The View from Everywhere" in which the deconstructionist assumes "seemingly inexhaustible vantage points none of which are owned" (p. 142).

Refusing to conceptualize the subject as entirely free-floating and indeterminate, and therefore capable of impersonation, requires recognizing that we read from one or more subject positions (however constructed and provisional). As Fuss (1989) explains, positionality is the essentialism that must inhere in constructionist discourse since the deconstruction of identity categories always occurs from some *place*. Likewise, Mohanty (1992) argues for a way of conceptualizing identity and politics that highlights the relationship between "location as I have *inherited* it" and the "self-conscious, strategic location as I *choose* it now" (p. 88, emphasis mine). Or as Hall (1989) explains, "Cultural identities come from somewhere, have histories," even as they "undergo constant transformation" (p. 70). Cultural identity is "not an essence, but a *positioning*" (p. 72). The critique of identity has gone too far when it is a "refusal to accept responsibility for one's implication in actual historical or social relationships, or a denial that positionality exists or matters, a denial of one's own personal history" (Martin and Mohanty 1986: 208).

The "politics of location" has been employed to represent a conceptualization of identity and politics that recognizes the historicized, constructed, and multiple character of identity but that doesn't forgo the political salience of identity altogether. It represents that identity is never wholly fixed, but neither is it wholly fluid because we are framed by the webs of power and meaning we are situated in. Those webs are historical and shifting but have a recuperative tendency that works to maintain preexisting relations of inequality. Antiessentialist thought, which "questions the authority of definitional cages," is not accurately understood as relativism but, rather, is "a challenge to *contextualize*" (Williams 1991: 109, emphasis mine), to recognize that there is "no transcendental location possible" (Mohanty 1992: 89). Speaking specifically about the dilemmas of male feminism, Harding (1991) suggests that just as "whites as whites can provide traitorous readings of the racial assumptions in texts" (p. 497), men's relationship with feminism is one whereby they must assume a "traitorous social location" (p. 501). The notion of traitor is useful because it recognizes that political actions are always read in relation to cultural identities, and it suggests that we might act from a "location" rather than impersonating the "other."[5]

Sameness, Difference, and Empathy

I find the exchange between Showalter and Eagleton emblematic of, and instructive to a discussion of identity politics in many ways. While Showalter's response to Eagleton's narrative appears wholly negative, my own response is somewhat different, which, at least in part, reflects the historical context of my reading. As a thirty-something white feminist, generationally, I enter feminist theory at a point where white feminists have been "humbled by two decades of criticism by feminists of color" and when current political conditions necessitate broad alliances and therefore "scrupulously constructive forms of criticism" (Newton and Stacey 1992: 54) of those who are at once "other" and "ally." Moreover, the emergent transdisciplinary field of cultural studies, where agendas for social justice along multiple axes come together, potentially provides a site for dialog rather than easy appraisals of each other's behavior.

I cannot agree, without qualification, that Eagleton simply changed the subject. Rather, I read Eagleton's class narrative as an instance of empathy by drawing an analogy between his own position to the one Showalter describes. That is, he claims to have some understanding and empathy for the position female feminists occupy: many want to see men engage in feminist critique but, for good reasons, are distrustful.

By saying this I don't mean to redeem Eagleton from Showalter's incisive critique. While this moment of empathy is important, and the analogy based on his own past experience of a subordinated identity might be a catalyst for his understanding, Eagleton fails to recognize the limits of the analogy, which is, perhaps, the source of Showalter's complaint. The subjective experience of class and gender identities is not identical nor separable. Neither are these two social formations entirely analogous. Such analogs suggest the need for further consideration of just how parallel or different are the various social formations of inequality. Eagleton reveals no recognition of these insights, insights that have been at the forefront of feminist theory. Because Eagleton does not push the analogy to its limits, his analog appears to be only an opportunity to divert attention from the critique Showalter has leveled against him. A more satisfactory response would include the recognition of difference and would therefore reveal the *specificity* of whatever similarity exists.

Discourse on sameness carries potential dangers. Spelman (1988) cautions us here when she points to the arrogance and power that inheres in white women's claims of sameness with women of color, explaining that "women of color have been distrustful of white women who point to similarities between them when it seems politically expedient to do so and to dissimilarities when it does not" (p. 139). Likewise, on the surface, according to Showalter's reading, Eagleton's analogy sounds disturbingly similar to the "equal victims" discourse of parts of the contemporary men's movement in the United States that fail to hear what women are saying about the specificity of their subordination and, instead, assert a knee-jerk "men are oppressed too" response. Juxtaposing this popular discourse with the trends in contemporary theory highlights the risk of such false equivalencies or "incorrect parallelisms" (Banner 1989) present in the latter. It is a cause for concern when the politics of theory leads too easily to a discourse of liberal pluralism where we are all different and we all suffer equally (so in a sense, we are again, all the same.) One attendant danger within antiessentialist discourse is the denial of the political histories of our differences as when "difference ceases to threaten or signify power relations" (Rutherford 1990: 11).

On the other hand, Showalter's critique reveals the tendency in feminist discussions of male feminism to presuppose that all men are "empowered to speak," that they are all straight, white, and class privileged (Owen 1987; Boone 1990). Here difference is conceptualized as "unmediated otherness" where, "on the other side of difference, they must be, they are, all alike" (Lazreg 1988: 93). The de-essentializing of identity categories, including those we readily label "dominant" ("men" in this case), is of course the necessary corrective to the problems of identity politics as conventionally conceived, and allows us to recognize the multiplicity of identity. But as we've seen, we should be equally cautious to avoid "identity skepticism," or in this case, the error of *always* refusing to conceptualize men as a class.[6] It is at times, of course, in the interest of feminist politics to consider men a class. Aside from the differences both *within* the category men and *within* the category women, "men and women stand in a political relationship to each other" (Brittan 1989). That this relationship is crosscut by other differences was revealed by Eagleton's narrative on class. Notably, neither author comments on the potential salience to their exchange of their own racialization or other constructs of identity.

I would like to briefly consider a second issue that the Showalter/Eagleton exchange raises for me; that is, how "class identity" might be conceptualized in relationship to gender, race, and sexuality. When we turn to the experience of identity as self-presence, the emotional investments people have in their identities and the experiences of differential treatment based on identity, what can we say about the specificity of a claim to subordination based on class? I hope here only to raise some questions about how the "class" is and is not theorized in work on the politics of identity and location.

Notes toward Class Identity and the Politics of Difference

Eagleton, by laying claim to a subordinated class identity, has implicitly responded to one of the questions that concerns Showalter: " 'with what organic social group [does] the straight white male intellectual [have] any particular affinities?' " (p. 118).[7] For Showalter, the organic group is the "Old Boys' Network" (p. 118). Quite possibly Eagleton's appeal to class identity seems disingenuous to Showalter because, as an academic, he has clearly left his proletarian origins behind. However, this may be a telling instance regarding how class is commonly conceptualized in relationship to gender, sexuality, and race in contemporary feminist theory. Gender, race, and sexual identities are not necessarily "lost" or changed by becoming an intellectual because one can remain without challenge (or at least with less challenge) a part of the organic community that is one's constituency.

To assume that because Eagleton is no longer a member of the working class, he has no claims to that experience or identity, is to suggest that he does not bring the cultural residue of his class background to the present. But intellectuals are shaped by their "*pre*-institutional histories" (Chabram 1990). Chabram, speaking specifically about working-class Chicana/o intellectuals, considers what it means to "bring [the ghetto] with you" to the institution (p. 234). She explains, "we must acknowledge the active presence of our sociocultural formation and class origins, origins that continue, yes continue, to linger in our talk (both spoken and written), and our cultural traditions. . . . [T]hese formations are replenished and sustained by the experiences of our families, our students, our colleagues, and our neighbors" (p. 234). What she suggests is that her race-ethnic-class identity is not something easily left behind but remains, if not through present connections to a constituency, then at least as cultural memory. Chabram (p. 237) goes on to say, "[w]e have never been able to escape our referent—the Chicano population—even when we have gained something in economic access and prestige. This is because Chicana/o intellectuals are seen as 'Chicanos first, and intellectuals second.' "

What is inescapable here is that color and ethnicity tend to signify a working-class referent because of the overrepresentation of people of color among the poor and working-class. In the United States, whiteness and middle-classness are linked in common sense and routinely stand in for each other (although inaccurately at times).[8] For white, previously working-class intellectuals, such as Eagleton claims to have been, the class referent is escapable precisely because of their whiteness and the subsequent potential invisibility of class. Class does not as easily appear encoded onto the body (although it certainly *can* be and often is) and therefore *may* be perceived and experienced as a less fixed identity than race and gender. Class, then, is a less easily essentialized category.

Takagi's (1994) explanation of the difference between race and sexuality as aspects of identity is instructional here. As she explains, one can choose to be in or out regarding sexual identity, but one does not as easily choose to be in or out regarding racial/ethnic identity, which is often (but not always) made apparent by phenotype. Sexual identity is not as transparent and scripted on the body. Likewise, academics from the working class, whose bifurcated experience allows them to know how to operate in multiple class spheres, can make a choice about passing. White working-class turned middle-class activists and intellectuals can more easily escape their working-class referent (and often do, and in a hurry). They can choose to pass, deploying "working-class" identity in the reverse economy of leftist circles only when it has currency and passing it when it does not. Passing, however, is not the same as forgetting and the anxiety of the performance and the pain of class longing often remain.[9] Class has not often been made salient in the politics of identity, and presents unique challenges to which I have only alluded here.

There are many possible reasons for the current, relative inattentiveness to the way class identity intersects with race, gender, and sexuality. The minimal exploration of class identity in contemporary U.S. feminism might reflect the current fashion of theory. As Pfeil (1994) suggests, there is a tendency in contemporary feminism to dismiss political economy as "one of a number of 'male-dominant discourses' feminists have too uncritically adopted for their work" (p. 218) and that can only go, along with "uneducable men," into the "permanent penalty box" (p. 219).[10] While Eagleton's comments might well reveal that gender analysis is commonly missing from the cultural critique of left-leaning white men, Showalter's easy dismissal of Eagleton's analogy might reflect an assumption that his claim to working-class experience can only be an artifice of an outdated, prefeminist Marxism.

Conclusion

I have briefly commented here on some of the challenges that arise in the attempt to create coalitions in the context of current thinking about identity and politics. That context includes the desire to both reject and affirm identity, and to acknowledge both sameness and difference across social identities. One challenge is to maintain a vigilant awareness of the inherent power relations present in such claims and to avoid the regeneration of privilege even in the very process of attempting such alliances.

What is at issue then, is *how* claims of similarity and difference are *used*. Making a claim to similarity or difference necessarily means doing so from some "place." That is, to suggest that someone's situation is similar or different requires relating that person and her or his experience to a subject-position one claims to occupy. The use of "incorrect parallelisms" can result in the erasure of the *political histories* of our differences. The result can be a gesture of cultural domination under the guise of unlearning privilege. As Newton and Stacey (1992: 71) put it, speaking to the dilemma of male feminism, "What is required, of course, is a greater challenge to patriarchal power relations than of performing them with greater sensitivity and better grace."

In the struggle to reconceptualize political community, we might keep in mind, on the one hand, that the alliances demanded by current political conditions require "not less incisive, but less self-righteous" criticism of those with "whom we share a commitment to cultural critique, multiculturalism, and a less unjust future" (Newton and Stacey 1992: 54). On the other hand, attempts at traitorous identities might wisely include the recognition that the "other's" acceptance of "us," "is always, *must* always necessarily be provisional" (Pfeil 1994: 226). Rather than forgoing alliance, we might create a "provisional solidarity" (p. 227) in the present.

NOTES

1. Showalter's essay first appeared in *Raritan* in 1983 as a review essay of Culler's *On Deconstruction* (1982) and Eagleton's *The Rape of Clarissa* (1982) and his *Literary Theory* (1983), as well as books by other authors

2. Showalter is quoting Larry Lipking here in "Aristotle's Sisters."

3. Identity politics has generally referred to "the tendency to base one's politics on a sense of personal identity." In this formulation, the "link between identity and politics is causually and teleologically defined," resulting in the belief that "identity necessarily determines a particular kind of politics" (Fuss 1989: 97, 99). A rethinking of conventional notions of identity politics has occurred within the overlapping fields of feminist studies, ethnic studies, cultural studies, and queer theory. For dialogues on essentialism and identity politics, see Hull et al. (1982); Moraga and Anzaldúa (1983); Bourne (1987); S. Epstein (1987); Adams (1989); de Lauretis (1989); Fuss (1989); Spivak (1989); Anzaldúa (1990); Alarcon (1990); Rutherford (1990); Mohanty et al. (1991); B. Epstein (1991); Sandoval (1991); Escoffier (1991); Duggan (1992); Scott (1992a, 1992b); Gamson (1995); and Nicholson and Seidman (1995). For offerings on the "politics of location," see Rich (1986); Frankenburg and Mani (1993); Mohanty (1992); and Kaplan's (1994) survey of the multiple uses of the phrase. See Wallace (1989) for a critique of its usage.

4. Fuss cites a long history on the "dispute over 'reading as a woman.' " See Kamuf (1980); Culler (1982); Scholes (1987); and Heath (1987).

5. The idea of identities as traitorous was perhaps initially expressed by Moraga (1986), who described how, as a Chicana, some of her identity labels, such as lesbian and feminist, resulted in her reception as a "traitor to her race." Her understanding of identity as multiple, and the possibility of acting as a traitor to identity components that are subordinate ones, is a corrective to Harding's conceptualization, which tends toward a too simple victim/perpetrator model where identities appear entirely subordinated or dominant.

6. Here I am paraphrasing Bordo (1990), who describes "gender skepticism" as eschewing the use of women as a category a priori on theoretical grounds.

7. Showalter is quoting Frederic Jameson here in *Diacritics*, Fall 1992.

8. White working-class identity is more clearly articulated in Eagleton's Great Britain than it is in Showalter's United States, which falsely prides itself on being "classless."

9. As described by many working-class academics across race; see Sennett and Cobb (1972); Rodriguez (1982); Ryan and Sackrey (1984); Tokarczyk and Fay (1993); Allison (1994); and Kadi (1996).

10. See also Brown (1993) for an account of the relationship between class politics and identity politics.

REFERENCES

Adams, Mary Louise. 1989. "There's No Place Like Home: On the Place of Identity in Feminist Politics," in *Feminist Review*, no. 31: 22–32.

Alarcon, Norma. 1990. "The Theoretical Subjects of This Bridge Called My Back," in *Making Face, Making Soul, Haciedo Caras: Creative and Critical Perspectives by Women of Color,* edited by G. Anzaldúa. San Francisco: Aunt Lute Foundation Books.

Allison, Dorothy. 1994. *Skin: Talking about Sex, Class and Literature.* Ithaca: Firebrand Books.

Anzaldúa, Gloria (ed.). 1990. *Making Face, Making Soul-Haciedo Caras: Creative and Critical Perspectives by Women of Color.* San Francisco: Aunt Lute Foundation Books.

Banner, Lois. 1989. Review of books on men and masculinity, in *Signs,* Spring: 703–708.

Boone, Joseph A. 1990. "Of Me(n) and Feminism: Who(se) Is the Sex That Writes?" in *Engendering Men: The Question of Male Feminist Criticism,* edited by Boone and Cadden. New York: Routledge.

Bordo, Susan. 1990. "Feminism, Postmodernism, and Gender-Scepticism," in *Feminism/Postmodernism,* edited by Linda Nicholson. New York: Routledge.

Bourne, Jenny. 1987. "Homelands of the Mind: Jewish Feminism and Identity Politics," in *Race and Class* 29, no. 1: 1–24

Brittan, Arthur. 1989. *Masculinity and Power.* New York: Basil Blackwell.

Brown, Wendy. 1993. "Wounded Attachments," in *Political Theory* 21, no. 3: 390–410.

Chabram, Angie. 1990. "Chicana/o Studies as Oppositional Ethnography," in *Cultural Studies* 4, no. 3, October: 228–247.

Chabram, Angie, and Rosa Linda Fregoso. 1990. "Chicana/o Cultural Representations: Reframing Alternative Critical Discourses," in *Cultural Studies* 4, no. 3, October.

Culler, Jonathon. 1982. *On Deconstruction: Theory and Criticism after Structuralism.* Ithaca: Cornell University Press.

de Lauretis, Teresa. 1989. "The Essence of the Triangle or, Taking the Risk of Essentialism Seriously: Feminist Theory in Italy, the U.S., and Britain," in *Differences: A Journal of Feminist Cultural Studies* 1, no. 2, Summer.

Duggan, Lisa. 1992. "Making It Perfectly Queer," in *Socialist Review* 22: 11–23.

Eagleton, Terry. 1982. *The Rape of Clarissa.* Oxford: Blackwell.

Eagleton, Terry. 1983. *Literary Theory: An Introduction.* Minneapolis: University of Minnesota Press.

Eagleton, Terry. 1987. "Response," in *Men in Feminism,* edited by A. Jardine and P. Smith. New York: Routledge.

Epstein, Barbara. 1991. "Political Correctness and Collective Powerlessness," in *Socialist Review* 21, no. 3–4: 13–35.

Epstein, Steven. 1987. "Gay Politics, Ethnic Identity: The Limits of Social Constructionism," in *Socialist Review* 17, no. 3–4.

Escoffier, Jeffrey. 1991. "The Limits of Multiculturalism," in *Socialist Review* 21, no. 3–4.

Frankenberg, Ruth, and Lata Mani. 1993. "Crosscurrents, Crosstalk: Race, 'Postcoloniality' and the Politics of Location," in *Cultural Studies* 7, no. 2: 292–310.

Fuss, Diana. 1989. *Essentially Speaking: Feminism, Nature and Difference.* New York and London: Routledge.

Gamson, Joshua. 1995. "Must Identity Movements Self-Destruct? A Queer Dilemma," in *Social Problems* 42, no. 3: 390–407.

Hall, Stuart. 1989. "Cultural Identity and Cinematic Representation," in *Framework* 36: 68–81.

Harding, Sandra. 1991. *Whose Science? Whose Knowledge? Thinking from Women's Lives.* Ithaca: Cornell University Press.

Heath, Stephen. 1987. "Male Feminism," in *Men in Feminism,* edited by A. Jardine and P. Smith. New York: Routledge.

Hennessy, Rosemary. 1993. *Materialist Feminism and the Politics of Discourse.* New York: Routledge.

hooks, bell. 1990. *Yearning: Race, Gender, and Cultural Politics.* Boston: South End Press.

Hull, Gloria T., Patricia Bell Scott, and Barbara Smith (eds.). 1982. *All the Women Are White, All the Blacks Are Men, but Some of Us Are Brave: Black Women's Studies.* Old Westbury, NY: Feminist Press.

Jardine, Alice, and Paul Smith (eds.). 1987. *Men in Feminism.* New York: Routledge.

Kadi, Joanna. 1996. *Thinking Class: Sketches from a Cultural Worker.* Boston: South End Press.

Kamuf, Peggy. 1980. "Writing Like a Woman," in *Women and Language in Literature and Society,* edited by S. McConnell-Ginet, R. Borker, and N. Furman. New York: Praeger.

Kaplan, Caren. 1994. "The Politics of Location as Transnational Feminist Practice," in *Scattered Hegemonies: Postmodernity and Transnational Feminist Practices,* edited by C. Kaplan and I. Grewal. Minneapolis: University of Minnesota Press.

Lazreg, Marnia. 1988. "Feminism and Difference: The Perils of Writing as a Woman on Women in Algeria," in *Feminist Studies* 14, no. 1.

Martin, Biddy, and Chandra Talpade Mohanty. 1986. "Feminist Politics: What's Home Got to Do with It?" in *Feminist Studies, Critical Studies,* edited by Teresa de Lauretis. Bloomington: Indiana University Press.

Modleski, Tania. 1991. *Feminism without Women: Cultural Criticism in a Postfeminist Age.* New York: Routledge.

Mohanty, Chandra Talpade. 1992. "Feminist Encounters: Locating the Politics of Experience," in *Destablizing Theory: Contemporary Feminist Debates,* edited by Michelle Barrett and Anne Phillips. Stanford, CA: Stanford University Press.

Mohanty, Chandra Talpade, Ann Russo, and Lordes Torres (eds.). 1991. *Third World Women and the Politics of Feminism.* Bloomington and Indianapolis: Indiana University Press.

Moraga, Cherríe. 1986. "From a Long Line of Vendidas: Chicanas and Feminism," in *Feminist Studies, Critical Studies,* edited by Teresa de Lauretis. Bloomington: Indiana University Press.

Moraga, Cherríe, and Gloria Anzaldúa (eds.). 1983. *This Bridge Called My Back: Writings by Radical Women of Color.* New York: Kitchen Table: Women of Color Press.

Morris, Meaghan. 1988. *The Pirates Fiance: Feminism, Reading, Postmodernism.* New York: Verso.

Newton, Judith, and Judith Stacey. 1992. "Learning Not to Curse, or, Feminist Predicaments in Cultural Criticism by Men: Our Movie Date with James Clifford and Stephen Greenblatt," in *Cultural Critique,* Winter 1992–93: 51–82.

Newton, Judith, and Judith Stacey. 1997. "The Men We Left Behind Us: Narratives around and about Feminism from White, Leftwing, Academic Men," in *From Sociology to Cultural Studies: New Perspectives,* edited by Elizabeth Long. Malden, MA: Blackwell Publishers.

Nicholson, Linda, and Steven Seidman (eds.). 1995. *Social Postmodernism: Beyond Identity Politics.* New York: Cambridge University Press.

Owen, Craig. 1987. "Outlaws: Gay Men in Feminism," in *Men in Feminism,* edited by A. Jardine and P. Smith. New York and London: Routledge.

Pfeil, Fred. 1994. "No Basta Teorizar: In-Difference to Solidarity in Contemporary Fiction,

Theory, and Practice," in *Scattered Hegemonies: Postmodernity and Transnational Feminist Practices,* edited by C. Kaplan and I. Grewal. Minneapolis: University of Minnesota Press.

Rich, Adrienne. 1986. *Blood, Bread and Poetry: Selected Prose, 1979–1985.* New York: Norton.

Rodriguez, Richard. 1982. *The Hunger of Memory: The Education of Richard Rodriguez.* New York: Bantam Books.

Rosaldo, Renato. 1994. "Whose Cultural Studies?" in *American Anthropologist* 6, no. 3.

Rutherford, Johnathon. 1990. "A Place Called Home: Identity and the Cultural Politics of Difference," in *Identity: Community, Culture, Difference,* edited by Rutherford. London: Lawrence and Wishart.

Ryan, Jake, and Charles Sackrey. 1984. *Strangers in Paradise: Academics from the Working-Class.* Boston: South End Press.

Sandoval, Chela. 1991. "U.S. Third World Feminism: The Theory and Method of Oppositional Consciousness in the Postmodern World," in *Genders,* no. 10, Spring.

Scholes, Robert. 1987. "Reading Like a Man," in *Men in Feminism,* edited by A. Jardine and P. Smith. New York: Routledge.

Scott, Joan. 1992a. "Experience," in *Feminists Theorize the Political,* edited by Judith Butler and Joan W. Scott. New York: Routledge.

Scott, Joan. 1992b. "Multiculturalism and the Politics of Identity," in *October,* no. 61: 12–19.

Sennett Richard, and Jonathan Cobb. 1972. *The Hidden Injuries of Class.* New York: Vintage Books.

Showalter, Elaine. 1987. "Critical Cross-Dressing: Male Feminists and the Woman of the Year," and "Elaine Showalter Replies," in *Men in Feminism,* edited by A. Jardine and P. Smith. New York: Routledge.

Spelman, Elizabeth. 1988. *Inessential Woman: Problems of Exclusion in Feminist Thought.* Boston: Beacon Press.

Spivak, Gayatri Chakravorty. 1989. "In a Word." Interview by Ellen Rooney in *Differences: A Journal of Feminist Cultural Studies* 1, no. 2, Summer.

Takagi, Dana Y. 1994. "Maiden Voyage: Excursion into Sexuality and Identity Politics in Asian America," in *Amerasia Journal* 20, no. 1: 1–17.

Tokarczyk, Michelle, and Elizabeth Fay. 1993. *Working-Class Women in the Academy: Laborers in the Knowledge Factory.* Amherst: University of Massachusetts Press.

Wallace, Michelle. 1989. "The Politics of Location: Cinema/Theory/Literature/Ethnicity/Sexuality/Me," in *Framework* 36: 42–55.

Williams, Patricia. 1991. *The Alchemy of Race and Rights: Diary of a Law Professor.* Cambridge: Harvard University Press.

Chapter Sixteen

Report from the Bahamas

June Jordan

I am staying in a hotel that calls itself The Sheraton British Colonial. One of the photographs advertising the place displays a middle-aged Black man in a waiter's tuxedo, smiling. What intrigues me most about the picture is just this: while the Black man bears a tray full of "colorful" drinks above his left shoulder, both of his feet, shoes and trouserlegs, up to ten inches above his ankles, stand in the also "colorful" Caribbean salt water. He is so delighted to serve you he will wade into the water to bring you Banana Daquiris while you float! More precisely, he will wade into the water, fully clothed, oblivious to the ruin of his shoes, his trousers, his health, and he will do it with a smile.

I am in the Bahamas. On the phone in my room, a spinning complement of plastic pages offers handy index clues such as CAR RENTAL and CASINOS. A message from the Ministry of Tourism appears among these travellers tips. Opening with a paragraph of "WELCOME," the message then proceeds to "A PAGE OF HISTORY," which reads as follows:

> New World History begins on the same day that modern Bahamian history begins— October 12, 1492. That's when Columbus stepped ashore—British influence came first with the Eleutherian Adventures of 1647—After the Revolutions, American Loyalists fled from the newly independent states and settled in the Bahamas. Confederate block-ade-runners used the island as a haven during the War between the States, and after the War, a number of Southerners moved to the Bahamas.

There it is again. Something proclaims itself a legitimate history and all it does is track white Mr. Columbus to the British Eleutherians through the Confederate Southerners as they barge into New World surf, land on New World turf, and nobody saying one word about the Bahamian people, the Black peoples, to whom the only thing new in their island world was this weird succession of crude intruders and its colonial consequences.

This is my consciousness of race as I unpack my bathing suit in the Sheraton British Colonial. Neither this hotel nor the British nor the long ago Italians nor the white Delta airline pilots belong here, of course. And every time I look at the photograph of that fool standing in the water with his shoes on I'm about to have a West Indian fit, even though I know he's no fool; he's a middle-aged Black man who needs a job and this is his job—pretending himself a servile ancillary to the pleasures of the rich. (Compared to his options in life, I am a rich woman. Compared to most of the Black Americans arriving for this Easter weekend on a three nights four day's deal of bargain rates, the middle-aged waiter is a poor Black man.)

We will jostle along with the other (white) visitors and join them in the tee shirt shops or, laughing together, learn ruthless rules of negotiation as we, Black Americans as well as white, argue down the price of handwoven goods at the nearby straw market while the merchants, frequently toothless Black women seated on the concrete in their only presentable dress, humble themselves to our careless games:

"Yes? You like it? Eight dollar."

"Five."

"I give it to you. Seven."

And so it continues, this weird succession of crude intruders that, now, includes me and my brothers and my sisters from the North.

This is my consciousness of class as I try to decide how much money I can spend on Bahamian gifts for my family back in Brooklyn. No matter that these other Black women incessantly weave words and flowers into the straw hats and bags piled beside them on the burning dusty street. No matter that these other Black women must work their sense of beauty into these things that we will take away as cheaply as we dare, or they will do without food.

We are not white, after all. The budget is limited. And we are harmlessly killing time between the poolside rum punch and "The Native Show on the Patio" that will play tonight outside the hotel restaurant.

This is my consciousness of race and class and gender identity as I notice the fixed relations between these other Black women and myself. They sell and I buy or I don't. They risk not eating. I risk going broke on my first vacation afternoon.

We are not particularly women anymore; we are parties to a transaction designed to set us against each other.

"Olive" is the name of the Black woman who cleans my hotel room. On my way to the beach I am wondering what "Olive" would say if I told her why I chose the Sheraton British Colonial; if I told her I wanted to swim. I wanted to sleep. I did not want to be harrassed by the middle-aged waiter, or his nephew. I did not want to be raped by anybody (white or Black) at all and I calculated that my safety as a Black woman alone would best be assured by a multinational hotel corporation. In my experience, the big guys take customer complaints more seriously than the little ones. I would suppose that's one reason why they're big; they don't like to lose money anymore than I like to be bothered when I'm trying to read a goddamned book underneath a palm tree I paid $264 to get next to. A Black woman seeking refuge in a multinational corporation may seem like a contradiction to some, but there you are. In this case it's a coincidence of entirely different self-interests: Sheraton/cash = June Jordan's short-run safety.

Anyway, I'm pretty sure "Olive" would look at me as though I came from someplace as far away as Brooklyn. Then she'd probably allow herself one indignant query before righteously removing her vacuum cleaner from my room; "and why in the first place you come down without your husband?"

I cannot imagine how I would begin to answer her.

My "rights" and my "freedom" and my "desire" and a slew of other New World values; what would they sound like to this Black woman described on the card atop my hotel bureau as "Olive the Maid"? "Olive" is older than I am and I may smoke a cigarette while she changes the sheets on my bed. Whose rights? Whose freedom? Whose desire?

And why should she give a shit about mine unless I do something, for real, about hers?

It happens that the book that I finished reading under a palm tree earlier today was the novel *The Bread Givers,* by Anzia Yezierska. Definitely autobiographical, Yezierska lays out the difficulties of being both female and "a person" inside a traditional Jewish family at the start of the 20th century. That any Jewish woman became anything more than the abused servant of her father or her husband is really an improbable piece of news. Yet Yezierska managed such an unlikely outcome for her own life. In *The Bread Givers,* the heroine also manages an important, although partial, escape from traditional Jewish female destiny. And in the unpardonable, despotic father, the Talmudic scholar of that Jewish family, did I not see my own and hate him twice, again? When the heroine, the young Jewish child, wanders the streets with a filthy pail she borrows to sell herring in order to raise the ghetto rent and when she cries, "Nothing was before me but the hunger in our house, and no bread for the next meal if I didn't sell the herring. No longer like a fire engine, but like a houseful of hungry mouths my heart cried, 'herring—herring! Two cents apiece!" who would doubt the ease, the sisterhood of conversation possible between that white girl and the Black women selling straw bags on the streets of paradise because they do not want to die? And is it not obvious that the wife of that Talmudic scholar and "Olive," who cleans my room here at the hotel, have more in common than I can claim with either one of them?

This is my consciousness of race and class and gender identity as I collect wet towels, sunglasses, wristwatch, and head towards a shower.

I am thinking about the boy who loaned this novel to me. He's white and he's Jewish and he's pursuing an independent study project with me, at the State University where I teach whether or not I feel like it, where I teach without stint because, like the waiter, I am no fool. It's my job and either I work or I do without everything you need money to buy. The boy loaned me the novel because he thought I'd be interested to know how a Jewish-American writer used English so that the syntax, and therefore the cultural habits of mind expressed by the Yiddish language, could survive translation. He did this because he wanted to create another connection between us on the basis of language, between his knowledge/his love of Yiddish and my knowledge/my love of Black English.

He has been right about the forceful survival of the Yiddish. And I had become excited by this further evidence of the written voice of spoken language protected from the monodrone of "standard" English, and so we had grown closer on this account. But then our talk shifted to student affairs more generally, and I had learned that this student does not care one way or the other about currently jeopardized Federal Student Loan Programs because, as he explained it to me, they do not affect him. He does not need financial help outside his family. My own son, however, is Black. And I am the only family help available to him and that means, if Reagan succeeds in eliminating Federal programs to aid minority students, he will have to forget about furthering his studies, or he or I or both of us will have to hit the numbers pretty big. For these reasons of difference, the student and I had moved away from each other, even while we continued to talk.

My consciousness turned to race, again, and class.

Sitting in the same chair as the boy, several weeks ago, a graduate student came to discuss her grade. I praised the excellence of her final paper; indeed it had seemed to me an extra-ordinary pulling together of recent left brain/right brain research with the themes of transcendental poetry.

She told me that, for her part, she'd completed her reading of my political essays. "You are so lucky!" she exclaimed.

"What do you mean by that?"

"You have a cause. You have a purpose to your life."

I looked carefully at this white woman; what was she really saying to me?

"What do you mean?" I repeated.

"Poverty. Police violence. Discrimination in general."

(Jesus Christ, I thought: Is that her idea of lucky?)

"And how about you?" I asked.

"Me?"

"Yeah, you. Don't you have a cause?"

"Me? I'm just a middle-aged woman: a housewife and a mother. I'm a nobody."

For a while, I made no response.

First of all, speaking of race and class and gender in one breath, what she said meant that those lucky preoccupations of mine, from police violence to nuclear wipe-out, were not shared. They were mine and not hers. But here she sat, friendly as an old stuffed animal, beaming good will or more "luck" in my direction.

In the second place, what this white woman said to me meant that she did not believe she was "a person" precisely because she had fulfilled the traditional female functions revered by the father of that Jewish immigrant, Anzia Yezierska. And the woman in front of me was not a Jew. That was not the connection. The link was strictly female. Nevertheless, how should that woman and I, another female connect, beyond this bizarre exchange?

If she believed me lucky to have regular hurdles of discrimination then why shouldn't I insist that she's lucky to be a middle class white Wasp female who lives in such well-sanctioned and normative comfort that she even has the luxury to deny the power of the privileges that paralyze her life?

If she deserts me and "my cause" where we differ, if, for example, she abandons me to "my" problems of race, then why should I support her in "her" problems of housewifely oblivion?

Recollection of this peculiar moment brings me to the shower in the bathroom cleaned by "Olive." She reminds me of the usual Women's Studies curriculum because it has nothing to do with her or her job: you won't find "Olive" listed anywhere on the reading list. You will likewise seldom hear of Anzia Yezierska. But yes, you will find, from Florence Nightingale to Adrienne Rich, a white procession of independently well-to-do women writers. (Gertrude Stein/Virginia Woolf/Hilda Doolittle are standard names among the "essential" women writers.)

In other words, most of the women of the world—Black and First World and white who work because we must—most of the women of the world persist far from the heart of the usual Women's Studies syllabus.

Similarly, the typical Black History course will slide by the majority experience it pretends to represent. For example, Mary McLeod Bethune will scarcely receive as much attention as Nat Turner, even though Black women who bravely and efficiently provided for the education of Black people hugely outnumber those few Black men who led successful or doomed rebellions against slavery. In fact, Mary McLeod Bethune may not receive even honorable mention because Black History too often apes those ridiculous white history courses which produce such dangerous gibberish as The Sheraton British Colonial "history" of the Bahamas. Both Black and white history courses exclude from their central consideration those people who neither killed nor conquered anyone as the means to new identity, those people who took care of every one of the people who wanted to become "a person," those people who still take care of the life at issue: the ones who wash and who feed and who teach and who diligently decorate straw hats and bags with all of their historically unrequired gentle love: the women.

> Oh the old rugged cross
> on a hill far away
> Well I cherish the old rugged cross

It's Good Friday in the Bahamas. Seventy-eight degrees in the shade. Except for Sheraton territory, everything's closed.

It so happens that for truly secular reasons I've been fasting for three days. My hunger has now reached nearly violent proportions. In the hotel sandwich shop, the Black woman handling the counter complains about the tourists; why isn't the shop closed and why don't the tourists stop eating for once in their lives. I'm famished and I order chicken salad and cottage cheese and lettuce and tomato and a hard boiled egg and a hot cross bun and apple juice.

She eyes me with disgust.

To be sure, the timing of my stomach offends her serious religious practices. Neither one of us apologizes to the other. She seasons the chicken salad to the peppery max while I listen to the loud radio gospel she plays to console herself. It's a country Black version of "The Old Rugged Cross."

As I heave much chicken into my mouth tears start. It's not the pepper. I am, after all, a West Indian daughter. It's the Good Friday music that dominates the humid atmosphere.

> Well I cherish the old rugged cross

And I am back, faster than a 747, in Brooklyn, in the home of my parents where we are wondering, as we do every year, if the sky will darken until Christ has been buried in the tomb. The sky should darken if God is in His heavens. And then, around 3 p.m., at the conclusion of our mournful church service at the neighborhood St. Phillips, and even while we dumbly stare at the black cloth covering the gold altar and the slender unlit candles, the sun should return through the high gothic windows and vindicate our waiting faith that the Lord will rise again, on Easter.

How I used to bow my head at the very name of Jesus: ecstatic to abase myself in deference to His majesty.

My mouth is full of salad. I can't seem to eat quickly enough. I can't think how I should lessen the offense of my appetite. The other Black woman on the premises, the one who disapprovingly prepared this very tasty break from my fast, makes no remark. She is no fool. This is a job that she needs. I suppose she notices that at least I included a hot cross bun among my edibles. That's something in my favor. I decide that's enough.

I am suddenly eager to walk off the food. Up a fairly steep hill I walk without hurrying. Through the pastel desolation of the little town, the road brings me to a confectionery pink and white plantation house. At the gates, an unnecessarily large statue of Christopher Columbus faces me down, or tries to. His hand is fisted to one hip. I look back at him, laugh without deference, and turn left.

It's time to pack it up. Catch my plane. I scan the hotel room for things not to forget. There's that white report card on the bureau.

"Dear Guests:" it says, under the name "Olive." I am your maid for the day. Please rate me: Excellent. Good. Average. Poor. Thank you."

I tuck this momento from the Sheraton British Colonial into my notebook. How would "Olive" rate *me*? What would it mean for us to seem "good" to each other? What would that rating require?

But I am hastening to leave. Neither turtle soup nor kidney pie nor any conch shell delight shall delay my departure. I have rested, here, in the Bahamas, and I'm ready to return to my usual job, my usual work. But the skin on my body has changed and so has my mind. On the Delta flight home I realize I am burning up, indeed.

So far as I can see, the usual race and class concepts of connection, or gender assumptions of unity, do not apply very well. I doubt that they ever did. Otherwise why would Black folks forever bemoan our lack of solidarity when the deal turns real. And if unity on the basis of sexual oppression is something natural, then why do we women, the majority people on the planet, still have a problem?

The plane's ready for takeoff. I fasten my seatbelt and let the tumult inside my head run free. Yes: race and class and gender remain as real as the weather. But what they must mean about the contact between two individuals is less obvious and, like the weather, not predictable.

And when these factors of race and class and gender absolutely collapse is whenever you try to use them as automatic concepts of connection. They may serve well as indicators of commonly felt conflict, but as elements of connection they seem about as reliable as precipitation probability for the day after the night before the day.

It occurs to me that much organizational grief could be avoided if people under-stood that partnership in misery does not necessarily provide for partnership for change: *When we get the monsters off our backs all of us may want to run in very different directions.*

And not only that: even though both "Olive" and "I" live inside a conflict neither one of us created, and even though both of us therefore hurt inside that conflict, I may be one of the monsters she needs to eliminate from her universe and, in a sense, she may be one of the monsters in mine.

I am reaching for the words to describe the difference between a common identity that has been imposed and the individual identity any one of us will choose, once she gains that chance.

That difference is the one that keeps us stupid in the face of new, specific information about somebody else with whom we are supposed to have a connection because a third party, hostile to both of us, has worked it so that the two of us, like it or not, share a common enemy. *What happens beyond the idea of that enemy and beyond the consequences of that enemy?*

I am saying that the ultimate connection cannot be the enemy. The ultimate connection must be the need that we find between us. It is not only who you are, in other words, but what we can do for each other that will determine the connection.

Part IV

Womanist/Black Feminist Perspectives

The histories of the women's movement in the United States have talked of the first wave when women, mostly white and middle class, fought for equal inheritance rights, dress reform, education, and the vote. This organizing began when black women in the South were still in slavery and the issues early feminism fought for had little meaning for them. By the turn of the twentieth century, when the campaign to win suffrage was the central issue the movement engaged in, it was still a white woman's movement. There were black women activists but they formed their own suffrage organizations and fought other issues too, such as the practice of lynching and racial injustice. After the vote was won, the women activists went home and the movement lay dormant until the upheavals of the 1960s saw it resurrected again (Ferree and Hess 1985; Rupp and Taylor 1990).

Bernice McNair Barnett contests this history through her work on black feminist organizations that emerged in the supposedly unorganized phase of women's activism. She shows that black women were politically active in the 1950s in spite of the triple constraints of gender, race, and class. They were the backbone of the civil rights movement, working behind the scenes while the male leaders spoke to the media. In addition, she distinguishes black women's organizations from black men's and reveals the collectivist form of organizing they engaged in. Using the perspective of a feminist politic, she views them in terms of their feminist values, goals, and practices.

One problem that arose for black women who involved themselves in white women's organizations was the antagonism they encountered from black men, who accused them of working with the enemy. Barbara Smith challenges the notion that to be a black feminist means one has somehow left the black race, is no longer part of the black community, and no longer cares about home. She examines the myths that black men developed to divert black women from working for their freedom. The accomplishments black women have made are noted, as well as the difficulties they have faced from within the black community, from white feminists, and from one another. Smith defines separatism as premised on fear rather than a position of strength. For her, black feminism crosses race and gender borders but is also autonomous, challenging both the sexism of black men and the racism of white women.

If we are to work together, African American and white women, can we trust each other? The attention issues of race have received is gratifying, according to Ann du Cille, but is it real? Do white women, who have taken up the mantle of research, writing, and speaking engagements on the interconnections of race, class, and gender, really understand it? Have they not come to the party a little late? Having spent most of her adult life working on these issues, du Cille finds herself suspicious of the motives of those people who are suddenly making a name for themselves on issues that were of little concern to them in the past. Who can or should study black people's lives, the intricacies of class, or gendered social structures? These are questions she considers in raising issues of women and black studies.

What does it feel like to be a woman of color? In her poem *ink: black on white,* Rubina Ramji evokes an image that transposes color and reminds us of the permutations these categories contain, the hidden realities, and the necessity of writing her "self" over and over again.

REFERENCES

Ferree, Myra Marx, and Beth B. Hess. 1985. *Controversy and Coalition: The New Feminist Movement.* Boston: Twayne.

Rupp, Leila J., and Verta Taylor. 1990. *Survival in the Doldrums: The American Women's Rights Movement, 1945 to the 1960s.* Columbus: Ohio State University Press.

Chapter Seventeen

Black Women's Collectivist Movement Organizations
Their Struggles during the "Doldrums"

Bernice McNair Barnett

> My arrest [in 1946] convinced me that my defiance alone would do little or nothing to remedy such situations. Only *organized* effort could do that. But where to start? . . . *I was a feminist before I really knew what the word meant* [emphasis added], and so I dismissed the hardfaced men . . . but I felt that I could appeal to some of the women. I played bridge with them, but more important, I knew that they [middle-class Black women] must suffer from the racial abuses and the indignity accorded to all Blacks, even though they were somewhat insulated from it. Their outward indifference was a mask to protect both their psyche and their sanity.
>
> —Mary Fair Burks, "Trailblazers" (1990)

In the 1970s, Freeman (1973, 1975, 1979) argued that the modern women's movement had a distinctively "feminist" mode consisting of two "branches" that differed in age, organizational structure, and style. The one branch comprised women who were older, had a certain amount of money and other resources, had some specialized time, developed organizational structures that were centralized, and had hierarchical leadership styles (for example, formal position leaders). The other branch comprised younger women who had little or no money, had much unspecialized time, developed organizational structures that were highly decentralized, and had nonhierarchical leadership styles (for example, grassroots leaders). Ferree and Hess (1985, 49) described these different feminist branches as a "bureaucratic strand" and a "collectivist strand" in the new women's movement and suggested that both

"emerged in the mid-1960s" and "intertwined" in the 1970s and 1980s but remained "two different organizational modes . . . reflecting the history and needs of
their members."

This scholarship on the organizational modes of the new women's movement
raises some crucial issues regarding modern Black women's collectivist movement
organizations and the origins of these "new" feminist modes.[1] First, the period that
Ferree and Hess (1985) have characterized as an unorganized phase in the women's
movement and Rupp and Taylor (1987) have referred to as "the doldrums" saw
the emergence of several Black women's collectivist organizations, two of which I
examine in detail here. Second, in spite of the triple constraints of gender, race, and
class, various groups of Black women (not just elite, educated Black women) were
far from passive or apolitical in the 1950s. In their homes, communities, churches,
and collectivist organizations, African American women actively engaged in protest
against the oppression they encountered on a day-to-day basis (Gilkes 1980, 1982,
1988; Giddings 1984; Sachs 1988a, 1988b; Barnett 1989, 1990, 1993; Collins
1990; Evans 1992). Third, African American women were never simply a homogeneous group. Black women political activists developed different organizational
modes that reflected their unique history and structural location within interlocking
systems of gender, race, and class stratification.

This research compares two Black women's collectivist movement organizations
located in Montgomery, Alabama: the Women's Political Council (WPC), founded
in 1946, almost ten years before the momentous 1955 Montgomery bus boycott;
and the Club from Nowhere (CFN), founded in 1956 during the bus boycott. The
Montgomery boycott set in motion one of the most significant protests in modern
American history. It was the first successful mass protest by African Americans in
modern times. And Black women, working in their communities and their voluntary
associations, served as initiators and organizers of this protest. Yet their stories as
"leaders" (Barnett 1989, 1990, 1993) and key activists are just beginning to be told
(Giddings 1984; Robinson 1987; Burks 1990; Crawford, Rouse, and Woods 1990;
Mueller 1990). Though not narrowly "feminist" in primary aim or manifest intent
(that is, in privileging gender oppression as the only or main target of political
action), these groups illuminate women's particular organizational preferences and
styles. I thus attempt to analyze their organizational modes (a) from the standpoint
of a *Black women's* movement organization (for example, to view their organizational forms as gendered politics, separate from the dominant Black, male-headed
civil rights movement organizations such as the NAACP and the Urban League)
and (b) from the standpoint of a modern *feminist* organization (for example, to
view these organizational modes in terms of their feminist values, goals and practices, and transformational outcomes for women).

My research utilizes data from a larger study of leadership in the civil rights
movement and the ongoing collection of data on Black women's leadership roles in
social protest. This essay is based on analysis of (1) archives, organizational records,
published works, and personal papers of civil rights activists and (2) sixteen in-
depth personal interviews with civil rights activists.[2] A major portion of the archival
data was collected between 1986 and 1987. Personal interviews were conducted

immediately thereafter and intermittently since 1988. Interviews with the women were conducted primarily in person in a variety of settings, including my hotel room and their homes and places of work (day care and community centers, universities, city council meeting places). Follow-up interviews were conducted over the telephone and during special civil rights movement commemorative events.

It is important to note several things about the sixteen Black women activists I interviewed.[3] First, these women came from diverse educational and socioeconomic class backgrounds. Some were public school teachers and college professors; some were lawyers and are now judges; some were office secretaries and insurance salespersons; some were the wives of elite Black professionals and did not work outside the home for pay; and some were, and remained, domestic workers and cooks, basically poor and working-class women. This last category is too often incorrectly assumed to be apolitical and thus inconsequential to social movement mobilization, maintenance, and success. But poor and working-class Black women as well as elite and middle-class Black women contributed to the success of the Montgomery bus boycott and many other protests (King 1958; Giddings 1984; Morris 1984; Barnett 1989, 1990). Second, though several of the women are nationally known, many are known only inside the movement and in their local communities. This may be true of most Black women activists. Third, all sixteen women were participants in multiple organizations. These community leaders were also active members of their churches, and most of them—especially the professional women—were members of the NAACP, the Urban League, the PTA, and several other voluntary associations as well. A few belonged to both the WPC and the CFN.

Finally, it is important to keep in mind that these Black women, even the most educated "elites," had to organize within the 1950s southern social structure (Bates 1962; Clark 1962, 1990; Giddings 1984; Robinson 1987; Barnett 1989; 1990; Burks 1990). The triple constraints imposed by interlocking systems of gender, race, and class stratification in this racist setting made a mockery of organizing on the basis of a common gender. As Black feminist scholars have pointed out, however, it is extremely important to understand that for Black women these multiple statuses cannot be separated or prioritized (hooks 1981; Hull, Scott, and Smith 1982; Gilkes 1988; King 1988; Collins 1990). Giddings's pioneering work (1984) illustrates that Black women's struggles for equality have been ignored by both Black men and White feminists. Anna Julia Cooper's 1892 declaration, "When and where I enter . . . then and there the whole race enters with me" (quoted in Giddings 1984, 13), puts Black women at the center of analysis and critiques the exclusionary tendencies of both Black men civil rights activists and White women feminists.

Women's Activism and Models of Movement Organizations

Social movement scholars have argued that social movement organizations (SMOs) are significant and even necessary vehicles for noninstitutionalized social change (Freeman 1979; McAdam 1982; Morris 1984). Scholars of the new women's movement have argued that the organizational modes developed by the movement of the

1960s and 1970s are very different from those employed by the movement in the late nineteenth and early twentieth centuries. These new organizational modes have been seen as uniquely "feminist" in their structure, values, and practices. As ideal types, they are nonbureaucratic, nonhierarchical, participatory, and democratic (Rothschild-Whitt 1979; Ferree and Hess 1985).

Recently, feminist scholars (see Martin 1990) have argued for reducing the emphasis on ideal-type organizational modes and broadening the focus to include organizations that perhaps do not claim to be feminist but do in fact employ feminist values, practices, and outcomes. I argue that Black women's movement organizations exhibited such "feminist" organizational patterns. Just as organizational modes in the women's movement emerged from unique structural and historical circumstances, each of these Black women's movement organizations emerged from unique historical circumstances and reflected the needs of its members. Moreover, Black women civil rights activists and leaders such as Ella Baker were important role models for the White women who later became activists and leaders in the new women's movement. The emphases on participatory democracy, community, collectivism, caring, mutual respect, and self-transformation that have been viewed as distinctive characteristics of White women's organizing in the late 1960s and 1970s can be found in Black women's political activism and organizing several decades earlier (Evans 1979, 1992; Morris 1984; McAdam 1988; Barnett 1989; Breines 1989; Mueller 1990; Sirianni 1993).

The origins of participatory democracy in Black women's organizing in the 1940s, 1950s, and 1960s have seldom been acknowledged (Evans 1992). Exclusion of Black women's political history from feminist accounts is not new. Terborg-Penn (1978, 27) writes of the lack of acknowledgment of Black feminists' contributions in the earlier waves of feminist mobilization as well.[4] Black feminist scholars view this neglect as a basic failure in the feminist movement to come explicitly to grips with its unwillingness to acknowledge the diversity and multiplicity of women's experiences and women's consciousness (Terborg-Penn 1978; hooks 1981; Terrelonge 1984; King 1988; Collins 1990):

> Sexism and racism have so informed the perspective of American historiographers that they have tended to overlook and exclude the effort of black women in discussions of the American women's rights movement. White female scholars who support feminist ideology have also ignored the contributions of black women. . . . An example of the trend can be found in June Sochen's work *Herstory,* where she discusses white women's organizations in a chapter titled "The Women's Movement" but discusses black women's organizations in a chapter titled "Old Problems: Black Americans." (hooks 1981, 160–61)

Certainly, Black women's experiences are unique, especially in the way that racism and sexism intersect in their lives, but their experiences *as women* are often overlooked (hooks 1981; Hull, Scott, and Smith 1982; Barnett 1989, 1993). Emphasis on their uniqueness should not result in a failure to recognize commonalities among women and their organizations. I believe that it would be a mistake to marginalize or exclude the movement activism and organizing strategies of modern

Black women in the scholarship on "feminist" organization simply because their environment demanded a focus on racial oppression.

Black women's roles as "organizers" in the churches, in work- and school-based associations, in sororities such as Delta Sigma Theta and Alpha Kappa Alpha, in male-dominated SMOs such as the Urban League, and in various clubs and associations such as the National Association of Colored Women and the National Council of Negro Women have long been recognized. Their tremendous organizing skills and effective practices served as the foundation of the civil rights movement and were later adopted by youth, peace activists, and White women (Evans 1979, 1992; Morris 1984; McAdam 1988; Barnett 1989; Mueller 1990; Payne 1990. Nonetheless, their roles as "leaders" in modern social movements have seldom been recognized. Elsewhere I argue for a rethinking of the traditional conception of leadership as formal, public "spokesman" because it is gender-biased and one-dimensional, and it limits both women's actual opportunities and their recognition as "leaders" (Barnett 1989, 1993).[5] My research on modern Black women civil rights leaders is an attempt to put leadership back onto the theoretical agenda of movement scholarship, to challenge the dominant male-centered assumptions, and to conceptualize the roles of women in grassroots community groups in terms of leadership. In my multidimensional view of leadership, organizing is a significant dimension. Black women of different socioeconomic classes were organizers of distinctively communal and participatory movement organizations, which in turn empowered them.

The Women's Political Council and the "Club from Nowhere"

In comparing the styles of two Black women's movement organizations, I focus on three main areas: (1) historical and political context (including founding date, purpose, scope of goals, membership, and strategies and tactics); (2) structural dimensions (including authority and leadership, social relations, and differentiation); and (3) feminist characteristics (including feminist values, goals and practices, and outcomes). . . .

The Women's Political Council and Its Middle-Class Base

The Women's Political Council (WPC) was founded in 1946 in Montgomery, Alabama, by Mary Frances Fair Burks, head of the English Department at a historically Black school, Alabama State College in Montgomery. This organization was headed by formally educated, middle-class, "elite" Black women who were college professors or the wives of elite professionals (dentists, professors, doctors, lawyers, ministers). The socioeconomically secure and "well-connected" women of Montgomery made up the membership core.

The WPC had a formal, somewhat hierarchical authority structure with a president, secretary, treasurer, and heads of assorted committees, or "groups." During the life of the organization there were only two presidents, both college professors and both formally elected by the membership. Leaders were formally chosen for the four main groups—also referred to as "chapters"—on the basis not of issues but of geographical coverage. A WPC officer recounts: "Issues really were not the main reason someone was chosen a group leader. . . . Normally the president chose a reliable and dedicated person to make sure everything got done on her side of town. Of course, the person was usually a professional woman. . . . We thought this was the best thing because we wanted to make sure that the north, south, east, and west sides of Montgomery were always covered and had a leader."

The circumstances surrounding the WPC's founding are ironic. It was established in response to White racism in Montgomery's League of Women Voters (LWV), which denied membership to women who were Black. Burks and most of the forty Black women who later formed the WPC had all experienced some mortifying incident, such as an unwarranted brutal arrest by White police, and initially tried to use the LWV as a means to empower themselves to improve their treatment, but were rebuffed. One WPC member described the particular circumstances surrounding its emergence:

> If the League of Women Voters had not denied our participation and membership in its organization, we wouldn't have had reason to establish the Women's Political Council. . . . When they refused to allow Black women to participate simply because of our race, we had no other alternative but to form our own if we wanted to be part of an organization that allowed us *as women* to participate in political life and to address our political concerns. . . . It seems so irrational as I look at it—they refused to allow Black women to be members of a *women's* organization. I guess they thought we were something *less than women*." (Emphasis added)

It was White women, rather than Black women, who placed their primary emphasis on race over gender by insisting on segregation. Hence, Black women organized the WPC to fight racial segregation practiced by White women as well as the oppressive White male power structure in Montgomery. The name of the group—which Burks successfully persuaded the members to adopt in a close vote over the alternative "Women's Human Relations Committee"—made its direct *political action* concentration manifest (Burks 1990). Between its founding in 1946 and its crucial role in the bus boycott in 1955, the WPC worked to improve conditions for all Blacks but especially for Black youth and Black women. Expressing Black women's orientation towards community and family, one WPC member recalled:

> Black children didn't have playgrounds and recreation areas in their neighborhoods. Our Black youth especially didn't have any places to go [for] recreation. Young people need these things. And then whenever they were together, we were always afraid for them because they were harassed by the law. The teenagers, very fine teenagers, couldn't participate in much because of the way they were treated by police officers, who didn't care that they were fine boys and girls who were active in the schools and the churches.

Black women often took the brunt of racially oppressive segregation laws and sexually oppressive behaviors in the South. Many, regardless of their socioeconomic class, experienced daily insults in their work settings and in public, especially on public transportation. When she traveled on the interstate bus home to Macon, Georgia, college professor JoAnn Robinson experienced the same kind of abuse as seamstress Rosa Parks when she traveled on the city bus in Montgomery. Constance Baker Motley and other Black women civil rights lawyers who were litigating in the southern courts faced public insult and physical abuse by the very people sworn to uphold the law and to provide equal protection under the law (Barnett 1991).

In 1950 JoAnn Robinson took over "Group One," the most politically active committee of the WPC, and led the WPC in lobbying and letter-writing campaigns, including threats of a refusal to pay for segregated parks and of a bus boycott (Robinson 1987, 22–24). In 1955, after news circulated that Rosa Parks had been arrested for refusing to give up her bus seat, Robinson put into action the boycott that the WPC had been planning as a response to the long list of insults directed against Black women in Montgomery. She called Burks, other faculty, and students to start the distribution of leaflets, which, together with word-of-mouth dissemination and newspaper headlines, resulted in almost 100 percent Black participation. The bus boycott began on Monday, December 5, 1955 (Morris 1984); in less than four days the arrest of Rosa Parks had precipitated a WPC-planned event that ushered in the most significant phase of Black protest ever to occur in the United States.

Such a leadership role was risky and demanding. One respondent recalled: "JoAnn could have been fired from her job at the college [Alabama State]. . . . Most of us [professors] had families to support and had to be careful about being openly involved. . . . JoAnn was something else . . . so determined . . . didn't even seem to be afraid if they [Black as well as white administrators] found out. . . . Hah! She used the mimeograph machines in the college to run off leaflets about the boycott!"

Like Ella Baker and many other Black women activists, Robinson was a behind-the-scenes leader (Barnett 1989, 1993). In her memoir (Robinson 1987, 10) she expresses a collectivist orientation and lack of self-promotion that are persistent themes in Black women's activism from slavery to modern times:

> I was one of the first persons arrested in the course of the boycott; that was my first direct experience of what takes place when people are incarcerated. In general, however, I kept a low profile and stayed as much as possible in the background. That I did so was not from fear for my own well-being, but rather out of deep respect for Dr. Trenholm, for Alabama State College, and for its faculty and student body—all of whom would have been unavoidably implicated in case of trouble.

When Robinson was forced to resign from Alabama State in 1960, after being investigated by a special state committee, she took a position in the English department of Grambling State University in Grambling, Louisiana (Robinson 1987, 168–69). One WPC member expressed admiration for Robinson and other activists employed in places of such high vulnerability:

> Many women had to be undercover for fear of losing their jobs. This was a real threat. Some of us who worked for Black businesses . . . didn't have to worry about this type of retaliation. I worked for [a Black business], . . . which encouraged me, supported

my activities, even donated money to the movement. Women such as Mrs. Robinson and Mrs. Burks and Mrs. Glass had to be careful or else they could lose their jobs. Being brave is one thing. Being sensible is another, especially when you have a family obligation. This is why I admire those women who did what they did.

Lamenting the loss of so many "good women" who risked their jobs and were forced to discontinue their activism, another activist and WPC officer explained: "The two or three remaining presidents of various auxiliaries were finally frightened out of operating. . . . It really just boiled down to about five of us who were left at the university. . . . We continued in the churches."

Such opposition reduced the historical visibility of the organization. Almost all the records of the WPC and the Montgomery Improvement Association (MIA), the organization headed by male ministers to coordinate boycott activities, were destroyed during this time: when White supremacists used the tactic of subpoenaing records for trial, leaders in the WPC countered by destroying the organization's records. When I asked to see the names of officers and committees in the WPC, one of the officers told me:

> We don't really have any records anymore. We had to destroy them during the boycott because we knew that this same thing had been used to try to run the NAACP out of town many years ago. The Whites subpoenaed the NAACP's records and publicized the membership lists. When we were subpoenaed to testify at the boycott trials, we knew that they were trying to use the same thing to get back at us. . . . So, we decided we had to destroy the minutes and our membership roster. . . . That's why I really can't tell you everything you want to know, especially who all were members. I have very few papers left.

Burks, Robinson, and others, such as Faustine Dunn, Thelma Glass, Geraldine Nesbitt, Irene West, Johnnie Carr, and Sadie Brooks, developed very ingenious ways of organizing. One respondent illustrates the creative and effective fund raising of these Black women: "In all my speeches I used to tell the people: if you are afraid, and I know you are, and you can't stand up, [then] George Washington, Abraham Lincoln, and Alexander Hamilton—all those boys are dead and they are not going to tell *nobody* . . . so just give us some of those boys' pictures and let us do the work. . . . The women in our organization will just get out there and do the work" (original emphasis).

The WPCers used a variety of tactics to obtain information and resources as well. For example, even though the White women in the LWV had denied the Black women membership, the WPC leadership nevertheless invited LWV leaders to WPC meetings and after-church gatherings to provide information on White candidates whenever there was an elected office to fill. Years before the 1955 boycott the WPC was seeking political empowerment through electoral politics, self-consciously using "subversive" tactics. One such tactic was to establish a Negro Youth Day, similar to the day set aside for the White high schools to elect students who replaced government officials for a day (Burks 1990). Like the adult citizenship education and training pioneered by Septima Poinsette Clark (1962, 1990) in the 1950s, this program was aimed at fostering in Black youth the desire for and belief in the efficacy of change through electoral politics. Many of the youth trained by WPC members and public school teachers later became SNCC activists and leaders who fearlessly initiated voter registration campaigns in Mississippi and other parts of the Deep South (Barnett 1989; Breines 1989; Burks 1990).

Finally, Robinson's use of the mimeograph machines in the public college, operated by the very power the WPC was fighting, is an excellent illustration of how the professional, college-based leadership had access to what Freeman (1979) labels "specialized resources." The WPC not only had status and access to decision-makers within the movement but also a little status and access to the mayor and other decision-makers in the larger White political structure. The leafleting that the WPC used so effectively required access to professional expertise, money from the city's affluent Blacks, and professor-teacher-student-government service networks. These resources had already been mobilized by the WPC to engage in direct political confrontations via letter-writing campaigns, taxation protests, and "hearings" before the mayor in the decade preceding the boycott. Both their willingness to take risks and their access to resources made the WPC women *leaders* in the civil rights movement in Montgomery, even though the gender dynamics of the movement tended to obscure their significant *contributions*.

The Club from Nowhere and Its Working-Class Base

In addition to the WPC, other movement organizations helped to sustain the boycott in Montgomery. The key organizers and leaders of some of the collectivist organizations were not professional women or wives of professionals, but rather poor and working-class Black women (Barnett 1990). One little-known activist organization that can serve as an example of the type was the "Club from Nowhere" (CFN), founded in 1956 by Georgia Gilmore, a domestic worker and restaurant cook, to support the boycott just then getting under way in Montgomery.[6] One leader of the Montgomery boycott tells of the innovative tactics used by Gilmore and other members:

> The Club from Nowhere was truly something Mrs. Georgia Gilmore should be proud of. She headed this club and even lost her job working in a cafe when she started it. The club went door to door asking for donations and selling dinner plates and baked goods. . . . [They] made weekly reports on all the money collected from all kinds of people—Blacks and Whites. Some of these people didn't want it known that they had given money to the movement, so they wouldn't give Mrs. Gilmore and the other ladies checks that could be traced, only cash. And Mrs. Gilmore made sure they didn't tell anybody who had made the donations. That's why it was called the Club from Nowhere, so that none of the people giving the money could be in the least bit accused of supporting the movement.

Unfortunately, Gilmore, like most southern Black women domestic workers, was especially vulnerable to economic retaliation. Her employer learned of her activism, fired her from her job as a cook, and blacklisted her from other jobs. Undaunted, however, she continued cooking and baking in her home, selling the items door to door, and turning over all the money to the boycott's organizing unit, the MIA.

While these poor and working-class women didn't have access to the specialized resources available to the WPC's professional women, the CFN did have access to other valuable resources. As Freeman (1979, 195) points out: "Movements that seem to be poor, that draw from seriously deprived constituencies, may in fact be rich in some less obvious, but still tangible resources," such as time and commitment. The maids, cooks, and service workers of the CFN also had access to information in the homes of their White employers. As they went invisibly about their domestic work, the CFNers were alert to news about the strategies and tactics of the White opposition. They had resources in their particular churches and neighborhoods as well. Although they had no status in the polity at large or even in the male-dominated organizations in the movement, the church conferred status on poor Black women who gave their time and personal commitment. These church networks were important for organizing boycott activities (Morris 1984).

The fluidity of status and the permeability of class boundaries among women in the Black community, especially before integration, is indicated by their common involvement in the Black churches and the occasional overlapping memberships of the activists. For example, Gilmore's and Robinson's mutual friend Johnnie Carr, a former cook and later a successful insurance salesperson, participated in both the WPC and the CFN. Carr was the youngest of seven children born to a farm family near Montgomery and for much of her early life was forced to earn her living by working as a cook and maid to White families—the typical low-level domestic service jobs available to most poor and working-class Black women in the South—though she had entered the insurance industry by the time of the boycott. Carr and the other women in the various "clubs" and "councils" in Montgomery were extremely active in the church, the community, and the NAACP. Carr and her close friend Rosa Parks served alternately as secretary of the local NAACP, headed by Pullman porter E. D. Nixon, and helped to organize for the bus boycott. Several years after the boycott, Carr became the only woman ever to serve as president of the MIA, which remains a viable organization in Montgomery and which Carr still heads today. The mobilization of the CFN in particular was a significant experience of empowerment for its participants.

Empowerment was in part a result of the deliberately nonhierarchical structure of the group. Unlike the somewhat formal, hierarchical structure of the Women's Political Council and the male-led Montgomery Improvement Association, the Club from Nowhere was a loosely structured network of neighborhood women who had no formal rules or regulations. Although Gilmore was referred to as the "head," authority and decision-making were vested in the group as a whole. Professionalism and expertise were not the basis of leadership. The CFN operated in an ad hoc manner, using "generally agreed upon ethics" (Rothschild-Whitt 1979; Martin 1990). On the east side of town (like the WPC, poor and working-class women divided the city into organizing sectors), Gilmore's counterpart Inez Ricks operated "the Friendly Club" in the same manner. There were no fixed rules, no supervision of member activities, no formal recruitment, no special incentives for membership, and no functional or hierarchical division of labor.

Such groups were not entirely independent, however. Whereas the WPC was a completely autonomous Black women's organization, separate from the male-headed MIA, NAACP, and Urban League, the CFN was a single-purpose Black women's organization that lacked power relative to the male-dominated civil rights organizations. Although the WPC often conferred with the male-dominated organizations, it did not see itself as an appendage of them; they in turn recognized the autonomy and influence of the WPC in the community. In contrast, the CFN "looked up to the MIA" for guidance and directives. Unlike the women of the WPC, the women of the CFN saw themselves only as an "arm" of the male-dominated movement organizations.

The short life span of the CFN reflected the organization's short-term, one-dimensional purpose, as described by one respondent: "The Club from Nowhere was really not an organization like the Women's Political Council. The Club from Nowhere was formed for the sole purpose of raising money to finance the Montgomery boycott. It went out when the movement died down." In contrast, the WPC's fourteen-year history reflected goals that were multiple, broad, and geared to structural change. The WPC as an organization, however, ultimately succumbed to the repressive effect of job retaliation by the opposition.

The Politics of Empowerment

The WPC and the CFN had tremendous impact on the lives of their members. Like the women described by Gilkes (1980, 1988), Giddings (1984), Jones (1985), and Collins (1990), the Black women in these two organizations were individuals of courage and inner strength, who were further empowered through their activism. Gilmore, for example, responded to being unemployed and blacklisted by going into business for herself with movement support. Recognizing the political vulnerability of being a renter, she used the organizing skills and contacts she developed during the movement to finance the purchase of her own home.[7] Her involvement in the boycott transformed not only her material conditions but her political consciousness (Barnett 1990). She continued to organize poor and working-class Black women around issues of day care and voting rights and inspired at least one of her children to pursue a formal career in politics.

The middle-class and affluent women of the WPC learned to be directly proactive for political change. In fact, one of the very first tasks of membership in the WPC was to succeed in registering to vote by passing the citizenship tests that the White opposition was using to keep Blacks from voting in the South (Robinson 1987; Burks 1990). The poor and working-class women aided and assisted the recognized movement leaders and engaged in self-help strategies and activities of their own as well. The women in the WPC and CFN considered it a duty to help one another and sacrifice for the cause. The middle-class women of the WPC and the working-class women of the CFN also shared a sense of community; they were willing to stand up for each other. One activist said: "I was always in a kind of position where I could stand up anywhere anytime. I was not afraid to ask people to volunteer their time or their money, but if they were afraid, I understood and did not push. I told them I'd do it for them. And I could get out there and do it because I was secure in my job [with a Black-owned business] and could afford to do it."

In summary, the Black women in these two organizations did much planning and organizing in the civil rights movement. The WPC and the CFN were founded at different times, had different purposes, and used different tactics. Their members' self-conscious quest for social justice, however, transformed not only their lives but also the structure of society. Yet these women and their organizations have received relatively little recognition, especially compared with the male activists and male-dominated movement organizations. One WPC member and longtime NAACP worker compared this exclusion and subordinate status of Black women in Montgomery during the time of the boycott to the historical exclusion of women throughout society's institutions:

> Throughout history, you'll see women being left out in almost every area. . . . If you read the Bible, of course you'll find mention of significant women, such as Esther and Ruth; however, you'll never find these women mentioned in the same glowing manner as Peter and Paul and Moses. . . . Women throughout the Bible and history had done outstanding things that they were not considered capable of doing, but when they did them, they simply were not recognized as much as the men.

Another activist suggested a relationship between racism and private patriarchy in Black man-woman relations in the South.[8] She pointed to Black women's cognizance of the "fragile" position of Black males:

> In the South, women still look to men as leaders when women are actually doing the work. . . . A lot of this comes from the tradition of the church and the male minister as the leader, the person whom you're suppose to obey. The movement was no different. . . . Women obeyed and supported their husbands, looked up to them as leaders, and didn't take any credit even if it was offered. . . . Black women especially had to work hard, but never ever threaten the fragile position of their Black men.

One veteran civil rights leader interviewed suggested an explanation beyond traditional gender role differences and expectations among Blacks and pointed to the larger problem of public patriarchy in American society: "When Europeans came to America, women had to take a back seat to males. . . . Men didn't do the work that women did, and yet they got all the praises. This European patriarchal influence is evident not just among Blacks but also among Whites. . . . Women don't get credit and praise for the work they do because that's how the White European tradition sets things up."

In her memoir, WPC president and Montgomery boycott organizer JoAnn Robinson (1987, 172) summarized Black women's courage and resolve in organizing for change:

> Those who stayed behind in Montgomery carried on what we had begun, as they should have. Since 1957, the WPC members, now retired and scattered around the country in various walks of life, still feel that a woman's duties do not end in the home, church, or classroom. Members have sought to determine the ills of dissatisfied Black people and, through intelligent approaches to proper sources, to find solutions

to the nagging problems that turn good men into beasts and kill the hopes, dreams, and faith of those who would strive toward something better.

Conclusion

There are both similarities and differences among Black women's social movement organizations. On the basis of conventional criteria, the middle-class women's organization, the WPC, is more recognizably "feminist" than the working-class organization, the CFN. Because African American women are not a homogeneous category, one does not fully challenge the definitions of what is feminist politics by simply adding studies of those African American women's organizations that look most like White feminist organizations. Both the WPC and the CFN were organizations that encouraged participation by all women. Such participation is a "feminist" goal, practice, and outcome. Though often unsung, the Black women who belonged to the WPC and the CFN fought for "their" rights as well as those of their children, husbands, fathers, mothers, sisters, and brothers. Certainly, those Black women, just like their White sisters in the "new women's movement," were empowered by their activism.

The class differences among African American women also mattered, however. From the beginning, the middle-class women of the WPC were prepared to take political action. For them, the boycott was an *opportunity*. It had been their idea and their initiative, and in that sense they were leaders from the start, however unacknowledged. But the CFN women needed more than an opportunity. They needed to learn that they could be effective political leaders, and the nonhierarchical structure of their organization both reflected this need and made it possible to overcome it. As an organization the CFN was never more than an auxiliary, but as members of the CFN poor and working-class women empowered themselves to become leaders. Their leadership was then evident in later years in Montgomery. Such grassroots empowerment of women was a common outcome of civil rights organizing in the poorest sectors of the Black community.

My research illustrates that when the standard categories of feminist organizations are applied to Black women's historical experiences, they are simply inadequate. Indeed, these standard questions point to the need to rewrite the history of women's organizing in a way that gives voice and visibility to the experiences of Black women, who were not "in the doldrums" in the 1940s and 1950s or newly mobilized in the 1960s. Instead, despite vigorous opposition, they provided leadership throughout this period.

In these Black women's movement organizations, founded during the period considered "pre-feminist," feminist organizing patterns and orientations emerge. Yet Black women's movement organizations have a different history from White women's movement organizations. The dimensions of gender and race and of self and family/community are not separable in their experience. These Black women's organizations were also different from the male-dominated civil rights organizations of the time—the MIA, SCLC, NAACP, CORE, and Urban League—which were all very hierarchical and bureaucratic. Collectivist in orientation, these women's groups offered innovative plans, took risks, and supported each other, as well as Black men, in the quest for justice and equality. The strategizing, organizing, fund raising, communicating, and leadership roles of the women of the WPC and the CFN were critical. Finally, Black women's SMOs differed from each other. They reflected diverse needs and ways of organizing within their community and differential access to specialized and unspecialized resources.

Black feminists have pointed out that "feminist" scholarship contradicts itself when Black women's activism is marginalized, seen only in terms of race, or excluded from feminist theorizing (hooks 1981; Hull, Scott, and Smith 1982; Collins 1990). Indeed, there is much to be learned from the organizing strategies of all women, particularly those who have been marginalized (Sachs 1988a, 1988b; Barnett 1989, 1990, 1993). As Giddings (1984, 5–6) has argued: "Despite the range and significance of our [Black women's] history, we have been perceived as token women in Black texts and as token Blacks in feminist ones. . . . Black women had a history of their own, one which reflects their distinct concerns, values and the role they have played as *both Afro-Americans and women. And their unique status has had an impact on both racial and feminist values*" (emphasis added). This research should be seen as a step not only toward reclaiming that history for its own sake but toward understanding the feminist implications of organizing on gender and race and class dimensions simultaneously.

NOTES

I want to express my sincere gratitude to the Black women civil rights activists who generously granted interviews and shared their organizing experiences with me. I am also grateful to many people who provided helpful comments on earlier versions of this essay, particularly Cheryl Townsend Gilkes, Hester Eisenstein, and Jo Freeman. Finally, I owe a very special debt to Myra Marx Ferree and Patricia Yancey Martin for their priceless encouragement, feedback, and editorial advice.

1. There has been considerable scholarship on White women's movement organizations such as NOW, on various women's liberation "first groups" (cf. Freeman 1975, 1979; Rothschild-Whitt 1979; Ferree and Hess 1985), and on both White male-dominated and Black male-dominated movement organizations such as SDS, the NAACP, SCLC, CORE, the Urban League, and SNCC (Zinn 1965; Morris 1984; Breines 1989; Stoper 1989). Explicit analysis of modern Black women's movement organizations, however, has been noticeably absent in the literature.

2. Time has taken its toll on veteran civil rights activists; the recent deaths of several of those I interviewed precluded follow-up on significant questions that their participation raised and insights that they provided for our initial interview. That some of those who are still living cannot readily recall the names and activities of all of the women involved makes the destruction of organizational records and membership rosters (to avoid their being subpoenaed; see below) all the more unfortunate.

3. The names of the women respondents are not used here because they were promised anonymity. I acknowledge my sincere appreciation to them for sharing with me their organizing experiences and their insights.

4. For example, Lottie Rollins and other Black feminists founded the racially integrated South Carolina Women's Rights Association (SCWRA) and attended the American Suffrage Association Convention of 1872. When the *History of Women's Suffrage* was written in 1900, however, the starting date of the movement was given as 1890, and no reference was made to the SCWRA, founded twenty years earlier (see discussion in Terborg-Penn 1978).

5. Though there is a rich historical and sociological literature on leadership, much contemporary social movement scholarship views "leaders" as one of many "resources" needed for and mobilized by a social movement organization. For additional discussion of this point, see Barnett (1993).

6. One might argue that this collectivity called a "club" is not an organization. In addressing this issue, however, Martin (1990, 185) defines an organization as any "relatively enduring" group of people (one that exists for more than a few meetings) structured to pursue goals that are collectively identified. By this criterion, the CFN was a movement organization; it was intentional and had an emergent plan of action and organized strategy.

7. The political as well as material transformation that ensued for her was similar to the effects that involvement in voter registration had on sharecroppers Fannie Lou Hamer and Unita Blackwell.

8. Research by Martin, Wilson, and Dillman (1991) makes the point that social, cultural, and structural conditions shape gender relations in the South. They argue that the intersecting of patriarchy and slavery in the antebellum South "fundamentally confounded gender and race relations" in the region and that slavery and White men's sexual "exploitation of Black women hindered the development of common bonds or identity among White and Black women" (105–6).

REFERENCES

Barnett, Bernice McNair. 1989. "Southern Black Women of the Civil Rights Movement: The Unsung Heroes and Leaders." Paper presented at the annual meetings of Sociologists for Women in Society, San Francisco.

———. 1990. "Sharecroppers, Domestics, and the Club From Nowhere: Poor and Working Class Women Organizing for Indigenous Collective Action." Paper presented at the annual meetings of the Southern Sociological Society, Louisville, Ky.

———. 1991. "Career Patterns of Black Women Civil Rights Lawyers: A Case of Triple Advantage or Triple Jeopardy?" Paper presented at the annual meetings of Sociologists for Women in Society, Cincinnati, Ohio.

———. 1993. "Invisible Southern Black Women Leaders in the Civil Rights Movement: The Triple Constraints of Gender, Race, and Class." *Gender & Society* 7:162–82.

Bates, Daisy. 1962. *The Long Shadow of Little Rock: A Memoir.* New York: David McKay.

Breines, Wini. 1989. *Community and Organization in the New Left: The Great Refusal.* Rev. ed. New Brunswick, N.J.: Rutgers University Press.

Burks, Mary Fair. 1990. "Trailblazers: Women in the Montgomery Bus Boycott." In *Women in the Civil Rights Movement: Trailblazers and Torchbearers,* ed. Vickie Crawford, Jacqueline Rouse, and Barbara Woods. New York: Carlson.

Clark, Septima Poinsette. 1962. *Echo in My Soul.* New York: Dutton.

———. 1990. *Ready from Within: Septima Clark and the Civil Rights Movement.* Trenton: Africa World Press.

Collins, Patricia Hill. 1990. *Black Feminist Thought: Knowledge, Consciousness, and the Politics of Empowerment.* Boston: Unwin Hyman.

Crawford, Vickie, Jacqueline Rouse, and Barbara Woods, eds. 1990. *Women in the Civil Rights Movement: Trailblazers and Torchbearers.* New York: Carlson.

Evans, Sara. 1979. *Personal Politics: The Roots of Women's Liberation in the Civil Rights Movement and the New Left.* New York: Random House.

———. 1992. "The Women's Movement in the United States in the 1960s." In *Challenging Times: The Women's Movement in Canada and the United States,* ed. Constance Backhouse and David Flaherty, 61–71. Montreal: McGill-Queens University Press.

Ferree, Myra Marx, and Beth B. Hess. 1985. *Controversy and Coalition: The New Feminist Movement.* Boston: Twayne.

Freeman, Jo. 1973. "The Origins of the Women's Liberation Movement." *American Journal of Sociology* 78(4): 792–811.

———. 1974. "The Feminist Scholar." Speech, Montclair, N.J. Published in *QUEST: A Feminist Quarterly* 5 (Summer 1979): 26–36.

———. 1975. *The Politics of Women's Liberation: A Case Study of an Emerging Social Movement and Its Relation to the Policy Process.* New York: David McKay.

———. 1979. "Resource Mobilization and Strategy: A Model for Analyzing Social Movement Actions." In *The Dynamics of Social Movements,* ed. Mayer N. Zald and John D. McCarthy, 167–89. Cambridge, Mass.: Winthrop. Rev. as "A Model for Analyzing the Strategic Options of Social Movement Organizations," in *Social Movements of the Sixties and Seventies,* ed. Jo Freeman (New York: Longman, 1983), 193–210.

Giddings, Paula. 1984. *When and Where I Enter: The Impact of Black Women on Race and Sex in America.* New York: Harper & Row.

Gilkes, Cheryl Townsend. 1980. "Holding Back the Ocean with a Broom: Black Women and Community Work." In *The Black Woman,* ed. La Frances Rodgers-Rose, 217–32. Beverly Hills, Calif.: Sage.

———. 1982. "Successful Rebellious Professionals: The Black Woman's Professional Identity and Community." *Psychology of Women Quarterly* 6(3): 289–311.

———. 1988. "Building in Many Places: Multiple Commitments and Ideologies in Black Women's Community Work." In *Women and the Politics of Empowerment,* ed. Ann Bookman and Sandra Morgan. Philadelphia: Temple University Press.

hooks, bell. 1981. *Ain't I a Woman: Black Women and Feminism.* Boston: South End Press.

Hull, Gloria T., Patricia Bell Scott, and Barbara Smith, eds. 1982. *All the Women Are White, All the Blacks Are Men, But Some of Us Are Brave.* Old Westbury, N.Y.: Feminist Press.

Jones, Jacqueline. 1985. *Labor of Love, Labor of Sorrow: Black Women, Work, and the Family from Slavery to the Present.* New York: Basic Books.

King, Deborah. 1988. "Multiple Jeopardy, Multiple Consciousness: The Context of a Black Feminist Ideology." *Signs* 14(1): 42–72.

King, Martin Luther, Jr. 1958. *Stride towards Freedom: The Montgomery Story.* New York: Harper.

McAdam, Doug. 1982. *Political Process and the Development of Black Insurgency.* Chicago: University of Chicago Press.

———. 1988. *Freedom Summer.* New York: Oxford University Press.

Martin, Patricia Yancey. 1990. "Rethinking Feminist Organizations." *Gender & Society* 4: 182–206.

Martin, Patricia Yancey, Kenneth R. Wilson, and Caroline M. Dillman, 1991. "Southern-Style Gender: Trends in Relations between Men and Women." In *The South Moves into Its Future: Studies in the Analysis and Prediction of Social Change,* ed. J. S. Himes, 103–48. Tuscaloosa: University of Alabama Press.

Morris, Aldon. 1984. *The Origins of the Civil Rights Movement: Black Communities Organizing for Change.* New York: Free Press.

Mueller, Carol McClurg. 1990. "Ella Baker and the Origins of Participatory Democracy." In *Women in the Civil Rights Movement: Trailblazers and Torchbearers,* ed. Vickie Crawford, Jacqueline Rouse, and Barbara Woods, 51–70. New York: Carlson.

Payne, Charles. 1990. "Men Led, But Women Organized: Movement Participation of Women in the Mississippi Delta." In *Women in the Civil Rights Movement: Trailblazers and Torchbearers,* ed. Vickie Crawford, Jaqueline Rouse, and Barbara Woods, 1–12. New York: Carlson.

Robinson, JoAnn Gibson. 1987. *The Montgomery Bus Boycott and the Women Who Started It.* Knoxville: University of Tennessee Press.

Rothschild-Whitt, Joyce. 1976. "Conditions Facilitating Participatory Democratic Organizations." *Sociological Inquiry* 46: 75–86.

———. 1979. "The Collectivist Organization: An Alternative to Rational-Bureaucratic Models." *American Sociological Review* 44 (August): 509–27.

Rupp, Lelia J., and Verta Taylor. 1987. *Survival in the Doldrums: The American Women's Rights Movement, 1945 to the 1960s.* New York: Oxford University Press.

Sachs, Karen. 1988a. *Caring by the Hour: Women, Work, and Organizing at Duke Medical Center.* Urbana: University of Illinois Press.

———. 1988b. "Gender and Grassroots Leadership." In *Women and the Politics of Empowerment,* ed. Ann Bookman and Sandra Morgen, 77–94. Philadelphia: Temple University Press.

Sirianni, Carmen. 1993. "Learning Pluralism: Democracy and Diversity in Feminist Organizations." In *Democratic Community: NOMOS XXXV,* ed. John Chapman and Ian Shapiro, 283–312. New York: New York University Press.

Stoper, Emily. 1989. *The Student Nonviolent Coordinating Committee.* Brooklyn: Carlson.

Terborg-Penn, Rosalyn. 1978. "Discrimination against Afro-American Women in the Woman's Movement, 1830–1920." In *The Afro American Woman: Struggles and Images,* ed. Sharon Harley and Rosalyn Terborg-Penn, 17–27. Port Washington, N.Y.: Kennikat Press.

Terrelonge, Pauline. 1984. "Feminist Consciousness and Black Women." In *Women: A Feminist Perspective,* 3d ed., ed. J. Freeman, 557–67. Palo Alto, Calif.: Mayfield.

Zinn, Howard. 1965. *SNCC: The New Abolitionists.* Boston: Beacon Press.

Chapter Eighteen

Introduction to *Home Girls: A Black Feminist Anthology*

Barbara Smith

In the fall of 1981, before most of this book was compiled, I was searching for a title. I'd come up with one that I knew was not quite right. At the time I was also working on the story which later became "Home" and thought that I'd like to get some of the feeling of that piece into the book. One day while doing something else entirely, and playing with words in my head, "home girls" came to me. Home Girls. The girls from the neighborhood and from the block, the girls we grew up with. I knew I was onto something, particularly when I considered that so many Black people who are threatened by feminism have argued that by being a Black feminist (particularly if you are also a Lesbian) you have left the race, are no longer a part of the Black community, in short no longer have a home.

I suspect that most of the contributors to *Home Girls* learned their varied politics and their shared commitment to Black women from the same source I did. Yet critics of feminism pretend that just because some of us speak out about sexual politics *at home,* within the Black community, we must have sprung miraculously from somewhere else. But we are not strangers and never have been. I am convinced that Black feminism is, on every level, organic to Black experience.

History verifies that Black women have rejected doormat status, whether racially or sexually imposed, for centuries. Not only is there the documented resistance of Black women during slavery followed by our organizing around specific Black women's issues and in support of women's rights during the nineteenth century, there is also the vast cultural record of our continuously critical stance toward our oppression. For example, in the late nineteenth and early twentieth centuries, poets Frances E. W. Harper (1825–1911), Angelina Weld Grimke (1880–1958), Alice Dunbar-Nelson (1875–1935), Anne Spencer (1882–1975), and Georgia Douglas Johnson (1886–1966) all addressed themes of sexual as well as racial identity in some of their work.

One of the best cultural repositories that repeatedly demonstrates Black women's desire for freedom and fair treatment inside and outside of the home is the Blues. In

Reprinted by permission from *Home Girls: A Black Feminist Anthology,* edited by Barbara Smith. New York, Kitchen Table. Women of Color Press, 1983.

her essay, "Slave Codes and Liner Notes," in *But Some of Us Are Brave: Black Women's Studies* Michele Russell analyzes the social-political commentary available in Black women's music. Of Bessie Smith she writes: ". . . dating from the early twenties, her advice to women is: 'Get a working man when you marry. Cause it takes money to run a business.' " As an example of this message, Russell quotes Smith's "Get It, Bring It, and Put It Right Here," which, as she writes, "speaks for itself":

> I've had a man for fifteen years
> Give him his room and his board.
> Once he was like a Cadillac
> Now he's like an old worn-out Ford.
>
> He never brought me a lousy dime
> And put it in my hand.
> Oh there'll be some changes from now on
> According to my plan.
>
> He's got to get it, bring it, and put it right here
> Or else he's gonna keep it out there.
> If he must steal it, beg it, or borrow it somewhere
> Long as he gets it, I don't care.
>
> I'm tired of buying pork chops to grease his fat lips
> And he'll have to find another place to park his ole hips
> He's got to get it, bring it, and put it right here
> Or else he's gonna keep it out there.[1]

Here is a practical approach for dealing with a basic problem. Smith's attitude also embodies the values of what anthropologist John Langston Gwaltney defines as "core Black culture" in his masterwork *Drylongso*. Most of the people Gwaltney interviews, whether female or male, describe marriage as a pragmatic partnership. Mabel Johns, a woman in her sixties, comments thusly on the fact that her white female employer had to get her husband's permission for every expenditure:

> Now, I just couldn't be so bothered with all that. I am a grown woman, so I buy what I think I should. I don't mean selfish buying. I know more about these things than my husband did. Now if you can't pull together then you best pull apart. I was lucky and unlucky in marriage. I will tell anyone I had a good husband. He was a man and I was a woman, so we didn't neither of us have to raise the other.[2]

I have always felt that Black women's ability to function with dignity, independence, and imagination in the face of total adversity—that is, in the face of white America—points to an innate feminist potential. To me the phrase "Act like you have some sense," probably spoken by at least one Black woman to every Black child who ever lived, is a cryptic warning that says volumes about keeping your feet on the ground and your ass covered. Alice Walker's definition of "womanist" certainly makes the connection between plain common sense and a readiness to fight for change. She writes:

WOMANIST: (According to Walker) From *womanish.* (Opp. of "girlish," i.e. frivolous, irresponsible, not serious.) A black feminist or feminist of color. From the colloquial expression of mothers to daughters, "You're acting womanish," i.e., like a woman. Usually referring to outrageous, audacious, courageous or *willful* behavior. Wanting to know more and in greater depth than is considered "good" for one. Interested in grown-up doings. Acting grown-up. Being grown-up. Interchangeable with other colloquial expression: "You're trying to be grown." Responsible. In charge. *Serious.* . . .

2. Also: Herstorically capable, as in "Mama, I'm walking to Canada and I'm taking you and a bunch of other slaves with me." Reply: "It wouldn't be the first time."[3]

Black women as a group have never been fools. We couldn't afford to be. Yet in the last two decades many of us have been deterred from identifying with a liberation struggle which might say significant things to women like ourselves, women who believe that we were put here for a purpose in our own right, women who are usually not afraid to struggle.

Although our involvement has increased considerably in recent years, there are countless reasons why Black and other Third World women have not identified with contemporary feminism in large numbers.[4] The racism of white women in the women's movement has certainly been a major factor. The powers-that-be are also aware that a movement of progressive Third World women in this country would alter life as we know it. As a result there has been a concerted effort to keep women of color from organizing autonomously and from organizing with other women around women's political issues. Third World men, desiring to maintain power over "their women" at all costs, have been among the most willing reinforcers of the fears and myths about the women's movement, attempting to scare us away from figuring things out for ourselves.

It is fascinating to look at various kinds of media from the late 1960s and early 1970s, when feminism was making its great initial impact, in order to see what Black men, Native American men, Asian American men, Latino men, and white men were saying about the irrelevance of "women's lib" to women of color. White men and Third World men, ranging from conservatives to radicals, pointed to the seeming lack of participation of women of color in the movement in order to discredit it and to undermine the efforts of the movement as a whole. All kinds of men were running scared because they knew that if the women in their midst were changing, they were going to have to change too. In 1976 I wrote:

Feminism is potentially the most threatening of movements to Black and other Third World people because it makes it absolutely essential that we examine the way we live, how we treat each other, and what we believe. It calls into question the most basic assumption about our existence and this is the idea that biological, i.e., sexual identity determines all, that it is the rationale for power relationships as well as for all other levels of human identity and action. An irony is that among Third World people biological determinism is rejected and fought against when it is applied to race, but generally unquestioned when it applies to sex.[5]

In reaction to the "threat" of such change, Black men, with the collaboration of some Black women, developed a set of myths to divert Black women from our own freedom.

Myths

Myth No. 1: The Black Woman Is Already Liberated

This myth confuses liberation with the fact that Black women have had to take on responsibilities that our oppression gives us no choice but to handle. This is an insidious, but widespread myth that many Black women have believed themselves. Heading families, working outside the home, not building lives or expectations dependent on males, seldom being sheltered or pampered as women, Black women have known that their lives in some ways incorporated goals that white middle-class women were striving for, but race and class privilege, of course, reshaped the meaning of those goals profoundly. As W. E. B. Du Bois said so long ago about Black women: "our women in black had freedom contemptuously thrust upon them."[6] Of all the people here, women of color generally have the fewest choices about the circumstances of their lives. An ability to cope under the worst conditions is not liberation, although our spiritual capacities have often made it look like a life. Black men didn't say anything about how poverty, unequal pay, no childcare, violence of every kind including battering, rape, and sterilization abuse, translated into "liberation." . . .

Myth No. 2: Racism Is the Primary (or Only) Oppression Black Women Have to Confront (Once We Get That Taken Care of, Then Black Women, Men, and Children Will All Flourish. Or as Ms. Luisah Teish Writes, We Can Look Forward to Being "the Property of Powerful Men")[7]

This myth goes hand in hand with the one that the Black woman is already liberated. The notion that struggling against or eliminating racism will completely alleviate Black women's problems does not take into account the way that sexual oppression cuts across all racial, nationality, age, religious, ethnic, and class groupings. Afro-Americans are no exception.

It also does not take into account how oppression operates. Every generation of Black people, up until now, has had to face the reality that no matter how hard we work we will probably not see the end of racism in our lifetimes. Yet many of us keep faith and try to do all we can to make change now. If we have to wait for racism to be obliterated *before* we can begin to address sexism, we will be waiting for a long time. Denying that sexual oppression exists or requiring that we wait to bring it up until racism, or in some cases capitalism, is toppled, is a bankrupt position. A Black feminist perspective has no use for ranking oppressions, but instead demonstrates the simultaneity of oppressions as they affect Third World women's lives.

Myth No. 3: Feminism Is Nothing but Man-Hating (and Men Have Never Done Anything That Would Legitimately Inspire Hatred)

It is important to make a distinction between attacking institutionalized, systematic oppression (the goal of any serious progressive movement) and attacking men as individuals. Unfortunately, some of the most widely distributed writing about Black women's issues has not made this distinction sufficiently clear. Our issues have not been concisely defined in these writings, causing much adverse reaction and confusion about what Black feminism really is.[8]

This myth is one of the silliest and at the same time one of the most dangerous. Anti-feminists are incapable of making a distinction between being critically opposed to sexual oppression and simply hating men. Women's desire for fairness and safety in our lives does not necessitate hating men. Trying to educate and inform men about how their feet are planted on our necks doesn't translate into hatred either. Centuries of anti-racist struggle by various people of color are not reduced, except by racists, to our merely hating white people. If anything it seems that the opposite is true. People of color know that white people have abused us unmercifully and it is only sane for us to try to change that treatment by every means possible.

Likewise the bodies of murdered women are strewn across the landscape of this country. Rape is a national pastime, a form of torture visited upon all girls and women, from babies to the aged. One out of three women in the U.S. will be raped during her lifetime. Battering and incest, those home-based crimes, are pandemic. Murder, of course, is men's ultimate violent "solution." And if you're thinking as you read this that I'm exaggerating, please go get today's newspaper and verify the facts. If anything is going down here it's woman-hatred, not man-hatred, a war against women. But wanting to end this war still doesn't equal man-hating. The feminist movement and the anti-racist movement have in common trying to insure decent human life. Opposition to either movement aligns one with the most reactionary elements in American society.

Myth No. 4: Women's Issues Are Narrow, Apolitical Concerns. People of Color Need to Deal With the "Larger Struggle"

This myth once again characterizes women's oppression as not particularly serious, and by no means a matter of life and death. I have often wished I could spread the word that a movement committed to fighting sexual, racial, economic, and heterosexist oppression, not to mention one which opposes imperialism, anti-Semitism, the oppressions visited upon the physically disabled, the old and the young, at the same time that it challenges militarism and imminent nuclear destruction is the very opposite of narrow. All segments of the women's movement have not dealt with all of these issues, but neither have all segments of Black people. This myth is plausible when the women's movement is equated only with its most bourgeois and reformist elements. The most progressive sectors of the feminist movement, which includes some radical white women, have taken the above issues, and many more, quite seriously. Third World women have been the most consistent in defining our politics broadly. Why is it that feminism is considered "white-minded" and "narrow" while socialism or Marxism, from verifiably white origins, is legitimately embraced by Third World male politicos, without their having their identity credentials questioned for a minute?

Myth No. 5: Those Feminists Are Nothing but Lesbians

This may be the most pernicious myth of all and it is essential to understand that the distortion lies in the phrase "nothing but" and not in the identification Lesbian. "Nothing but" reduces Lesbians to a category of beings deserving of only the most violent attack, a category totally alien from "decent" Black folks, i.e., not your sisters, mothers, daughters, aunts, and cousins, but bizarre outsiders like no one you know or *ever* knew.

Many of the most committed and outspoken feminists of color have been and are Lesbians. Since many of us are also radicals, our politics, as indicated by the issues merely outlined above, encompass all people. We're also as Black as we ever were. (I always find it fascinating, for example, that many of the Black Lesbian-feminists I know still wear their hair natural, indicating that for us it was more than a "style.") Black feminism and Black Lesbianism are not interchangeable. Feminism is a political movement and many Lesbians are not feminists. Although it is also true that many Black feminists are not Lesbians, this myth has acted as an accusation and a deterrent to keep non-Lesbian Black feminists from manifesting themselves, for fear it will be hurled against them.

Fortunately this is changing. Personally, I have seen increasing evidence that many Black women of whatever sexual preference are more concerned with exploring and ending our oppression than they are committed to being either homophobic or sexually separatist. . . .

Home Truths

Above are some of the myths that have plagued Black feminism. The truth is that there is a vital movement of women of color in this country. Despite continual resistance to women of color defining our specific issues and organizing around them, it is safe to say in 1982 that we have a movement of our own. I have been involved in building that movement since 1973. It has been a struggle every step of the way and I feel we are still in just the beginning stages of developing a workable politics and practice. Yet the feminism of women of color, particularly of Afro-American women, has wrought many changes during these years, has had both obvious and unrecognized impact upon the development of other political groupings and upon the lives and hopes of countless women.

The very nature of radical thought and action is that it has exponentially far-reaching results. But because all forms of media ignore Black women, in particular Black feminists, and because we have no widely distributed communication mechanisms of our own, few know the details of what we have accomplished. The story of our work and contributions remains untold. One of the purposes of *Home Girls* is to get the word out about Black feminism to the people who need it most: Black people in the U.S., the Caribbean, Latin America, Africa—everywhere. It is not possible for a single introduction or a single book to encompass all of what Black feminism is, but there is basic information I want every reader to have about the meaning of Black feminism as I have lived and understood it.

In 1977, a Black feminist organization in Boston of which I was a member from its founding in 1974, the Combahee River Collective, drafted a political statement for our own use and for inclusion in Zillah Eisenstein's anthology, *Capitalist Patriarchy and the Case for Socialist Feminism*. In our opening paragraph we wrote:

> The most general statement of our politics at the present time would be that we are actively committed to struggling against racial, sexual, heterosexual, and class oppression and see as our particular task the development of integrated analysis and practice based upon the fact that the major systems of oppression are interlocking. The synthesis of these oppressions creates the conditions of our lives. As Black women we see Black feminism as the logical political movement to combat the manifold and simultaneous oppressions that all women of color face.

The concept of the simultaneity of oppression is still the crux of a Black feminist understanding of political reality and, I believe, one of the most significant ideological contributions of Black feminist thought.

We examined our own lives and found that everything out there was kicking our behinds—race, class, sex, and homophobia. We saw no reason to rank oppressions, or, as many forces in the Black community would have us do, to pretend that sexism, among all the "isms," was not happening to us. Black feminists' efforts to comprehend the complexity of our situation as it was actually occurring, almost immediately began to deflate some of the cherished myths about Black womanhood, for example, that we are "castrating matriarchs" or that we are more economically privileged than Black men. Although we made use of the insights of other political ideologies, such as socialism, we added an element that has often been missing from the theory of others: what oppression is comprised of on a day-to-day basis, or as Black feminist musician Linda Tillery sings, ". . . what it's really like/To live this life of triple jeopardy."[9]

This multi-issued approach to politics has probably been most often used by other women of color who face very similar dynamics, at least as far as institutionalized oppression is concerned. It has also altered the women's movement as a whole. As a result of Third World feminist organizing, the women's movement now takes much more seriously the necessity for a multi-issued strategy for challenging women's oppression. The more progressive elements of the left have also begun to recognize that the promotion of sexism and homophobia within their ranks, besides being ethically unconscionable, ultimately undermines their ability to organize. Even a few Third World organizations have begun to include the challenging of women's and gay oppression on their public agendas.

Approaching politics with a comprehension of the simultaneity of oppressions has helped to create a political atmosphere particularly conducive to coalition building. Among all feminists, Third World women have undoubtedly felt most viscerally the need for linking struggles and have also been most capable of forging such coalitions. A commitment to principled coalitions, based not upon expediency, but upon our actual need for each other is a second major contribution of Black feminist struggle. Many contributors to *Home Girls* write out of a sense of our ultimate interdependence. Bernice Johnson Reagon's essay, "Coalition Politics: Turning the Century," should be particularly noted. She writes:

> You don't go into coalition because you just *like* it. The only reason you would consider trying to team up with somebody who could possibly kill you, is because that's the only way you can figure you can stay alive. . . . Most of the time you feel threatened to the core and if you don't you're not really doing no coalescing.

The necessity for coalitions has pushed many groups to rigorously examine the attitudes and ignorance within themselves which prevent coalitions from succeeding. Most notably, there has been the commitment of some white feminists to make racism a priority issue within the women's movement, to take responsibility for their racism as individuals, and to do antiracist organizing in coalition with other groups. Because I have written and spoken about racism during my entire involvement as a feminist and have also presented workshops on racism for white women's organizations for several years during the 1970s, I have not only seen that there are white women who are fully committed to eradicating racism, but that new understandings of racial politics have evolved from feminism, which other progressive people would do well to comprehend.[10]

Having begun my political life in the Civil Rights movement and having seen the Black liberation movement virtually destroyed by the white power structure, I have been encouraged in recent years that women can be a significant force for bringing about racial change in a way that unites oppressions instead of isolating them. At the same time the percentage of white feminists who are concerned about racism is still a minority of the movement, and even within this minority those who are personally sensitive and completely serious about formulating an *activist* challenge to racism are fewer still. Because I have usually worked with politically radical feminists, I know that there are indeed white women worth building coalitions with, at the same time that there are apolitical, even reactionary, women who take the name of feminism in vain.

One of the greatest gifts of Black feminism to ourselves has been to make it a little easier simply to *be* Black and female. A Black feminist analysis has enabled us to understand that we are not hated and abused because there is something wrong with us, but because our status and treatment is absolutely prescribed by the racist, misogynistic system under which we live. There is not a Black woman in this country who has not, at some time, internalized and been deeply scarred by the hateful propaganda about us. There is not a Black woman in America who has not felt, at least once, like "the mule of the world," to use Zora Neale Hurston's still apt phrase.[11] Until Black feminism, very few people besides Black women actually cared about or took seriously the demoralization of being female *and* colored *and* poor *and* hated.

When I was growing up, despite my family's efforts to explain, or at least describe, attitudes prevalent in the outside world, I often thought that there was something fundamentally wrong with me because it was obvious that me and everybody like me was held in such contempt. The cold eyes of certain white teachers in school, the Black men who yelled from cars as Beverly and I stood waiting for the bus, convinced me that I must have done something horrible. How was I to know that racism and sexism had formed a blueprint for my mistreatment long before I had ever arrived here? As with most Black women, others' hatred of me became self-hatred, which has diminished over the years, but has by no means disappeared. Black feminism has, for me and for so many others, given us the tools to finally comprehend that it is not something we have done that has heaped this psychic violence and material abuse upon us, but the very fact that, because of who we are, we are multiply oppressed. Unlike any other movement, Black feminism provides the theory that clarifies the nature of Black women's experience, makes possible positive support from other Black women, and encourages political action that will change the very system that has put us down.

The accomplishments of Black feminism have been not only in developing theory, but in day-to-day organizing. Black feminists have worked on countless issues, some previously identified with the feminist movement and others that we, ourselves, have defined as priorities. Whatever issues we have committed ourselves to, we have approached them with a comprehensiveness and pragmatism which exemplify the concept "grassroots." If nothing else, Black feminism deals in home truths, both in analysis and in action. Far from being irrelevant or peripheral to Black people, the issues we have focused on touch the basic core of our community's survival.

Some of the issues we have worked on are reproductive rights, equal access to abortion, sterilization abuse, health care, child care, the rights of the disabled, violence against women, rape, battering, sexual harassment, welfare rights, Lesbian and gay rights, educational reform, housing, legal reform, women in prison, aging, police brutality, labor organizing, anti-imperialist struggles, anti-racist organizing, nuclear disarmament, and preserving the environment. Frustratingly, it is not even possible to know all the work Black and other Third World women have done, because as I've already stated, we have no consistent means of communication, no national Third World feminist newspaper, for example, that would link us across geographic boundaries. It is obvious, however, that with every passing year, more and more explicitly feminist organizing is being done by women of color. There are many signs:

- Women of color have been heavily involved in exposing and combatting sterilization abuse on local, state, and national levels. . . .
- For a number of years, health issues, including reproductive freedom, have been a major organizing focus. . . .
- Black and other Third World women have been centrally involved in all aspects of organizing to combat violence against women. Many women of color first became involved in the women's movement through this work, particularly working/volunteering in battered women's shelters. . . .
- Third World women are organizing around women's issues globally. Activists in the Caribbean, Latin America, Africa, India, New Zealand, England, and many other places are addressing issues which spring simultaneously from

sexist, heterosexist, racist, imperialist, and economic oppression. Some of these individuals and groups specifically identify as feminist. . . .

- A number of Black and Third World Lesbian organizations are addressing a variety of issues as "out" Lesbians, such as Salsa Soul Sisters in New York City and Sapphire Saphos in Washington, D.C. They are doing education and challenging homophobia in their various communities as well as working on issues that affect Lesbians, women, and people of color generally. . . .
- Black feminist cultural work is flourishing, particularly in literature and in music. . . .

We have done much. We have much to do. Undoubtedly the most pressing work before us is to build our own autonomous institutions. It is absolutely crucial that we make our visions real in a permanent form so that we can be even more effective and reach many more people. I would like to see rape crisis centers, battered women's shelters, women's centers, periodicals, publishers, buying co-operatives, clinics, artists' collectives, and ongoing political organizations started and run by women of color. The Third World Women's Archives and Kitchen Table: Women of Color Press, both founded in 1981, are examples of institutions controlled by women of color. We need more. I believe that everything is possible. But there are challenges we face as Black feminists that we can neither bury nor ignore.

Challenges

By challenges I do not mean what we face from out there, the familiar insults and "isms," I want to write about the challenges we face in each other, to broach the subject of accountability in Black women. The raw material comes directly from my life, especially those excruciating places where I have abandoned, and been abandoned by, other women, when our anger about our differences seemed insurmountable, and we gave up on each other. Writing this is frightening because I must mention things about which I know we disagree. It is not the first time.

I was an outsider when I was growing up. I am still not sure of all the reasons. From an early age Bev and I were very shy, or as the Black ladies who tried to coax us to talk called it, "bashful." My over-protective, old-fashioned grandmother, who was primarily in charge of me until I started high school, never let me stray too far from home. In school I was quiet and "too smart" to win the approval of anybody except the other "too smart" Black girls, who formed a solid little core in elementary school at least. I was already serious and inward-turning, but when my mother died when I was nine, whatever trust I had in the workings of the world evaporated. Besides her loss, I felt as if everybody knew about the tragedy that had befallen me and saw me as an object of pity, which I, of course, despised. Looking back on those years, I realize that I was in a state of constant fury. I was furious that such a horrible thing could have happened to me and that I had absolutely no say-so about it. Adolescence was worse, a time when my awkwardness increased, my anger became less easy to conceal, and not fitting in became a crime. No matter what I did or how I tried to disappear, my classmates could sense something fundamentally unsettling about me. They knew that I was different.

Difference is at the crux of the challenges I am writing about here. Without Audre Lorde, who has so often examined in her work the implications of difference, I would not understand nearly as well the positive and negative power difference can have among us. Lorde writes:

> As women, we have been taught to either ignore our differences or to view them as causes for separation and suspicion rather than as forces for change. Without community, there is no liberation, only the most vulnerable and temporary armistice between an individual and her oppression. But community must not mean a shedding of our differences, not the pathetic pretense that these differences do not exist.[12]

Although these remarks were made to a predominantly white, straight, academic audience to alert them to the racism, classism, and homophobia which pervade their perceptions, Lorde's words have at least equal resonance for us, "between ourselves."[13]

Black women, especially those of us who are feminists and/or Lesbians, are not supposed to differ with each other. We may revel in our nonconformity vis-à-vis the world at large and any fool looking at us could tell us how unique each of us is. But, perhaps because there are not that many Black women who view both their racial and sexual identities politically, a tacit assumption exists that we must be fundamentally alike and, at all costs, we must not disagree. There is a kind of conformity that is typical of the Black community, perhaps because we have so often had to define ourselves in opposition to our opppressors, that we as Black feminists are also no doubt heir to. We transform cultural beliefs and habits that may indeed characterize many of us into requirements and use them as proof of our own and others' full membership in the race.

I will never forget the period of Black nationalism, power, and pride which, despite its benefits, had a stranglehold on our identities. A blueprint was made for being Black and Lord help you if you deviated in the slightest way. I'm sure many Black women reading this hardly fit during those times. How relieved we were to find, as our awareness increased and our own Black women's movement grew, that we were not crazy, that the brothers had in fact created a sex-biased definition of "Blackness" that served only them. And yet, in finding each other, some of us have fallen into the same pattern—have decided that if a sister doesn't dress like me, talk like me, walk like me, and even sleep like me, then she's really not a sister. Conformity. I am not saying that any particular group of Black women does this more than others, because at times we can all fall prey to the "jugular vein" mentality, as Lorde terms it, and want to kill or erase from our universe anyone unlike us.

But how do we meet the challenge of what is not known? How do we avoid, when threatened, falling back on the easiest of solutions? I have often addressed the pitfalls of Lesbian separatism as practiced by mostly white women, which makes an ideology out of distance and the exclusion of the "other," even if that "other" is ostensibly their white male oppressor. But I am even more disturbed by the racial separatism of some Black women. Although I understand the compelling motivations for not wanting to deal constantly with those who oppress us—the desire that we all have for some peace—separatism as a strategy often takes a "to hell with it" stance as opposed to a directly confrontational one. Instead of working to challenge the system and to transform it, many separatists wash their hands of it and the system continues on its merry way. Political change is difficult. Sometimes it seems impossible, but it will not come about, as Bernice Johnson Reagon puts it, inside our "little barred rooms." Reagon's words about coalitions, her warning to watch out for "mono-issued people," have just as much meaning for Black women as for anybody else.

Autonomy and separatism are fundamentally different. Whereas autonomy comes from a position of strength, separatism comes from a position of fear. When we're truly autonomous we can deal with other kinds of people, a multiplicity of issues, and with difference, because we have formed a solid base of strength with those with whom we share identity and/or political commitment. Often, Black women who adopt racial separatism as an ideology say that we must take that position because, if we don't, white women (and even non-Afro-American women of color) will take over "our" movement. It is hard for me to conceive of this. Although racist white women may temporarily undermine our efforts or annoy us with their ignorance, they cannot sway us if we are actually autonomous and independent. They can neither tell us what to do nor stop us from doing it. The weakest white women in the movement are those who are most racist and self-serving. They may play power games for the moment, but their effect is quite limited. Political experience enables us to avoid them and to determine how and with whom to form coalitions worth making. As for other Third World women usurping "our" movement, *understand that movements are not owned and that ethnocentrism is ethnocentrism no matter whose face it wears.*

Black women can legitimately choose not to work with white women. What is not legitimate is ostracizing other Black women who have not made the same choice. The worst effect of separatism is not upon whomever we define as "enemy," but upon ourselves as it isolates us from each other. I have seen the wreckage of these sister-to-sister rejections far too many times. In "Lesbianism as an Act of Resistance," Cheryl Clarke writes:

> I personally am tired of going to events, conferences, workshops, planning sessions that involve a coming together of black and other lesbians of color for political or even social reasons and listening to black lesbians relegate feminism to white women, castigate black women who propose forming coalitions with predominantly white feminist groups, minimize the white woman's oppression and exaggerate her power, and then finally judge that a black lesbian's commitment to the liberation of black women is dubious because she does not sleep with a black women. All of us have to accept or reject allies on the basis of politics not on the specious basis of skin color. *Have not black people suffered betrayal from our own people?*[14]

We can be so cruel to each other for so many reasons; this cruelty is something we must begin to examine and diminish. Eradicating it is one aspect of Black women's accountability.

Another challenge closely linked to these issues is our relationship with other women of color. To me, the single most enlivening and hopeful development in the 1980s has been the emergence of so many Third World feminists. Often, both Black and white women in the U.S. have equated the term "Third World" with "Afro-American." This collapsing of identities has created falseness in our own understandings and in those of white women, who are unable to make distinctions. Like Black women, Native American, Asian American, and Latina women are involved in autonomous organizing at the same time that we are beginning to find each other. Certainly *This Bridge Called My Back: Writings by Radical Women of Color* co-edited by Cherríe Moraga and Gloria Anzaldúa, has been a document of and a catalyst for these coalitions. I think that more than any other single work, *This Bridge* has made the vision of Third World feminism real. But with the reality of connection among women of color, we confront again the fact of difference. In the introduction to the section of *This Bridge* which deals with differences, "Between the Lines: On Culture, Class, and Homophobia" Cherríe Moraga writes:

> What lies between the lines are the things that women of color do not tell each other. There are reasons for our silences: the change in generation between mother and daughter, the language barriers between us, our sexual identity, the educational opportunities we had or missed, the specific cultural history of our race, the physical conditions of our bodies and the labor. . . .
>
> We begin by speaking directly to the deaths and disappointments. Here we begin to fill in the spaces of silence between us. For it is between these seemingly irreconcilable lines—the class lines, the politically correct lines, the daily lines we run down to each other to keep difference and desire at a distance—that the truth of our connection lies.[15]

Like many Black women, I know very little about the lives of other Third World women. I want to know more and I also want to put myself in situations where I *have* to learn. It isn't easy because, for one thing, I keep discovering how deep my own prejudice goes. I feel so very American when I realize that simply by being Black I have not escaped the typical American ways of perceiving people who are different from myself. For example, I catch myself falling back on stereotypes in order to feel less awkward in a cultural context unfamiliar to me or I make chauvinistic assumptions about the "universal" accessibility of the English language. I also have been stymied at times by other Third World women's verifiably negative attitudes toward Black people, the fact that some of them have also bought the culture's values about race. We all have work to do and changing is a true challenge. In my own favor, I hope, is that I have a thorough knowledge of what it feels like to be dismissed because of one's physical being, language, and culture. I also rely on the inspiration I get from glimpsing the possibilities that bridging our differences as women of color holds. We cannot permit separatism or fear to deny those possibilities or to crush that future.

Some issues being raised in the context of the larger women's movement also present challenges. The growth of Jewish feminist organizing and the exposure of anti-Semitism in the women's movement must be supported by Black and other Third World women. Whatever the convoluted and painful history between Black and Jewish people in particular, anti-Semitism is real; it is one form of actual oppression. It is our responsibility to understand and oppose it. The devastating situation in the Middle East, Israel's policies there, and the reality that there are Jews who have undeniably functioned as racists do not justify anti-Semitism. We might also keep in mind that although the majority of Jews in America are of European background, there are Jews in the U.S., the Middle East, Ethiopia, and elsewhere, who are people of color and victims of anti-Semitism.

In response to a confrontation between Jewish and Third World women at the 1981 New England Women's Studies Association conference, Cherríe Moraga, Julia Pérez, Beverly Smith, and I wrote the following, in a letter to *Gay Community-News*:

> As women of color, we feel it's essential to examine our own understanding about how oppression works in this country. It's often hard for us to believe that we can be both oppressed and oppressive at the same time. Anti-Jewish feelings on the part of women of color and racism on the part of Jewish women are examples of this very reality. (Those of us who are Lesbians know very well that the most personally devastating homophobia comes from straight people within our own communities, to name another example of the oppressed being oppressive.) We are not trying to side-step the pervasive fact of color oppression in this country and are committed to confronting white racism, whether practiced by Jews or non-Jews. However, we feel it is critical for women of color not to fall into the trap of countering racism on the part of Jews with anti-Semitism. . . .
>
> We don't have to be the same to have a movement, but we *do* have to admit our fear and pain and be accountable for our ignorance. In the end, finally, we must refuse to give up on each other.[16]

I have seen some Black women be blatantly anti-Semitic with a self-righteousness they would probably not exhibit in any other case. I have also seen some Jewish women single out Black women as anti-Semitic, with a depth of accusation that would make it appear that non-Jewish Black people are more responsible for Jewish oppression than the white gentile power structure. Letty Cottin Pogrebin's recent "Anti-Semitism in the Women's Movement" evidences such an attitude. She writes:

> Many Jewish women specifically resent that for years, they have talked openly about "confronting" their racism, while with a few noteworthy exceptions black women's anti-Semitism has been largely unmentionable.[17]

White Jewish women who are aware of, and sensitive to, the implications that *both* racism and anti-Semitism have for forming fruitful alliances can best encourage Black and other Third World women's comprehension of, and accountability to-ward, the issue of anti-Semitism. But I am more concerned with the responses of other Black women and I question whom it serves when we permit internal hostility to tear the movement we have built apart. Who benefits most? Undoubtedly, those outside forces that will go to any length to see us fail.[18]

Another issue which is currently causing a great deal of turmoil in the women's movement is sexuality. I do not mean by *sexuality* a mere euphemism for Lesbian-ism. A furious debate is being staged as to what is acceptable or unacceptable sexual

behavior, period—whether Lesbian or heterosexual. In other words, sex itself—
how women experience or fantasize sexual pleasure—is at the core of the controversy, along with an examination of what values we attach to it.

Until now, Black women have been peripheral to these debates and I am not sure
that it will be helpful to us to step into the middle of "white-rooted interpretations"
of these issues.[19] And yet, the existence and outspokenness of some women who are
making principled explorations of desire, need, identity, and power have pushed me
to examine my own reluctance to look at sexuality as a Black woman. It seems so
terrifying to me to talk about these things, coming from a home and culture where
sexual matters of any kind were seldom discussed, at least across the generations.
Black women have traditionally been reluctant to talk about sex with their daughters. "Keep your dress down and your drawers up," is a homily of this reticence. At
the very same time, all Black women have been viewed as sexual animals by the
society as a whole and at times by Black men as well. In such a charged context,
considering the dimensions of Lesbian sexuality has been totally taboo. Sexual
repression, coupled with blatant sexual exploitation, has contributed to a complex
psychological mix. Who knows what we think and, more importantly, feel? But it
is up to us, with each other's help, to find out. Such a dialogue will only enrich us
and our movement and ultimately strengthen our defense against increasing sexual
exploitation. The better we understand ourselves, the less vulnerable we are to other
people's violent interpretations of our sexual motives and behavior.

Since Black Lesbian issues are addressed in a variety of ways in this anthology, I
had not planned to bring up this last area of difference, the divisions caused by
homophobia. A few days ago, however, as I was working on this introduction, the
homophobia of Black women against Black women once more brought me low and
I decided I wanted to get very specific about the constant level of attack all Lesbians
and gay men face.

Most readers know, at least theoretically, what homophobia is. Cheryl Clarke's
"The Failure to Transform: Homophobia in the Black Community" astutely analyzes many of its dimensions. What I think many heterosexual Black people don't
know, and don't want to know, is the toll homophobia takes on a day-to-day basis.
Too many pretend that Lesbian and gay oppression is an inconsequential matter,
not a real oppression, one that could easily be alleviated by merely being "discreet"
or, better still, by "reforming" completely. Don't bring it up, be closeted. In other
words, become straight. . . .

When someone asks, "Why do you have to bring it up? Why can't you just do
whatever you want in the privacy of your own home?" they are ignoring oppression. They are, in fact, suggesting that we not exist.

I am more than a little tired of Black women who say they are political, who say
they are feminists, who rely on Black Lesbians' friendship, insights, commitment,
and work, but who, when it comes down to the crunch and the time to be accountable, turn their backs. The oppression that affects Black gay people, female and
male, is pervasive, constant, and not abstract. Some of us die from it. I've already
said, "There's nothing to compare with how you feel when you're cut cold by your

own."[20] I guess I'll keep on saying it until some other Black women who are not Lesbians begin with compassion to say it too.

The gulfs between us hurt and they are deeply rooted in the facts of difference. Class and color differences between Black women have divided us since slavery. We have yet to explore how riddled we are by this pain. Not surprisingly, antagonisms over class and color operate among Black feminists, but unfortunately more back-biting has occurred about it than thoughtfulness or healing. But who better than Black feminists to take on the challenge of exposing and analyzing these centuries old chasms? In December of 1981 I wrote in my journal:

> And then I think of the eighty-nine year old Black woman who Sharon interviewed for her dissertation. A "domestic" who had lost a finger in a laundry accident; who still rode three buses every day to get back and forth to her job, her home. I imagine her poverty, her loneliness, the depths of her faith and perhaps her capacity to love and I think: Wasn't this movement supposed to be about her? Wasn't it?

Color, class, age, sexual identity, religion, politics, and the fact that sometimes we plain do not agree result in undeniable differences. The question is whether we will let these differences kill our movement. It would not be the first time, yet I fervently hope that for us it will not come to this. We can take courage from Lorde's words:

> *I urge each one of us here to reach down into that deep place of knowledge inside herself and touch that terror and loathing of any difference that lives there. See whose face it wears.* Then the personal as the political can begin to illuminate all our choices.[21]

NOTES

1. Russell, Michele. "Slave Codes and Liner Notes," in *All the Women Are White, All the Blacks Are Men, but Some of Us Are Brave: Black Women's Studies,* eds. Hull, Scott & Smith. Old Westbury, N.Y.: Feminist Press, 1982, pp. 132 and 133.

2. Gwaltney, John Langston. *Drylongso: A Self-Portrait of Black America.* New York: Random House, 1980, p. 167.

3. Walker, Alice. *In Search of Our Mother's Gardens.* (Forthcoming, 1983.) Cited from manuscript, n.p.

4. The terms *Third World women* and *women of color* are used here to designate Native American, Asian American, Latina, and Afro-American women in the U.S. and the indigenous peoples of Third World countries wherever they may live. Both the terms *Third World women* and *women of color* apply to Black American women. At times in the introduction Black women are specifically designated as Black or Afro-American and at other times the terms *women of color* and *Third World women* are used to refer to women of color as a whole.

5. Smith, Barbara. "Notes for Yet Another Paper on Black Feminism, or Will the Real Enemy Please Stand Up?" in *Conditions: Five, The Black Women's Issue,* eds. Bethel & Smith, 2, no. 2 (Autumn, 1979), p. 124.

6. Du Bois, W. E. B. *Darkwater, Voices from Within the Veil.* New York: AMS Press, 1969, p. 185.

7. Teish, Luisah. "Women's Spirituality: A Household Act," in *Home Girls,* ed. Smith. Watertown, Mass.: Persephone Press, Inc., 1983. All subsequent references to work in *Home Girls* will not be cited.

8. See Linda C. Powell's review of Michele Wallace's *Black Macho and the Myth of the Super Woman* ("Black Macho and Black Feminism") in this volume and my review of bell hooks's (Gloria Watkins's) *Ain't I a Woman: Black Women and Feminism in New Women's Times Feminist Review* 9, no. 24 (November, 1982), pp. 10, 11, 18, 19 & 20 and in *Black Scholar* 14, no. 1 (January/February 1983), pp. 38–45.

9. Tillery, Linda. "Freedom Time," *Linda Tillery,* Oakland: Olivia Records, 1977, Tuizer Music.

10. Some useful articles on racism by white feminists are Elly Bulkin's "Racism and Writing: Some Implications for White Lesbian Critics." *Sinister Wisdom 13* (Spring, 1980), pp. 3–22; Minnie Bruce Pratt's "Rebellion." *Feminary* 11, nos. 1 & 2, (1980), pp. 6–20; and Adrienne Rich's "Disloyal to Civilization: Feminism, Racism, Gynephobia." *On Lies, Secrets and Silence: Selected Prose 1996–1978.* New York: W. W. Norton, 1979, pp. 275–310.

11. Hurston, Zora Neale. *Their Eyes Were Watching God.* Urbana: University of Illinois Press, 1937, 1978, p. 29.

12. Lorde, Audre. "The Master's Tools Will Never Dismantle the Master's House," in *This Bridge Called My Back: Writings by Radical Women of Color,* eds. Moraga and Anzaldúa. Watertown: Persephone Press, Inc., 1981, p. 99.

13. "Between Ourselves" is the title of a poem by Lorde which appears in her book *The Black Unicorn.* New York: W. W. Norton, 1978, pp. 112–114. This poem also appeared in an earlier volume by the title, *Between Our Selves.* Point Reyes, Calif.: Eidolon Editions, 1976.

14. Clarke, Cheryl. "Lesbianism as an Act of Resistance," in *This Bridge,* p. 135.

15. Moraga, Cherríe. In Moraga and Anzaldúa, *This Bridge,* pp. 105 & 106.

16. Moraga, Cherríe et al., *Gay Community News* 8, no. 32, (March 7, 1981), p. 4.

17. Pogrebin, Letty Cottin. "Anti-Semitism in the Women's Movement," in *Ms.* 9, no. 12 (June, 1982), p. 70.

18. See " 'The Possibility of Life Between Us': A Dialogue Between Black and Jewish Women," ed. Beverly Smith with Judith Stein and Priscilla Golding in *Conditions: Seven* 3, no. 1 (Spring, 1981), pp. 25–46.

19. Moraga, Cherríe. "Played between White Hands: A Response to the Barnard Sexuality Conference Coverage," in *Off Our Backs* 12, no. 7 (July, 1982), p. 23.

20. Smith, Barbara, and Beverly Smith. "Across the Kitchen Table: A Sister-to-Sister Dialogue," in Moraga and Anzaldúa, *This Bridge,* p. 124.

21. Lorde, Audre. In Moraga and Anzaldúa, *This Bridge,,* p. 101.

Chapter Nineteen

The Occult of True Black Womanhood
Critical Demeanor and Black Feminist Studies

Ann duCille

*The Black Woman; The Black Woman: An Anthology;
The Black Woman in America; The Black Woman in
American Society; The Black Woman Cross-Culturally;
Black Women in America; Black Women in White
America; Black Women in the Nineteenth Century;
Black Women in Nineteenth-Century American Life;
Black Women Writers; Black Women Writers at Work;
Black Women Writing Autobiography; Black Women
Writing the American Experience; Black Women Nov-
elists; Black Women Novelists in the Wake of the Civil
Rights Movement; Black Women, Fiction, and Literary
Tradition; The Sexual Mountain and Black Women
Writers; Ain't I a Woman; Arn't I a Woman*

For reasons that may already be obvious, the books named above and numerous others like them have led me to think of myself as a kind of sacred text. Not me personally, of course, but me black woman object, Other. Within and around the modern academy, racial and gender alterity has become a hot commodity that has claimed black women as its principal signifier. I am alternately pleased, puzzled, and perturbed—bewitched, bothered, and bewildered—by this, by the alterity that is perpetually thrust upon African American women, by the production of black women as infinitely deconstructable "othered" matter. Why are black women always already Other? I wonder. To myself, of course, I am not Other; to me it is the white women and men so intent on theorizing my difference who are the Other. Why are they so interested in me and people who look like me (metaphorically speaking)? Why have we—black women—become the subjected subjects of so much contemporary scholarly investigation, the peasants under glass of intellectual inquiry in the 1990s?

Abridged by permission from *Signs: Journal of Women in Culture and Society* 19, no. 3 Spring 1994): 591–629. Copyright © 1994, University of Chicago Press.

The attention is not altogether unpleasant, especially after generations of neglect, but I am hardly alone in suspecting that the overwhelming interest in black women may have at least as much to do with the pluralism and perhaps even the primitivism of this particular postmodern moment as with the stunning quality of black women's accomplishments and the breadth of their contributions to American civilization. It is not news that by virtue of our race and gender, black women are not only the "second sex"—*the Other,* in postmodern parlance—but we are also the last race, the most oppressed, the most marginalized, the most deviant, the quintessential site of difference. And through the inversionary properties of deconstruction, feminism, cultural studies, multiculturalism, and contemporary commodity culture, the last shall be first. Perhaps.

I say *perhaps* because we have experienced the problematic of such inversions before: the preoccupation with black women, with the blues, the black folk, the authentic, the real colored thing in the 1920s, for example, a preoccupation fueled at least in part by the primitivist proclivities of the historical moment. In the twenties, the fascination with the black female body, in particular, and the primitive sexual anatomy and appetite attributed to the African woman increased the degree to which the black female functioned as an erotic icon in the racial and sexual ideology of Western civilization.

Black feminist theorist bell hooks calls the contemporary version of this preoccupation with alterity "the commodification of Otherness" or "eating the Other." "Within commodity culture," she writes in *Black Looks,* "ethnicity becomes spice, seasoning that can liven up the dull dish that is mainstream white culture." Mass culture, then, in hooks's view, perpetuates the primitivistic notion "that there is pleasure to be found in the acknowledgment and enjoyment of racial difference" (1992, 21).

Where gender and racial difference meet in the bodies of black women, the result is the invention of an other Otherness, a hyperstatic alterity. Mass culture, as hooks argues, produces, promotes, and perpetuates the commodification of Otherness through the exploitation of the black female body. In the 1990s, however, the principal sites of exploitation are not simply the cabaret, the speakeasy, the music video, the glamour magazine; they are also the academy, the publishing industry, the intellectual community. In the words of black male theorist Houston Baker, who is among those who have recently taken up African American women (and taken on black feminist critics): "Afro-American women's expressivity and the analyses that it has promoted during the past two decades represent the most dramatically charged field for the convergence of matters of race, class, and gender today" (1991, 1–2). Of course, one of the dangers of standing at an intersection— particularly at such a suddenly busy, three-way intersection—is the likelihood of being run over by oncoming traffic.

Michele Wallace likens the traffic jam that has built up around Zora Neale Hurston, in particular, to a "rainbow coalition" of critics, who, "like groupies descending on Elvis Presley's estate," are engaged in "a mostly ill-mannered stampede to have some memento of the black woman" (1990, 174), who is, at least to some degree, a figment of their individual and collective critical imaginations.

Precisely the question I want to explore in this essay is what it means for black women academics to stand in the midst of the "dramatically charged field"—the traffic jam—that black feminist studies has become. Are we in the way of the critical stampede that accompanies what I am calling here "the occult of true black womanhood"? Are we in danger of being trampled by the "rainbow coalition" of critics—"black, white, male, female, artists and academics, historicists and deconstructionists"—that our own once isolated and isolating intellectual labors have attracted to the magnetic field of black feminist studies? . . .

Within the realm of literary studies alone, the names making up even a partial list of pioneering black feminist scholars are, as Houston Baker has said, "legion" (1991, 10): Deborah McDowell, Nellie McKay, Hortense Spillers, Gloria Hull, Patricia Bell Scott, Cheryl Wall, Valerie Smith, Mae Henderson, Gloria Wade-Gayles, Thadious Davis, Trudier Harris, Frances Smith Foster, Hazel Carby, Joyce Joyce, and Claudia Tate, as well as Christian, Washington, Smith, and many many others.[1] Both as an inspiration to aspiring young black women writers and as an editor at Random House in the 1970s, Toni Morrison, too, has played a particularly dramatic role in opening up spaces for and directing critical attention toward African American women.

While I, as a beneficiary of their research and writing, am anxious to give credit where credit is long overdue, this essay is not intended as a praisesong for black women scholars, critics, and artists, or even as a review of the literature they have generated.[2] Rather, I would like to examine critically some of the implications and consequences of the current explosion of interest in black women as literary and historical subjects. Among the issues I hope to explore are the ways in which this interest—which seems to me to have reached occult status—increasingly marginal-izes both the black women critics and scholars who excavated the fields in question and their black feminist "daughters" who would further develop those fields.

What does it mean, for example, that many prestigious university presses and influential literary publications such as the *New York Times Book Review* regularly rely not on these seasoned black women scholars but on male intellectuals—black and white—to read, evaluate, and review the book manuscripts of young black women just entering the profession? What does it mean for the black female profes-soriate that departments often ask powerful senior black male scholars to referee the tenure and promotion cases of the same black women scholars who have challenged or affronted these men in some way? What does it mean for the field in general and for junior African Americanists in particular that senior scholars, who are not trained in African American studies and whose career-building work often has excluded (or at least not included) black women, are now teaching courses in and publishing texts about African American literature and generating supposedly "new scholarship" on black women writers? What does it mean for the future of black feminist studies that a large portion of the growing body of scholarship on black women is now being written by white feminists and by men whose work frequently achieves greater critical and commercial success than that of the black female scholars who carved out a field in which few "others" were then interested?

My questions are by no means new; nor do I claim to have any particular insightful answers. I only know that as an African Americanist who has been studying the literature and history of black women for almost thirty years and teaching it for more than twenty, I have a burning need to try to work through on paper my own ambivalence, antipathy, and, at times, animosity over the newfound enthusiasm for these fields that I readily—perhaps too readily—think of as my own hard-won territory. I feel a little like the parent who tells the child she is about to reprimand that "this hurts me more than it hurts you." But lest anyone think that this is an easily authored Portnoy's complaint in blackface—yet another black womanist indictment of white feminists who can do no right and men who can do only wrong—I want to make explicit my own dis-ease with the antagonism to which I have admitted and by which I am myself somewhat baffled.

Elsewhere I have argued against territoriality, against racial, cultural, and gender essentialism, against treating African American studies as the private property of what Gayatri Spivak calls "black blacks" (Spivak 1989).³ Yet questions of turf and territoriality, appropriation and co-optation persist within my own black feminist consciousness, despite my best efforts to intellectualize them away. Again, this is not a new dilemma. The modern, academic version of the ageless argument over who owns the sacred text of me and mine is at least as old as the work of white anthropologists Melville and Frances Herskovits dating back to the 1920s and reaching a controversial peak in 1941 with the publication of *The Myth of the Negro Past,* a study of African cultural retentions scorned by many black intellectuals (Herskovits [1928] 1985, 1938, 1941; Herskovits and Herskovits 1936). It was in the fifties, however, that white scholars began to loom large in the realm of black historiography and literary criticism, often receiving within the academy a kind of attention and credibility that the pioneering work of many black historians and literary critics had not enjoyed. Black historian Darlene Clark Hine noted in 1980 that "most of the highly-acclaimed historical works were, with few exceptions, written by white scholars." In fact, in her estimation, the legitimization of black history as a field proved a "bonanza for the [white] professional historians already in positions [as university professors and/or recognized scholars] to capitalize from the movement" (Hine 1980, 115, as quoted in Meier and Rudwick 1986, 294). . . .

Asked about the explosion of interest in the lives and literature of black women among male scholars and white feminists, Barbara Christian responded in part: "It is galling to me that after black women critics of the 1970s plowed the neglected field of Afro-American women's literature when such an act was academically dangerous, that some male and white feminist scholars now seem to be reaping the harvest and are major commentators on this literature in influential, though not necessarily feminist journals such as *The New York Review of Books.* Historical amnesia seems to be as much a feature of intellectual life as other aspects of American society" (Christian et al. 1990, 61).

Historical amnesia may displace her at any time, but for this moment anyway, the black woman writer has become a bonanza. Her near phenomenal popularity as subject matter has spawned a wealth of critical scholarship and has spontaneously generated scores of scholars determined to claim her material and cultural production—what Houston Baker calls "Afro-American women's expressivity"—as their intellectual discourse. But as Barbara Christian's remarks imply, black women's expressivity is not merely discourse; it has become lucre in the intellectual marketplace, cultural commerce. What for many began as a search for our mothers' gardens, to appropriate Alice Walker's metaphor (1974), has become for some a Random House harvest worth millions in book sales and prestigious university professorships. Sensitive as the issue is, it must be said at some point and even at the risk of hurt feelings that the explosion of interest in the black female subject is at least in some measure about economics—about jobs. White feminist scholar Elizabeth Abel has acknowledged as much. "This new attentiveness [to texts by women of color] has been overdetermined," she argues, "by the sheer brilliance and power of this writing and its escalating status in the literary marketplace and, consequently, the academy; [and] by white feminist restlessness with an already well-mined white female literary tradition" (1993, 478). For many scholars trained in these well-mined fields, the shift to African American studies has yielded more prominent positions at more prestigious institutions.

But is this, as it seems to be for Barbara Christian, necessarily a bitter harvest? We—"we" being here African American women scholars—have complained long and loud about exclusion, about the degree to which white feminists and male critics have ignored the work of black women. Can we now legitimately complain that they are taking up (and taking over?) this important work? And what do such complaints tell us about ourselves and our relationship to what many of us continue to speak of as *our* literature?[4] . . .

Undeniably critical contributions to the study of black women and their literature and history have been made by scholars who are neither black nor female. The name of William L. Andrews comes to mind immediately, as does that of Robert Hemenway (Hemenway 1977; Andrews 1986). That we have increased access to the autobiographical writings of nineteenth-century African American women is due in part to Andrews's effort. That Hurston's work is now so readily accessible is due in no small measure not only to the efforts of black feminist writer Alice Walker, but also to those of white male scholar Robert Hemenway. Through the research and publishing efforts of white feminist scholar Jean Fagan Yellin and black male theorist Henry Louis Gates, to cite two other examples, we now have authentification of and access to two fundamental texts from the nineteenth century: Harriet Jacobs's *Incidents in the Life of a Slave Girl, Written by Herself* ([1861] 1987) and Harriet Wilson's *Our Nig* ([1859] 1983). Moreover, since 1988 the Schornburg Library of Nineteenth-Century Black Women Writers, of which Gates is general editor, has made available to critics and scholars dozens of previously lost texts. The recent work of white feminist scholar Elizabeth Ammons also represents a positive turn in literary studies. In its inter-cultural readings of works by African, Asian, Native, Jewish, and white American women, her book *Conflicting Stories: American Women Writers at the Turn into the Twentieth Century* (1992) represents a model we all would do well to follow.

Surely this is great work and good news. Why, then, am I and so many other black feminist scholars left wrestling with such enduring questions about co-optation and exploitation? Why are we haunted by a growing sense that we are witnessing (and perhaps even have inspired in some way) the commodification of the same black womanhood we have championed? It is a mistake, I think, to define this persistent (but perhaps inherently unresolvable) debate over who can read black female texts as strictly or even perhaps primarily racial or cultural or gendered: black/white, male/female, insider/outsider, our literature/your theory, my familiar/their foreign. The most important questions, I have begun to suspect, may not be about the essentialism and territoriality, the biology, sociology, or even the ideology about which we hear so much but, rather, about professionalism and disciplinarity; about cultural literacy and intellectual competence; about taking ourselves seriously and insisting that we be taken seriously not as objectified subjects in someone else's histories—as native informants—but as critics and as scholars reading and writing our own literature and history.

Disciplinary Matters: When Demeanor Demeans

So I have arrived at what for me is at the heart of what's the matter. Much of the newfound interest in African American women that seems to honor the field of black feminist studies actually demeans it by treating it not like a discipline with a history and a body of rigorous scholarship and distinguished scholars underpinning it, but like an anybody-can-play pick-up game performed on a wide-open, untrammeled field. Often the object of the game seems to be to reinvent the intellectual wheel: to boldly go where in fact others have gone before, to flood the field with supposedly new "new scholarship" that evinces little or no sense of the discipline's genealogy. Moreover, many of the rules that the academy generally invokes in doing its institutional business—in making appointments, assigning courses, and advancing faculty—are suddenly suspended when what is at stake is not the valorized, traditional disciplines of Western civilization but the more marginal, if extremely popular, fields within African American studies.

Among those elements considered when English departments hire medievalists, Victorianists, Americanists, and so on, at least in my experience in the academy, are school(s) attended, the nature of one's graduate training, the subject of one's dissertation, and not only what one has published but where one has published as well. Were the articles refereed? Were they published in reputable academic journals? Are the journals discipline-specific, edited and juried by experts in the candidate's field, scholars who know whereof they read? I have seen these valorized criteria relaxed time and time again, however, when these same traditionally trained, nonblack scholars are being hired not in the fields in which they were educated but in African American studies. Interestingly enough, the same loosening of standards does not readily occur when black scholars—particularly young black scholars—apply for positions as generalists in American or world literature. The fact that the educational system is such that it is still largely impossible to specialize in African American literature without first being trained in the European and Anglo-American canons does not keep the powers that be from questioning the preparedness of blacks who apply for jobs as generalists. A dissertation on Toni Morrison or C. L. R. James or W. E. B. Du Bois does not necessarily qualify one as an Americanist, but a thesis on Chaucer or the Brontës or Byron is not an impediment to an appointment as an African Americanist.

Indeed, the question of who is authorized to teach African American discourse is riddled with ironies, paradoxes, and contradictions. Black scholars duly and properly trained and credentialed in traditional fields—medieval studies, for example— are often assumed or expected to be ready, willing, and able to teach black studies courses. African American studies programs and departments are not supposed to be intellectual ghettos populated exclusively by black scholars, particularly when white scholars want to enter such programs, but the field of African American studies often is treated like a black ghetto—like the one right and proper place for black intellectuals—when black scholars dare to step out of it, dare to be medievalists or classicists or British Victorianists.

Moreover, while many of our white colleagues and administrators may theorize African American and black feminist studies as open fields, as acquirable tastes ("You don't have to be one to teach one," as someone put it), this intellectual position often is not lived up to institutional practice. For when these same individuals want someone to provide a black reading of their work or black representation on a committee or black resources for their students or information about a particular black author or details about an event in black history, more times than not it is to black faculty that they turn, and not to the white Victorianists they have hired as African Americanists and have authorized to teach courses in black literature and history. . . .

Of course, my point is that for many of us, for many black women scholars, questioning the race, ethnicity, culture, and credentials of those the academy authorizes to write *our* histories and to teach and interpret *our* literature is anything but petty. Rather, it is a concern that rises from the deepest recesses of who we are in relation to where we live and work. Black women have pioneered a field that even after more than twenty years remains marginalized within the university, regardless of how popular both the field and its black women practitioners are with students. Our at once precarious and overdetermined positions in the academy and our intimate knowledge of social, intellectual, and academic history prompt us not simply to guard our turf, as often accused, but also to discipline *our* field, to preserve its integrity and our own.

I have emphasized the pronoun *our* in order to problematize the admitted possessiveness of our disciplinary concerns. For no matter how compelling—no matter how historically resonant—the sense of personal stake that permeates the scholarship by black women about black women just may be an aspect of the insider/outsider problematic for which African American women academics have to take responsibility. It may be time for us to interrogate in new and increasingly clinical ways our proprietary relationship to the field many of us continue to think of as *our own*.

Such internal review presents its own problematic, however. To claim privileged access to the lives and literature of African American women through what we hold to be the shared experiences of our black female bodies is to cooperate with our own commodification, to buy from and sell back to the dominant culture its constitution of our always already essentialized identity. On the other hand, to relinquish claim to the experiences of the black body and to confirm and affirm its study purely as discourse, simply as a field of inquiry equally open to all, is to collaborate with our own objectification. We become objects of study where we are authorized to be the story but have no special claim to decoding that story. We can be, but someone else gets to tell us what we mean.

This conundrum operates, of course, in realms beyond the either/or options I have established here. But how to find the middle ground, that happier medium? How do we negotiate an intellectually charged space for experience in a way that is not totalizing and essentializing—a space that acknowledges the constructedness of and the differences within our lived experiences while at the same time attending to the inclining, rather than the declining, significance of race, class, culture, and gender? . . .

Critical Apologia: The Driving Miss Daisy Crazy Syndrome

Yet. Still. And but. If a Ph.D. in British literature is not a title deed to the African American text, neither is black skin. Romantic fantasies of an authentic, cohesive, magical, ancient, all-knowing black female folk are certainly not unique to white academics who would read black women. Some might argue that what is at issue is not simply the color or culture of the scholar but the kind, quality, and cultural competence of the scholarship. Black historian Carter Woodson reportedly welcomed the contributions of white scholars, "so long as they were the products of rigorous scholarship and were not contaminated by the venom of racial [and, I would add, gender] bias" (quoted by Meier and Rudwick 1986, 289). Unfortunately, however, such biases are ideologically inscribed and institutionally reproduced and as such are not easily elided—not even by the most liberal, the most sensitive, the most well-intentioned among us. I think, for example, of Adrienne Rich.

I had long been a fan of Rich's poetry, but I was rather late in coming to her prose. Of Woman Born: Motherhood as Experience and Institution (1986), originally published in 1976, was more than a dozen years old before I gave myself the pleasure of reading it. For once, however, my timing could not have been better, for I "discovered" this essential book at a critical moment in my life and in the development of my feminism: on the eve of my fortieth birthday, as I wrestled with the likelihood of never having a child. Rich's brilliant analysis of motherhood as an instrument of patriarchy helped me come to terms with the constructedness of what I had been reared to believe were natural maternal instincts without which I was no woman. But for all that Rich's book gave me, it also took something away; and what it snatched from me, ironically and perhaps a little unfairly, has come to mean almost as much to me as what it gave.

For a moment in the penultimate chapter of this passionate and painful critique of motherhood, Rich turns her remarks toward the black woman who helped raise her. To this woman, who remains nameless, Rich assigns the designation "my Black mother." "My Black mother was 'mine,' " she writes, "only for four years, during which she fed me, dressed me, played with me, watched over me, sang to me, cared for me tenderly and intimately" ([1976] 1986, 254). Rich goes on to describe poetically the physical presence of her Black mother, from whom she "learned— *nonverbally*—a great deal about the possibilities of dignity in a degrading situation" (254; my emphasis). Unaware of the degrading situation she creates with her words, she continues: "When I began writting this chapter I began to remember my Black mother again: her calm, realistic vision of things, her physical grace and pride, her beautiful soft voice. For years, she had drifted out of reach, in my searches backward through time, exactly as the double silence of sexism and racism intended her to do. She was meant to be utterly annihilated" (254–55).

To the double silences of sexism and racism Rich adds a third; the silence (and the blindness) of feminism. . . . Adrienne Rich no doubt means to honor the woman who cared for her as a child. But the poetry of her prose should not disguise the paternal arrogance of her words or mask the annihilating effect of her claim on the being she resurrects and recreates as "my Black mother." Silent and nameless in Rich's book, "my Black mother" has no identity of her own and, in fact, does not exist beyond the care and nurture she gave exclusively to the young Adrienne.

" 'Childless' herself, she *was* a mother," Rich writes of her objectified subject. Her claim to "my Black mother" and her attempt to thrust motherhood upon a childless black woman domestic worker are all the more ironic because of what she claims for all women in the introduction to the anniversary edition of *Of Woman Born*: "The claim to personhood; the claim to share justly in the products of our labor, not to be used merely as an instrument, a role, a womb, a pair of hands or a back or a set of fingers; to participate fully in the decisions of our workplace, our community; to speak for ourselves, in our right" (xxviii). Even in the midst of her own extended critique of the mystification of motherhood and the objectification of women as mothers, Rich has both mystified and objectified someone she can see only in the possessive case as "my Black mother." "My Black mother" is a role, a pair of hands; her function is to instruct the white child "nonverbally" in the ways of the world, even as she cannot speak "in [her] own right."[5]

The kind of transformative move Rich makes in invoking the silent racial, maternalized Other is in no way unique to her prose. The child may be father of the man in poetry, but frequently when white scholars reminisce about blacks from their past it is black mammy (metaphorically speaking, even where the mammy figure is a man) who mothers the ignorant white infant into enlightenment. Often as the youthful, sometimes guilty witness to or cause of the silent martyrdom of the older, Other, the privileged white person inherits a wisdom, an agelessness, perhaps even a racelessness that entitles him or her to the raw materials of another's life and culture but, of course, not to the Other's condition.

Such transformative moves often occur in the forewords, afterwords, rationales, even apologias white scholars affix to their would-be scholarly readings of the black Other—discussions that methinks just may protest too much, perhaps suggesting a somewhat uneasy relationship between author and objectified subject. These prefaces acknowledge the "outsider" status of the authors—their privileged positions as white women or as men—even as they insist on the rightness of their entry into and the significance of their impact on the fields of black literature and history.

Gerda Lerner offers such a rationale in her preface to *Black Women in White America:* "Black people at this moment in history need above all to define themselves autonomously and to interpret their past, their present and their future" (1972, xviii). Having called upon the black "physician" to heal her/himself, Lerner then goes on to explain her presence in the operating room: "Certainly, historians who are members of the culture, or subculture, about which they write will bring a special quality to their material. Their understanding and interpretation is apt to be different from that of the outsider. On the other hand, scholars from outside a culture have frequently had a *more challenging vision* than those closely involved in and bound by their own culture. Both angles of vision are complementary in arriving at the truth about the past and in finding out 'what actually happened' " (xix; my emphasis). A more challenging vision? Why does the perspective of the white scholar reading "the black experience" represent a more challenging vision? . . .

I know I am misbehaving. I know I should be more patient, more sisterly, more respectful of other people's discoveries. I know my bad attitude comes from what in this instance might be called the arrogance of "black privilege": after all, I—whose earliest childhood memories include finding a snake in our mailbox shortly after we moved into an all-white neighborhood and being called "nigger" on my first day at an all-white elementary school—did not learn my racial consciousness from reading Richard Wright's "Big Boy Leaves Home" as an adult. But I mean my criticism as a kindness. Perhaps if I can approximate in words—however haltingly—what is so inexplicably problematic and profoundly offensive about these *Driving-Miss-Daisy*/some-of-my-best-friends-are-black/I-once-was-a-racist confessionals, I will do the field and all those who want to work in it a genuine favor. Perhaps if I can begin to delineate the difference between critical analysis that honors the field and guilty conscience rhetoric that demeans it, I can contribute something positive to the future production of scholarship on African American women. Unfortunately, the words do not come easily and the heart of what's the matter is a difficult place to get to. How do you tell people who do not get it in the first instance that it is only out of the arrogance of white privilege and/or male prerogative that they assume that it is an honor for a black woman to be proclaimed their black mother or their black friend or their black guardian or their black conscience? . . .

Toward a Conclusion

I am not quite certain what to make of the ground I have covered in this article or where to go from here. More bewitched, bothered, and bewildered than ever by my own problematic, I find myself oddly drawn to (gulp) William Faulkner. The griefs of great literature, Faulkner suggested in his Nobel Prize acceptance speech, must grieve on universal bones. I realize that I have heard this before—and not just from Faulkner. . . . In the words of three white feminist academics who claim to identify closely with the explicit depiction of physical and psychic abuse in the fiction of black women writers such as Toni Morrison, Alice Walker, and Gayl Jones: "We, as white feminists, are drawn to black women's visions because they concretize and make vivid a system of oppression." Indeed, they continue, "it has not been unusual for white women writers to seek to understand their oppression through reference to the atrocities experienced by other groups" (Sharpe, Mascia-Lee, and Cohen 1990, 146). . . . The lure of black women's fiction is, at least in part, its capacity to teach others how to endure and prevail, how to understand and rise above not necessarily the pain of black women but their own.

Is this usage of black women's texts a bad thing? If Faulkner is right—if it is the writer's duty to help humankind endure by reminding us of our capacity for courage and honor and hope and pride and compassion and pity and sacrifice and survival— black women writers have done the job particularly well. The griefs of African American women indeed seem to grieve on universal bones—"to concretize and make vivid a system of oppression." But it also seems (and herein lies the rub) that in order to grieve "universally," to be "concrete," to have "larger meaning," the flesh on these bones ultimately always must be white or male.

This, then, is the final paradox and the ultimate failure of the evidence of experience: to be valid—to be true—black womanhood must be legible as white or male; the texts of black women must be readable as maps, indexes to someone else's experience, subject to a seemingly endless process of translation and transference. Under the cult of true black womanhood, the colored body, as Cherríe Moraga has argued, is "thrown over a river of tormented history to bridge the gap" (1981, xv), to make connections—connections that in this instance enable scholars working in exhausted fields to cross over into the promised land of the academy.

Both black women writers and the black feminist critics who have brought them from the depths of obscurity into the ranks of the academy have been such bridges. The trouble is that, as Moraga points out, bridges get walked on over and over and over again. This sense of being a bridge—of being walked on and passed over, of being used up and burnt out, of having to "publish while perishing," as some have described their situations—seems to be a part of the human condition of many black women scholars. While neither the academy nor mainstream feminism has paid much attention to the crisis of black female intellectuals, the issue is much on the minds of black feminist scholars, particularly in the wake of the Thomas/Hill hearings, the critique of professional women and family values, and the loss of Audre Lorde and Sylvia Boone in a single year. So serious are these issues that the state and fate of black women in and around the university were the subjects of a national conference held at the Massachusetts Institute of Technology in January 1994. Entitled "Black Women in the Academy: Defending Our Name, 1894–1994," this conference, the first of its kind, drew together nearly two thousand black women from institutions across the country. The conference organizers have said that they were overwhelmed by the response to their call for papers: they were instantly bombarded by hundreds of abstracts, letters, faxes, and phone calls from black women describing the hypervisibility, superisolation, emotional quarantine, and psychic violence of their precarious positions in academia.

I do not mean to imply that all black women scholars see themselves as what Hurston called "tragically colored," but I think that it is safe to say that these testimonies from across the country represent a plaintive cry from black women academics who see themselves and their sisters consumed by exhaustion, depression, loneliness, and a higher incidence of such killing diseases as hypertension, lupus, cancer, diabetes, and obesity. But it also seems to me that Jane Gallop's anxieties about African American women, Nancy K. Miller's fear that there is no position from which a middle-class white woman can speak about race without being offensive, and Houston Baker's desire for dialogue with black women scholars also represent plaintive cries. Clearly both white women and women and men of color experience the pain and disappointment of failed community.

As much as I would like to end on a positive note, I have little faith that our generation of scholars—black and nonblack, male and female—will succeed in solving the problems I have taken up in this article. We are too set in our ways, too alternately defensive and offensive, too much the products of the white patriarchal society that has reared us and the white Eurocentric educational system that has trained us. If ever there comes a day when white scholars are forced by the systems that educate them to know as much about "the Other" as scholars of color are required to know about so-called dominant cultures, perhaps black women will no longer be treated as consumable commodities.

Until that day, I see a glimmer of hope shining in the bright eyes of my students who seem to me better equipped than we to explore the intersection of racial and gender difference. I was impressed by the way young women—black and white—and one lone white man in a seminar I offered on black feminist critical theory were able to grapple less with each other and more with issues, to disagree without being disagreeable, and to learn from and with each other. I wonder if there is a lesson for us older (but not necessarily wiser) academics in their interaction. I wonder what it would mean for feminist scholarship in general if "woman" were truly an all-inclusive category, if "as a woman" ceased to mean "as a white woman." I wonder what it would mean for women's studies, for black studies, for American studies, if women of color, white women, and men were truly able to work together to produce the best of all possible scholarship. . . .

NOTES

1. Most of the black feminist critics Baker lists have produced essays, articles, and books too numerous to name. In addition to a wealth of critical essays, Thadious Davis, Trudier Harris, and Deborah McDowell, e.g., have made tremendous contributions to the fields of African American and black feminist literary studies through their editorial work on a number of important projects, including vol. 51 of the Dictionary of Literary Biography series (Harris 1986) and Beacon Press's Black Women Writers Series (McDowell). See among many other pivotal essays, introductions, and books, McDowell (1980) 1985; Tate 1981;

Hull, Scott, and Smith 1982; Wall 1982; McKay 1984; Wade-Gayles 1984; Carby 1986, 1987; Joyce 1987; Smith 1987; Spillers 1987.

2. For such a review of the critical literature, see Carby 1987 and Wall 1989.

3. See, e.g., the introduction and conclusion to my study *The Coupling Convention: Sex, Text, and Tradition in Black Women's Fiction* (1993).

4. White deconstructivist Barbara Johnson has called Henry Louis Gates on his repeated use of the term "our own." Johnson notes that in a single discussion "Gates uses the expression 'our own' no fewer than nineteen times." She goes on to query the meaning behind his ambiguous phrase: "Does Gates mean all black people (whatever that might mean)? All Afro-Americans? All scholars of Afro-American literature? All black men? All scholars trained in literary theory who are now interested in the black vernacular?" See Gates 1989 and Johnson 1989.

5. In the tenth anniversary rev. ed. of *Of Woman Born*, a wiser, reflective Adrienne Rich attempts to expand and adjust her vision in light of 1980s concerns and considerations. To her discussion of "my Black mother" she appends a footnote that reads in part: "The above passage overpersonalizes and does not, it seems to me now, give enough concrete sense of the actual position of the Black domestic worker caring for white children" ([1976] 1986, 255). Even ten years later, Rich has failed to recognize that she is talking about another woman—another woman who is not her black mother but a laborer whose role as mammy is also socially, politically, and economically constructed.

REFERENCES

Abel, Elizabeth. 1993. "Black Writing, White Reading: Race and the Politics of Feminist Interpretation." *Critical Inquiry* 19 (Spring): 470–98.

Ammons, Elizabeth. 1992. *Conflicting Stories: American Women Writers at the Turn into the Twentieth Century*. New York: Oxford University Press.

Andrews, William L., ed. 1986. *Sisters of the Spirit: Three Black Women's Autobiographies of the Nineteenth Century*. Bloomington: Indiana University Press.

Baker, Houston, Jr. 1991. *Workings of the Spirit: The Poetics of Afro-American Women's Writing*. Chicago: University of Chicago Press.

Carby, Hazel. 1986. "It Jus' Be's Dat Way Sometime: The Sexual Politics of Women's Blues." *Radical America* 20(4):9–22.

———. 1987. *Reconstructing Womanhood: The Emergence of the Afro-American Woman Novelist*. New York: Oxford University Press.

Christian, Barbara. (1975) 1985. "Images of Black Women in Afro-American Literature: From Stereotype to Character." In her *Black Feminist Criticism: Perspectives on Black Women Writers*, 1–30. New York: Pergamon.

———. 1980. *Black Women Novelists: The Development of a Tradition, 1892–1976*. Westport, Conn.: Greenwood.

Christian, Barbara, Ann duCille, Sharon Marcus, Elaine Marks, Nancy K. Miller, Sylvia Schafer, and Joan W. Scott. 1990. "Conference Call." *differences* 2 (Fall): 52–108.

duCille, Ann. 1993. *The Coupling Convention: Sex, Text, and Tradition in Black Women's Fiction*. New York: Oxford University Press.

Gates, Henry Louis, Jr. 1989. "Canon-Formation and the Afro-American Tradition." In *Afro-American Literary Studies in the 1990s*, ed. Houston Baker, Jr., and Patricia Redmond, 13–49. Chicago: University of Chicago Press.

Harris, Trudier, ed. 1986. *Afro-American Writers from the Harlem Renaissance to 1940.* *Dictionary of Literary Biography,* vol. 51. Detroit: Gale Research.

Hemenway, Robert. 1977. *Zora Neale Hurston: A Literary Biography.* Urbana: University of Illinois Press.

Herskovits, Melville J. (1928) 1985. *The American Negro: A Study in Racial Crossing.* Westport, Conn.: Greenwood.

———. 1938. *Dahomey.* New York: Augustin.

———. 1941. *The Myth of the Negro Past.* Boston: Beacon.

Herskovits, Melville J., and Frances Herskovits. 1936. *Suriname Folklore.* New York: Columbia University Press.

Hine, Darlene Clark. 1980. "The Four Black History Movements: A Case for the Teaching of Black History." *Teaching History: A Journal of Methods* 5 (Fall): 115. Quoted in Meier and Rudwick 1986.

hooks, bell. 1981. *Ain't I a Woman.* Boston: South End.

———. 1992. *Black Looks: Race and Representation.* Boston: South End.

Hull, Gloria, Patricia Bell Scott, and Barbara Smith, eds. 1982. *All the Women Are White, All the Blacks Are Men, but Some of Us Are Brave.* Old Westbury, N.Y.: Feminist Press.

Jacobs, Harriet. (1861) 1987. *Incidents in the Life of a Slave Girl, Written by Herself,* ed. Jean Fagan Yellin. Cambridge: Harvard University Press.

Johnson, Barbara. 1989. Response to Gates. In *Afro-American Literary Studies in the 1990s,* ed. Houston Baker, Jr., and Patricia Redmond, 39–44. Chicago: University of Chicago Press.

Joyce, Joyce A. 1987 "The Black Canon: Reconstructing Black American Literary Criticism." *New Literary History* 18 (Winter): 335–44.

Lerner, Gerda. 1972. *Black Women in White America: A Documentary History.* New York: Random House.

McDowell, Deborah. (1980) 1985. "New Directions for Black Feminist Criticism." In *The New Feminist Criticism: Essays on Women, Literature, and Theory,* ed. Elaine Showalter. New York: Pantheon.

McKay, Nellie. 1984. *Jean Toomer, Artist: A Study of His Literary Life and Work, 1894–1936.* Chapel Hill: University of North Carolina Press.

Meier, August, and Elliot Rudwick. 1986. *Black History and the Historical Profession, 1915–1980.* Urbana: University of Illinois Press.

Moraga, Cherríe. 1981. "Preface." In *This Bridge Called My Back: Writings by Radical Women of Color,* ed. Cherríe Moraga and Gloria Anzaldúa, xiii–xix. New York: Kitchen Table: Women of Color Press.

Rich, Adrienne. (1976) 1986. *Of Woman Born: Motherhood as Experience and Institution.* Tenth anniversary ed. New York: Norton.

Sharpe, Patricia, F. E. Mascia-Lee, and C. B. Cohen. 1990. "White Women and Black Men: Different Responses to Reading Black Women's Texts." *College English* 52 (February): 142–53.

Smith, Valerie. 1987. *Self-Discovery and Authority in Afro-American Narrative.* Cambridge: Harvard University Press.

Spillers, Hortense. 1987. "Mama's Baby, Papa's Maybe: An American Grammar Book." *Diacritics* 17 (Summer): 65–81.

Spivak, Gayatri Chakravorty. 1988. *In Other Worlds: Essays in Cultural Politics.* New York: Routledge.

———. 1989. "In Praise of *Sammy and Rosie Get Laid.*" *Critical Quarterly* 31(2):80–88.

Tate, Claudia. 1981. *Interviews with Black Women Writers*. New York: Continuum.

Wade-Gayles, Gloria. 1984. *No Crystal Stair: Visions of Race and Sex in Black Women's Fiction*. New York: Pilgrim Press.

Walker, Alice. 1974. "In Search of Our Mothers' Gardens." *Ms.* 2 (May): 64–70, 105.

Wall, Cheryl A. 1982. "Poets and Versifiers, Singers and Signifiers: Women Writers of the Harlem Renaissance." In *Women, the Arts, and the 1920s in Paris and New York,* ed. Kenneth W. Wheeler and Virginia Lee Lussier, 74–98. New Brunswick, N.J.: Transaction.

———, ed. 1989. "Taking Positions and Changing Words." In her *Changing Our Own Words: Essays on Criticism, Theory, and Writing by Black Women,* 1–15. New Brunswick: Rutgers University Press.

Wallace, Michele. 1990. "Who Owns Zora Neale Hurston? Critics Carve Up the Legend." In her *Invisibility Blues,* 172–86. New York: Verso.

Wilson, Hatriet. (1859) 1983. *Our Nig; or, Sketches from the Life of a Free Black*. New York: Vintage.

ink
black on white

rubina ramji

to be my poet
is to spit dark words onto white paper
using black ink
black on so much white
worth so little (on white) doing so much (for white)
revealing truths   lies   seconds of reality
as it rushes through my fingers
putting more black on white
till there is no space
to say   write   think   more

so i open my eyes to the reality i have created
expecting justice (blind)   freedom (colonized)
to be what i can be
today
different at any moment
woman   coloured   intelligent   lonely   vicious   carefree
me

instead the white paper
has absorbed all of my beautiful black ink
washing this poet away
white rules
condescending   paternal   intelligent   consuming   vicious   carefree

so i use a stronger pen
writing myself over and over again

Reprinted by permission.

carving my space through the white paper
destroying it
leaving no reality
to be judged by

Part V

Deconstructing Sex and Gender

Even before African American women began to challenge the notion of undifferentiated womanhood, lesbians were raising issues of sexual orientation within feminist organizations and consciousness-raising groups. The notion that the "woman-identified woman" was the core of feminist identity led to purges on both sides of this debate. In the early 1970s the small-group sector had lesbian-focused groups that limited membership to a small percentage of women who were "giving their energy to men." In the mass-movement sector, organizations like the National Organization for Women (NOW) were purging outspoken lesbians from their ranks (Ryan 1992).

Over time these practices gave way to the recognition that one's sexual orientation was a matter of legitimacy for one's lifestyle decisions. Other questions arose, though, connected to identity, desire, and difference. Lesbianism became something beyond physical desire to political position, including the provision that sex be egalitarian. Following from notions of "correct" forms of intimacy were denial and repression, particularly related to pornography and sadomasochism, where efforts were made to regulate female sexuality (Phelan 1989). Articles in this section look at some of those questions, as well as the construction and reconstruction of identity, the unsettled nature of sexual identity, and boundary construction.

Eileen Bresnahan's article reveals the difficulty of accepting new interpretations of lesbian feminism when conceptions of what that meant failed to include a radical feminist ideology. Her feminist group knew the connection to radical thought and a lesbian feminist lifestyle but was confronted with a visitor from another part of the country who did not conform to these expectations. What had seemed so evident was now being contested. The humor Bresnahan includes in her writing adds a telling comment to what was shocking in that situation and time to what today would seem commonplace. It is a good example of the challenges to identity politics yet to arise and why resistance was the first response to this occurrence.

In a different setting Trisha Franzen offers another look at lesbian identity conflicts, this time based on class, education, and age differences. The conflict between university students and bar lesbians over appropriate dress, role behavior, and feminist consciousness shows the depth of meaning connected to an identity politics of lesbianism that transcends sexuality. Acceptable behaviors and nonacceptable behaviors and the ideological underpinnings connected to them created a gulf between these two groups of lesbians. What before was assumed—butch/fem roles—new lesbians, using a morally righteous tone, were now contesting. The conflict was offensive and, being an early one, failed to allow for the different life experiences each group had confronted and managed in the construction of reality their lives reflected.

The fissures these early confrontations revealed led to more concerted efforts to create a community of like thinking, behaving, and "being" than had seemed necessary before. But even in a lesbian separatist community, cracks emerged. As Marilyn Frye shows in her article "Lesbian Community: Heterodox Congregation," there are more disagreements than agreements in living and surviving within one's group. For instance, she cites things her lesbian separatist community does not agree on:

- sexual practices and what separatism means
- working against U.S. imperialism and nuclear weapons
- recycling, having Christmas trees, hamburgers
- appropriate dress, shaving, wearing makeup

The list goes on. The point is, there are many things some members feel passionately about that others oppose or could not care less about. Yet, they continue to exist and to experience a strong sense of shared accomplishments. This she feels is natural when women are able to support one another's lives and when they recognize and honor what has kept them apart in the outside world.

There are some questions, though, that continue to tear apart a sense of women's unity. Joshua Gamson reports on one such issue from the Michigan Womyn's Music Festival. Each year thousands of women, mostly lesbian feminists, camp out for a week of music, lecture, and community at this annual event. Rules of admittance developed related to the feeling that women should be free to experience themselves without the presence of men, that this should be a woman-only space. The question of allowing transsexual women into the conference created heated discussion. The rejection of this "suspect" class of participants is analyzed by Gamson in terms of boundary divisions and the meaning such boundaries imply. The article also highlights the ongoing process of decision making that identity politics entails.

In the final article of this section, Arlene Stein discusses the fissures 1970s lesbian feminism opened up. Ex-lesbians, bisexuality, transgendered women, and the challenges of queer theory are part of the deliberation lesbian feminists engage in today. She calls this the search for both sexual identities and politics that avoids the pitfalls of "an identity politics that refuses difference or a politics of difference without collected identity" (Stein 1997:199). Stein makes the point that identities are not permanently settled and that recognizing the problematic nature of group boundaries can lead to a new inclusiveness where many women who felt excluded can begin to feel they belong, and to participate on their own terms.

REFERENCES

Phelan, Shane. 1989. *Identity Politics: Lesbian Feminism and the Limits of Community*. Philadelphia: Temple University Press.

Ryan, Barbara. 1992. *Feminism and the Women's Movement: Dynamics of Change in Social Movement Ideology and Activism*. New York: Routledge.

Stein, Arlene. 1997. *Sex and Sensibility: Stories of a Lesbian Generation*. Berkeley: University of California Press.

Chapter Twenty-one

The Strange Case of Jackie East
When Identities Collide

Eileen Bresnahan

I clearly remember the first time I saw her, an obviously lesbian woman, in silver studs and leather, wearing a jacket with "DYKETACTICS" emblazoned across the back. The year was 1976, the place Denver's Woman to Woman Feminist Bookcenter (WtW), and the question in my mind, "Who on earth is this woman, and where the hell did she come from?"

I was, you see, a radical-feminist "movement heavy," on the *Big Mama Rag* (*BMR*) collective, with many organizations, demonstrations, and actions under my belt. I'd been a founding member of a university women's center, had lived in a feminist collective (with the two women who were most instrumental in founding Woman to Woman), had worked on the "Women Everywhere" radio collective, and generally knew—or, at least, knew of—most everyone who was part of what we called the Denver "Women's Community," i.e., the collection of more-or-less countercultural feminists, both radical and cultural, both lesbian and straight, who showed up at radical-feminist actions and at *BMR* and WtW community meetings. I also knew most of the faces, if not the names, of the local people "on the Left," in the various socialist and Marxist groups and collectives who "did politics" in an orbit that intersected with ours. I was, in other words, "connected"—I even knew a few women from NOW.

This woman was no one—and, indeed, like no one—I'd seen before: Like no one in the Women's Community, whose members, with our Levis and "ethnic" prints, probably would have been taken for working-class "hippies" as much as lesbians—at least until some of us started cutting our hair shorter and shorter.[1] Nor like the "bar dykes" we would see when we went dancing, who sometimes affected a much "harder" look, but whom we scorned for their lack of political consciousness and involvement. We'd tried to reach out to these other lesbians when doing our organizing, too often only to be rebuffed by comments like "I'm a lesbian, what's an action about abortion rights got to do with me? I don't worry about pregnancy." We would try to reply to these rejections dressed up as questions—to ignore their unmistakably hostile edge and to reach some common understanding—but usually before we'd begun, the women were gone, in search of companionship, a drink, or a dancing partner, leaving us to fume and to wonder what we were doing wasting our energy like this.

But this woman in the bookstore was apparently political: at least her DYKE-TACTICS jacket seemed to argue for that interpretation, since no one at the time who was not also a radical feminist (at some level) would ever claim the word "dyke," especially in such an "in your face" way as it was capitally studded into that leather jacket. Most of the bar dykes, even in Denver, were still fairly closeted. We radical lesbian feminists would walk around holding hands or kiss our lovers and partners on the lips on the street (nonmonogamy was still the rule of the day), but what lesbian self-identification we wore in printed form was largely confined to buttons and t-shirts. A leather jacket with "DYKE" in studded letters, three inches high, was a bit beyond our pale, for reasons both of fashion and finances. Who the hell was she? Where had she come from? And, more important, what did she want?

The answers were not very long in coming. After I got home, I telephoned my lover at the time (now my partner of twenty-two years), Kate, who was working in the *BMR* office. I told her about the strange woman I had seen, and asked if she were anyone Kate knew. Kate said no, and then, in the course of conversation, told me about two articles in the latest issue of Hera, a new radical-feminist newspaper, published in Philadelphia. (*BMR,* like most women's movement publications, exchanged subscriptions with other women's movement and Left periodicals. Because of this, we got almost all of them, and often received first issues as overtures to such exchanges; that was how we'd gotten *Hera.*) The first of these articles was called something like "My Boyfriend Dropped Me Off at the Lesbian Bar" and was a defense of bisexuality.

In 1976, to defend bisexuality in an avowedly radical-feminist periodical was quite daring, at least in our corner of the world. This was past the stage when most radical-feminist projects had become separatist and, indeed, *BMR* officially supported a feminist separatist line (though it did not mandate separatism for collective members). As *BMR* understood it, feminist separatism required separating from men in all important areas of both political work and private life as a *strategy* having a twofold purpose. First, it was intended as a woman-centered strategy, meant to provide women space in which to get strong and to learn to take care of and lead ourselves—without the burden (as a friend of mine used to put it) of having to "breast-feed feminism to men." We saw this distance as needed to allow women to hear our own voices and to work on our own oppression—without having to worry over what men, especially leftist men, thought about that or about what we "really" should be doing. Second, it was a message and an action directed toward men, intended explicitly to withhold women's energies from them as a "strike against men" or a "strike against the Left." Feminist separatism put both men and the Left on notice that women no longer would tolerate either personal or institutionalized sexism, telling the Left as well that its own internal sexist oppression was dividing and weakening the larger movement. Until leftist men got their own acts together and began confronting their own sexism, they could forget about counting on feminist women to work in their projects (though not necessarily to show up at their demonstrations, which we might choose to attend just as any other "outside" person might). In both aspects the goal was *strategic,* designed to accomplish specific, time-limited goals. We were very careful to maintain that we considered ourselves part of the larger Left, but that we just could not work within it at that time. However, we also let it be known that we stood with the Left against any external attacks. We did not believe that our separatism would be terribly long-term, but saw it only as something we needed to do for a while, until we could feel stronger and be assured that feminist issues would be taken seriously and that we would not be personally mistreated within the larger Left.

In adopting this version of separatism *BMR* was swimming against the tide of the time, which increasingly demanded lesbian separatism, that is, that radical-feminist groups should be lesbian-only. Although we agreed that lesbianism could be a radical refusal to participate in patriarchally organized heterosexual relations—and, indeed, most of us had "come out" in the women's movement—we also realized that sexuality was a very complicated and personal issue. Perhaps because for us feminism was so much a matter of getting women—always including ourselves—free from oppression, we were very reluctant to turn around and try to impose some sexual orthodoxy on other women. We knew well enough that lesbian relationships, just like heterosexual ones, could be troubled or even sick, replicating within them power relations learned in the larger society. We had chosen them for ourselves but realized that in many ways this was a privileged choice. We considered our politics working-class based, and so understood that many women could not make the choices we had. We therefore did not consider lesbian separatism to be politically progressive.

Women who supported lesbian separatism, however, argued that working with straight women was really to give power up to men. As the logic went, because women who were in relationships with men were always having gendered sorts of trouble in these relationships, and always whining about it to their lesbian-feminist sisters and demanding aid and sympathy, they were a conduit of lesbian energy to men. Lesbian separatists felt that straight women were unwilling to give up their heterosexual privilege and always were primarily oriented toward men, yet demanded that their lesbian sisters support them through their troubles, putting lesbians in the position of helping to facilitate the straight women's continued participation in heterosexuality. Since lesbian feminists had figured out that heterosexuality was unhealthy and politically oppressive to women, why should they continue to facilitate some women's participation in it (by being friends and sisters to straight women), in effect allowing their energy to be sapped by women who, before everything else, were obsessed with men? Lesbianism in a patriarchal society was itself dangerous and costly enough. Better to cut the heterosexual women off and to keep lesbian energy for lesbians.

With that much of the lesbian separatist argument—to be honest—many of us on *BMR* could agree. We had little personal sympathy for, or interest in, many of the young straight women we knew, who often seemed to us to revel in the dysfunction of their relationships with men. However, we also saw a difference between these women "who should know better" and women who, because of class, or race, or age, were really stuck in heterosexual relationships. In our more lucid moments, when we came up with our group politics, we realized that we could not sit in judgment of women who continued to relate sexually to men, since they were the ones who had to live their own lives. Though we thought lesbianism was the correct position, to demand it as a prerequisite for political involvement seemed unfair, because all of us had many areas of our lives in which we were unable to live up to what we thought were the best strategies for change. We had been through some struggles over this, but they had generally died down by this time.[2]

For us another underlying problem with lesbian separatism was that—at least as it was usually advanced at the time—the arguments for it seemed fairly "fascist," usually depending on some sort of biological determinism. The cultural feminists who were then the leading proponents of lesbian separatism usually argued for it on the basis of assertions that males are inherently defective. Some argued that men are mutants, crippled by a defective Y-chromosome and so inferior to women. Others believed that male aggressiveness is inherent, making men fundamentally incapable of sustained civilized behavior. All lauded some apparently essential and eternal feminine principle that made women clearly superior to men. Because of this analysis, for lesbian separatists separatism was not a strategy so much as a permanent necessity.[3]

Because *BMR* saw lesbian separatism as based in the notion that some people are essentially superior to others, it clashed with our basic view of feminism as committed to the deconstruction of all social hierarchy, which we saw as a social creation, the manifestation of illegitimate privilege. We didn't think men were inherently different; to admit that would have been to let them off the hook. It also would have been to repeat the mistake we wanted to correct. We instead asserted that men are personally responsible for their roles in perpetuating oppression. Just because we were mad at them, didn't mean we were ready to write them off. To do that would have been to give up on creating a better world.

But this woman writing in *Hera* was mounting a frontal attack on the idea that separatism was a correct strategy, both in terms of something women needed for ourselves and in terms of the idea that women should stay away from men until men got their act together. And, in claiming bisexuality, she was clearly one of the women "who should know better"—not trapped in heterosexuality by the pressures of class and race and patriarchy, but choosing to continue it in the face of a demonstrated ability to be lesbian if she really wanted to. This was shocking: she was claiming the label "radical feminist" while "scabbing"—on the basis of personal willfulness—on the strike against men. Kate told me that she and some collective members who had just left the office had discussed whether *BMR* should write a response to the *Hera* article. We would have to see if a consensus could be reached on this at the next meeting.

Kate went on to say, however, that this article was only the tip of the iceberg that was *Hera*. Indeed, the assertion that one could be a radical feminist and also bisexual was small potatoes compared to another article that the issue contained. This article espoused the virtues of something of that most of us on the *BMR* collective to that point had never even heard: "lesbian-feminist sadomasochism." Kate said this article had left her, and the other collective members who had read it, totally aghast. I should be sure to read it before the next meeting, since we might well want to write a response to it as well. Then we said goodbye, and I went off to work. During the shift that followed (I was working in the intensive care unit of a local hospital), I can't say I gave the matter of the strange woman or the matter of *Hera* a great deal of thought.

Upon arriving home late that night, however, I found Kate fairly bursting to tell what had happened in the *BMR* office within moments of our telephone conversation. "Your woman," she said, "walked right in the door. I knew it had to be her; who else could it have been, dressed like that?"

"Did she have the DYKETACTICS jacket?" I was surprised she would have ventured into our offices, since we were not really that kind of project.

"That's how I was sure it was her," Kate replied. "We didn't really talk much: she didn't have much to say, and I didn't want to let on that we were overly curious about her, since I didn't want to freak her out. But she did say her name is Jackie East.[4] And then she says she's from Philadelphia. And you know that new paper I was telling you about, *Hera*? Well, it's out of Philadelphia, too. I thought at first it must be just a coincidence. But after she told me she was from Philadelphia, and from the look of her, and from what they're writing out there—well, as soon as she left the office, I said to myself, 'She's trouble.' And, you know, I'll bet she is."

I couldn't argue; I was betting that, too. But any speculation about Jackie East was immediately pushed to the rear by the demands of the project, and specifically by the need to respond to what *Hera* had published. Over the next few days, it became apparent that whatever unease we might feel over "My Boyfriend Dropped Me Off at the Lesbian Bar," it was minor in comparison with the major queasiness we all felt over the very idea of something like "lesbian-feminist sadomasochism." We decided we had to respond in print.[5]

The process of creating such responses generally included charging everyone on the collective to read the offending piece, and then having a meeting at which we would discuss the issues and begin formulating our response to it. At this meeting, everyone would take detailed notes, and at some point we would collectively decide what member, or group of members—sometimes with assistance from interested nonmembers—would write the response. This selection process usually turned on who most wanted to do the actual writing (if such a person existed) and, failing that, who was willing to do it and had the time to do it. In any case, the actual writer or writers were charged with representing the perspective of the whole collective. She would bring back the finished piece to a later meeting to be approved for publication.

This process, as it might be imagined, encouraged a lot of talking, both within the project among collective members and "friends" and outside the project in the Women's Community as a whole. No attempt was ever made to keep these things and our intentions toward them secret and, in the case of any major controversy, it wouldn't be long before the entire Women's Community was buzzing about a given issue. It soon became obvious that this one was destined to be such a major controversy. Almost before we knew it, "players" in the political life of the Women's Community—some of whom were former *BMR* collective members or current or former WtW collective members—were dropping by our office to read the sado-masochism piece and to let us know what their opinions were on it. Many heated discussions ensued, in the *BMR* offices, in WtW Bookcenter, on the streets of Capitol Hill, and in the local bars. It was immediately obvious that, although the *BMR* collective was solidly united in our position on the issue, this unity was not shared throughout the Women's Community.

In brief, the *BMR* collective's position on the possibility of a lesbian-feminist sadomasochism was that this construction was a clear oxymoron. We were quick to concede that we cared little what women chose to do in the privacy of their bedrooms (or whatever), but that we did not see how any sadomasochistic sexual practice could be called "feminist." For us feminism was about eliminating relations of domination, not about "playing" with them or reconstructing them. We would never condemn the participants in sadomasochistic sexual games—since we realized that we had all been reared in a power-saturated culture, and it would be "ultra-left"[6] of us to expect people to behave as if they had not—but we also did not think such practices deserved the designation "feminist." What could be feminist about getting-off on dominating another or on being dominated by another?

One of the women who stopped by the *BMR* offices to share her views with us was Jackie East. She did, indeed, know the women who published *Hera* and the woman who had written the sadomasochism article. Further, she did not like the direction in which our collective reasoning on sadomasochism was tending. She had been going about the Denver Women's Community advancing a pro-lesbian-feminist-sadomasochism position, and this position was finding a number of local women who strongly agreed, showing every sign of hardening into a coherent group. We became more concerned.

At least in part, some of the women who supported the possibility of calling sadomasochism "feminist" did so because they thought *BMR* was trying to enforce a feminist orthodoxy and was picking on Jackie East in the process. There was always a group of women in the feminist community upset with the *BMR* collective because we had control of the sole media outlet that could advance a "Denver feminist" position and were adamant that we would publish only what the collective decided to publish (though this included letters to the editor from women who disagreed with us, and we in fact generally published every letter to the editor that we received). The *BMR* collective saw this insistence on ultimate control as a reasonable feminist position: we were doing the work (tons of it, all unpaid) and taking the responsibility for keeping the project viable (not a small thing on the subshoestring budget on which we operated), so we were determined that we also made the final decisions—while being careful to provide avenues of accountability and openings for criticism. Some women, however, felt that we should publish everything submitted to us, without political or other judgment, and saw us as somehow violating some fuzzy feminist principle if we declined. Among these women Jackie East found supporters, but she also drew the support of some women who just agreed with the *Hera* article that sadomasochistic sexual practices could rightly be called "feminist." Those of us on the *BMR* collective, along with some of those of the WtW collective, began to fear that a "split" in the Women's Community was shaping up. We decided it was time to take positive steps to head off such destructive infighting, if this could still be done.

Taking the lead in the attempt to avoid a rupture in the Women's Community was one of the women who had been instrumental in founding WtW, Peggy. Peggy decided, as a first step, to have a few women from *BMR* sit down with Jackie East, on the neutral ground of Denver's Cheesman Park, to see if a compromise could be forged. Kate and I agreed to represent the *BMR* collective, with Peggy along as well, while only Jackie East represented the pro-feminist-sadomasochism side. In retrospect, I can see that this was unfair and a mistake. Because Peggy agreed with the *BMR* perspective, this left Jackie East, whom we had found out was relatively new to radical politics, alone to oppose three experienced women's movement organizers (all of whom had also had at least some experience in the Left). Though we had every good intention, it's no wonder we could not arrive at a mutually agreeable conclusion (although I still have to wonder if such a possibility ever existed). Jackie East felt isolated and outnumbered, while we felt frustrated and impatient.

In essence, the theory part of the conversation went nowhere. Jackie East was unwilling to accept that sadomasochism could not be seen as feminist. From her perspective, it allowed women to experience power and that was feminist in itself. She was not swayed by the argument that because this power was exercised over another woman; that even at this level of analysis it was difficult for us to see how such an experience of power could be called "feminist." She just insisted that it was.

In the course of talking, though, we did learn some surprising things (to us, anyway) about Jackie East and Dyketactics. One of these was that she and the group were very active in antipornography activism. This was novel to us; we had never thought of pornography as a political feminist issue. We knew there were some groups beginning to deal with the whole issue of violence against women, but to us this was more about rape and battering and woman killing than about anything to do with pornography. As lesbians, we knew that our ordinary sexual practices were seen as themselves pornographic by most of the population. As feminists, we knew that much of what the movement had historically done about disseminating information on sexuality and abortion and birth control and self-health had been, and could still be, attacked by the mainstream of society as pornographic. As radicals, we knew that the state could not be trusted to be the gatekeeper of the flow of information throughout society. All of these things militated against our becoming involved in any campaign to encourage the state to restrict any flow of information. We worked outside the system, not for it; we made demands, not compromises.

A second thing that surprised us about Jackie East was that she saw the police as allies in the fight to free women. From our point of view, the police were agents of the state, whose primary purposes were to protect property and to keep people like us in our proper "place." When we demonstrated, we wouldn't even talk to the police who came along with the parade permit—it just wasn't done, and besides, we really didn't like them. But Jackie East told stories of how much the police liked Dyketactics' antipornography campaigning, and how friendly the police were to them, and how the police gave them tips on ways of sabotaging sex businesses.

Looking back, I can see now that a large part of why we couldn't come to an agreement was because we were representative of completely different developments in feminism. The women on *BMR,* like Peggy from WtW, were radical feminists, committed to an autonomous women's movement but with roots in the radical politics of the Left. Jackie East, on the other hand, was one of the new women who had come into feminism after its split from the larger Left. To her, feminism was about female self-improvement and the empowerment of individual women. She was a cultural feminist, though it wasn't obvious to us at the time.

Part of what concealed this from us was that cultural feminism had been around for a while—perhaps as long as there had been a movement—though not in the activist form represented by Jackie East. Most of the feminists we at that time called "cultural"—a term that was *always* applied pejoratively by women who identified as radical feminists—were into feminist spirituality and goddess worship and other things we saw as irredeemably apolitical. We criticized them for pursuing "individual solutions," whether in their quest for "women's land," in their inquiries into parthenogenesis, or in their lesbian separatism. Even though we radical feminists were not at that time in the Left, we saw ourselves as of the Left: We believed that women could *never* be truly liberated in a capitalist society and that revolution was *impossible* without the participation of men. Our goal was to transform society, but cultural feminists wanted to leave society behind, to create better lives for themselves and women like them, but not necessarily to bring everyone else along in the process.

Because of this orientation, the cultural feminists we knew were only rarely politically active. That was a large part of our problem with them: to us it seemed that they never really *did* anything useful to anybody but themselves and a very few others. As radical feminists, we believed that no one could be free until everybody else was. This didn't mean that we thought women should sacrifice themselves to the cause—that was the "service-orientation" we rejected—but that they should understand that freedom was always a collective good and that to really work on getting oneself free implied working on freeing everybody.

Jackie East and her group, though, were a new kind of cultural feminists. They were politically active, but with only women's narrow interests in mind. This gave them the status of "Exhibit A" in any case designed to prove that the Left was right to argue that autonomous feminism would inevitably become bourgeois. These women had forgotten that the state was not to be trusted, indeed could never work in the interests of the oppressed because its allegiance always lay with capital and patriarchy. Instead, they believed that they could use the state for their own purposes. This idea, to radical feminists of the time, was utter anathema.[7]

So, given the ideological gulf that existed between our perspectives, it is hardly surprising that rather than heal the growing controversy, the meeting in the park actually did more to exacerbate it. Jackie—who by this time was calling herself

Jackie West, in honor of her new region of residence[8]—apparently feeling put upon as a result of our having "ganged-up" on her, must have decided she needed reinforcements. So she telephoned her friends in Philadelphia, and whatever she said to them, it must have been plenty persuasive, because before too many more days had passed—to our utter and abject horror and dismay—a minor gaggle of them turned up in Denver, having hitchhiked across the country to come to the support of their embattled compatriot.

I don't know what I can say to communicate adequately how appalled and amazed we Denver radical feminists were when these women popped up in our midst. We knew that some radical feminists did a lot of hitchhiking—we'd done some of it ourselves—but this really was too much! Why on earth would they come half way across the country just to fight with us? How could we make this controversy go away?

We decided to do the only thing we knew to do when the Women's Community was in the throes of some ideological crisis: we called a community meeting. Such community meetings were relatively commonplace in the women's movement; BMR and WtW both had them irregularly as a mechanism to encourage feedback and to maintain accountability between the projects and other feminists. But such meetings were usually sparsely attended—unless for some reason some subset of the community was angry at something one of the projects had done or contemplated doing.[9] But community meetings over controversies like this one were not-to-be missed events, drawing in virtually every woman even peripherally connected to the Women's Community.

At this time in Denver, absolutely the only place to hold a community meeting was in the basement of WtW. Designated women-only space—"womanspace" in the parlance of the movement—this basement was large and dim, furnished with a number of tables, couches, and chairs that had been scavenged from area alleyways and dumpsters. It was the closest thing we had to a community common room, and we hung out in it, held meetings of political groups and support groups and consciousness-raising groups in it, used it for child care, and just generally occupied it. It was comfortable, neutral space, into which everyone in the Women's Community could come. But men could not, conferring the added advantage of enabling us to air our internal grievances free of male interference without having to go to the additional step of making a point of closing a meeting to them (since scheduling in WtW basement automatically excluded men), a considerable advantage when the issues were touchy, but also nice in general.[10]

When I walked into the community meeting, I knew we were in for a scene. I had never seen that basement that full—women were everywhere, on all the surfaces and lining all the walls; women were even sitting on the steps going down into the basement. Usually, meetings would only occupy a quarter, even a sixth, of this large space, but when the meeting circle extended to the stairs, encompassing the entire basement, you knew that the issue was hot. By that measure, this one was red hot, since the back of the space was several women deep. There were women in the room I hadn't seen in months, women I'd never seen, and women whom I could swear had sworn they would die before they set foot in this space again. All relevant feminist constituencies were represented: radical, cultural, liberal, and socialist—there were even a few women from NOW. This was going to be a long one.

If I could, I would reconstruct the conversation but it was a long time ago, and anyway, as I remember it now, it didn't get much beyond the impasse in the park. I do remember saying, though, something like "Well, I suppose torturing kittens to death might also make some women feel powerful, but I still don't think that would allow us to call it 'feminist.' " This seemed to me the essence of the matter but, predictably, the point was misunderstood, and I was accused of alleging that feminist sadomasochists enjoy torturing kittens to death. The women from Philadelphia became outraged because such an allegation (had I actually made it) would indeed have been damning—especially considering that in my experience the only thing the majority of feminists have ever been able to agree on is that we are really, really, seriously fond of cats.

So, things, as we say, deteriorated, and the meeting didn't end so much as explode. *BMR* published its anti-lesbian-feminist-sadomasochism piece, just as we had always intended, but some local women who supported Jackie East stayed mad at us for a very long time—for all I know, they may still be mad. The Philadelphia women hitchhiked back to Philadelphia, taking Jackie East with them, and peace descended once again over the Denver Women's Community.

That would be the end of our story, except for one strange fact. Kate, my partner, just happens to have been born in Philadelphia, and a couple of years later we visited her family there. While in town, Kate decided to look up a few friends whom she had known from the years when she was active in the Philadelphia Women's Community. As we visited with these friends, eventually the conversation turned to Jackie East. Did they know her, we inquired. Oh, yes, they replied; they actually knew her fairly well. Had they then heard the story of her foray to Denver? They allowed they'd heard something about it, but asked us to tell the story as we knew it. So we went through the whole thing, pretty much as I have laid it down here.

After we finished, they were silent for a moment. Then one of them said, "Well, the story Jackie East is telling around Philadelphia is that, when the *Big Mama Rag* people in Denver found that she was a Philadelphia supporter of lesbian-feminist sadomasochism, they asked her to come to a meeting."

"Yes, we did that," I said.

"But, as Jackie East tells it, the meeting was not in a park, but in a secluded mountain cabin. She says that as soon as she arrived, the *BMR* collective jumped her, tied her to a chair, and held her there for days, without food or water, trying to get her to recant her support for lesbian-feminist sadomasochism."

"What?" Kate said. "You can't be serious."

"I am serious," the woman replied. "I've heard her tell the story more than once. Quite a few people around here seem to believe it."

"But," I said, "the *BMR* collective has to have a series of meetings just to decide whether or not to change the name of a section of the paper. How would we ever be able to decide to do something like lure a woman to the mountains and tie her to a chair? Besides, none of us can afford to rent a cabin in the mountains and none of us has a car."

The women listened patiently as we sputtered, but I've always had the nagging feeling that they never quite believed us. So ever afterward I have had to live with the realization that, despite the strong ethical commitments and the deep respect for people that always drove my political activism, somewhere there might be some woman or group of women who think I was party to imprisoning and torturing a woman because of her beliefs. For me, this has been an object lesson in the fact that, no matter how good are your intentions, some people are going to get them wrong—or even willfully misrepresent them—and there's often nothing you can do about that. So, in politics, do the best you can, but never lose your sense of the absurd, because, sister, you're gonna need it.

As time has passed, I've learned to be grateful to Jackie East for providing this story with such an inventive ending. But I've also gained the perspective to see that the emergence of lesbian-feminist sadomasochism was but one symptom of a new emphasis on individual self-improvement and individualistic forms of liberation that infused the women's movement after its disengagement from the organized Left, and ultimately destroyed it. Eventually, it became impossible to say that any given practice was or wasn't "feminist" or "radical feminist," since the only criteria by which something could be judged feminist came to be whether it was preferred by a woman who identified herself as a such. Increasingly, the emphasis shifted to "lifestyle" and female self-affirmation, and away from the attempt to create a feminist politics. Indeed, to many of the new women, for someone even to suggest that the term "radical feminist" meant something very specific, was to "oppress" them by trying to limit their freedom to define themselves, and their "right" to be "validated" in whatever that definition entailed.

When I first became active in the women's movement, however, to be a radical feminist meant something specific. Groups that identified as radical feminist spent long hours developing "points of unity" and "manifestos," and if a woman who wanted to join said she couldn't support the principles laid down, she was invited to apply elsewhere. But if she said she wasn't sure, and needed to know more, then we invited her to be a provisional member, and learn what we meant by our politics. She had to be willing to acknowledge that she didn't already know all there was to know about radical feminism, to be willing to learn what had led us to the commitments we held.

Lately, it has become fashionable for women who have never in practice organized politically to advance the theory that what feminism needs is to build a movement around no starting principles. But in my experience, such organizing is impossible because, though you might be able to get women into the same room on just the mere premise of a nonspecific feminism, you can't get them to decide what to *do* on that basis. And, given what we've seen happening lately, it's apparent that more women are comfortable identifying with feminism's issues than with calling themselves feminists. Points of unity provide a basis on which we may be the same thing, supporting the same politics. Without them, sadomasochism can be as lesbian-feminist as is organizing against cuts in welfare or for lesbian and abortion rights.

So, even though the story of Jackie East reminds me of the funny side of political activism, it also reminds me of what killed the women's movement. Once we could no longer say what was—and wasn't—radical feminist, we could no longer decide what to do to accomplish our agenda. Indeed, we could no longer even have a collective agenda because political agendas must be based on a sense of who you are as a member of a group and therefore of who your allies and your enemies are. It is impossible to pick one strategy or another, one tactic or another, unless you know where you, and the people who are your allies, want to go. And where you want to go differs according to who you currently are, what has made you that, and what is continuing to oppress people like you.

After the Jackie East business, I felt different about calling myself a radical lesbian feminist. I felt then that I should really explain what I meant by it when I said it. I thought attaching it to a sexual practice was trivializing, and for me—though I always insisted, and still believe, that politics, when done right, is an awful lot of fun—there was nothing trivial about my feminist identity. Largely because I'm a working-class woman who grew up in the 1950s and 1960s, the women's movement was the first time I took myself seriously and the first time I was taken seriously by others whom I could also respect. Through it, I first saw that many of the problems I had thought were personal were in fact social in origin; in it I found the strength to stand up and say what I thought.

Movements often attract damaged people, but they also give these people a space to try to create something new, both out of ourselves and out of society. But, to do that, they also have to provide us with vision of something better than we have and a sense of all that we might have been and might still become. The identity of radical feminist was a pretty good start on that: it let us know who we were and also who we wanted to be, in a movement we women made ourselves, in defiance of all the people who thought we could never do such a thing.

This movement, when it worked, could be truly beautiful—and those times that it did work were almost enough to make up for all the times it didn't. Our good times provided us a glimpse into everything we, and human society, might be. In the process, they also confirmed us in the conviction that a radical feminist was a very worthy thing to be, an identity more than worth fighting for.

NOTES

1. It is important to emphasize that we did not all identify as lesbian, though most of us did. Perhaps a third of the women in the Denver Women's Community identified as heterosexual and a much smaller number as bisexual.

2. There was always some contention among collective members about which form of separatism was correct, and some individual members did not always toe the collective line. For example, when I first became active on *BMR*, I was working on production (getting the paper ready to go to press) when another collective member, whom I had barely met, began

"putting down" straight women. I informed her that I thought such behavior was unfeminist and unacceptable because it was divisive and we needed to be a movement of all women. She made little response but subsequently proceeded to spread the rumor around the Women's Community that *I* was straight (apparently, this was the only reason she could imagine to explain my objection to "straight-bashing"). When I found this was happening, I was horrified and went to some pains to straighten it out (no pun intended).

(Within two years the woman who had been straight-bashing was a practicing heterosexual, living with a man and working in a white auxiliary to a black liberation group. In an interesting mirroring of the case of people who gay-bash, her hostility to the sexually different was apparently rooted in the uncertainty she felt about her own sexuality. For me, this has always served as an object lesson that because feminists can't count on being any better than anyone else, we have to be sure that we're politically more principled.)

3. I remember sitting in a WtW community meeting with members of the Olivia Records collective who were at that time militantly lesbian-separatist (ironic, considering the path they have taken since then). Did they, I asked, see this separatism as a short-term strategy or as something more long lasting? The Olivia woman replied, "Well, I suppose you could say our separatism is a strategy, but only if by short-term you mean the next two or three hundred years." I remember thinking that, for the Olivia woman, this probably seemed a concession to moderation. But to my eyes, it was politically wacko.

4. Jackie East's birth name, we subsequently learned, was Jackie Something-long-and-Eastern-European, now lost to the sands of time. Jackie East was a "liberation name" or *nom de guerre,* a self-invention fairly common in the women's movement. Sometimes women would use for their last name their mother's first name combined with "daughter" or "child," as in Marysdaughter or Ellenchild; in this way a woman named Kate Green became Kate Bertiesdaughter, while another was known only by the single name, Dorothychild. Still others took their "family" name from an admired female historical figure, as in the case of Jackie St. Joan. Sometimes women would construct something, often a single name, from scratch, as in the case of a woman I once met as Moonrabbit, or the *BMR* collective member called Woodwoman, or the woman who went only by Pandora. Sometimes these names stuck and became more or less permanent; other times they were a thing of the moment.

5. Responding in print to one another, or in general to current theoretical or theoretical-practical movement controversies, was something most feminist journal-projects did. *BMR,* as was typical of these projects, saw its primary missions as building a strong and lasting independent (of both the Left and of academic feminism) women's movement. To this end, the building of radical-feminist theory was integral, and reporting the news only secondary (though we did do a lot of reporting, since women wanted and needed to know what was going on and such reporting might "radicalize" more women and—we hoped—thereby get them involved in the movement). *BMR*'s orientation toward theory building reflected, at least in part, our conscious rejection of a "service orientation" toward what we were doing. We did not conceive of our mission as one of serving some feminist clientele "out there" but, rather, one of engaging in the collective creation of a radical-feminist movement.

6. "Ultra-left" was a movement designation for analyses and demands that expected people to behave as though they had been reared in and lived in a postrevolutionary society, even though no revolution had yet occurred. An ultra-left analysis or demand was idealistic and moralistic, rather than material; as such it was unsophisticated, unrealistic, and probably mean-spirited.

7. Lest anyone be confused, it is important to remember that what has been called "radical feminism" in recent times, since Catharine MacKinnon and Andrea Dworkin appro-

priated the term to describe their peculiar perspective, is not what the term meant in 1976. In 1976, a radical feminist was someone who opposed *both* patriarchy *and* capitalism from a very "out-system" perspective. No radical feminist of the time would advocate trusting the state to regulate something we cared about, such as the flow of information. Indeed, it was actively debated whether or not we should trust the state to deal with rapists, since we knew it was not able to do even that fairly. And in our personal lives most of us were so distrustful of the state that were we to be robbed, we didn't even report it to the police. The less contact with them, the better. When someone broke into the *BMR* office and vandalized it, we did (after some discussion) call the police, but only because we thought it was important to make public what had happened. Resorting to the police or to the courts, in any context, was certainly far from the first thing that came to our minds.

8. Most of us on *BMR* always subsequently called her Jackie East-West (among ourselves, at any rate) as an expression of our displeasure with what we felt was her tendency toward fuzzy thinking and capricious action. (We also, frankly, didn't much like her, and resented all the trouble she was causing us.)

9. Or unless someone was being set up to be "trashed." Trashing was an informal women's movement practice in which an activist woman—who was perceived by someone or some group of someones as being "too much of a leader" or as having "too much power" or as having made "mistakes"—was singled out to be personally attacked. It was ugly. Usually the victim had no idea that this was coming (the shock-element being part of the point); however the "trasher" was commonly accompanied by a number of her friends (who might be people that the "trashee" had also until that moment thought of as *her* friends). As well, some women would show up just to watch. Usually only one or two women present, if that, would speak up against what was going on (in part because it took some experience to recognize what was happening, in part because there are cowards everywhere). It left its victims, most of whom were women who had given their life's blood to the women's movement, utterly devastated, and it frequently drove them away (which is what it was designed to do). Fortunately, it was a relatively rare occurrence but, when it did happen, always a memorable one for all concerned.

10. Contrary to the assertions of a certain recent biographer of the celebrity currently known as "Roseanne," WtW never excluded men from the bookstore proper nor was a baseball bat with which to hit on the head men who objected to this nonexistent policy ever kept on the premises. Indeed, like *BMR*, WtW was very happy to accept men's money and to try to expand their minds. The basement, though explicitly womanspace, was likewise free of baseball bats or other weapons of mayhem, as was the *BMR* office. (Given that conservatively a quarter of the women's community was explicitly pacifist, I can't imagine how either project would have collectively decided to physically assault people. It took a three-hour meeting just to decide on the wording for a leaflet.)

Chapter Twenty-two

Differences and Identities
Feminism and the Albuquerque Lesbian Community

Trisha Franzen

This article is about the politicization of the Albuquerque, New Mexico, lesbian community. It is also very much about race, class, sexuality, and difference. It traces how three subcommunities of lesbians in this southwestern city defined themselves and each other during the period 1965–80, the years when feminism became a significant influence among them.

I came out in Buffalo, New York, in a lesbian community where I perceived continuity between members of the older lesbian community, gay liberation activists, and lesbians active in the women's movement. In that environment, many of us "new" lesbians learned the social and political lessons of lesbian culture from our "elders," that is, from those women who had lived as lesbians before the emergence of contemporary feminism and the articulation of lesbian theory. Among our core lessons was to listen to women's life stories and not to privilege the written word over the lived experience. Feminist and lesbian theory were accepted only if validated by lesbians' own lives. Issues of race and class were raised and debated as they connected with our lives. The process was, to use Cherríe Moraga and Gloria Anzaldúa's term, "theory in the flesh" (1981, 23).

When I moved to Albuquerque in 1980, I did not find analogous connections within its lesbian community. I soon became part of a feminist lesbian network, the core of which was overwhelmingly Anglo in a city where Anglos are barely the majority. Most of the women I met had moved to New Mexico as adults and had come to their lesbian identities within the women's movement. There did not seem to be much connection between this part of the Albuquerque lesbian community and an indigenous pre–women's movement one. There were no elders within the feminist lesbian circles, no women who had been active in the public bar community and were now involved in the feminist lesbian activities.

I found the absence of women of color and lesbian elders startling. The stratification I found between newly out feminist lesbians and native-born Albuquerque lesbians challenged my personal experience and my understanding of the emerging

Abridged by permission from *Signs: Journal of Women in Culture and Society* 18, no. 4 (Summer 1993):891–906. Copyright (c) 1993, University of Chicago Press.

works in lesbian and gay history that suggested that politicization follows a sense of shared identity and community consciousness (see, e.g., D'Emilio 1983). The lack of racial integration was disturbing in light of the increasingly strong challenges being made to feminist theory and activism by poor and working-class women and women of color.[1] Within lesbian studies, the invisibility of less-privileged lesbians was being countered by writers, activists, and scholars who were demanding that lesbians too examine the assumption that "all women's issues are the same" (Gibbs and Bennett 1980, 49).

Concurrent with these discussions were the feminist sexuality debates that asked, among other questions, who rightfully could claim lesbian and feminist identities and whether there are politically correct and incorrect sexual behaviors.[2] The relevance of this last controversy to issues of diversity and interconnections within the lesbian community was not immediately clear. What was clear was that it was not easy to talk about sex within feminist lesbian circles in Albuquerque. Even discussions concerning sexual behavior, roles, and S/M were suspect and were often met with silencing sarcasm and ridicule. An attempt to hold a public forum at the feminist bookstore on what was termed at the time "the sexual fringe" deteriorated into a battle between two hostile camps and a years-long public silence on these issues.

All these issues made me want to know why the Albuquerque lesbian community had split the way it had. This curiosity led to a formal research project based on interviews with lesbians who were involved with this community between 1965 and 1980. The interviews were open-ended and semistructured, focusing on each woman's experience as a lesbian in this southwestern city. Throughout this project I attempted to balance my sample on the factors of race/ethnicity and class as well as between lesbians who were born and raised in New Mexico and those who settled there as adults. Therefore, when I refer to native New Mexicans I am talking not about Native Americans but women of all races from New Mexico. The result provided diversity though it does not completely match the racial/ethnic composition of the city. I supplemented this data with newspaper articles, findings from a 1981 community survey, and records from the National Lesbian Feminist Organization and Siren, an early women's music production and education group. . . .

For the purpose of this article I have had to impose a static framework on what were dynamic divisions within a complex community. The three groups I compare are defined only on the basis of their public lesbian activities: women who were socially and politically active as lesbians within feminism; women who were socially active as lesbians, usually through the bars, but were not politically active or were not politically active as lesbians; and closeted women who were not socially or politically active as lesbians. What is important to remember is that there were active feminists in all three groups. The differentiating identifications for women in this article are not their feminist identities but, again, their public lesbian activities or "outness." Some women from all three groups, for example, were associated with the Women's Center at the University of New Mexico, but many more of the women from the first group than from the second or third. I did not ask any of the feminists in my sample to define themselves by any particular theoretical position—

radical feminist, liberal feminist, socialist feminist, etc.—nor did I delve into the sexual attitudes or behaviors of any of the women in this study. . . . The earliest gay bar remembered by my narrators was the Newsroom, which later became Duke's Cave. According to Paula: "It was pretty awful looking. Very small, very smoky. It was down under [a straight bar]. The bathroom leaked into the . . . I mean I don't know what was leaking exactly, but the bathroom was above and it never worked right. It wasn't scary, but a horrible dump. But I had a lot of fun there." The Newsroom fits the stereotype of early gay bars: smoky, dark, and a little sleazy. The police came regularly, sometimes stopping action throughout the bar to check IDs. To add to the risk and excitement, there were occasional fights. According to my informants, however, the limits of this bar were far overshadowed by the relief patrons felt in finding a lesbian/gay community.

During this period, gay men also gathered at the coffee houses that served the Albuquerque "beat" crowd; although comfortable and accepted in these public places, they made up only a small percentage of the clientele. For their part, Albuquerque lesbians frequented a jazz bar in Santa Fe, sixty miles to the north. This establishment was owned and managed by a French woman named Claude, who set the tone for nonconforming gender behavior by appearing some evenings in a flamboyant evening gown and full makeup and other nights in a tuxedo and slicked-back hair. This bar attracted a mature, mixed crowd—women and men, gay and straight—and was a favorite of middle-class lesbians.[3]

These gathering places were followed by what came to be called the Old Heights, the first of several bars run by a gay couple, Bill and Larry. One woman remembered it as opening in 1958. While their first bar was not a great improvement over the Newsroom, the New Heights, which opened several years later, was. It was attached to one of the most elegant restaurants in the city, which employed a number of gay men. Bill and Larry are remembered with great fondness as being, according to Barbara, "extremely gracious": "I felt real safe in the New Heights. With them I always felt safe. If people got tossed in jail, they'd go and do your bail."

The number of bars continued to grow. By the mid-1960s, lesbians could choose from the Wellington, a relatively fancy bar and restaurant; the Limelight, a large, rustic establishment located in the mountains east of the city; Mildred's, an in-town bar; the Upstairs Lounge, an afterhours club; and Crickets, a women's private club. Part of a family bar in the town north of Albuquerque also served as a gay bar for a short period of time.

Except for Crickets, these were all mixed bars (i.e., serving lesbians and gay men) with full liquor licenses. Crickets, owned by a Native American woman, operated under a private club liquor license, as does a lesbian bar that opened later. . . .

Albuquerque lesbians remember the late sixties and early seventies as good times. While the bars ranged from plush to sleazy, lesbians felt they had choices about where to socialize, and they recall harassment as minimal. Public lesbian culture in Albuquerque, according to the women who frequented the bars, shared many of the features identified by other lesbian historians (Nestle 1987; Kennedy and Davis 1993). One's social and sexual lives involved butch-femme roles with the accompanying dating etiquette and dress codes. Private parties supplemented nights at the bars. At these parties, the lesbians who did go to the bars socialized with their more closeted friends. Softball was a very important lesbian activity and teams drew women of all races and classes from across the city. . . .

Across the board, lesbians active in the bars and the closeted networks in the 1960s emphasize the solidarity they felt among themselves and between lesbians and gay men. The lesbians not only shared the public bar space with gay men but also considered them their friends. For some lesbians these men provided compatible dates for those occasions that called for a heterosexual cover.

While the bars were the centers of gay life in Albuquerque as elsewhere, many lesbians who frequented the bars were also in contact with closeted lesbians. As my research progressed, I became increasingly conscious of the interconnections and overlappings among the various lesbian social networks through friendships, school, softball, and parties, convincing me that the closeted lesbians were important players in the history of the public community and the growth of feminism.

My research suggests that in this community during this period, the bar-going lesbians and the lesbians who did not socialize at the bars defined themselves in part against each other, but in an opposition free of hostility. They saw in each other two ways to be lesbian, one based on safety and passing and one based on risk and an identity that was articulated and affirmed by a community. While one group's identity was centered at the bars, the closeted women kept theirs private within their homes and the homes of their closest friends.

To understand how these two subgroups related to each other, it is important to recognize that within each were individuals who had known each other often from childhood on. They had gone to school together, played sports with each other, and worked with each other. From these shared histories they could identify with each other. It also was not unusual for women to move back and forth between these two groups. . . .

When asked, most closeted women gave concerns about their jobs as their reason for avoiding public lesbian spaces. They felt they had to struggle hard enough as women to achieve economic self-sufficiency and accepted remaining in the closet as the price they had to pay for it. Only a few of the women mentioned that they did not like the bars or could not identify with the women in them.

It appears therefore that the decisions of the closeted women served as constant reminders to the public/bar lesbians of the dangers involved in participating in public gay life as well as demonstrating another, less risky way to be gay. Nevertheless, the lesbians I interviewed who were part of these social networks before the reemergence of the women's movement did not convey any sense of resentment or judgment toward each others' choices about the bars. In several cases, younger lesbians mentioned older, closeted lesbians who had served as on-the-job mentors, passing on survival strategies and warnings about the dangers of not being discreet. Although the lessons were not always appreciated immediately, they were respected in retrospect. Several quite out lesbians strongly stated their support for the decisions of closeted women, especially those in educations. As one Chicana stated, there was a "live and let live attitude" within the community.

The respectful acceptance of different choices and different ways to be lesbian was strongest among women who had grown up and gone to school together, regardless of differences in race and class. On the other hand, the closeted networks of women who were not native Albuquerqueans conveyed a sense of distance from bar lesbians. Nor did the "natives' " sense of solidarity extend to the feminists who became part of the Albuquerque lesbian scene in the late sixties and early seventies. The bar lesbians were confused and put off by their actions and ideas. The extent to which the bar lesbians viewed feminism as foreign is best captured by the name given the women most frequently credited with introducing feminist lesbianism to Albuquerque. Consistently this group is referred to as the "Boston crazies." What was clear about these feminists, according to one bar lesbian, was that they were "not us."

If one group of lesbians discussed in this article centered their lesbian identities at the bars and the other in their homes, this third group built their identities around the Women's Center at the University of New Mexico. While straight women and lesbians from the other categories were important in the development of the center, according to my informants, feminist lesbianism was centered there. The women in this third network connected with each other on the basis of their feminism and lesbianism. Many of them were students at the University of New Mexico as undergraduates, graduate students, and law students. . . .

Although feminist lesbianism was centered at the university, tensions between feminist lesbians and other lesbians were clearest at the bars. Several of the feminist lesbians remember the arrangements in the early 1970s as "old gays on one side, new gays on the other." When asked if there was much interaction, one feminist stated, "Very little between old gay and new gay. Very little. Only old gays we saw were those at the bar. And I think they viewed us as interlopers into their space. That we were dilettantes and eating pussy just to see what it tasted like and would go home to our hubbies. I mean they felt their area was being invaded." . . .

The split between these two sectors of the community can also be seen around specific issues. As I mentioned earlier, bar lesbians had often socialized with gay men and felt a sense of solidarity with them. Barbara, for example, stated that she preferred mixed bars. When her friends started going to the lesbian bar in the 1970s, she went with them but missed the guys. In contrast, Joan, a feminist lesbian, does not recall knowing any gay men. "We hated all men. Just hated them because the political rhetoric was that gays got together with other men because they hated women."

This difference may have more complex roots than separatist rhetoric. The differing histories of the individuals in these groups suggest that the extent of their earlier relationships with men influenced their acceptance of and interaction with gay men. Few of the bar or closeted lesbians I interviewed had ever been seriously involved with men in romantic or sexual ways. The males in their lives, besides family and work colleagues, had been these gay men with whom they shared public gay spaces and a sense of refuge from straight society. In contrast, many of the feminist lesbians had been married or recently involved in heterosexual relationships. For example, one feminist recalls that at its inception all of the women in her consciousness-raising group identified themselves as heterosexual and several were married. Looking back, she realizes that all these women eventually came out. In short, while the older lesbians tended to confront sexism and their lack of heterosexual privilege in the public sphere—in school, on the job, when trying to get a mortgage—the feminist lesbians had struggled over gender issues in intimate relationships with husbands and boyfriends.

Feminist lesbians also had a disdain for butch/femme roles and the dress and etiquette codes associated with them. On the other side, bar lesbians saw the feminist uniform of Levis, flannel shirts, work boots, and short hair as unattractive, even sloppy. Interestingly, while the feminist lesbians were reacting strongly against such roles, among the bar lesbians there was some sense that the importance and rigidity of these roles had diminished by this time. . . .

After 1978 the divisions within the lesbian community became even more pronounced with the opening of a second lesbian bar. While the first exclusively lesbian bar originally had been downtown, it soon moved and remained for the rest of its existence on the predominantly Hispanic, working-class west side. In the late 1970s a native New Mexican Chicana who had worked in the first lesbian bar opened a new bar in the predominantly Anglo Northeast Heights. The owner of this new bar stated that she opened her establishment to "provide women with a nicer place." What resulted was a self-segregation based on class and race, with middle-class and Anglo women going to the new bar and the older bar's clientele becoming increasingly working-class or poor women and women of color.

Not surprisingly, the feminist lesbians generally abandoned the older bar and patronized the newer one. But this arrangement did not have a long honeymoon. As stated earlier, both of these "women's" bars were run under private club licenses that made the clubs nonprofit organizations in which individuals bought memberships. These "members" theoretically had some say in the management of "their club." This situation appears to have produced higher expectations for these clubs than for gay bars generally, and even higher ones for the new bar and its owner. The feminists assumed that the owner of the new bar would run it more democratically and expected what was to the owner's mind a private business to be run according to feminist principles. Not long after the bar opened, a group of feminist lesbians asked for a meeting with the owner and confronted the owner about certain of her management decisions, claiming that they were frustrated by the owner's lack of support for their activities and their politics. On her part, the owner claims that "they wanted a share of the profits." Whatever happened, whatever the motives, these differences were not resolved amicably, and to this day the owner identifies the feminists as "trouble-making radicals."

Another example of the difficulties between these groups can be seen in a story I first heard as part of the oral history of the feminist lesbian community. I had been told about a great party that had been held, the highlight of which was two popular women appearing dressed only in cowboy boots, hats, and guns and holsters. This story was passed on as hilarious, a celebration of the outrageous behavior that was part of the early days of feminist lesbianism. I had no reason to doubt this analysis until I heard a very different version from the woman whose home was the site of the party. This Anglo, native New Mexican lesbian had only recently discovered feminism and had become part of a central feminist lesbian circle. She ran her business, which involved giving lessons mostly to children, out of her home. Her feminist friends had wanted to have a party at her house but she resisted because she was afraid it would hurt her business. They held the party anyway when she was away on a business trip. She only found out about the party when women she barely knew came up to her at the bar and said how much they liked her house. When she finally figured out the connection between the drop in her business and the people who claimed to have been in her home, she tried to confront her feminist friends about the party. They refused to hear her and shunned her afterward as being too bourgeois and closeted.

But these particular instances of suspicion and overt hostility needed to be contextualized within a greater sense of separation between the two networks sharing the public lesbian space. Although the feminist lesbians frequented the bars, they did so with other feminists, straight, gay, and undecided. This group was very much caught up in the excitement of the women's liberation movement. Their activism centered around the University of New Mexico, and they were instrumental in founding and maintaining the U.N.M. Women's Center and Women Studies Program, the Albuquerque Rape Crisis Center, and the Shelter for Victims of Domestic Violence. As lesbians, they had to struggle for recognition of their lives and lesbian issues within these organizations as well as in others such as the National Organization for Women and the New Mexico chapter of the National Women's Political Caucus. They were an important presence at a left-feminist sit-in at the campus newspaper in the early 1970s and at the state hearings for the Equal Rights Amendment. In 1976 an out lesbian was elected homecoming queen at the University of New Mexico (although the governor refused to crown her).

It was often in the political arena that the third category of lesbians, the women in the closeted networks, came into contact with the feminist lesbians. A significant number of closeted lesbians became leaders in women's political organizations and worked alongside the out feminist lesbians, though they themselves remained closeted. In spite of this shared work, women from each group had suspicions about the other. The closeted lesbians did not feel that the open lesbians understood and respected their decisions to remain closeted. They also felt that the feminist lesbians were interested only in the sexuality issue, the lesbian perspective, and would not support them in their struggles around less specifically lesbian concerns, especially those based on class and race. On their part, the feminist lesbians felt betrayed by the closeted lesbians' less-than-wholehearted support of their position, support that frequently would have necessitated abandoning their closets. The feminist lesbians interpreted the closeted lesbians' personal and political decisions as internalized oppression.

Significantly, no specifically lesbian formal organization was founded in Albuquerque until a chapter of the National Lesbian Feminist Organization was begun in 1978. The gay student organization at the University of New Mexico, founded in 1970, has been and remains a predominantly male group.

As far as the indigenous lesbian community was concerned, feminist lesbianism as political theory and practice might just as well have dropped from a spaceship. That is how alien these new lesbians, these new ways of being lesbians were to the women who made up the early public community and closeted networks. The more important question, however, is why this combination of political philosophy and personal identification was greeted with suspicion and resistance and perceived of as imposed and invasive in Albuquerque. When there appeared a group of lesbians articulating an analysis of lesbian oppression, why was this group rejected by the native community? And what does this history of the lesbian community in Albuquerque have to contribute to lesbian history and theory?

In Albuquerque, neither shared lesbian identities nor shared feminist identities were sufficient bases for solidarity across the lesbian community. Why? This research suggests that sexuality is at the core of all the issues involved and that sexuality is a problematic basis for political solidarity among women. The feminist sexuality debates made this point clear. Among other complications, women have been divided into good and bad, esteemed or despised, protected or exploited, all on the basis of sexuality. And in the dominant culture's portrayals of female sexuality, that very sexual Other that all women should fear becoming has often been the poor woman, the woman of color, and the lesbian.

Did lesbian theory and practice take these issues into account when lesbians were confronting each other in Albuquerque? In a limited way, yes. Feminists knew how calling women lesbians was a threat used to divide women and keep women in their places, but there was no recognition of how sexuality interacted with racism and classism to separate women from each other within lesbian communities. Albuquerque feminist lesbians could not talk about sex, but without talking about sex they could not really talk about being lesbians. Only now is the diversity of lesbian voices being heard, and it has taken time for lesbians to research and reveal the history needed to build theory and examine how race and class differences are entwined with sexuality and issues of trust and power. Now lesbians are asking if we feared identifying with each other because in that identity would be claiming a sexuality that was threatening.

What does it mean that for lesbians claiming one's sexuality makes us sexual outlaws? Joan Nestle (1987) describes the struggle against this labeling and speaks of how feminism appeared to offer a comforting respectability to lesbians. Lesbians could be the best feminists, but only if we discarded all in lesbianism that might be seen as tainted by heterosexuality. In Albuquerque there was certainly that sense that feminist lesbians wanted other lesbians to "clean up their acts." This included, for example, discarding both the behavior and appearances associated with butch/femme roles. Feminist lesbians in Albuquerque interpreted these roles as pseudo-heterosexuality rather than what Elizabeth Lapovsky Kennedy and Madeline Davis, from their study of the Buffalo lesbian community, see as an authentically lesbian-developed set of sexual norms (1993). Feminist lesbians in Albuquerque also wanted to rid lesbianism of its overt sexuality, of sexual desire based on difference seen clearly in roles but also associated with working-class lesbians and lesbians of color.

On the other side of this hostility were the bar lesbians' views of feminist lesbians. In a state where civil rights struggles had produced a heightened awareness of race and class privilege and where longtime New Mexicans felt their material and cultural lives threatened by a rapid influx of newcomers, having a group of newly out, newly New Mexican, middle-class, educated, Anglo women start telling them how to be lesbians understandably might antagonize the women who had made up the public lesbian community in Albuquerque, many of whom were lesbians of color and from poor and working-class backgrounds.

In mutual suspicion, these groups confronted each other over who defined "real" lesbians. The feminist lesbians came informed, and in their eyes validated, by feminist and lesbian-feminist theory that viewed lesbians as superior feminists. Yet few of them had much experience living as lesbians, negotiating the realities of being self-supporting women while finding a positive sexual identity in a society that condemned lesbians. The public and the closeted lesbians had that practice, had "theory in the flesh," but little articulated analysis of their lives and their oppression. There were few links between these two groups to foster a dialogue.

Such a dialogue might have been possible if there had been any other organized group within the gay/lesbian community. The lack of any community-based homophile or Gay Liberation activities is important here. There was no gay civil rights activism in Albuquerque up to the emergence of feminism: no Mattachine chapter, no Daughters of Bilitis, or any other group that might have provided a base for a shared political consciousness or even a sense of an organized political community. This absence of a grass-roots, sexuality-based movement kept Albuquerque from following the pattern of politicization historians have identified in cities in which there was greater continuity between the public gay/lesbian communities and gay/lesbian political activism. The consequence was the splits I saw when I entered this community.

But such tensions were not all that existed in the Albuquerque lesbian community. It seems equally important that differences based on race and class had always existed, and yet solidarity within the sexuality-based community had been possible before lesbian feminism was introduced. This appears to be due to the long history lesbians in Albuquerque had had with each other before feminism. The women who had grown up, gone to school, and played ball together knew each other well enough across class and racial lines that even when they made different choices on how to live as lesbians, those choices could be understood and respected without denying each others' subjectivity. To me, what existed between these two groups is an example of what Marilyn Frye (1983) and Maria Lugones (1990) termed "loving perception," as opposed to the "arrogant perception" that existed between them and the feminist lesbians.

Although this brief history of the Albuquerque lesbian community demonstrates how race, class, and other power issues interconnect with sexuality in our lives, it also warns of the limitations of theory. Trying to be both activists and theorists, the feminist lesbians of Albuquerque proceeded in the best way they knew how, given both their reliance on theory and the state of lesbian and feminist theory at that point in time. Today, unfortunately, those roles are becoming increasingly separate, and, if anything, academically based feminists are even more dependent upon theory as the means to gain status within their professional lives. All feminists need to heed the critiques of our dependence on theory and to keep our theory connected with the realities of women's lives. (See, e.g., Christian 1990 and Rebolledo 1990.)

In Albuquerque, many of the early feminist lesbian leaders left; a couple became important theorists, one helped found Olivia Records (a lesbian-owned recording company), another headed a national gay organization, a few are again living straight lives. The lesbians who remained in Albuquerque found that the city is too small and the need for one another too great for lesbians to ignore each other. Additionally, the Albuquerque lesbian community has been too dynamic a scene for these earlier divisions to solidify. With new leaders and the time for trust to grow through continuing interaction and dialogue, lesbians in Albuquerque are perhaps in the vanguard in building a multicultural feminist lesbian community.

NOTES

1. Some of the early works include Bethel and Smith 1979; Davis 1981; Moraga and Anzaldúa 1981.

2. See, e.g., Cook 1977, 42–61; Rich 1980, 631–60; Faderman 1981; SAMOIS 1981; Ferguson, Zita, and Addelson 1982, 147–88; Linden et al. 1982; Snitow, Stansell, and Thompson 1983; and Vance 1984.

3. Many of the women I interviewed spoke of knowing of a separate Santa Fe lesbian network of older wealthy women who had settled in Santa Fe or Taos and participated in the artistic circles of those cities.

REFERENCES

Bethel, Lorraine, and Barbara Smith, eds. 1979. *Conditions: five,* the black women's issue.

Christian, Barbara. 1990. "The Race for Theory." In *Making Face, Making Soul*—Haciendo Caras: *Creative and Critical Perspectives by Women of Color,* ed. Gloria Anzaldúa, 335–45. San Francisco: Aunt Lute.

Cook, Blanche Weisen. 1977. "Female Support Networks and Political Activism: Lillian Wald, Crystal Eastman, and Emma Goldman." *Chrysalis* 3:43–61.

Davis, Angelo Y. 1981. *Women Race and Class.* New York, Vintage.

D'Emilio, John. 1983. *Sexual Politics, Sexual Communities: The Making of a Homosexual Minority in the United States.* Chicago: University of Chicago Press.

Faderman, Lillian. 1981. *Surpassing the Love of Men.* New York: Morrow.

Ferguson, Ann, Jacquelyn Zita, and Kathryn Pyne Addelson. 1982. "On 'Compulsory Heterosexuality and Lesbian Existence': Defining Terms." In *Feminist Theory: A Critique of Ideology,* ed. Nannerl O. Keohane, Michelle Z. Rosaldo, and Barbara C. Gelpi, 147–88. Chicago: University of Chicago Press.

Frye, Marilyn. 1983. *The Politics of Reality: Essays in Feminist Theory*. Trumansburg, N.Y.: Crossing.

Gibbs, Joan, and Sara Bennett, eds. 1980. *Top Ranking: A Collection of Articles on Racism and Classism in the Lesbian Community*. Brooklyn, N.Y.: February Third Press.

Kennedy, Elizabeth Lapovsky, and Madeline Davis. 1993. *Boots of Leather, Slippers of Gold: The History of a Lesbian Community*. New York: Routledge & Kegan Paul.

Linden, Robin Ruth, Darlene R. Pagano, Diana E. H. Russell, and Susan Leigh Star, eds. 1982. *Against Sadomasochism: A Radical Feminist Analysis*. East Palo Alto, Calif.: Frog in the Well.

Lugones, Maria. 1990. "Playfulness, 'World'-Travelling and Loving Perception." In *Making Face, Making Soul-Haciendo Caras: Creative and Critical Perspectives by Women of Color*, ed. Gloria Anzaldúa. San Francisco: Aunt Lute.

Moraga, Cherríe, and Gloria Anzaldúa, eds. 1981. *This Bridge Called My Back: Writings by Radical Women of Color*. Watertown, Mass.: Persephone.

Nestle, Joan. 1987. *A Restricted Country*. Ithaca, N.Y.: Firebrand.

Rebolledo, Tey Diana. 1990. "The Politics of Poetics: Or, What Am I, a Critic, Doing in This Text Anyhow?" In *Making Face, Making Soul*-Haciendo Caras: *Creative and Critical Perspectives by Women of Color*, ed. Gloria Anzaldúa, 346–55. San Francisco: Aunt Lute.

Rich, Adrienne. 1980. "Compulsory Heterosexuality and Lesbian Existence." *Signs* 5(4): 631–60.

SAMOIS, ed. 1981. *Coming to Power: Writings and Graphics on Lesbian S-M*. Boston: Alyson.

Snitow, Ann, Christine Stansell, and Sharon Thompson, eds. 1983. *Powers of Desire: The Politics of Sexuality*. New York: Monthly Review.

Vance, Carole, ed. 1984. *Pleasure and Danger: Exploring Female Sexuality*. Boston: Routledge & Kegan Paul.

Chapter Twenty-three

Lesbian Community
Heterodox Congregation

Marilyn Frye

(On Saturday, April 29, 1989, at the Mountainmoving Coffeehouse in Chicago, I was a member of a panel of nine lesbians who had contributed to the new anthology *For Lesbians Only,* a collection of lesbian separatist writings.[1] Each of us did a reading or made a short presentation. This is the statement I composed and read for the occasion.)

I live in Lansing, Michigan. I have lived there for almost fifteen years. There's a lesbian community there which I, along with many others, have worked to create, grow, and maintain. This community has been shaped in many ways by lesbians who are separatist—though being separatist does not mean the same thing to all of us. I'm proud of the lesbian community in the town I live in. I move in that community with a strong and satisfying sense of shared accomplishments. I want to talk a bit about that community tonight.

Two things have happened recently in my community that have generated a lot of feeling and a lot of talk. The two things weren't causally connected with each other; they just happened to happen close to each other. About a week ago, a lesbian in my town committed suicide. She did it decisively and deliberately. The other thing is that Sarah Hoagland's recent presentation in Lansing triggered open conflict about the value of twelve-step programs to individual dykes and as an influence in the community. Both of these things, the suicide and the conflict, focused my attention on lesbian community—what it is, how it works, what kind of glue holds it together.

Probably the most obvious thing about what makes this community a community is that it is *not* that we agree on everything. There is, in fact, much disagreement on practically everything. Here's a list of some things there is *not* agreement on in my community:

- we do not agree on the importance of recycling jars and paper, or on whether it's OK to have christmas trees;

Reprinted by permission of the author from *Willful Virgin: Essays in Feminism, 1976–1992,* by Marilyn Frye. Freedom, Calif.: Crossing Press, 1992. Copyright © 1990 by Marilyn Frye.

- we do not agree about what the priority is on working against U.S. imperialism in Central America or on working against nuclear power and nuclear weapons, or on working for legal and available abortions;
- we do not agree on whether the practice of friendship requires remaining supportive, or even civil, to lesbians who go straight, or requires active support of lesbians who have male babies;
- we all say that we are against racism, but we do not agree at all about what it is or what to do about it;
- we don't agree about whether it's OK to wear skirts and dresses, to shave our legs, to get permanents, to wear make-up; we don't agree about whether twelve-step programs are wholesome for dykes, or whether it's OK to practice or to purchase therapy;
- we do not agree about how much of the Lesbian Alliance's funds should be donated to the Sharon Kowalski fund, or about whether the Lesbian Alliance and the Ambitious Amazons should try to work together more;
- we don't agree about what kinds of behavior between lovers are OK and what kinds are terrible;
- we do not agree about whether there is still any such thing women's music or about whether the Olivia Caribbean cruises are absurd;
- we don't agree about how important it is to have events, activities, and homes accessible to wheelchair users, or about whether it's OK to drink alcohol, to go to weddings, to like your father or brother, to de-dyke your house when your parents visit, to get a hot-tub or a nice car if you can afford it, to watch tv, or to go to a male dentist;
- we do not agree about hamburgers.

And this is only a few of the things we don't all agree about in my community. I'm sure I don't even know what some of the things are that we don't agree about.

You might suppose that there is agreement among us on some other level, and I supposed it too. But the issues about 12-step programs have made me doubt it. I thought that in spite of all our differences about specific actions and practices, what held us together was something some of us have called "ethical compatibility"—some deep likeness of ethical and political intuition. I have thought something like that underlay our *lesbianism,* our *desire* for each other. But now I'm thinking that within my community there is not even a significant likeness of basic ethical and political intuition.

So what is there? What holds us in community? The answer seems to be either (1) nothing holds us in community, or (2) I've asked the wrong question. I opt for (2).

What I'm getting at here is that it's the natural normal thing for women to be connected and sustained in community with each other, and it has nothing in particular to do with agreeing about anything, or even liking each other. It certainly doesn't have anything in particular to do with approving of each other. Instead of looking for something like common values to account for what holds us together, we should consider whatever kept us apart or works to keep us apart. . . . And this brings me to the topic of separatism.

Heteropatriarchal forms of social organization keep women apart from women, separate women from women. And that, I would say, is unnatural. I spoke at the beginning of creating and maintaining lesbian community. But when I think about the actual activities and behaviors we do, what they mostly add up to is not *building* something, but just *clearing space* for something. Almost all the organizing adds up to nothing more than making space and getting a whole bunch of lesbians in that space all at once. That is, we separate lesbians from separation from each other and then community happens. It is anarchic, often strife-ridden and stressful, not always fun, not always affirming of whatever we think about things or about ourselves, but it's also just the normal thing for women—to be in lesbian connection with each other. It doesn't have to be explained.

Now, what about the suicide? It is terribly sad and awful, and I grieve for the life that might have been. It makes everyone wonder what we could or should have done to make living tolerable, not to mention joyful, for that woman. But one of my friends (with whom I disagree about some very important things) noted that in the almost fifteen years we've known this community of many hundreds of lesbians, this is only the second suicide she knew of (only the first that I had known of). Before the current era of lesbian feminist consciousness and gay rights, suicide was epidemic among lesbians, so my older friends have told me. But it is not, among us. In the time I have known this community, we have fought and quarreled, and trashed, and bashed, and made love and made hate, had parties and played and flowed through shifting patterns of affiliation and ostracism, and had powerful feelings of solidarity and powerful feelings of alienation from each other, and put out a zillion newsletters and fliers and organized fund-raisers and gossiped, and felt great and felt terrible. And lesbians in my community have survived in large numbers.

What I'm saying is that lesbian community is possible—a community that is "separate" in the sense that there is a lesbian center of gravity (or of hilarity, perhaps), a force field, in which natural lesbian connection happens, which sustains and protects lesbians in many ways and varying degrees from the ravages of misogyny and heterosexualism, even, for some and in some ways from the violences of racism and poverty.

In my community, lesbians don't agree about anything and *lesbians survive in droves.*

NOTE

1. *For Lesbians Only: A Separatist Anthology,* edited by Julia Penelope and Sarah Lucia Hoagland (London: Onlywomen Press, 1988).

Chapter Twenty-four

Messages of Exclusion
Gender, Movements, and Symbolic Boundaries

Joshua Gamson

Begin with two strange, apparently unrelated moments of conflict in sex and gender movement histories.

CNN's *Larry King Live* was blaring on television. "You won't believe who's won the right to advise the United Nations," the announcer crowed to his audience. "A gay-rights alliance with UN standing that includes groups that advocate sex with children. The debate starts here, live," he promised (*Larry King Live* 1993). Within the International Lesbian and Gay Association (ILGA), granted consultative status to the United Nations Economic and Social Council earlier in 1993, the debate had already exploded. Within a year, the North American Man/Boy Love Association (NAMBLA) was expelled from ILGA. "NAMBLA is not a gay organization," said Gregory King of the Human Rights Campaign Fund, the largest U.S. gay and lesbian lobbying group, in support of the ouster. "They are not part of our community and we thoroughly reject their efforts to insinuate that pedophilia is an issue related to gay and lesbian civil rights" (in Tsang 1994, 15). His statement, echoed elsewhere throughout the debate, sidesteps a fact no one disputed: NAMBLA had been a member of the ILGA for a decade. An old stasis was demolished: NAMBLA's practical if awkward inclusion, now public, was undermined as it threatened the existing symbolic boundaries of the *gay and lesbian* collective.

Around the same time, the 19th Annual Michigan Womyn's Music Festival (MWMF) was in full swing, and several attendees were meeting with the festival's communications coordinators. Having set themselves up outside the gates under the banner "Camp Trans: For Humyn-Born Humyns," they were lodging their protest of a policy limiting attendance at the festival to "womyn-born womyn." Writer Leslie Feinberg introduced herself as a person born anatomically female but "who passes and lives as a man and has a driver's license showing her sex as male." Would she be allowed entry under the policy? Kodi Hendrix self-identified as a person born with both male and female genitalia asked, "Will only half of me be allowed in?" James Green, a female-to-male transsexual activist, asked if

Abridged by permission from *Gender & Society* 11, no. 2 (April 1997):178–199. Copyright (c) 1997 by Sociologists for Women in Society.

"he would be considered a woman by the festival owners using the same logic by which they consider male-to-female transsexuals to be men even after sex-change surgery" (Camp Trans 1994). Eventually, although no change was made in the policy under which transsexuals had been ejected in the past, transsexual protesters entered the festival grounds without resistance. In a mirror of the ILGA/NAMBLA dispute, a new equilibrium had been reached, at least temporarily: Transsexual women remained excluded from the lesbian feminist collective, even as they gained entry.

Political battles like these within movements, many of them ending in similar expulsions, are nothing new. (Consider, for example, the factionalization in the early years of the contemporary women's movement [Buechler 1990; Echols 1989; Ryan 1989, 1992].) Nor are these kinds of disputes, at least on the face of it, terribly difficult to understand. Scholars now routinely note that social movements depend on the active, ongoing construction of collective identity, and that deciding who *we* are requires deciding who we are not (Phelan 1993; Taylor and Whittier 1992). All social movements, and identity movements in particular, are thus in the business, at least sometimes, of exclusion.[1] Their reasons, in addition to the general advantages of group solidarity, are good ones at both strategic and expressive levels. In political systems that distribute rights and resources to groups with discernible boundaries, activists are smart to be vigilant about those boundaries; in cultural systems that devalue so many identities, a movement with clarity about who belongs can better provide its designated members with the strength and pride to revalue their identities.

Maintenance of group boundaries involves movements in bitter disputes not only with those everyone agrees is not a member (that is, with antagonists) but also in often uglier conflicts with those who might reasonably be considered members or protagonists. The *us* is solidified not just against an external *them* but also against *thems* inside, as particular subgroups battle to gain or retain legitimate *us* standing. Yet, despite a renewed interest in the cultural dynamics of social movements (Johnston and Klandermans 1995), these internal contests are still only rarely analyzed as movement phenomena in their own rights, and for what they reveal about collective identity construction (Cohen 1996; Gamson 1995). For scholars of gender, moreover, these movement processes are especially significant: The construction of a collective gender identity is in part a movement outcome (Taylor 1996; Taylor and Whittier 1992).

In this article, I take a closer look at two internal movement disputes to shed a brighter light on inclusion/exclusion processes and their place in the construction of collective identity. I first review some of the perspectives already circulating, emerging from literatures on collective identity, which emphasize the ways *boundary negotiation* reinforces the solidarity necessary for collective action, and note the benefits of solid boundaries. Then, drawing on extensive primary documents from the two debates, I develop and revise those perspectives, arguing for greater attention both to communication contexts and to the gendered aspects of movement identity building.

The cases examined here, which both involved the explicit expulsion of some members, emerged in sex and gender movements in the early 1990s: over the involvement of the NAMBLA in the organizing of the ILGA, and over the participation of transsexuals in the MWMF. The ILGA and MWMF cases provide important evidence that dynamics of exclusion depend only partially on the expressive and instrumental needs for group solidarity. In both cases, significantly, it is not the *participation* of particular people (boy lovers, transsexuals) that is threatening. In fact, NAMBLA members were active in the international lesbian and gay organization long before they were excluded, and transsexuals were quietly allowed into the women's music festival just after they were officially expelled. This gap between practice and public discourse suggests that internal movement debates over inclusion and exclusion are best understood as *public communications*. They depend heavily on the communicative environment, I will argue, especially the location and nature of the primary *audience*.[2]

Practical participation in the collective, in each case, coexisted—often uncomfortably, but coexisted just the same—with public silence about that participation for a period. That stasis was disrupted, however, when interested parties called public attention to the collective's symbolic boundaries; those boundaries were then renegotiated publicly, with groups fighting to define true membership. These public definitions, and redefinitions, may or may not change the ways participation happens. The cases examined amount to different versions of the same process: In one, the challenge came from outside (as right-wing political organizations attempted to publicly undermine gay and lesbian boundaries), and the communication was primarily geared toward a broad American public; and in the other, the challenge came from within (as transsexuals publicly disputed *lesbian feminist* boundaries), and the public communication was primarily between members. In each case, the *we* of collective identity shifted through a similar and revealing process, shaped primarily by the communication environment.

This analysis triggers further questions, taken up in the conclusion, about the gendered nature of these collective identity processes: Are these dynamics somehow unique to gender and sexuality movements, or are movement dynamics gendered in some more general, discernible ways? Drawing on the model of gendered institutions and organizations (Acker 1990; Gordon 1990; Lorber 1994), and especially on the call to come to terms with the gendered nature of social movements (Taylor 1996), I return to the ILGA and MWMF cases to suggest that gendered communication environments are central to understanding collective identity construction not only in sex and gender movements but also in social movements more generally. The cases of explicit expulsion of group members in sex and gender movements, in the end, put the spotlight on the issue of whether and how "all social movements—regardless of whether they are focused on issues pertaining specifically to women and irrespective of their gender composition—are engaged in the social construction of gender" (Taylor 1996, 166).

Collective Identity, Exclusion, and Solidarity

Among the ways in which collective identities are created and maintained, clarifying boundaries of membership is plainly central. Put simply, identity requires difference; building collective identities requires not simply pointing out commonalities but also marking off who we are not (Phelan 1993; Spelman 1988).[3] The "achievement" of collective identity is inevitably tied to some degree of boundary patrol. Clear membership boundaries are, moreover, useful for mobilization (one knows who is a potential participant and who is not), for collective grievances (one knows for whom a claim is being made), and for group solidarity (one knows to whom one is tied).

Although there are important exceptions, especially from those writing about women's movement factionalization, for the most part scholars have pointed to the relationship between movement actors and those explicitly opposed to them as the site of boundary negotiation.[4] Verta Taylor and Nancy Whittier, for instance, in building their important analytical framework for understanding collective identity construction, point to "the social, psychological and physical structures that establish *differences between a challenging group and dominant groups*" (1992, 111, emphasis added; see also Gerson and Peiss 1985). The conflict among the challengers is here underplayed, in favor of that between challenger and dominator. In a related effort, Scott Hunt, Robert Benford, and David Snow (1994) emphasize the ways collective identity construction is linked to the framing of issues by social movements. In their analysis, movements construct three sets of identities: protagonists (sympathizers, beneficiaries, advocates), antagonists (opposition actors), and audiences (neutral or uncommitted observers). In the course of making claims about "countermovements, countermovement organizations, hostile institutions, inimical publics, and social control agents," movements establish "antagonist identity fields" (Hunt, Benford, and Snow 1994, 197).

Certainly, this is the case. Movement actors solidify their boundaries by defining themselves against those they agree are enemies. Yet, while Hunt, Benford, and Snow (1994) note the elasticity and overlap between these identity categories, this fluidity remains overlooked. As in Taylor and Whittier's (1992) analysis, the process by which a collective defines its identity against those claiming to already be members is overshadowed. That process of *contested membership* and *indigenous policing* (Cohen 1996), that muddle in which members fight for the title of protagonist, is crucial for understanding collective identity. Indeed, it is the fact that movements often fight internally over who is the antagonist, and that audiences are sometimes committed antagonists or protagonists, that needs careful attention. And as Cathy Cohen has shown in her discussion of Black gay identities and AIDS politics, there is much at stake in these fights, since "contestation of identity has tangible effects, influencing the distribution of resources, services, access, and legitimacy within communities" (1996, 6).

Looking closely at debates over expulsion or inclusion, then, takes us a step further toward clarifying the dynamics of collective identity construction. Direct exclusion is not the only way such boundaries are drawn. Many forms of exclusion are more coded or less visible (Cohen 1996). Some white-dominated gay bars, for instance, exclude African American patrons by requiring three forms of identification; more broadly, many have pointed out that much "universal" women's organizing excludes by making assumptions reflecting white, heterosexual, middle-class women's experience (Ryan 1992; Spelman 1988). Looking at cases, as I do here, in which exclusion is not just uncoded but loud and clear, highlights the process by which in-groups become out-groups, and vice versa. . . .

Transsexuals, Lesbians, and the Internal Audience: The Michigan Womyn's Music Festival

The MWMF, one of many women-only events and institutions that grew out of the lesbian feminist movement of the 1970s (Echols 1989; Ryan 1992; Taylor and Rupp 1993), began in 1976 and has grown into an event that annually attracts several thousand women to a 650-acre plot of land for five days of camping, cooking, music, and workshops. Although it is of course built on music, it is explicitly a political event, built on the lesbian feminist philosophy of the woman-oriented woman as feminist vanguard and related community-building strategies, many of them involving separation from men (Phelan 1989; Ryan 1992; Taylor and Rupp 1993; Whittier 1995). The festival, in the words of one longtime participant, is part of the project of maintaining "male-free spaces" as spots for the development of women's culture in opposition to male domination:

> Standing naked "downtown" at the Michigan Womyn's Music Festival, I have thought of myself as "inside" and of the patriarchal world as "out there" somewhere beyond the borders of the womyn-owned land. (Penelope 1990, 15)

For this experience of an "inside" safe from patriarchy to work, there must be no ambiguity about who is female and who is not. Of course, femaleness is not a sufficient condition for inclusion and is, like gayness in ILGA, one among many boundaries being simultaneously negotiated in and through lesbian feminism (see Whittier 1995); the presence of certain kinds of females (vocally antifeminist women, for example) would also be likely to trigger policing, and the presence of certain kinds of females (sadomasochists, for instance) does trigger controversy (Festival forum 1990; Taylor and Rupp 1993). Still, for a lesbian feminist cultural event like this, drawing as it does on "female values, separatism, the primacy of women's relationships, and feminist ritual" (Taylor and Rupp 1993, 34), the delineation of male from female would seem to be a necessary condition. Transsexuals make that delineation unclear.

While the presence of transsexual women in women-only spaces was an issue of dispute periodically during the 1970s, especially with the publication of Janice Raymond's *The Transsexual Empire* (Raymond 1979; Stone 1991), at the MWMF the question of who qualified as a woman did not explode until 1991, when Nancy Jean Burkholder was expelled from the 16th annual festival. As she tells it, Burkholder had attended the festival the previous year without incident but was approached as she waited to enter in 1991 by two women, asking to speak to her about "a serious and difficult matter."

> Chris said that the Michigan Womyn's Music Festival was a woman-only event and she wanted to know if I were a man. I replied that I was a woman and showed her my New Hampshire picture ID driver's license. Then she asked me if I were a transsexual. I asked her what was the point of her questioning and she replied that transsexuals were not permitted to attend the festival. She said that MWMF policy was that the festival was open to "natural womyn-born womyn" only. (Burkholder 1993, 4)

Told that the policy "was for the benefit of transsexuals' safety and the safety of women attending the festival," Burkholder asked to see the policy in writing. "I said I was willing to submit to a genital examination in order to satisfy her concerns about my sex," Burkholder (1993, 4) recalls, but this was refused. Although no written policy was produced, after the festival producers were consulted, Burkholder was expelled from the festival (Burkholder 1993; Keen 1991).

Although no transsexuals were expelled from the next year's festival, Burkholder's expulsion set in motion a controversy over transsexual inclusion within the festival that has continued for several years.[5] More important, it set in motion an organizing effort by a group of transsexual women and their supporters, aiming specifically to publicly challenge the festival's "womyn-born womyn only" policy, to "raise consciousness among festival participants" about the policy, and to "demonstrate that not only could [the policy] not be enforced, but that there is, in fact, no rational justification for its existence" (Fredrickson 1993; Gabriel 1993, 8). Their efforts involved holding workshops and setting up a literature table including Burkholder's account of the previous year's events, 24 "gender myths" ("common misperceptions about transsexuality within the lesbian community with rebuttals"), and buttons such as "Where's Nancy?" "I Might Be Transsexual," and "Bisexual, Transsexual, Meat Eating, Lipstick Wearing Leatherdyke from Hell" (Gabriel 1993, 8). One participant announced herself as transsexual at two workshops, later declaring her presence there "to be in the same tradition of civil disobedience as that of African Americans who conducted sit-ins at segregated lunch counters in the early 1960s" (Gabriel 1993, 11).

This organizing effort emerged, not coincidentally, during the growth period of a small but vocal, radical transsexual movement (Bornstein 1994; Brown 1994; International Conference on Transgender Law and Employment Policy 1994; Stone 1991). Many of those involved in transsexual organizing identify as feminist, and many as lesbian, and have explicitly asserted recognition as openly transsexual feminists as a political goal. (One of the women expelled from MWMF, Davina Anne Gabriel, is publisher and editor of *TransSisters: The Journal of Transsexual Feminism.*) As transsexual activists, these women had good reason to push at the public boundaries of the lesbian feminist *we.* They *wanted* their exclusion publicized among the women present at MWMF. Once Burkholder was expelled, transsexual women directed their efforts toward keeping the issue of feminist boundaries in public view for festival goers. In fact, one track of a "multi-track strategy" during the 1992 festival was to "create suspicion" that a nontranssexual woman was actually transsexual, to "see if she would be expelled"; she was not (Gabriel 1993, 8). Provoking expulsion, if it directed public attention toward the exclusion of transsexuals, was itself a strategy. "The Michigan Womyn's Music Festival is, quite simply," one group of women wrote, "the frontline in the struggle for inclusion of transsexual womyn within the lesbian/feminist community" (Burkholder et al. 1994, 11).

It was precisely the terrain of "who is a woman?" (and, therefore, "who is a lesbian?") and, perhaps most of all, "who is a feminist?" on which transsexuals waged their public battles.[6] One argument was simply that transsexuals are women, and the policy is, therefore, discriminatory. If they are indeed "legally, hormonally, socially and anatomically female," one woman wrote, the festival organizers have no more right to the policy "than they do to exclude differently abled women, fat women, old women, young women, or left handed women" (Malone 1992). Taking another tack, Nancy Burkholder argued that since medical history is the only way to distinguish transsexual women from nontranssexual women, the policy is "not based on any real difference" but on "a gut feeling—like racism or homophobia" (Burkholder 1991, 15).

Beyond establishing the commonality between transsexual and nontranssexual women, antiexclusion arguments claimed the ground of feminism. As Davina Gabriel put it, the justifications for exclusion

> are rooted in patriarchal assumptions and practices. All of the justifications cited for the exclusion of transsexual womyn prove to be inadequate because, ultimately, they are all based on patriarchal concepts of *determinism,* either biological, environmental, or a combination of both. Determinism, in turn, proves to be based on another patriarchal concept, that of *reductionism.* Likewise, arguments favoring the exclusion of transsexual womyn also prove to be fundamentally founded in patriarchal concepts of gender *binarism.* (Gabriel 1994, 12)

Not only do transsexuals belong within the boundaries of feminist community, but their exclusion is antifeminist, contrary to "universal sisterhood" and "feminist values" (Severns 1992, 2). Expanding the boundaries to include transsexual women affirms feminist community. *We are you; you are us.*

Transsexual organizing against the "womyn-born womyn only" policy met with a strong response from the festival producers.[7] In 1992, the producers defended their response to the presence of "a known transsexual man" at the festival (refusing, interestingly, Burkholder's self-definition) and reaffirmed their commitment to "keep our focus and energy on womyn and on presenting the best week of womyn's culture and community that we know how to create." The issue of transsexual inclusion was "processed" by the festival working community, the producers reported, and those discussions revealed that "the group of womyn who come together to create this gathering supports this Festival policy" (Vogel and Price 1992, 10). The Michigan festival, they argued.

> is and always has been an event for womyn, and this continues to be defined as womyn-born womyn. We respect everyone's right to define themselves as they wish. ... We mean only to define *who this event is for.* We hold dearly our right to make

this determination and in the same regard we believe that it is the right of every other womyn's institution and community to define these issues depending on their own particular needs and concerns. (Vogel and Price 1992, 10, emphasis added)

Other supporters of the newly revealed policy argued similarly. As one writer to the lesbian feminist magazine *Lesbian Connection* put it,

One of the benefits of festivals is that we can fully explore—even glorify—our identities as women, without the trappings and traps this culture imposes upon those of us born with the XX chromosome. To argue that anyone who decides to become a woman has undergone the same oppression, and has the same bond of common experience as those born to it, is to flatten the experience of those who came to it by birth, and who have lived it since. (Festival responses 1992, 8)

Another writer, similarly arguing that *woman* is an identity that cannot be taken on later in life, recategorizes male-to-female transsexuals even more dramatically, arguing that "the fuss about 'transsexual women' exists because our society has no role for castrated, feminized men—'eunuchs.' "

I can understand how American eunuchs would think of themselves as women—one has to think of oneself in the terms available. However, surgery doesn't make a eunuch a woman, any more than melanin implants and a wish for African ancestors would make me Black. Transgendered people are part of the queer community, and ought to be valued for their individuality and able to make friends on the same basis as anyone else. However, *women as a group have no obligation to take care of eunuchs as a group.* (Festival responses 1992, 9, emphasis added).

Transsexuals, as castrated men clearly outside the bounds of women's *we,* are justifiably excluded.

In keeping with their policy, three days into the 1993 festival, producers expelled three transsexual women who had gained admittance and, on the second day, had set up a table with literature about transsexual exclusion. Although womyn-born womyn was never defined, the message was always clear: *You are not women, you are not us.*

The objection here, it is crucial to note, was not so much to the presence of transsexual women nor to any terribly rigid version of what womanhood, which comes in many expressions and shapes and colors at the festival, can look like. The objection was any movement in the publicly noted boundaries; what was at stake was what public inclusion of transsexuals communicated to the feminist community members gathered at the festival. According to one account, in fact, the security coordinator told the tablers that "if we had not revealed our transsexuality to anyone then we would have been allowed to remain at the festival" (Gabriel 1993, 20).

The priority on symbolic rather than actual boundaries becomes even more clear as the story continues. In 1993, the expelled transsexuals, along with their supporters, set up camp across the road from the festival's front gate, calling it Camp Trans. This protest camp was reinstated the following year, with 13 transsexual women, 12 nontranssexual women, one transsexual man, one nontranssexual man, and one intersexed person in attendance. The organizers held workshops, speeches, readings, and religious services, and distributed statements. After extensive meetings that year with festival producers, a new compromise was reached. While they refused the demand to replace "womyn-born womyn" with "nontranssexual" in their policy, the producers declared that they were leaving it up to individuals to decide whether they were womyn-born womyn. Declaring that their group consisted of transsexual women, nontranssexual women, an intersexed person, and transgendered women, and "that each of them interpreted the term 'womyn born womyn' to include them," the protesting group entered the festival. None among them was refused tickets or asked questions (Camp Trans 1994, 3).

As in the NAMBLA case, the renegotiation of collective identity takes place not because loose membership boundaries threatened the operation of the festival, as the looking-the-other-way inclusion attests. Instead, it is pushed by a party for whom the current formulation no longer works—in this case, by transsexuals for whom visibility has come to be seen as a political necessity and who have garnered enough personnel to wage a challenge. Again, a stasis is disrupted by the publicness of the inclusion, and long-standing divisions within lesbian feminist politics are reopened.

Here, too, the communication context, the targeting of an internal audience of feminist women at the festival, shapes both the identity claims and the resolution. As opposed to, say, using transsexualism to muddy or take apart the category of *woman* (Bornstein 1994; Gamson 1995), transsexuals in this context aimed primarily at expanding the boundaries of *woman, feminist,* and *lesbian,* while reaffirming the categories. And as long as the category *woman* was left loose but intact, allowing both separation (we know who we are) and community (we are diverse), actual participation by the "excluded" was not disturbing to producers. As long as the symbolic boundaries communicated what they needed to—that *woman* is a clearly designated category—the physical gates are open. A new compromise is reached, in which the question of who is female, and, therefore, potentially lesbian and feminist, is no longer up for grabs.

Conclusion: Audiences, Identity Patrol, and Gendered Movements

These cases of conflict within sex and gender movements indicate that building and maintaining collective identity boundaries takes place not just vis-à-vis clearly designated antagonists (Helms and the antigay right, men demanding access to women's bodies and spaces) but largely on the unstable terrain of contested membership. Moreover, I have argued, with their odd incongruence of on-the-ground inclusion and public exclusion, the stories point to the importance of the *symbolic* aspect of symbolic boundaries. As in the current U.S. "don't ask, don't tell" compromise for lesbians and gays in the military, what gets publicly communicated by inclusion or expulsion trumps the question of actual participation. As this examination of internal disputes in sex and gender movements illustrates, "Transsexuals are not women" and "Man-boy lovers are not gay," however heartfelt, are not so much permanent positions on identity as elastic, directed communications about identity.

When and how exclusion takes place, then, is closely tied to the specific conditions under which the collective boundaries are being used politically; those boundaries are, in a sense, cultural resources (Williams 1995), communication tools in specific political struggles. Understanding collective identity construction thus requires careful, grounded analysis of these communication environments, the conditions under which various actors fight for "true" membership status (Lichterman 1995): Who is calling the question of public exclusion and for what political purposes? Who are the audiences being targeted, and how do they (or the perception of them by those attacking and defending versions of collective identity) shape the outcome?

As this analytical framework suggests, these dynamics of course differ for different movements, shaped as they are by the particular political concerns and environments. The two cases presented here may help us see more clearly some of the important conditions affecting the opening and closing of movement boundaries. To begin with, it is plain that a shift in the communication environment can come from either outside or inside the existing movement boundaries. The use of NAMBLA and ILGA by outsider antagonists (Helms and his allies) to communicate to nongay and nonpedophile audiences set in motion a set of events not at all unlike the attempts by insider transsexuals in Michigan to communicate to women within the collective we of (lesbian) feminism: bitter arguments, expulsions, a narrowing of the identity category.

That boundary contestation can take place with or without the involvement of external adversaries is unsurprising, but it matters: primarily because the audience for the subsequent communication-by-expulsion differs. ILGA's key audience, for instance, was those in a position to rescind UN status (or pressure others to rescind it), and the tightening of the gay-and-lesbian identity boundary was prompted by the need to communicate respectability to those decision makers. As I have pointed out, when the audience was gay-and-lesbian membership organizations alone, NAMBLA's participation prompted no dramatic boundary patrol. At the MWMF, at which the primary audience is other lesbian feminist–identified women, the commitment to narrower public boundaries came about because of a perceived threat to the organizing principle by which the festival's participant-audience is attracted: that those born to female bodies experience similarly oppressive (and empowering) experiences.

Clearly in these cases, what is being communicated is not just generic boundary drawing but has much to do with gender: with distinguishing male from female, with defining appropriate relationships between adult men and male children, with making or unmaking the link between same-sex desire and men as sexual predators. This suggests that we need to think more carefully about the gendered nature of movement activity—in this case, the process through which identity boundaries stretch and contract in response to particular communication environments. Are these communications gendered simply because the movements initiating them are gender-based ones, or might inclusion/exclusion processes and identity patrols be gendered in other sorts of movements as well?

The literature thus far is largely silent on these sorts of questions. Although the strong turn in the last decade to "the idea that social structure and social processes are gendered" (Acker 1990, 145; see also Lorber 1994) has been amply applied to the state (e.g., see Gordon 1990) and organizations (e.g., Acker 1990), it has made only small ripples in the approach to social movements. Scholars have certainly recognized gender divisions within movements and carefully analyzed gender as a basis for mobilization and the gender system as a movement target, but the notion that "the concept of a two-gender system that constructs women to be the subordinates of men is central to the emergence, nature, and outcomes of social movements" (Taylor 1996, 166) remains largely unexplored.

The stories I have recounted here provide some initial directions. If the argument holds that exclusions are most prominently public communications and thus that identity boundaries shift in response to particular audiences, it is fruitful to consider how communication settings are themselves gendered. Beyond the genders of the speakers and listeners, the resonant gender symbolism of a communication environment (ideas and images about masculinity and feminity, the links between sexuality and gender, distinguishing male from female) crucially shapes boundary patrol.

For instance, ILGA (and NAMBLA) were very quickly enmeshed in a scene in which particular images of men could be easily deployed to discredit cogendered lesbian and gay organizing. In the highly rhetorically oriented sites of Congress and television, the image of the predatory, child-molesting man was easy to evoke— especially at a time when "family values" have been symbolically opposed to gay and lesbian rights. Given its association with the predatory homosexual, this image threw a dark shadow over gay men and lesbian women both. ILGA, directed by the gender symbols deployed by others, cast itself as pro-child in opposition to the male predator, using expulsion of NAMBLA as its means of communicating, and thus tightening, the collective identity boundaries.

The gendered communication setting shaped identity-patrol activities at MWMF in a different way. Rather than particular discrediting imagery, at MWMF it was male-female categorization more generally that was at stake. It was public confidence in female difference that was being protected. Of course, the emphasis on rigid gender categories is hardly a lesbian feminist invention, but it is nonetheless central to lesbian feminist culture (Taylor and Rupp 1993). The expulsion of transsexuals has been much less about some need to deny participation to transsexuals than about reinforcing the clear difference between women and men in a setting in which *woman* cannot stop making sense. If the "drawing of boundaries between male and female promotes the kind of oppositional consciousness necessary for organizing one's life around feminism" (Taylor and Rupp 1993, 43) and transsexuals make the boundary harder to draw, their expulsion communicates its clarity anew. Exclusion and inclusion, here again, are largely patterned by gendered meanings circulating most strongly.

It might appear that this is a dynamic peculiar to sex and gender movements, and the significance of gendered communication is certainly more overt in these cases that it might be elsewhere. But to stop at that appearance would be to miss the point. It is hard to imagine a public communication setting that does not link up in significant ways to the doing of gender—and the identities that social movements of all kinds constantly create and re-create are significantly molded by those settings. In the Nazi movement, for instance, gender oppositions "served as the metaphor for the polarization of Jews as weak and emotional and 'Aryans' as strong and rational," Verta Taylor (1996, 171) reminds us. The systematic, gender-specific stigmatizing associations of "the abnormal sexuality of both black men and women," used "historically and currently in this country to support and justify the exploited position of black people," Cathy Cohen points out, have critically influenced the indigenous definitions of who is or is not "really" Black, and in particular to partially exclude Black gay men from communal membership and, therefore, from access to community resources (Cohen 1996, 376).

The lesson from all this arguing, then, goes much beyond the difficult skirmishes over ancient Greek pedophiles and UN influence, eunuchs and woman's culture: If all communication environments are gendered, and inclusion/exclusion processes shift in response to communication settings, collective identity construction and deployment are, in general, necessarily gendered processes. We need to look much more closely at the subtle and not-so-subtle intersections, then, between gendered communication environments and social movement dynamics. Turning *us* into *them, them* into *us,* be they environmentalists, fundamentalists, men, women, or in between, is a process never divorced from the gendered meaning structures in which all movements operate.

NOTES

1. Exclusions and symbolic boundary-patrol activities, I would argue, are more visible and more critical for identity-based organizing: Whereas collective identity building is necessary for any movement to mobilize participants and build solidarity (Friedman and McAdam 1992), identity-based movements make their claims on the basis of, and on behalf of, a particular collective (as opposed to, say, peace movement activists making more universal grievances).

2. By *public communication,* I mean simply the sending, receiving, and exchange of ideas, information, and symbols (via speech, gesture, visual representation, and so on) that operate independent of specific, personal relationships. By *communicative environment,* I mean the loosely structured arena in which such exchanges take place: the interacting characteristics of "senders" and their institutional or social location, of the actual "receivers" and intended audiences and their institutional or social location, and of the medium through which symbols are carried. By distinguishing *symbolic* from *practical* inclusion/exclusion, I do not mean to suggest that practices are not symbol carriers, but to distinguish rhetorical exclusion from the actual closing off of active participation.

3. I am using *collective identity* to mean simply the "shared definition" of a group that derives from members' common interests, experiences, and solidarity" (Taylor 1989, 771). Alberto Melucci has recently expanded on this definition in ways that directly inform this article, emphasizing that collective identity is "process" rather than product, an "interactive

and shared definition" that is "constructed and negotiated through a repeated activation of the relationships that link individuals" (Melucci 1995, 44). For extended discussions of the concept of collective identity, see Friedman and McAdam (1992) and Melucci (1989, 1995). On symbolic boundaries more generally, see Lamont and Fournier (1992).

4. Much of the literature on women's movement factionalization has described and analyzed internal divisions within feminism, including such events as the "purge" of the lesbian "lavender menace" from the National Organization for Women in the 1970s and the often bitter tensions between "cultural feminists" and various others within the women's movement (Echols 1989; Ryan 1992; Taylor and Rupp 1993). While these writings focus important attention on internal disputes, they either are primarily descriptive or have a somewhat different analytical focus than the one taken here. That is, they tend to be more concerned with explaining the emergence and workings of specific women's movement divisions than with making use of those divisions to understand collective identity construction; Barbara Ryan's analysis, for instance, concerns how feminist ideology "was used by leaders and activists as a mobilizing resource during the organizing stage and why, at the same time, the feminist groups making up the movement experienced antagonistic relations based on ideological conflict" (1992, 54). Although her book is primarily concerned with movement persistence and transformation, Nancy Whittier's recent discussion of conflicts within the radical women's movement in Columbus, Ohio, is closest to mine, examining the contribution of such conflicts to changes in movement identities and group boundaries (Whittier 1995; see esp. pp. 100–14).

5. Similar debates have emerged in diverse locations, including Seattle (O'Hartigan 1994), Brisbane, Australia (Griffin 1994), and the lesbian S/M conference Powersurge (Powersurge drops 1994).

6. These debates echo long-standing discussions within lesbian feminism about "who is a lesbian?" and within feminism more generally about the relationship between feminism and lesbianism (Echols 1989; Ryan 1992; Taylor and Rupp 1993). Adrienne Rich's (1980) now-classic "Compulsory Heterosexuality and Lesbian Existence," for instance, set off rounds of definitional debates among feminist intellectuals (Ferguson, Zita, and Addelson 1981). The Michigan Womyn's Music Festival (MWMF) debates, interestingly if unsurprisingly, are more focused on defining the statuses of woman and feminist than that of lesbian—although, of course, those statuses are all tightly linked in the radical-feminist framework of the festival. As Whittier and others have pointed out, as lesbians became more visible in the 1970s radical women's movement, "lesbian ideology developed, and in practice activists often conflated the categories 'lesbian' and 'radical feminist' " (Whittier 1995, 107). Thus, while *woman* and *feminist* are explicitly debated in the transsexual disputes (see also Gamson 1995), in the lesbian feminist context the boundaries between lesbian and nonlesbian are also implicitly being negotiated through inclusion and exclusion of transsexuals.

7. This dispute is only one of several related ones over the years at the MWMF, most notably over the presence of male children and sadomassochists at the festival (Baker 1990; Braeman 1989; Briggs 1990; Festival forum 1990; Festival responses 1990; Johnson 1989; Rodriguez and Booky 1990).

REFERENCES

Acker, Joan. 1990. Hierarchies, jobs, bodies: A theory of gendered organizations. *Gender & Society* 4:139–58.

Baker, Victoria. 1990. A discussion of sadomasochism at the Michigan festival. *off our backs,* September, 29–33.

Bornstein, Kate. 1994. *Gender outlaw.* New York: Routledge.

Braeman, Elizabeth. 1989. In defense of separatists. *off our backs,* November, 20.

Briggs, Laura. 1990. Gearing up for Michigan. *Gay Community News,* 12–18 August, 1, 12.

Brown, Katie. 1994. Gender outlaws. *Deneuve,* October, 42–4, 50.

Buechler, Steven M. 1990. *Women's movements in the United States.* New Brunswick, NJ: Rutgers University Press.

Burkholder, Nancy. 1991. Letter to the editor. *Washington Blade,* 29 November, 15, 31.

———. 1993. A kinder, gentler festival? *TransSisters,* November/December, 4–5.

Burkholder, Nancy, Rica Ashby Fredrickson, Davina Anne Gabriel, and others. 1994. Protest against Michigan Womyn's Music Festival's exclusionary policy will continue this year. *TransSisters,* summer, 11.

Camp Trans. 1994. Transsexual protesters allowed to enter Michigan Womyn's Music Festival. Hart, MI. Unpublished.

Cohen, Cathy. 1996. Contested membership: Black gay identity and the politics of AIDS. In *Queer Theory Sociology,* edited by Steven Seidman. Oxford, UK: Blackwell.

Echols, Alice. 1989. *Daring to be bad: Radical feminism in America 1967–1975.* Minneapolis: University of Minnesota Press.

Ferguson, Ann, Jacquelyn N. Zita, and Kathryn Pyne Addelson. 1981. On "Compulsory heterosexuality and lesbian existence": Defining the issues. *Signs: Journal of Women in Culture and Society* 7:158–99.

Festival forum. 1990. *Lesbian Connection,* January/February, 9–11.

Festival responses. 1990. *Lesbian Connection,* May/June, 11–4.

———. 1992. *Lesbian Connection,* March/April, 8–10.

Fredrickson, Rica Ashby. 1993. How I spent my Michigan vacation. *TransSisters,* November/December, 25–7.

Friedman, Debra, and Doug McAdam. 1992. Collective identity and activism: Networks, choices, and the life of a social movement. In *Frontiers in social movement theory,* edited by Alan D. Morris and Carol M. Mueller. New Haven, CT: Yale University Press.

Gabriel, Davina Anne. 1993. Mission to Michigan. *TransSisters,* November/December, 8–12, 19–24.

———. 1994. Of transsexuals and transcendence. *TransSisters,* winter, 12–6.

Gamson, Joshua. 1995. Must identity movements self-destruct? A queer dilemma. *Social Problems* 42:390–407.

Gays: No NAMBLA. 1992. *Washington Blade,* 13 March, 29.

Gerson, Judith M., and Kathy Peiss. 1985. Boundaries, negotiation, consciousness: Reconceptualizing gender relations. *Social Problems* 32:317–31.

Gordon, Linda, ed. 1990. *Women, the state, and welfare.* Madison: University of Wisconsin Press.

Green, Jesse. 1994. The men from the boys. *Out,* September, 75–83, 128–36.

Griffin, Aidy. 1994. Politics or prejudice at confest. Unpublished.

Hunt, Scott A., Robert D. Benford, and David A. Snow. 1994. Identity fields: Framing processes and the social construction of movement identities. In *New social movements: From ideology to identity,* edited by E. Laraña, H. Johnston, and J. R. Gusfield. Philadelphia: Temple University Press.

International Conference on Transgender Law and Employment Policy. 1994. The international bill of gender rights. Unpublished.

Johnson, Angela. 1989. There must be a better way. *off our backs,* November, 20.

Johnston, Hank, and Bert Klandermans, eds. 1995. *Social movements and culture.* Minneapolis: University of Minnesota Press.

Keen, Lisa M. 1991. Michigan festival expels transsexual in middle of the night. *Washington Blade,* 13 September, 17.

Lamont, Michele, and Marcel Fournier. 1992. Introduction. In *Cultivating differences: Symbolic boundaries and the making of inequality,* edited by M. Lamont and M. Fournier. Chicago: University of Chicago Press.

Larry King Live. 1993. Cable News Network, October 13.

Lichterman, Paul. 1995. Piecing together multicultural community: Cultural differences in community building among grass roots environments. *Social Problems* 42:513–34.

Lorber, Judith. 1994. *Paradoxes of gender.* New Haven, CT: Yale University Press.

Malone, Patricia. 1992. Letter to the editor. *off our backs,* February, 28.

Melucci, Alberto. 1989. *Nomads of the present: Social movements and individual needs in contemporary society.* Philadelphia: Temple University Press.

———. 1995. The process of collective identity. In *Social movements and culture,* edited by H. Johnston and B. Klandermans. Minneapolis: University of Minnesota Press.

O'Hattigan, Margaret Dierdre. 1994. A rose is a rose: The nomenclature of sex and oppression. *TransSisters,* summer, 39–44.

Penelope, Julia. 1990. Women- and lesbian-only spaces: Thought into action. *off our backs,* May, 14–6.

Phelan, Shane. 1989. *Identity politics: Lesbian feminism and the limits of community.* Philadelphia: Temple University Press.

———. 1993. (Be)Coming out: Lesbian identity and politics. *Signs: Journal of Women in Culture and Society* 18:765–90.

Powersurge drops "woman-born women" only policy. 1994. *TransSisters,* summer, 10.

Raymond, Janice. 1979. *The transsexual empire: The making of the she-male.* Boston: Beacon.

Rich, Adrienne. 1980. Compulsory heterosexuality and lesbian existence. *Signs: Journal of Women in Culture and Society* 5:631–80.

Rodriguez, Tomasita, and Kathleen Booky. 1990. Letter to the editor. *off our backs,* June, 27.

Ryan, Barbara. 1989. Ideological purity and feminism: The U.S. women's movement from 1966 to 1975. *Gender & Society* 3:239–57.

———. 1992. *Feminism and the women's movement: Dynamics of change in social movement ideology and activism.* New York: Routledge.

Severns, Tamara. 1992. An open letter to the organizers of the Michigan Womyn's Music Festival. *Gay Community News,* 19 April-8 May, 2.

Spelman, Elizabeth. 1988. *Inessential woman: Problems of exclusion in feminist thought.* Boston: Beacon.

Stone, Sandy. 1991. The empire strikes back: A posttranssexual manifesto. In *Body guards,* edited by J. Epstein and K. Straub. New York: Routledge.

Taylor, Verta. 1989. Sources of continuity in social movements: The women's movement in abeyance. *American Sociological Review* 54:761–75.

———. 1996. *Rock-a-by baby: Feminism, self-help, and postpartum depression.* New York: Routledge.

Taylor, Verta, and Leila J. Rupp. 1993. Women's culture and lesbian feminist activism: A reconsideration of cultural feminism. *Signs: Journal of Women in Culture and Society* 19:33–61.

Taylor, Verta, and Nancy Whittier. 1992. Collective identity in social movement communities: Lesbian feminist mobilization. In *Frontiers in social movement theory,* edited by Alan D. Morris and Carol M. Mueller. New Haven, CT: Yale University Press.

Tsang, Daniel C. 1994. Unanimous senate vote threatens gay group, United Nations. *Frontiers,* 25 February, 15, 20.

van Hertum, Aras. 1993. U.S. gay leaders urging ILGA to oust NAMBLA. *Washington Blade,* 5 November, 1, 19.

Varnell, Paul. 1993. No more free rides for NAMBLA from the gay rights movement. *Lesbian and Gay News-Telegraph,* December, 10–23.

Vogel, Lisa, and Barbara Price. 1992. Letter to the editor. *off our backs,* January, 10.

Whittier, Nancy. 1995. *Feminist generations: The persistence of the radical women's movement.* Philadelphia: Temple University Press.

Williams, Rhys H. 1995. Constructing the public good: Social movements and cultural resources. *Social Problems* 42:124–44.

Chapter Twenty-five

Seventies Questions for Nineties Women

Arlene Stein

In 1991 news circulated in San Francisco that Amelia's, a lesbian bar which had been located on a busy street in the Mission District for thirteen years, was preparing to close. Bars had come and gone before, reflecting shifts in sexual politics and population. Maud's, the city's longest-running lesbian bar, had closed down two years earlier in the Haight District on the other side of town. Amelia's was the last lesbian bar in San Francisco, so its closure seemed particularly poignant. It marked, some suggested, the end of an era, the end of a time when the community possessed a spatial center. "In the old days," Robin Ward told me, referring to the 1970s, "one could go to a particular place"—a cafe, women's center, or bar—"to find the lesbian community." Fifteen years later, when she broke up with a longtime lover, she went out searching for that community and couldn't find it.

Yet even while Robin and others lamented what they saw as the loss of a "home base" for lesbians, women continued to pour into San Francisco and other cities and towns in search of sexual freedom and community. A columnist in the *San Francisco Examiner* observed that "more lesbians than ever live in San Francisco but the last lesbian bar is set to close." Some explained this in economic terms: unlike gay men, they suggested, lesbians lacked the capital necessary to support a commercial infrastructure. But the owner of Amelia's, a longtime participant in San Francisco's lesbian scene, put it best: "It's a victim of the lesbian community becoming more diverse," she said. "There is an absence of a lesbian community in the presence of a million lesbians."[1] Paradoxically, it was the growth and diversification of lesbian communities, rather than their decline, that destroyed the neighborhood bar.

In the early 1990s, in major urban centers across the nation one could find lesbian parenting groups, support groups for women with cancer and other life-threatening diseases, lesbian sex magazines, organizations for lesbian "career women" and lesbians of color, and mixed organizations in which out lesbians played visible roles. Gay/lesbian newspapers contained notices advertising hiking clubs for lesbians and their dogs, support groups for adult children of alcoholics, "leather and lace" motorcycle clubs, groups for lesbian-identified transsexuals, and many others. A multiplicity of lesbian groupings emerged, each representing a smaller subculture and special interest. There was no longer any hegemonic logic or center; lesbian culture seemed *placeless*. It had become more and more difficult to speak of "lesbian" identity, community, culture, politics, or even sexuality in singular terms. "I don't think there is one lesbian community," said Sunny Connelly, reflecting on nearly twenty years of change. "The community is getting bigger and smaller. Some of the infrastructure is going, bars are closing. In that way it's getting smaller. In the sense that more women are able to feel good about leading lesbian lives, it's getting bigger. But it's spreading out and becoming decentralized, which is good and bad."

Laments about the loss of lesbian community spoke to the loss of a center, of a sense of certainty and unity. For a brief period in the early 1970s, there was a burst of extraordinary solidarity, a feeling that lesbians shared a common oppression and a collective sense of identity. Lesbianism seemed to offer a settled, stable source of identification, affording membership in a bounded group with a common history, which offered both a refuge in a male and heterosexual world and a base for political action against male domination and compulsory heterosexuality. Lesbians were thought to possess one shared culture, "one true self," which was hidden inside a multiplicity of more superficial or artificially imposed "selves." Their common historical experiences and shared cultural codes were believed to provide them, as "one people," with unchanging frames of reference and meaning that continued beneath the vicissitudes of their actual history. This "oneness," underlying all other, more superficial differences, was thought to be the truth, the essence.[2]

But as the lives of the baby boom cohort became more settled, a younger cohort of women emerged, stamping their own generational sensibility upon the contours of lesbian culture and calling into question these earlier notions of collective identity. Like those before them, they constructed their lesbian identities in opposition as much to their lesbian predecessors as to the dominant heterosexual culture. Unlike their older sisters, however, who believed that together they could forge a unified sense of what it meant to be "a lesbian," young women coming of age in the 1990s had to establish lesbian identities at a time when many of the apparent certainties of the past had disappeared.

Questions of Identity Revisited

As a 1970s-influenced feminist studying women psychoanalysts from the 1930s, Nancy Chodorow found that a lack of attunement to gender characterized her interviewees' interpretation of their professional lives. Early women psychoanalysts were highly accomplished individuals who defied standard expectations of women. They had, it seemed, every reason to be conscious of themselves as women. But they were not. This indicates, observes Chodorow, the "variable and situated quality of gender."[3] For some women, and at some historical moments, consciousness of oneself as having a "gender" is more central than for other women at other times.

As a 1980s-influenced researcher looking at the experience of baby boom lesbians, who came of age in the 1970s, I was struck by how salient were their gender and sexual identities. Could the same be said of women coming out today? How, I wondered, do "nineties women"—young lesbians coming of age now—make sense of "*seventies questions*"? How do they understand their sexual identities, and does this understanding vary significantly from that of their baby boom predecessors? With these broad queries in mind, I interviewed ten lesbian-identified women, ranging in age from nineteen to twenty-nine, whose median year of birth was 1967, asking many of the same questions I had posed to women of the baby boom.

I imagined that I would find that for these younger women, sexual identifications do not play as central a role as they did for the older cohort. Twenty years of feminism, I surmised, had to some extent normalized lesbianism, making it less stigmatized and therefore less central to their lives. However, with some qualifications, I did not find this to be the case. Though the small number of interviews makes any claims speculative, it appears that among those coming out as lesbians today, as for their predecessors, sexuality is typically a highly salient, central aspect of the self. Becoming a lesbian entails placing oneself outside the dominant heterosexual culture, and all that that implies. Young women in particular, who must construct a sense of personhood as they establish a sexual understanding of themselves, face a complicated and frequently difficult task.

However, while the *salience* of lesbian identification among younger women did not seem significantly different from that of baby boomers at the same age, the *meaning* of this identification did. For example, among baby boomers, talk of "community" embodied the belief that lesbians all shared some basic common ground: a common marginality and a shared project of liberation. They believed that out of the diversity of women's lives and experiences they could construct a collective sense of what it meant to be a lesbian, developing subcultures that could nurture that vision. In contrast, when asked whether they considered themselves members of a "lesbian community," most of the younger women equated the idea of "community" with the imposition of "rules" and with the construction of idealized conceptions of lesbianism with which they could not fully identify.

Speaking of her knowledge of feminist theory and culture, twenty-four-year-old Lucia Hicks told me,

> I went through a period where I identified with "sisterhood is powerful" and all. I learned about it in school. I think that there are some really positive things I can take from that. But as I get older, I think that that whole era was simplistic in a lot of ways. There are a lot of rules. When you read the literature from that period there are a lot of ways of being in the world, and not being in the world. And you fit that picture, or you don't. And that's a little too simplistic for me.

Though criticizing feminism for its alleged simplicity, Lucia is quick to acknowledge that the existence of lesbian feminist culture—book ideas, music, and simply lesbian visibility—made her own coming out much easier. "I have to attribute my coming out in part to getting a grasp on feminism," she said. While keeping their distance from lesbian feminism, she and other younger women have also been profoundly influenced by it. "My sense is that a lot of younger dykes don't reject lesbian feminism, but they do take it for granted, not in a bad way. They just don't have to particularly announce it," said Lucia. "They just live it." This sensibility is evident in *Go Fish,* a 1994 film about a circle of lesbian friends in Chicago, which enjoyed mass distribution. The story starts from the assumption of an inherent acceptability, and even respectability, of lesbian lives. There are no painful coming out stories, the hallmark of lesbian narratives of the 1970s and 1980s. There are no painstaking justifications for lesbianism. It is the perspective of filmmakers who are in their twenties today, who have come of age two decades after Stonewall.

Nineties women have little hope of constructing a unified, collective sense of what it means to be a lesbian or a feminist. They are leery of attempts to define the "lesbian community," doubting if any one image could possibly represent the complexity of lesbian experiences. Twenty-five-year-old Judy Thomas told me, "What I am is in many ways contradictory. . . . I feel that I'm postfeminist, which isn't to say that I don't think we live in a male-dominated world. I just don't know whether the way to undermine it is to establish new expectations of what we should be. Everything is out there to be sliced and diced and put under the fine microscope." Judy's sense of indeterminacy and contradiction is related to shifts in the relationship between margin and mainstream. To become a lesbian in the 1970s was to stand outside the dominant culture. To affirm and celebrate lesbian lives, feminists were compelled to create an alternative culture. Lesbians of the baby boom went outside the music industry to make a women's music defined against commercial imperatives and "cock rock." They produced films, literature, and theories to make sense of their lives, to make themselves visible. Thanks to these efforts, nineties women have greater access than any previous generation to cultural images, narratives, and other resources that mirror their desires. Today, young women can learn about lesbian lives in women's studies courses, feminist fiction, and, increasingly, in mass-produced popular culture, such as the television show *Roseanne,* or the music of k. d. lang.

Because of these expanded opportunities, women of the postfeminist generation do not feel as strong a sense of loyalty to "feminist" or "women's" culture. They believe that they should be represented in mainstream culture, and they long for that representation. When I asked her what types of music she listened to, nineteen-year-old Ann Carlson answered, "I like 'cock rock' and women's music. I like both. But I like mainstream women's music the best." Rather than listen to "out" lesbian musicians recording on alternative women's music labels, "I like music that speaks to women but isn't only about women. . . . Tracy Chapman, Melissa Etheridge, Michelle Shocked. They don't use pronouns, proper nouns. To us that's cool. And we notice that men don't listen to that music." Ann subverts the feminist critique of masculinist music by embracing cock rock as a symbol of power *and* women's music as a reminder of her feminist roots. At the same time, however, she prefers "mainstream women's music": women musicians who employ lesbian and feminist imagery but perform for a mass audience. These performers' sexual ambiguity allows for the double appeal of the music—to the subculture, as well as to the mass audience. It permits audience members such as Ann to listen to music they consider to be "lesbian" and know that millions of other people are also listening to it. For her, the ambiguity is part of the appeal.[4] But the pluralization and "mainstreaming" of lesbian images are themselves ambiguous signs of progress: the increasing importance of mass-produced lesbian culture means that while lesbian images are much more plentiful than they ever were before, their production is much more reliant upon the whims of Hollywood and the culture industries, and thus lesbian lives are being commodified.[5] Nonetheless, many younger lesbians welcome this mainstreaming.

Other important differences between the seventies and nineties cohorts concern their views of the sexualization of women's bodies. While the older women claimed power by renouncing lipstick, coquettishness, and sexually explicit representations and by opposing the commercialization of beauty and sex, by 1990 many younger lesbians were asserting their sexual power by reclaiming these practices and withholding access from the conventional male beholder. As the decade wore on, the debates that emerged in bars, in coffee houses, and in the pages of community newspapers often appeared as a generational clash: Were the full-color spreads, in the glossy fashion magazines from *Elle* to *Vanity Fair,* that touted the joys of "lesbian chic" furthering lesbian visibility, or were they creating new, idealized, airbrushed versions of a genteel sapphism? Were younger women, who were pioneering a new roving club scene and unabashedly embracing sexual imagery, the rightful heirs of lesbian feminism or evidence of its demise?

When I first arrived in the Bay Area in 1981, lesbian bars, clubs, and social events were frequented by women who embraced lesbian feminist antistyle—work-shirts, jeans, and "sensible shoes." But through the next few years, many lesbians began to dress up. In night clubs and on the street it was not unusual to see younger women flaunt high heels, short skirts, and other trappings of femininity, often consciously evoking the butch-femme codes of the 1950s. Twenty-eight-year-old Jill Dinkins wears her "butch" identity proudly. Whenever she goes out with her girlfriend, they adopt sharply differentiated gender styles. Jill wears leather jackets, short-cropped hair, and men's vests; her girlfriend has long hair and wears makeup and skirts.

As Jill describes these forms of self-presentation, they sound very different from the butch-femme roles practiced by earlier working-class lesbians. For her, adopting a role is more a matter of play than necessity. "I like to play with power and sexuality. It's all a game." She and other nineties women selectively and self-consciously take on elements of butch-femme style. Some interpret the roles in an essentialized way, as showing their "true" nature and refusing the constraints of straight society, but for many these roles are more ambiguous and less naturalized than in the past. They are an aesthetic practice, a self-reflexive performance.[6]

This commitment to individual choice often also extends to sexual practices. Members of the nineties cohort tend to be much more tolerant of "slippages" of identity in general—of inconsistencies among identity, desires, and sexual practices —than their baby boom predecessors. Judy Thomas, who felt attracted to women and girls at a very early age, and who calls herself a "lesbian virgin" because she has never had a heterosexual experience, told me that she was toying with the idea of sleeping with a man, "just for the experience," and that she did not see this as a threat to her lesbian identity. She related a story about her best friend, a lesbian, who recently told her that she was having an affair with a man, fearing Judy's response. She reassured her friend that this news was not a threat to their friendship. "I was so shocked that she even asked me," she said. If there is a greater tolerance for inconsistencies of identity, this may be related to the greater propensity of younger lesbians to speak openly about their sexual practices.

Certainly, the sexual practices and politics of feminist lesbians were more diverse in private than was publicly admitted. As my interviewees suggested, frank sexual talk was muted in the interest of constructing lesbian solidarity. Recall Cindy Ross's description of lesbian sexuality in the 1970s: "Nobody knew what anyone else was doing." For nineties women, particularly members of urban lesbian subcultures, the gap between theorizing and practicing sexuality has seemingly narrowed. The belief that lesbian sexuality is radically different from and superior to other forms of sexuality, and that sexuality and desire are only peripheral aspects of the lesbian experience, is no longer widely held. As Jill Dinkins told me, "I've heard many conversations about sex recently in social settings. Not necessarily in a lovey-dovey manner, or in a clinical manner, but in an experimental sense. That's what a lot of young women are going through right now. They're not modeling themselves after older women." Nineties women were more likely to know about different types of sexual practices and to be aware of sexual and relational problems such as "lesbian bed death," the tendency for long-term lovers' sexual interests to wane. They are also far more likely than their baby boom predecessors to consider sexual fringe groups, such as sadomasochists, to be a legitimate part of the lesbian community. Most striking, perhaps, is the tolerance for—and even celebration of—bisexuality.

Women of the baby boom. I have argued, often suppressed their bisexuality in the interest of identifying as lesbian and challenging compulsory heterosexuality. Today, anecdotal evidence suggests that many young women, particularly on college campuses, have come to openly identify as bisexual rather than exclusively lesbian. Twenty-two-year-old Cindy Yerkovich explained that while she is attracted to men, she feels most comfortable with and sexually fulfilled by women. The label that best expresses who she is is "bi-dyke," signifying that her "sexual orientation is bisexual but [her] identity is lesbian." Cindy, who has long hair and a traditionally feminine appearance, said that she fights against the tendency to place her and others "in boxes": "A lot of stuff that has come down on me has been really looksist. People will call me bisexual not knowing whether I've ever slept with a man. Just because I have long hair. It bugs me that people assume I'm bisexual just because I pass. Gay people assume that I'm bisexual, if they don't assume that I'm straight." When I asked my younger interviewees if they were currently friends with or would choose to be friends with a bisexual woman, or how they would feel if a lesbian friend decided to become involved with a man on either a short-term or long-term basis, their responses tended, on the whole, to be quite positive. Some even suggested that lesbians and bisexual women have much in common by virtue of their "queerness."

Sometimes Cindy calls herself "queer," signifying a fluid sense of sexual orientation and a refusal to fully embrace the term "lesbian." For her, the term signifies a loose but distinguishable set of political and intellectual movements that are quite distinct from an "ethnic" style of lesbian/gay identity politics. *Queer* signifies the possibility of constructing a nonnormative sexuality that includes all who feel disenfranchised by dominant sexual norms.[7] Thus, on the Kinsey scale, Cindy says, "queer means anything that is not a 1 or completely heterosexual. . . . I think that 1s are just as abnormal as 6s, whatever abnormal means. Queer implies ambiguity. It implies that you can't define things in terms of us and them—it's not that easy. I don't want to define my identity in terms of exclusion." She and others who have been influenced by the queer critique insist that the refusal of lesbian/gay identity, rather than its affirmation, is the radical act. "We have a lesbian identity, a lesbian culture now. It's established. We don't have to fight to establish it. Now's the time to question what we've taken for granted." The presence of people with ambiguous sexual desires, such as bisexuals, challenges the faith in sexual object choice as a master category of sexual and social identity and offers the greatest potential to disrupt the normative heterosexual/homosexual binary.[8]

Armed with poststructuralist and postmodern theories of gender and sexuality, some also suggest that cross-gender practices such as butch-femme and drag are subversive acts that undermine the illusion of a coherently gendered self, therefore providing an alternative to a politics grounded in identity. They quote Judith Butler's claim: gender identities are "performative acts" that are always on uncertain ground.[9] The lengths to which we must go, through dress, demeanor, and all manner of social practices, to prove our masculinity or femininity attest to their tenuousness. Once differences *within* the categories—"woman" and "man," "heterosexual" and "homosexual"—are exposed, the old dichotomous conceptions are called into question.

In major cities, young "queers" infiltrated straight bars, carrying on "kiss-ins" designed to upset "normal" heterosexuality. Relying largely on the decentralized, cultural activism of street posturing, their styles and tactics were a pastiche of images and elements from popular culture, communities of color, AIDS activism, hippies, MTV, feminism, and early gay liberation.[10] At the 1993 march on Washington, marchers chanted in front of the White House: "We're here; we're gay; can Bill come out and play?"[11] Queer activists traveled to shopping malls, proclaiming, "We're here, we're queer, and we're not going shopping." They rejected civil rights strategies in favor of a politics of carnival, transgression, and antiassimilation, blending the in-your-face stance of gay liberationists with a parodic sense of the limits of identity politics.

Describing a short-lived but influential organization that embodied these ideas, one analyst wrote: "In its resistance to social codes (sexual, gender, race, class) that impose unitary identities, in rebelling against forces imposing a repressive coherence and order, Queer Nation affirms an abstract unity of differences without wishing to fix and name these."[12] In other words, the preference for the label *queer* represents "an aggressive impulse of generalization; it rejects a minoritizing logic of toleration or simple political interest-representation in favor of a more thorough resistance to regimes of the normal." Such generalization "suggests the difficulty in defining the population whose interests are at stake in queer politics."[13]

My conversations with young lesbians indicate that while relatively few—only the most highly educated and theory-savvy—claim the term *queer* wholeheartedly, many more, if not most, identify with the indeterminacy and irony at the heart of the queer project. They oppose the construction of an identity founded upon exclusions and are uncertain about the content of the category *lesbian*. Yet they tend to qualify their allegiance to "queerness" by retaining a critique of gender inequality. Judy Thomas, who works for a predominantly gay male organization in San Francisco, cautioned that among the men she works with "there is a complete lack of knowledge about lesbians."

> I don't think straight men know us, or gay men. . . . There is a very profound fear or kind of terror toward women that have any kind of sense of self, and there is a terrible resistance on the part of men to look at their own sexism. Some of my friends say that there's not a whole lot of common ground [between gay men and lesbians]. I don't really believe that, actually. But I do know that sexism is alive and well and living in gay male communities, just the same as racism is alive and well and living in my life, and my friends' lives.

Judy and her peers inherit a world in which women still lag far behind men with respect to all common measures of structural equality—pay equity, child care provisions, and the like—while at the same time feminist ideas have made considerable cultural headway. They were far from convinced that their loyalties stood with men. Indeed, among political activists in San Francisco and other cities, gay men and women often coexisted uneasily: ACT UP and Queer Nation chapters in many cities were marred by gender (and racial) conflicts.[14] The new "co-sexual" queer culture could not compensate for real, persistent, structural differences in style, ideology, and access to resources among men and women. This recurrent problem underscored that while the new queer politics asserted the sexual difference that could not be assimilated into feminism, gender, too, resisted being completely subsumed within sexuality.

Even as they integrate feminism into their daily lives, young lesbians seem to reject the view that lesbianism is *the* feminist act and the belief that any sexual identity is more authentic and unmediated than any other. Talk of "lesbian community," "lesbian identity," or "women's culture" and the global theories that underlie such language hold little appeal. When asked whether she identifies as a member of a lesbian community, Jill Dinkins replied: "I feel a sense of community with my friends who are lesbians. But I don't feel a sense of community with all lesbians. We agree on some things: that we love women, and that we want to live our lives as openly as we can. But we disagree on a lot of things: worldviews, political concerns, you name it." Jill spoke of refusing ghettoization, of acknowledging internal group differences, and of affirming individual choice of style and political and sexual expression. In this sense, she is "postfeminist," if that term describes women and men who, while holding their distance from feminist identities or politics, have been profoundly influenced by them.[15] She and other nineties women simultaneously locate themselves inside and outside the dominant culture, and they feel a loyalty to a multiplicity of different projects—some of them feminist oriented, others more queer identified. They recognize that while marginalized groups construct symbolic fictions of their experience as a means of self-validation, and thus compulsory heterosexuality necessitates the construction of lesbian/gay identities, nevertheless such identities are constraining as well as enabling.

Necessary Fictions

There is no doubt in my mind that the feminist movement has radically changed, in an important way, everybody's concept of lesbianism, straight or gay. There's not a dyke in the world today (in or out of the bars) who can have the same conversation that she could have had ten years ago. It seeps through the water system, you know?
—Amber Hollibaugh, in Hollibaugh and Moraga, "What We're Rollin' Around in Bed With" ([1951] 1983)

A veteran activist and early gay liberationist told me a story about going on a shopping expedition with several older relatives to a suburban mall outside San Francisco. The year was 1990. When they arrived at the mall, she and her relatives encountered some young "queers," dressed in ripped t-shirts and buzz-cut hairdos: they were chanting and holding a "kiss-in," an action designed to break the calm of compulsory heterosexuality and generally cause a stir. She looked at the young queer activists and saw her younger self. "I've always felt stifled by people who want to put me into a kind of strait jacket. There's a part of me that always wants to throw things in for shock value and stir them up a bit."[16]

Twenty years earlier, she had joined gay liberation and feminism out of a similar impulse to "smash the categories" and deconstruct reified notions of gender and sexuality. She judges her generation's efforts to be a qualified success: "We made homosexuality much more visible, we created a presence for gay life in this country. But we were young, naive, and very bold." Though they problematized heterosexuality, activists of her generation failed to problematize the constructed, indeed fragile, nature of their own collective self-concepts. "We wanted to turn everything upside down. Sometimes we failed to see that we were very much a part of the system we were trying to change. Sometimes we asked for too much. We ended up demanding too much of people."

Lesbians of the baby boom passionately affirmed their sexual identities, insisting, at least initially, that such identities are open-ended, evolving, and often situational. They found inadequate the conventional view that sexual identity is, for all intents and purposes, consolidated early in life. It could not account for the experiences of housewives who had never harbored desires for women, but who in the boundary-breaking times of the 1960s and 1970s left their husbands and took up with women. As Jeffrey Weeks put it, sexuality is "provisional, even precarious, dependent upon, and constantly challenged by an unstable relation of unconscious forces, changing social and personal meanings, and historical contingencies."[17]

Having revealed the contingent character of sexuality, however, many women of this generation, particularly those who had been touched by feminist ideas, began to seek stability, closure, and certainty, keeping a watchful eye on the boundaries of the "lesbian community." Over time, the impulse toward consistency won out. They sought congruence between individual and collective identities, even while placing great value upon achieving authenticity, being "true" to oneself. They believed that by achieving a stable sense of identity, they could maintain a sense of coherence and commitment despite external flux, instability, and change and their own passage through different periods of life. They downplayed internal differences: different desires, different self-conceptions, and different varieties of lesbian identification.

By externalizing difference and developing a gender separatism that policed the boundaries around the lesbian group, lesbian feminists came to reinforce the differences—between insider and outsider, normal and abnormal, male and female, heterosexual and homosexual—that they had originally sought to erase. This had the unintended effect of strengthening the notion of sexual minorities as "other," which left the "center"—heterosexuality—intact. The problem with this "ethnic" conception of homosexuality, writes Barbara Ehrenreich, is that "it denies the true plasticity of human sexuality and, in so doing, helps heterosexuals evade what they fear. And what heterosexuals really fear is not that 'they'—an alien subgroup with perverse tastes in bedfellows—are getting an undue share of power and attention, but that 'they' might well be us."[18]

Perhaps the eventual resurgence of essentialism and sexual binaries, both of which lesbian feminists had initially attacked, was inevitable, given the contradictions within feminists' reconceptualizing of lesbianism in the 1970s. They downplayed desire in the interest of political identity, while making sexual consistency and commitment a test of membership. They imagined lesbianism as an identification that transcended sexuality and, at the same time, defined women according to their sexual relationships. They tried both to undo the old categories and to form stable, consistent sexual identities, to embrace a universalizing conception of identity and unify lesbians as a minority group. But ultimately, they failed to escape dominant conceptions that saw sexuality in binary terms, as either heterosexual *or* homosexual, thus neglecting the diversity within each category and the variability of the boundaries separating them.

It appears that social movements organized around sexual identities are caught in a troubling paradox. "We are," observes Jeffrey Weeks, "increasingly aware that sexuality is about flux and change, that what we call 'sexual' is as much a product of language and culture as of nature. But we earnestly strive to fix it, stabilize it, say who we are by telling of our sex."[19] Perhaps stability and predictability are basic human needs, particularly for those of us living through rapid social transformations, whose identities are accordingly under great pressure to change. Yet the effort spent on keeping collective sexual identities intact may do no more than expose their ultimate instability and impermanence.

The history of lesbianism is the history of the progressive growth of knowledge, reflexivity, and group self-consciousness. Whereas knowledge accumulated about sexuality, as about human life in general, was once believed to clarify our understanding of the world, we have found instead that this knowledge has actually come to undermine our sense of certainty. The more we know, the less we can take for granted. Our capacity to reflect upon everything around us now actually threatens the stability of our institutions, and the resulting uncertainty has become a constituent element of modern institutions.[20] In particular, the more we know, the more we've come to see sexuality as fleeting, unstable, and up for grabs. Queer politics and poststructuralist-inspired queer theory may represent the latest stage in the development of greater and greater reflexivity and indeterminacy.

Today's queer activists enact a new universalizing move, a new attempt to smash the categories; while not unlike the early lesbian/gay liberation impulse, theirs seems more keenly aware of the provisional nature of *all* identities. As they wrestle with the tensions between identity and difference, they too have had heated boundary disputes. "They are trying to combine contradictory impulses: to bring together people who have been made to feel perverse, queer, odd, outcast, different, and deviant, and to affirm sameness by defining a common identity on the fringes," two veteran gay liberation activists note.[21] But at least these young activists seem to be highly sensitive to the contradictory nature of their project. Problematizing homosexuality along with heterosexuality; they are wary of engaging in fights over who belongs in the lesbian/gay/queer community and skeptical about "the possibility and desirability of a clear criterion of belonging."[22]

So while the contested nature of lesbianism is familiar, there is also something new; in Biddy Martin's words, "the irreducibly complex and contested status of identity has itself been made more visible."[23] This is deeply troubling to many women, particularly those who once held out the hope of constructing a unified lesbian feminist movement. The element of uncertainty here is bound to be unsettling: in contrast, carving out a sense of space, forming a community, and drawing boundaries, however precarious they may be, promote a sense of security. Indeed, the persistence of institutionalized and culturally reproduced normative heterosexuality, as well as the heterosexism that accompanies it, makes it necessary to continue the construction of a sense of difference based on (homo)sexual object choice.

As long as individuals are defined as different and inferior on the basis of their sexual desires or practices, they will need to develop a sense of collective identity and maintain institutions that counter stigma. This seems particularly true today, as a powerful and well-organized right wing in the United States mobilizes to deny lesbian and gay rights, along with the economic and political rights of other marginalized groups.[24] Without an organized and self-conscious movement, these rights cannot be defended. A collective identity requires that boundaries be established by setting forth at least minimal criteria for claiming that identity. The alternative is a vague pluralism that speaks only of "difference" and views all differences as equal and good. This "hundred lifestyles" strategy, which calls for "a pluralism of sexual choice," as Margaret Cerullo says, "doesn't represent an adequate response to the one lifestyle that has all the power"—heterosexuality.[25]

Today many of us, queer and not-so-queer, are searching for a way of talking about (and acting on) sexual identities and politics that avoids the twin pitfalls: an identity politics that refuses difference or a politics of difference without collected identity.[26] As individuals we are members of social groups yet remain ultimately irreducible to categories. "We are," writes Shane Phelan, "specific individuals as well as members of multiple groups."[27] As lesbians, we share differences *and* commonalities. We need to affirm what we share in common without feeling compelled to deny what makes each of us unique.

Individual differences will always exist. We have seen that even among self-identified lesbians, sexualities vary widely. For example, for some women, sexual object choice is open to choice and change. Others experience their sexual desires as relatively fixed. As long as we live in a society in which heterosexuality is normative, women who have early homosexual desires or experiences will develop a more deeply felt sense of difference than those who do not. But this difference is not of paramount significance and should not be used to determine who does and does not belong in our communities. Instead, we need to tolerate ambiguity. We need to question assumptions about who and what constitutes the lesbian community, deliberately courting greater uncertainty rather than seeking closure. This politics is already emerging in practice.

I have described how women of the baby boom, as they enter middle age, are combining commitment to lesbian communities with a greater sense of individualism. They are reconstituting lesbian identity in new, decentered ways as their responsibilities to work and family increase. Many younger women coming of age and coming out today are also reconstituting lesbian identity, in ways that tolerate inconsistency and ambiguity. They simultaneously locate themselves inside and outside the dominant culture as they pursue a wide range of projects. Their strategic deployment of lesbian/gay identities is balanced against their recognition of the limits of such identities.

In the decentered conception of identity that is emerging, individuals are comfortable in multiple contexts. They embody what Kathy Ferguson calls "mobile subjectivities," which are temporal, always in motion, and contingent. Identities, she suggests, are "deceptive homogenizations" that always conceal "some turbulence." If we simply identify on the basis of race, class, or sexuality, we cannot make sense of the used-to-be-working-class-now-professional, the woman of mixed race parentage who appears white, the divorced-mother-now-lesbian, or the former-lesbian-turned-straight. Many of us experience ourselves *between* rather than *within* existing categories of identification.

As part of this process, "coming out" may be losing its appeal as the guiding narrative of lesbian self-development. The coming out story may no longer be the central narrative of lesbian existence. Bonnie Zimmerman notes that lesbian writers today, as opposed to twenty years ago, have a different focus: "How I came out—how I discovered my real self—no longer engages our attention. We are out, and it's time to get on with our lives."[28] Coming out was once seen as a linear, developmental, goal-driven process, but today it is more likely to be conceptualized as an ongoing, dynamic social interaction, a process of self-creation that is both collective and individual, a "be-coming" rather than a "coming out."[29] This decentered model of identity formation mirrors the decentering of lesbian culture and communities, making it possible for us to imagine lesbian identities and communities that are more inclusive, less demanding, less confining, and more able to satisfy our desires for choice and autonomy.

If we understand the permanently unsettled nature of identities and group boundaries, we will be less apt to see this decentering as a sign that the lesbian feminist project has failed. Indeed, it may present new democratic potential. Many women who felt excluded by totalizing conceptions of lesbian identity may find that they can finally participate on their own terms. For example, those who experience their sexuality as fluid may claim lesbian identifications or not, as they find such identifications useful. Women who choose to move from homosexuality to heterosexuality (and back again, perhaps) may not experience that move as quite so threatening to their sense of self.

Sexual identities are fictions. But they are, as Jeffrey Weeks puts it, "necessary fictions." Lesbianism is now conceived as a collective and increasingly public basis of identity. Today, its emerging forms are broadening the range of possibilities for women. The future will undoubtedly bring yet new and different possibilities.

NOTES

1. Rob Morse, editorial, *San Francisco Examiner,* 12 November 1991, p. A$_3$. For similar trends in other cities, see Kelly Harmon and Cindy Kirschman, "Women behind Bars: Lesbians Lock Horns over the Changing Generational Face of the Lesbian Bar Business," *Advocate,* 31 December 1991, pp. 36–38.

2. This derives from Stuart Hall's work on Black identities (1989).

3. *Nancy Chodorow,* "Seventies Questions for Thirties Women," in Chodorow 1989, 217.

4. In the early 1990s, a few women were able to "cross over" and achieve mainstream success as out lesbians, integrating their sexuality into their art without allowing it to become either *the* salient fact or else barely acknowledged. k. d. lang and Melissa Etheridge, who had previously coded their sexuality as "androgyny," came out as lesbians, to great fanfare within lesbian/gay circles and to even greater commercial success. On the phenomenon of the "crossover" artist in popular music, see my "Crossover Dreams: Lesbianism and Popular Music since the 1970s" (Stein 1994).

5. For a more detailed explanation of the political implications of this mainstreaming, see Stein 1994. On the recent commodification of lesbian culture, see Clark 1993.

6. For a longer version of this argument, see Stein 1992.

7. On queer theory and politics, see Bérubé and Escoffier 1991; Duggan 1992; Fuss 1991.

8. Seidman 1993, 122.

9. Butler 1990.

10. Gamson 1995.

11. Phelan 1994, 153.

12. Seidman 1993, 133.

13. Warner 1991, 16.

14. On the checkered history of recent queer organizing, see Dan Levy, "Queer Nation in S.F. Suspends Activities," *San Francisco Chronicle,* 27 December 1991, p. 21; Michele DeRanleau, "How the Conscience of an Epidemic Unraveled," *San Francisco Examiner,* 1 October 1990, p. 24.

15. For a discussion of postfeminism that articulates this sense of continuity along with change, see Stacey 1990. As Mannheim [1928] 1952 suggests, the transition from one generation to another takes place continuously, through interaction between the two.

16. Martha Shelley, interview with author, 1990.

17. Weeks 1985, 186.

18. Barbara Ehrenreich, quoted in the *Guardian* (U.K.), 4 May 1993, p. 5. See also de Lauretis 1991.

19. Weeks 1985, 186.

20. Giddens 1991.

21. Bérubé and Escoffier 1991, 14.

22. Gamson 1995.

23. Martin 1992, 100.

24. On recent right-wing challenges to lesbian/gay rights, see Patton 1993; Johnston 1994.

25. Cerullo 1987, 71.

26. This is close to Stuart Hall's (1989) conception. Similarly, North American feminists have drawn upon the vocabulary of poststructuralism to problematize any simple notion of the category "woman" or "woman's experience" as the point of departure for late-twentieth-century sexual politics. See, for example, Scott 1989; Butler 1990.

27. Phelan 1994, 11.

28. Zimmerman 1990, 210.

29. Phelan 1994. Perhaps what is needed, as Rust 1993 suggests, is a social construction-ism that "allows for the possibility that individuals who are creating their identities will introduce their own goals" (71). Identity is here conceptualized as more open-ended and evolving, not as "what is, only what is becoming," and often as situational (Cass 1984). Psychoanalytic support for this view is offered by Schafer 1973, who argues that "empirically self-sameness is usually a rather inconstant idea in that it can change markedly in content with a significant change in mood and circumstance" and that in part it changes because one views oneself and one's identity at different times, for different reasons, and from different vantage points (52); *see also Lacan 1982, who restores to prominence the Freud who discovered* the bisexuality and polymorphous perversity of children, emphasizing that re-pressed versions remain in the unconscious and constantly destabilize the ego's wish to keep these lost possibilities at bay.

REFERENCES

Bérubé, Allan, and Jeffrey Escoffier. 1991. "Queer/Nation." *Outlook,* Winter, pp. 12–14.

Butler, Judith. 1990. *Gender Trouble: Feminism and the Subversion of Identity.* New York: Routledge.

Cass, Vivienne. 1984. "Homosexual Identity Formation: Using a Theoretical Model." *Journal of Social Research* 20: 143–67.

Cerullo, Margaret. 1987. "Night Visions: Toward a Lesbian/Gay Politics for the Present." *Radical America* 21 (March–April):67–71.

Chodorow, Nancy. 1989. *Feminism and Psychoanalytic Theory.* New Haven: Yale University Press.

Clark, Danae. 1993. "Commodity Lesbianism." In *The Lesbian and Gay Studies Reader,* ed. Henry Abelove, Michele Barale, and David Halperin. New York: Routledge.

de Lauretis, Teresa. 1991. "Queer Theory: Lesbian and Gay Sexualities." *differences* 3(2): iii–vviii.

Duggan, Lisa. 1992. "Making It Perfectly Queer." *Socialist Review* 22(1): 11–31.

Fuss, Diana, ed. 1991. *Inside/Out: Lesbian Theories, Gay Theories.* New York: Routledge.

Gamson, Joshua. 1995. "Must Identity Movements Self-Destruct? A Queer Dilemma." *Social Problems* 42:390–407.

Giddens, Anthony. 1991. *Modernity and Self-Identity: Self and Society in the Late Modern Age.* Stanford: Stanford University Press.

Hall, Stuart. 1989. "Cultural Identity and Cinematic Representation." *Framework,* no. 36: 65–72.

Hollibaugh, Amber, and Cherríe Moraga. [1981] 1983. "What We're Rollin' Around in Bed With: Sexual Silences in Feminism: A Conversation toward Ending Them." In *Powers of Desire,* ed. Ann Snitow, Christine Stansell, and Sharon Thompson, New York: Monthly Review.

Johnston, Susan. 1994. "On the Fire Brigade: Why Liberalism Can't Stop the Anti-Gay Campaigns of the Right." *Critical Sociology* 20(4): 3–19.

Lacan, Jacques. 1982. *Feminine Sexuality: Jacques Lacan and the "école freudienne,"* ed. Juliet Mitchell and Jacqueline Rose, trans. Jacqueline Rose. New York: Norton.

Mannheim, Karl. [1928] 1952. "The Problem of Generations." In *Essays on the Sociology of Knowledge,* ed. Paul Kecskemeti. New York: Oxford University Press.

Martin, Biddy. 1992. "Sexual Practice and Changing Lesbian Identities." In *Destabilizing Theory: Contemporary Feminist Debates,* ed. Michèle Barrett and Anne Philips. Palo Alto: Stanford University Press.

Patton, Cindy. 1993. "Tremble, Hetero Swine." In *Fear of a Queer Planet: Queer Politics and Social Theory,* ed. Michael Warner. Minneapolis: University of Minnesota Press.

Phelan, Shane. 1994. *Getting Specific: Postmodern Lesbian Politics.* Minneapolis: University of Minnesota Press.

Rust, Paula. 1993. "Coming Out in an Age of Social Constructionism" *Gender & Society,* 7(1):50–77.

Schafer, Roy. 1973. "Concepts of the Self and Identity and the Experience of Separation-Individuation in Adolescence." *Psychoanalytic Quarterly* 42: 42–59.

Scott, Joan. 1989. *Gender and the Politics of History.* New York: Columbia University Press.

Seidman, Steven. 1993. "Identity and Politics in a Postmodern Gay Culture." In *Fear of a Queer Planet: Queer Politics and Social Theory,* ed. Michael Warner. Minneapolis: University of Minnesota Press.

Shelley, Martha. [1969] 1970. "Notes of a Radical Lesbian." In *Sisterhood Is Powerful: An Anthology of Writings from Women's Liberation,* ed. Robin Morgan. New York: Random House.

Stacey, Judith. 1990. *Brave New Families.* New York: Basic Books.

Stein, Arlene. 1992. "All Dressed Up, But No Place to Go? Style Wars and the New Lesbianism." In *The Persistent Desire: A Femme-Butch Reader,* ed. Joan Nestle. Boston: Alyson.

Stein, Arlene. 1994. "Crossover Dreams: Lesbians and Popular Music since the 1970s." In *The Good, the Bad, and the Gorgeous: Popular Culture's Romance with Lesbianism,* ed. Diane Hamer and Belinda Budge. London: Pandora.

Warner, Michael. 1991. "Fear of a Queer Planet." *Social Text* 29:3–17.

Weeks, Jeffrey. 1985. *Sexuality and Its Discontents.* London: Routledge.

Zimmerman; Bonnie. 1990. *The Safe Sea of Women: Lesbian Fiction, 1969–1989.* Boston: Beacon.

Part VI

Lessons on Inclusiveness

The whole point to identity politics is to identify oneself as a member of a group with particular interests that need to be addressed. What starts out as a simple enough goal becomes complex as people begin to see that their interests are not always the same and that, because of competing identity claims, they have some interests in common and some that are opposed. To use a group consciousness of such scope as "women" as an organizing concept almost by design creates a unity composed of immense distinctions. Comprehending this reality took time. Early organizations merely thought of themselves as women's groups. However, over time women from other backgrounds challenged Western concepts of generic womanhood. By the 1990s, the women's movement was using terms like *inclusive* to indicate recognition and respect for differences among women. In this section, authors take us through early-twentieth-century organizing to contemporary times and the successes and failures of women's groups in confronting the changing nature of what the term *women* means.

Leila Rupp provides a historical perspective as she looks at international women's organizations from the late nineteenth century to the mid-twentieth century. There were many such groups that emerged in this period because of the growing recognition of the interconnections of trade and the threat of war on a global scale. Some organizations were interested in raising women's rights issues; others were more connected to peace efforts among nations; and still others adopted a single-issue agenda such as women's employment or the elimination of prostitution. Western-identified women who claimed to be transnational in membership and goals originated these organizations. Rupp takes us through the ideals of these groups and the confrontations that emerged as women from other nations, many former colonies, raised their voices and concerns. These were not easy exchanges, and the policies that resulted from them were mixed, some with more progressive responses than others. This look back in time provides an interesting background from which to examine the types of issues that have emerged since the more recent UN Conferences on Women began in 1975.

On a more current and experiential level, June Corman describes the process of inclusion in the planning of International Women's Day in the Niagara Peninsula. Corman covers the process of planning this event over a number of years, which reveals the learning that took place through both the mistakes that were made and the corrections that came out of those experiences. In spite of the difficulties and misunderstandings, the benefits she describes are encouraging signs that such efforts are worthwhile for all concerned.

Rosa María Pegueros takes up another issue of inclusiveness. What if you are the token member of your group, a visible symbol of the multicultural nature of a progressive women's organization? She was an activist in the National Organization for Women and had risen to a high leadership position when she began to question the nature of her status in NOW. Women are well aware of what tokenism means because they have always been subjected to the theorem that the exception makes the rule. And because sociologically the opposite is the case—the exception does not make the rule, it merely represents an exception to the rule—it seemed natural for her to doubt the sincerity of her warm welcome to the hierarchy of power. Tokens do not usually question their status; rather, they accept it as their due. That is, they like to think they are the exceptional woman or Hispanic or black person in a sea of white. But Pegueros was in a feminist organization where token status for women was a part of her political consciousness. The uncertainties and confusion over the meaning of her position are well explored in this writing.

Diane Fowlkes takes a very different tactic in her exploration of the origins of identity politics. She is interested in the many forms it takes, when it arose, how it became paramount in the women's movement, and why it was not named or emphasized in earlier movements, like the civil rights movements, that clearly hinged on race identity for movement organizing. She notes the actions of black women who chose to expand the movement through coalition work rather than fragment it through separation. Fowlkes uses the Combahee River Collective as an example of changing the terms of identity, such that its identity was multidimensional rather than unidimensional, allowing it to remain committed to the black liberation movement and to the women's movement. Her description of herself as a "writing spider" is meant to convey her sense of attempting to find ways that identity politics can create solidarity, with the women's movement and among all people committed to change. Fowlkes's review of other writings on this topic is informative and encourages working through the web of confusion often inherent in understanding how it might be possible to create unity with diversity in the multicultural reality of women's lives.

How are we to present ourselves to others so that they understand us, and how are they to present themselves to us so that we know them, too? First, according to Liza Grandia, we have to know ourselves. Second, we have to be able to get to the place where this conversation is taking place. If we are attempting to gain mutual understanding, imagine the difficulty when representational problems become magnified on an international level. Grandia did this by living in a mud hut in a Third World country for a period of time, but she recognizes that most people are not going to go to this extreme to understand Third World poverty. Yet, she still wants us to attempt the task of developing empathetic understanding of other people's lives, particularly those who live in circumstances vastly different from those of most people in the developed world. Her paper focuses on the roles of international activists and the contributions they make to cross-cultural empathy and emphasizes Non-Governmental Organizations (NGO) at the 1995 UN Conference on Women in Beijing. It was there that she felt the possibility of women's building a global community for restructuring people's lives through economic and spiritual empowerment.

Chapter Twenty-six

Challenging Imperialism in International Women's Organizations, 1888–1945

Leila J. Rupp

At the International Congress of Women in Chicago in 1933, Muthulakshmi Reddi, head of the All-Asian Women's Conference, proclaimed the women's movement "from its infancy, . . . international in character, crossing all barriers of caste, color, creed, or race."[1] Such an optimistic description echoed the International Council of Women's self-presentation as a "federation of women of all races, nations, creeds, and classes," the International Woman Suffrage Alliance's 1911 welcome to women "of whatever race, nativity, or creed," and the claim of the Congress of Women at The Hague in 1915, which gave birth to the Women's International League for Freedom, to speak for the "women of the world."[2]

In fact these transnational women's organizations originated and grew primarily in Europe and what have been called the "neo-Europes," countries such as the United States, Canada, and Australia, where European settler colonies flourished.[3] And within these countries, the women who joined were primarily of European origin, although elite African American women, long active on the national scene, participated at international gatherings even before the turn of the century. Calling attention to racial discrimination as practiced in different parts of the world and giving organizational expression to the solidarity of women of color around the globe, a group of activists, primarily members of the U.S. National Association of Colored Women, created the International Council of Women of the Darker Races in 1920, although the organization remained largely American in membership.[4] Only after the First World War, which shook the foundations of European dominance of the world system, did the international groups add sections in Latin America, the Middle East, Asia, and Africa.

Despite their grand proclamations of universality, women from neither the imperialist nor the dependent and colonized countries could free themselves from global relations of dominance. Nevertheless, challenges from what we now call "Third World women" provided a check to the imperialism of the international women's organizations, paving the way for a more global internationalism in the

Reprinted by permission from *NWSA Journal* 8.1 (Spring 1996):8–27. Copyright © 1996 by Indiana University Press.

late twentieth century. I focus here on interactions at the centers of the major transnational groups in order to understand both the limitations and the possibilities of internationalism in the first wave of the women's movement. Such a consideration also provides a context for the tensions within contemporary international feminism, tensions manifested most notably at the conferences sponsored by the United Nations during the Decade for Women, in Mexico City in 1975, Copenhagen in 1980, and Nairobi in 1985.[5]

Imperialist Internationalism

With roots in transatlantic contacts reaching back to the first half of the nineteenth century, the first wave of the international women's movement took organizational shape with the founding of the International Council of Women (ICW) in Washington, D.C., in 1888.[6] Designed to incorporate existing women's groups of every variety—from literary clubs to labor unions—the ICW avoided taking positions on controversial issues, including women's suffrage, which led to the spinoff of the International Woman Suffrage Alliance (IWSA, later IAW) in Berlin in 1904.[7] In turn, the IWSA gave birth to the Women's International League for Peace and Freedom (WILPF) when international suffragists could not agree on the advisability of holding a peace congress in time of war. The IWSA members who met in The Hague in 1915 to try to stop the Great War convened, after the carnage, in Zurich, where the WILPF took shape.[8]

These three major groups, in conjunction with a wide array of bodies organized on a regional basis or made up of particular constituencies of women or devoted to single issues, formed coalitions in the years between the wars to coordinate international collective action on such issues as peace, women's political rights, women's employment, and the abolition of prostitution (see Rupp, "Zur Organisationsgeschichte, Reinalda and Verhaaren). Spurred by the horrors of the First World War, internationally minded women held congresses, produced journals, organized political actions, and lobbied at the League of Nations. The outbreak of the Second World War nearly, but not entirely, severed connections among women. In the years of bipolar conflict after 1945, the growth of a Soviet-sponsored international women's organization that competed with existing groups, the rise of national liberation movements throughout the Third World, and the resurgence and emergence of national women's movements contributed to the swell of a second, and more global, wave of the international women's movement.[9]

But during the first wave, all three major organizations remained heavily Euro-American in composition and leadership (see Rupp, "Constructing"). Not only did Europe and-the neo-Europes contribute all but one of the national sections until 1923, but women from the United States, Great Britain, and western and northern Europe controlled the leadership of the three groups. This pattern perpetuated itself through the choice of official languages—English, French, and German—and the location of congresses primarily in Europe, with a few excursions to North America.

European imperialism and the historic shifts from one dominant Great Power to another ensured that large numbers of elite women from across the globe could indeed communicate in one or another of the official languages. But, as Alice Masaryk of Czechoslovakia pointed out in 1921 at the WILPF congress in Vienna, "sometimes a peasant has some idea that is well worth listening too *[sic]*," or, as Danish WILPF member Clara Tybjerg put it, "many working women would have liked to be here if it had not been for the difficulty of the different languages."[10] An article in *Jus Suffragii,* the journal of the IAW, proudly announced in 1932 that language presented no obstacle to publication of news submitted from different countries, thus overlooking the significance of the fact, as the article stated flatly, that the publication could not handle non-Roman alphabets.[11]

Likewise, suggestions or plans to hold meetings in locations other than Europe provoked shocked outcries that "such a far away *[sic]* place has been chosen."[12] In response to a proposal to meet in Honolulu, Marguerite Gobat, a Swiss WILPF member, explained why it was impossible for her to consider it: "We have, we women of Europe, better things to do—alas, too much to do on our continent—to go so far, at enormous expense."[13] When Brazilian IAW member Bertha Lutz invited the Alliance to meet in her country in 1936, U.S. leader Carrie Chapman Catt doubted that the leadership "would ever accept an invitation to go so far away from most of the countries that are members."[14] Although the German WILPF co-chairman Gertrud Baer in 1940 noted that "we know only too well that Europe is not the world" and an Australian member of the Pan Pacific Women's Association predicted in 1941 that Honolulu would become the Geneva of the future, only after the Second World War did the international women's organizations begin to meet beyond the confines of Europe and North America.[15]

As a result of such membership patterns, the dominant discourse within the transnational organizations—what has been called "feminist orientalism"—lauded "Western" societies as the pinnacle of progress for women in contrast to backward, repressive "Eastern" ways.[16] The very constructs of "West" and "East," of course, polarized the world in a way that had little to do with geography and obscured the much more complex hierarchical rankings embodied in the dominant assumptions about progress, civilization, and the emancipation of women. For the women in charge, western and northern Europe and the United States represented the core, southern and eastern Europe a semiperiphery, and Latin America, the Middle East, Asia, and Africa the periphery of a feminist world system.[17] Such a perspective forged the image of women of European origin in the lead, offering a hand to their more oppressed sisters. When Carrie Chapman Catt of the United States and Dutch IWSA leader Aletta Jacobs traveled around the world in 1911–12, they reported back on "women's awakening in the East," finding it "touching to think of these women, who lacked the simplest rights, seeking for help" (Deutsch).[18] Although no "Asiatic" delegates came to the 1913 congress of the International Woman Suffrage Alliance in Budapest, *Jus Suffragii* expressed confidence that "these sisters of ours will come some day." In the meantime, "we must make them understand" that women's cause is the same throughout the world.[19] At the 1915 Hague Congress, in the discussion of a resolution asserting the rights of "weaker and backward peoples," U.S. leader Jane Addams explained that this "applies to savage nations, such as the Congo and other places where civilisation is not established. It cannot apply to a European nation."[20] The "women of primitive race," African women "sold" to their husbands, veiled Muslim women, Asian women "more bound by tradition and faith than are we," and timid Latin American women controlled by their husbands and fathers all served to mark women of European origin as well on their way to emancipation.[21] Such depictions, as Antoinette Burton has argued powerfully in the case of British feminists, served the dual purpose of justifying imperialism and supporting Euro-American women's demands for their own rights. Women of European origin shouldered the burden of protecting the women of the world and at the same time implicitly accused "Western" men of seeming "Eastern" if they persisted in oppressing women at home.

But was internationalism necessarily imperialist? Despite the origins and patterns of growth of the transnational bodies, despite the decisions about where to hold conferences and what languages to speak, challenges to feminist orientalism mounted, particularly after the First World War. As national sections of the international organizations proliferated, and as colonized and dominated countries began to shake loose from Europe's grip, diverse voices rose to challenge imperialism within the international women's organizations.

Challenging Imperialism

The process of recruiting members and sections in parts of the world where the groups were not well represented came to be called making the movement "truly international."[22] Using whatever contacts they had, leaders sought names of potential supporters in unaffiliated countries, sent members on organizing tours, made use of women from other continents (often students) visiting or living in Europe, and offered subsidies to help delegates come to congresses. Thus *Jus Suffragii* called on its readers in 1913 to supply the names of correspondents in South America "longing for the liberation of their sex from the thraldom of outgrown custom", the WILPF sent a mission to China and Indochina in 1927 and followed up with an interim congress in Honolulu; the Alliance Board in 1933 co-opted Dhanvanthi Rama Rau, an Indian woman then living in England, to fill a vacancy; and the League office in Geneva asked local members to offer hospitality to the delegates of the Egyptian section during the 1937 congress in Luhacovice, Czechoslovakia.[23]

In addition, the groups made some attempts to adjust their structures to suit conditions in other parts of the world. The IWSA changed its constitution in 1913 at the recommendation of Carrie Chapman Catt and Aletta Jacobs, following their world tour, to allow the formation of auxiliaries where there were no suffrage organizations because such agitation would be impractical.[24] Eager for broader representation at the 1921 Vienna congress, the WILPF admitted delegates at large from Japan, China, and Mexico, all countries lacking sections, and in 1924 assured Japanese women that they had only to adopt the substance and spirit, not the letter, of the constitution in order to affiliate.[25] In the 1930s, the ICW considered the possibility of admitting "countries not entirely self-supporting and in different stages of development" and amended the constitution to allow the Executive Committee to co-opt additional members "drawn from any Continent or geographical group of countries outside Europe."[26]

Leaders of the transnational bodies sometimes recognized that they could not themselves organize outside the Euro-American arena. As an ICW member who visited Japan in 1907–08 put it, "as the movement must necessarily be conducted by Japanese, the ladies of other nationalities could only render passive assistance."[27] Likewise Catt argued that "Asia is not reaching out its weak hands to the West like a little child asking guidance of a strong man."[28] She was less optimistic about Latin America, on a tour with her Dutch colleague Rosa Manus in 1923, she found the women "slow" and doubted that her efforts would attain lasting results.[29] When the WILPF, through its U.S. section, undertook organizing work in Latin America in the 1930s, Emily Greene Balch warned of the "political reasons for preventing any shadow of an impression that the U.S. section regards itself as in any position of authority towards the independent countries of Latin America."[30]

But the leaders of European origin were not always sure that women from other continents could handle the job themselves. Catt noted in 1925 that "the Latin Americans do not at all like to be told or shown how to do things, so I am planning to show them some things that I think will be useful without appearing to do so."[31] When the Alliance held its 1935 congress in Istanbul, the leadership worried about the ability of the local Turkish committee to organize properly but recognized that the Turkish women might be "rather sensitive to any attempts to regard them as needing advice on matters affecting their local organisation."[32] Reporting on a special international conference organized by the National Council of Women of India in 1936, the ICW *Bulletin* rather patronizingly noted that "we are sure our Indian friends themselves realized that the questions thus chosen covered too wide a range to be considered with the thoroughness each of them deserved."[33] And belying a lack of confidence, Catt commented with regard to a suffrage campaign in the Philippines, "We have taken the position that they know quite well how to run their own campaign, and we have not offered any women to them, but have asked them if they would like to have a woman provided if we could find one to go."[34]

Whatever doubts the leaders harbored, they welcomed the expansion of their groups' international reach. A special resolution at the 1913 Budapest congress of the IWSA celebrated the addition of the auxiliary from China, the first Eastern nation to form one: "A movement which can thus unite Eastern and Western women in one aspiration may be truly said to go to the roots of humanity."[35] Somewhat less optimistically, *Jus Suffragii* described the "effort at understanding between the East and West" at the 1920 congress as "harder than any other."[36] The president of the Union of Turkish Women welcomed the International Alliance of Women to Istanbul in 1935, noting the location as a symbolic union of East and West, "the junction of two continents."[37] And the International Council of Women rejoiced that a special conference in Calcutta in 1936 was cementing "personal contacts between the women of the East and West and the North and South."[38]

In the process of making their organizations "truly international," women of

European origin faced insistent challenges from their new coworkers. When the organizers of the WILPF congress in Grenoble in 1932 invited Chiyin Chen, a Chinese woman living in Berlin, to come and speak briefly in Chinese, she responded, in German, that she could not undertake a lengthy interruption of her work "merely to speak for a few minutes in a language that probably all of the congress participants could not understand." She found this an "unreasonable demand that I cannot reconcile with my self-respect," and pointedly refused to be used in that way.[39] Such a response suggests that even well-meaning attempts by women of European origin to recognize, if not topple, the barrier of language could alienate rather than include women from other parts of the world.

Women from the colonial and dependent countries also insisted that they alone could represent themselves, explicitly rejecting the practice of women of European origin standing in for the women of countries in which they had settled.[40] Taraknath Das warned Jane Addams that it would be "a great mistake" to allow British women to organize an Indian section of the WILPF.[41] On behalf of Pandurgang Khanko, the secretary of the Indian News Service and Information Bureau, American Agnes Smedley emphasized that "we do not wish British women to speak for the women of India. They are quite uncapable of it," adding a note at the bottom of the letter directing a reply to the Bureau rather than Smedley.[42] That the WILPF took such criticisms to heart is suggested by the fact that it dropped "India (British)" as a listed section after 1919, hoped to add "a truly Indian Section" in 1921, and in 1936 turned down the request to affiliate from a British-headed peace organization in Calcutta, seeking instead to see "whether an Indian Section of the League could be started by Indians themselves."[43] Margaret Cousins, an Irish woman known as the "mother" of Indian feminism, herself recognized in 1942 that "Indian national consciousness is much more touchy nowadays about non-Asians like myself taking any initiative or prominent part in Indian progressive movements."[44] Elsewhere, the WILPF leadership seemed to come to recognize the need for indigenous sections as well, working "to get the Turkish women themselves" in 1929.[45] The Tunis section of the WILPF, founded that same year as a sort of subset of the French group, had as its original members almost all "Europeans or Jews," but a growing Muslim membership led to the acceptance of an independent section in 1932 "as a concession to the Arabs."[46]

Expanded representation brought new kinds of conflicts into the European-centered international bodies. In the 1920s and 1930s, women of European origin kept trying to form existing Jewish and Arab women's groups in Palestine into a single national section but found differences between Jewish and Muslim women insurmountable. In 1935, when a delegation of European women traveled to Palestine on behalf of the Alliance, they pronounced the Jewish Women's Union "small and intensely feminist" and the Arab Women's Union "nationalist to the exclusion of all other interests, violently anti-British and anti-Jewish." "We tried hard to persuade the Arab Women's Union to affiliate to the alliance," president Margery Corbett Ashby reported, "but," a classic understatement, "difficulties are very great."[47] Huda Shaarawi, whom Corbett Ashby describes as "terrifically nationalist

& tyrannical," took the lead in voicing the concerns of the Muslim women of Palestine within international women's movement circles.[48] A member of the Alliance Board, Shaarawi proposed in 1933 that the Disarmament Committee of the Women's International Organisations, a coalition group, support the Arab demand for an end to Jewish immigration, and in 1938 she called a Muslim women's congress on Palestine, prompting *Jus Suffragii* to editorialize that because of "our standing policy of neutrality on all national questions" and the fact that the IAW had "a faithful feminist group among the Jewish women of Palestine . . . , we could not express any opinion on the policy of the conference."[49] The issue of Palestine came to a head in the Alliance at the 1939 Board meeting. In response to a call for a protest against anti-Semitism, Shaarawi pointed out that the Muslims, too, suffered grave indignities and "the Arab women sharply resent that the Alliance would not come to their aid in protesting the injustices and persecutions that they suffer in Palestine."[50] Discussion of the question of further Jewish immigration to Palestine pitted Shaarawi against Dutch Jew Rosa Manus, who died in Auschwitz in 1942.[51] Although both the IAW and the WILPF developed an analysis of the situation in Palestine that emphasized economic over religious conflict and held Britain responsible both for its contradictory promises to the Jews and Palestinians and for its role in holding Palestine as a mandate for the League of Nations, efforts to organize in Palestine opened the door for conflict that could not be resolved within the international women's organizations.[52]

A different kind of controversy erupted in 1937 in the case of the Egyptian section of the WILPF. Provisionally accepted in April, the new section sent proposals for the upcoming conference in Czechoslovakia, making clear that it could not accept disarmament until Egypt had the capability to defend itself and that the issue of limiting and regulating state sovereignty had different ramifications for Egypt than for a country such as Britain. "The great imperialist powers . . . have often abused their state sovereignty to conduct an egoistic politics dangerous to peace," the Egyptian representative asserted.[53]

This position provoked consternation at WILPF's Geneva headquarters, since the joint chairmen did not want to discourage the section but could not accept its support of the Egyptian army.[54] In response to a letter from Geneva explaining that if the section advocated armament it would not be in accord with the principles of the WILPF, Egyptian spokeswoman Alice Jacot denied any conflict, insisting that universal disarmament did not mean unilateral disarmament without regard for whether a country was weak or strong, free or oppressed, aggressive or pacifist.[55]

At the request of the Egyptian section, the Executive Committee took up the question. Anna Tuby explained for Egypt that the Anglo-Egyptian Treaty called for, among other things, occupation by the British until Egypt could itself defend the Suez Canal, leaving Egyptian women with the unpleasant choice of supporting an Egyptian national army or the British occupation. Egyptian women advocated the complete independence of Egypt, which alone would make possible peace and disarmament. In the end, the Executive Committee voted to admit the section.[56] What is clear from this incident is that Egyptian women had a very different perspective on the meaning of disarmament, sovereignty, and internationalism than did women from countries with secure national identities and independence, and that they asserted themselves in interactions with the European leadership.

New sections of the transnational groups also raised the issue of work with men. Although all three of the major international women's organizations remained single-sex bodies, national and local sections could admit men, and women involved in a struggle for national independence sometimes insisted on the necessity of working with their male compatriots. WILPF member Eva Fichet, who belonged to the Tunis section, planned to bring her member husband to the 1934 international congress but recognized that "his presence will offend some of our collaborators" so promised that "he will only make an appearance at public meetings, if there are any."[57] Margery Corbett Ashby reported in 1935 that the enormous difficulties facing the nationalist struggle in Egypt "bring the men and women nearer together," and an unnamed Arab woman, speaking at the 1935 Istanbul congress of the IAW, asserted her belief in the necessity of working shoulder to shoulder with men in her country for prosperity and freedom: "The economic and political situation of my country is so desperate that it is extremely difficult for us women to give our wholehearted energies to the cause of feminism alone," she insisted.[58]

Women from colonized countries spoke out most forcefully against imperialism, directly or indirectly tangling with women of European origin, who defended their own countries' actions. At the 1933 International Congress of Women in Chicago, Syrian Alice Kandaleft denounced imperialism in the form of the mandate system, provoking a French delegate to speak positively about her country's rule by pointing to Syria's history of external control and to the infrastructure the French had built. "The points that were taken by our friend, the French lady, that they have always been under some other authority is certainly no excuse, and you all know that. The second thing is the hospitals and schools and all that—again, you know that old story. We all know it," Kandaleft replied. At the 1935 Alliance congress in Istanbul, Shareefeh Hamid Ali of India, on behalf of "we of the East," warned "you of the West that any arrogant assumption of superiority or of patronage on the part of Europe or America, any undue pressure of enforcement of religion or government or of trade or economic 'spheres of influence' will alienate Asia and Africa and with it the womanhood of Asia and Africa."[59] Likewise, at the 1937 WILPF congress, Egyptian Anna Tuby protested a Swedish proposal appealing to Great Britain to encourage and hasten development in the colonies, arguing that colonies could develop on their own and that "help" served only as a pretext for colonization. Even more forcefully, Hamid Ali denounced the pretext that imperial powers civilized backward peoples as "hypocritical and wrong." The "Ethiopians might as well some day pretend to go and civilize Italy, or China to civilize Japan. The civilization of peoples in Africa and Asia may be different from the European, but it has the same right of existence as that of Europe." Indians, she stated flatly, did not admire European civilization.[60] Hers was a particularly powerful voice questioning the very foundation of European imperialism.

In all of these ways, then, women from beyond the borders of Europe challenged imperialism and the feminist orientalist division of the "downtrodden" from the "emancipated." By making their voices heard, by refusing to be used as "local color," by questioning assumptions about the superiority of European civilization, by bringing their issues before an international audience, by insisting on self-representation and autonomy and by denouncing imperialistic global relations, women from what would come to be called the Third World opened a dialogue within the EuroAmerican-dominated transnational women's organizations.

Conclusion

Something happened "when guests from [the] antipodes sidled in—as if direct from Gilbert & Sullivan & Mikado," as an American participant in the 1924 WILPF congress put it in fine orientalist style.[61] Challenges to imperialism raised by women from Latin America, the Middle East, Asia, and Africa had an impact on the international women's movement. Beginning in the 1910s, prompted within the IWSA by the Catt-Jacobs world tour, the transnational groups manifested their first aspirations to become "truly international." Contact with women from other parts of the world had the potential to shake traditional assumptions, although that did not necessarily occur. Carrie Chapman Catt, glimpsing that the world was a more complex place than a feminist orientalist vision might suggest, could write in 1912 of Burmese women's right to own property, engage in business, and vote in municipal elections as making them better off than women in the West. But in the same breath she could note the languor of people in such sunshine.[62] "There are millions of women in the Orient who are held in the most pitiful tutelage, and denied every vestige of personal liberty, but we are finding that there are other millions who have always enjoyed more personal freedom than was accorded to most European women a century ago, and more than is now permitted to thousands of women under our boasted Western civilization," she concluded.[63] In the 1920s and 1930s, when the process of expansion began in earnest, the organizations' journals reported that women on the Gold Coast of Africa were independent, engaged in trading, and sometimes very wealthy; that Islam was not inherently oppressive to women; that "the projecting of the concepts and ideas of Western feminists upon the women whose lives we wish to study" had distorted research; and that African women were probably losing status under European influence as they were pushed out of agriculture and trade, kept out of local government, and "protected" morally.[64] Such a counterdiscourse to feminist orientalism is important and would not have developed without the challenges of women from the colonized and dependent countries.

Furthermore, the process of looking beyond the borders of Europe brought the issue of imperialism out into the open. It was not just a question of conflict between women from the imperial and colonized countries: women of European origin disagreed among themselves. Conflict simmered within the WILPF, on the whole the most staunchly anti-imperialist of the three groups, over what it called "Colonial Imperialism." The Executive Committee in 1933 resolved unambiguously that the organization "would have no right to express its strong condemnation of the terrible outrages committed by the Fascist regimes" if it did not also condemn the crimes of the imperial powers, even those that claimed the label "democratic."[65] But not all sections and members felt the same about raising their voices against their own governments, although the WILPF prided itself on this very practice.[66] The French section, noted for its radicalism, took a special interest in fighting imperialism, organizing a summer school in 1927 on the interracial problems of imperialism, contributing actively to the Colonial Commission established in 1931 "in view of the growing menace of imperialism and the sufferings and unrest among colonised peoples," and calling for independence and an end of military repression in the French colonies and mandates.[67] Likewise the U.S. section took the lead in investigating and condemning the U.S. occupation of Haiti in 1926.[68] The British section, however, held more ambivalent views on the question of empire. In 1924, members protested a telegram sent by the Hungarian international secretary Vilma Glücklich denouncing the "merciless enforcement" of British reprisals in Egypt, newly independent and struggling to wrest control of its destiny from England.[69] Taking a similar line with regard to India, the British section in 1930 argued that British imperialism was wrong but not particularly cruel, an affront to those who could not forget the Amritsar incident of 1919, in which British troops fired on and killed nearly four hundred unarmed Indians celebrating a Hindu festival.[70] Although internationally minded women did not all share an anti-imperialist position, neither was internationalism necessarily imperialist.

Faced with the crumbling system of colonialism and their own contradictory discourses on the nature of global relations, women of European origin struggled to come to grips with a changing world. The First World War, which undermined European control of the world system in countless ways, also stimulated attempts to expand the reach of the women's movement. In the 1920s and 1930s, the transnational women's groups added sections in Chile, Brazil, Egypt, India, Jamaica, Palestine, Haiti, Japan, Peru, Bermuda, Cuba, Puerto Rico, Turkey, Mexico, Tunis, and South West Africa. Spanish became a "semiofficial" language of the ICW in 1930, meaning that Spanish-speaking members could correspond with the international headquarters in their mother tongue and a Spanish edition of the *Bulletin* would appear when enough subscriptions had been gathered.[71] Huda Shaarawi and Dhanvanthi Rama Rau joined the Board of the International Alliance, the Alliance held its congress in Istanbul and the International Council put its seal of approval on a special congress in Calcutta, the WILPF recognized the inappropriateness of allowing British women to speak for India and accepted the Egyptian section despite its position on disarmament. Such developments resulted from the movement of Third World women into international spaces. Certainly those such as Chiyin Chen, refusing to speak a few words of Chinese for ceremonial purposes, or Huda Shaarawi, voicing the concerns of the Muslim women of Palestine, or Shareefeh Hamid Ali, calling attention to the arrogance of Western ways, challenged the structures and attitudes that formed barriers to the participation of women from beyond Europe and the neo-Europes. Thus the discussion that took place at the Decade for Women conferences in the 1970s and 1980s about what was or was not a "feminist" issue—a discussion that tended to pit "First World" against "Third World" women—can be seen as a continuation of the dialogue prompted by the first querying of imperialism within the international women's movement earlier in the century.

NOTES

1. On the All-Asian Women's Conference, see Basu and Ray.

2. "The Constitution and Standing Orders of the ICW," ICW papers, box 1, Sophia Smith Collection (SSC), Smith College, Northampton, MA, [Martina Kramers], "Announcements," *Jus Suffragii* 5.6 (15 Feb. 1911); Emily Hobhouse, foreword, International Committee of Women for Permanent Peace, *International Congress of Women, The Hague—April 28th to May 1st 1915, Report,* ix.

3. The term comes from Crosby.

4. Barnett; Neverdon-Morton; Minutes, Special Urgency Meeting, Joint Standing Committee, Feb. 29, 1928, Liaison Committee papers, no. 1, International Institute voor Sociale Geschiedenis (IISG), Amsterdam.

5. See Barry, Çagatay, Grown, and Santiago; Johnson-Odim, "Common Themes."

6. On early contacts, see McFadden, "Weaving the Cloth" and "Weaving the Delicate Web", Holton; Anderson; Klejman; Wikander Wiltshire, *Women in a Changing World* is a useful in-house history of the organization.

7. On the history of the Alliance, see Whittick; Bosch. In 1926, the IWSA changed its name to International Alliance of Women for Suffrage and Equal Citizenship.

8. On the Hague Congress and WILPF, see Bussey and Tims, Costin, Foster, Vellacott, "Feminist Consciousness" and "Place", Wiltsher, *Most Dangerous Women.*

9. On early postwar organizing in Africa and the role of the Soviet-sponsored Women's International Democratic Federation, see Johnson-Odim, "On Behalf."

10. Emily Greene Balch to Jane Addams, 12 Apr. 1921, Addams papers, University Microfilms International, reel 13, Minutes, [WILPF] Third International Congress of Women, Vienna, 10–16 July 1921, WILPF papers, reel 18.

11. "The Paper," *Jus Suffragii* 27.1 (Oct. 1932).

12. Annie Furuhjelm to Aletta Jacobs, 12 Feb. 1920, box 1, Jacobs papers, Internationaal Informatiecentrum en Archief voor de Vrouwenbeweging (IIAV), Amsterdam.

13. Marguerite Gobat to Gabrielle Duchêne (French), 7 Mar. 1927, Dossiers Duchêne, Fol. Rés. 206, Bibliothèque de documentation internationale contemporaine (BDIC), Universités de Paris, Nanterre.

14. Carrie Chapman Catt to Bertha Lutz, 6 May 1936, National American Woman Suffrage Association (NAWSA) papers, reel 12, Library of Congress (LofC).

15. Gertrud Baer, "A Christmas Letter to International Members and Sections," 25 Nov. 1940, WILPF papers, reel 11, Bessie M. Rischbieth, "The Geneva of the Future," *Jus Suffragii* 35.3 (Dec.–Jan. 1940–41).

16. Zonana coins the term "feminist orientalism," with reference to Said's classic work *Orientalism.* Other scholars use the term "imperial feminism" to describe the same phenomenon. See Mohanty; Amos and Pramar; Tyrrell; Burton, *Burdens,* "Feminist Quest," and "White Woman's Burden"; Ramusack; Donaldson; Sinha; Badran, *Feminists.*

17. In the terms of Immanuel Wallerstein's world system, the core is the dominant region of the world system, the semiperipheries intermediate zones, and the peripheries economically and/or politically subordinated regions.

18. On the Catt-Jacobs world tour, see Bosch 95–98.

19. "Editorial Notes," *Jus Suffragii* 7.10 (15 July 1913).

20. "Report of Business Sessions," 30 Apr. 1915, International Committee of Women for Permanent Peace, *Report*, 143.

21. Minutes, Liaison Committee, 25 July 1939, Liaison Committee papers, no. 2, IISG; "Congo," *Jus Suffragii* 18.11 (Aug. 1924); Nour Hamada, "The Oriental Women's Congress in Damascus," *Jus Suffragii* 24.12 (Sept. 1930); Deutsch; Carrie Chapman Catt to Lady Aberdeen, 27 June 1927, NAWSA papers, reel 12, LofC.

22. See, for example, Carrie Chapman Catt, "India" [part 2], *Jus Suffragii* 6.11 (15 July 1912); "Stenographic report of 2nd Congress," 24 Oct. 1921, International Federation of Working Women papers, Schlesinger Library (SL), Radcliffe College, Cambridge, MA; "Second Annual Convention of the International Association of Medical Women," *Jus Suffragii* 16.12 (Sept. 1922); "India," *Jus Suffragii* 19.6 (Mar. 1925); Minutes, International Conference of Business and Professional Women, Meetings of Delegation Leaders, 23 Aug. 1930, Phillips papers, carton 3, SL. I am grateful to Anene Ejikeme, who first noted the use of the term "truly international" for a later period.

23. "Editorial Notes," *Jus Suffragii* 7.10 (15 July 1913); "A Message to Chinese Women," *Pax* 2.6 (Apr. 1927); and "The Honolulu Congress," *Pax* 3.5 (Apr. 1928); "The Alliance Board," *Jus Suffragii* 27.8 (May 1933); Lotti Birch to Congress Committee [German], 28 Apr. 1937, WILPF papers, reel 21.

24. "Proposed Amendments to the Constitution," *Jus Suffragii* 7.7 (15 Mar. 1913); "Editorial Notes," *Jus Suffragii* 7.10 (15 July 1913).

25. Minutes, WILPF Executive Committee, Vienna, 4–9 July 1921, WILPF papers, reel 9; M.T. [Myrrha Tunas], "National Sections: 1924," WILPF papers, reel 2.

26. Ishbel Aberdeen, *President's Memorandum Regarding the 8th quinquennial Meeting of the ICW*, 1930, 11; "List of Resolutions passed by the Council Meeting," ICW, *President's Memorandum Regarding the Council Meeting of the ICW*, 1938, 85.

27. Sophie Sanford, "Mrs. Sanford's Visit to India and Japan," ICW, *Annual Report*, 1907–08.

28. Carrie Chapman Catt, untitled ms., 1913, Carrie Chapman Catt collection, box 7, Rare Books and Manuscripts Division, New York Public Library (NYPL), Astor, Lenox and Tilden Foundations.

29. Carrie Chapman Catt to Friends, 6 Mar. 1923, Catt papers, reel 5, LofC.

30. Emily Greene Balch to Clara Ragaz and Gertrud Baer, 15 Aug. 1934, WILPF papers, reel 20.

31. Carrie Chapman Catt to Margery Ashby, 7 Feb. 1925, NAWSA papers, reel 10, LofC.

32. Katherine Bompas to Louisa Fast, 6 Nov. 1934, Margery Corbett Ashby to Louisa Fast, 6 Nov. 1934, IAW papers, box 1, SSC.

33. Elisabeth Zellweger, "International Women's Conference in Calcutta," ICW *Bulletin* 14.7 (Mar. 1936).

34. Carrie Chapman Catt to Katherine Bompas, 21 Jan. 1937, NAWSA papers, reel 10, LofC.

35. Minutes, 21 June 1913, IWSA, *Report of Seventh Congress* (Manchester: Percy Brothers, 1913).

36. "The Eighth Congress of the I.W.S.A.," *Jus Suffragii* 14.9 (July 1920).

37. Bayan Latife Bekir, "Accueil de la Turquie," *Jus Suffragii* 29.7 (Apr. 1935).

38. Ishbel Aberdeen and Temair, "President's Letter," ICW *Bulletin* 14.4 (Dec. 1935).

39. Chiyin Chen to Anne Zueblin [German], 14 May 1932, WILPF papers, reel 20.

40. See Tyrrell on the WWCTU use of missionaries or other women of European origin to represent Japan, India, and China.

41. Taraknath Das to Jane Addams, 12 Apr. 1921, Addams papers, reel 13.

42. Agnes Smedley for the secretary, Pandurgang Khanko, Indian News Service and Information Bureau, to Emily Greene Balch; 28 Apr. 1921, WILPF papers, reel 1.

43. "Report of Secretary-Treasurer," May 1920–July 1921, WILPF papers, reel 9; Lotti Birch, "Report on Activities at Geneva Headquarters since September 1936," WILPF papers, reel 21.

44. Margaret Cousins to Alice Paul, 17 Mar. 1942, World Woman's Party papers, in the National Woman's party papers, reel 174. On Cousins, see Candy.

45. [Mary Sheepshanks] to Caris E. Mills, 12 Mar. 1929, WILPF papers, reel 19.

46. "Survey of the Activities, 1915–1937," typescript, n.d., WILPF papers, reel 11; "Tunis Branch," *Pax* 5.7 (May 1930), Camille Drevet, "The Women of Tunis," *Pax* 6.7 (June 1931); Minutes, WILPF International Congress, Grenoble, 15–19 May 1932, WILPF papers, reel 20.

47. M. Corbett Ashby to Josephine Schain, 5 Feb. 1935, Schain papers, box 4, SSC; G. Mallaterre-Sellier and C. Bakker van Bosse, "Rapport de notre voyage en Proche-Orient," 1935, Schain papers, box 4, SSC; M.I. Corbett Ashby, "An International Pilgrimage," *Jus Suffragii* 29.6 (Mar. 1935). The WILPF sent Elisabeth Waern-Bugge, a Swedish member, to Palestine in 1931.

48. Margery Ashby to Carrie Chapman Catt, 9 June 1926, NAWSA papers, reel 11, LofC. See Shaarawi, Badran, "Dual Liberation" and Badran *Feminists*.

49. Minutes, Disarmament Committee, 31 Oct. 1933, ICW papers, box 2, LofC; "Palestine," *Jus Suffragii* 33.2 (Nov. 1938).

50. Minutes [French], International Alliance of Women for Suffrage and Equal Citizenship Executive Committee, Copenhagen, 5 July 1939, IAW papers, Fawcett Library (FL), London Guildhall University, London.

51. Rosa Manus to Carrie Chapman Catt, 31 July 1939, Catt papers, reel 4, LofC; on this incident, see Bosch 221–22, 251; Whittick 144.

52. See Lucy Mair, "The Conflict in Palestine," *Jus Suffragii* 24.5 (Feb. 1930); [Mary Sheepshanks] to Yella Hertzka [German], 13 Mar. 1930, WILPF papers, reel 2; Minutes, WILPF International Executive Committee, Geneva, 23 Apr. [1930], WILPF papers, reel 10; "Resolutions and Appeals Not Included in the Text of the Minutes" [1930], WILPF papers, reel 10; Emily G. Balch, "Impressions of the Palestine Situation," *Pax* 5.7 (May 1930); [Mary Sheepshanks] to Yella Hertzka [German and English], 1 May 1930, WILPF papers, reel 2.

53. A. Jacot to Madame [French], 15 Apr. 1937, WILPF papers, reel 3; Egyptian section, "Propositions pour le Congrès de Luhacovice," n.d. [Apr. 1937], WILPF papers, reel 2.

54. Lotti Birch to Clara Ragaz and Cor Ramondt-Hirschmann [German], 1 May 1937, WILPF papers, reel 3; Cor Ramondt-Hirschmann to Lotti Birth [German], 7 May 1937, WILPF papers, reel 3; Clara Ragaz to Alice Jacot [French], 12 May 1937, WILPF papers, reel 3; Lotti Birch to Congress Committee [German], 12 May 1937, WILPF papers, reel 21; Cor Ramondt-Hirschmann to Clara Ragaz [German], 20 May 1937, WILPF papers, reel 3.

55. Alice Jacot to Clara Ragaz [French], 22 May 1937, WILPF papers, reel 3.

56. Clara Ragaz to Cor Ramondt-Hirschmann [German], 24 June 1937, WILPF papers, reel 3; Minutes, Executive Committee meeting, 26 July–3 Aug. 1937, WILPF papers, reel 21.

57. Eva Fichet to Emily Balch [French], 19 Aug. 1934, WILPF papers, reel 20.

58. Margery Corbett Ashby to Josephine Schain, 5 Feb. 1935, Schain papers, box 4, SSC; "Delegates and Friends," 1935, IAW papers, box 1, SSC.

59. Shareefeh Hamid Ali, "East and West in Co-operation," 1935, IAW papers, box 1, SSC.

60. Minutes, WILPF Ninth World Congress, Luhacovice, 27–31 July 1937, WILPF papers, reel 21.

61. Grace Johnson, notes on WILPF conference, May 1924, Woman's Rights Collection, box 25, SL.

62. Carrie Chapman Catt, "Burmah," *Jus Suffragii* 6.10(15 June 1912) and 6.11 (15 July 1912). Catt noted the economic and political rights of women in Sumatra and Java as well, a phenomenon that she attributed to the vestiges of an older matriarchal society.

63. Carrie Chapman Catt, "Java," *Jus Suffragii* 7.1 (15 Sept. 1912).

64. "Women of the Gold Coast," *Jus Suffragii* 18.6 (Mar. 1924), "The Turkish Woman of To-Day," *Jus Suffragii* 20.4 (Jan. 1926, E. S. Stevens, "The Woman Movement in Iraq," *Jus Suffragii* 24.2 (Nov. 1929), Kodsieh Ashraf, "Some Glimpses of the Past History and Present Progress of the Woman's Movement in Persia," ICW *Bulletin* 9.5 (Jan. 1931); "Position of Women of Native Races," *Jus Suffragii* 29.10 (July 1935), Eleanor Hawarden, "The Status of Women in Africa," *Jus Suffragii* 30.4 (Jan. 1936).

65. "Repression in the Colonies," *Pax* 8.9 (Oct. 1933).

66. "A New Peace: Report of the International Conference of Women at The Hague, 7 to 9 December 1922," WILPF papers, reel 9.

67. Gabrielle Duchêne to Madeleine Doty [French], 10 Nov. 1925, WILPF papers, reel 2, "International Summer School of the W.I.L. for 1927," *Pax* 2.4 (Feb. 1927); Madeleine Rolland, "Report of the Colonial Commission," draft, [1932], WILPF papers, reel 20; Minutes, WILPF International Executive Committee, Grenoble, 21–22 May 1932, WILPF papers, reel 10, Minutes, Ninth World Congress, Luhacovice, 27–31 July 1937, WILPF papers, reel 21.

68. On Haiti, see Bussey and Tims 58–59.

69. Hilda Clark to Jane Addams, 13 Dec. 1924, Jane Addams to Vilma Glücklich, 31 Dec. 1924; Jane Addams to Dorothy Evans, [Dec. 1924], Vilma Glücklich to Jane Addams, 19 Dec. 1924 and 19 Jan. 1925, Addams papers, reel 16.

70. Minutes, WILPF International Executive Committee, Geneva, 25 April [1930], WILPF papers, reel 10.

71. "Eighth Quinquennial Meeting of the International Council of Women," ICW *Bulletin* 8.10 (June 1930).

WORK CITED

Amos, Valerie, and Pratibha Pramar. "Challenging Imperial Feminism." *Feminist Review* 17 (1984):3–19.

Anderson, Bonnie S. "Joyous Greetings to Distant Lands: Creating an International Women's Movement, 1840–1860." Paper presented at the American Historical Association conference. Atlanta, 1996.

Badran, Margot. "Dual Liberation: Feminism and Nationalism in Egypt, 1870s–1925." *Feminist Issues* 8 (1988):15–34.

———. *Feminists, Islam, and Nation: Gender and the Making of Modern Egypt*. Princeton: Princeton UP, 1994.

Barnett, Evelyn Brooks. "Nannie Burroughs and the Education of Black Women." *The Afro-American Woman*. Ed. Sharon Harley and Rosalyn Terborg-Penn. Port Washington, NY: National University Publications, 1978. 97–108.

Barry, Kathleen. "International Feminism: Sexual Politics and the World Conference of Women in Copenhagen." *Feminist Issues* 1 (1981):37–50.

Basu, Aparna, and Bharati Ray. *Women's Struggle: A History of the All India Women's Conference, 1927–1990.* New Delhi: Manohar, 1990.

Bosch, Mineke, with Annemarie Kloosterman. *Politics and Friendship: Letters from the International Woman Suffrage Alliance, 1902–1942.* Columbus: Ohio State UP, 1990.

Burton, Antoinette. *Burdens of History: British Feminists, Indian Women, and Imperial Culture.* Chapel Hill: U of North Carolina P, 1994.

———. "The Feminist Quest for Identity: British Imperial Suffragism and 'Global Sisterhood,' 1900–1915." *Journal of Women's History* 3 (1991):46–81.

———. "The White Woman's Burden: British Feminists and 'The Indian Woman,' 1865–1915." Chaudhuri and Strobel 137–57.

Bussey, Gertrude, and Margaret Tims. *Women's International League for Peace and Freedom. 1915–1965.* London: George Allen and Unwin, 1965.

Cagatay, Nilüfer, Caren Grown, and Aida Santiago. "The Nairobi Women's Conference: Toward a Global Feminism?" *Feminist Studies* 12 (1986):401–12.

Candy, Catherine. "Margaret Cousins, 'Mother India' and the ideal 'femaculine': An Irish Orientalist Feminist in India." Paper presented at the American Historical Association conference. Chicago, 1991.

Chaudhuri, Nupur, and Margaret Strobel, eds. *Western Women and Imperialism: Complicity and Resistance.* Bloomington: Indiana UP, 1992.

Costin, Lela B. "Feminism, Pacifism, Internationalism, and the 1915 International Congress of Women." *Women's Studies International Forum* 5(1982):301–15.

Crosby, Alfred. *Ecological Imperialism: The Biological Expansion of Europe. 900–1900.* New York: Cambridge UP, 1987.

Deutsch, Regina. *International Woman Suffrage Alliance: Its History from 1904–1929.* London: IWSA, 1929.

Donaldson, Laura E. *Decolonizing Feminisms: Race, Gender, and Empire Building.* Chapel Hill: U of North Carolina P, 1992.

Ejikeme, Anene. " 'One Big Family': Nigerian Women and WILPF, 1950–70." MA thesis, Ohio State U, 1992.

Foster, Catherine. *Women for All Seasons: The Story of the Women's International League for Peace and Freedom.* Athens: U of Georgia P, 1989.

Holton, Sandra Stanley. " 'To Educate Women into Rebellion': Elizabeth Cady Stanton and the Creation of a Transatlantic Network of Radical Suffragists." *American Historical Review* 99 (1994):1112–36.

Johnson-Odim, Cheryl. "Common Themes, Different Contexts: Third World Women and Feminism." Mohanty, Russo, and Torres 314–27.

———. "On Behalf of Women and the Nation: Funmilayo Ransome-Kuti and the Struggles for Nigerian Independence and Women's Equality." *Expanding the Boundaries of Women's History.* Ed. Cheryl Johnson-Odim and Margaret Strobel. Bloomington: Indiana UP, 1992. 144–57.

Kandaleft, Alice. "The World as It Is and as It Could Be—Continued." *Our Common Cause — Civilization: Report of the International Congress of Women.* New York: National Council of Women of the U.S., 1933. 148–54, 161, 168–69.

Klejman, Laurence. "Les Congres féministes internationaux." *Mil neuf cent: Cohiers Georges Sorel: Revue d'histoire intellectuelle* 7 (1989): 71–86.

McFadden, Maggie. "Weaving the Cloth of International Sisterhood." Paper presented at the National Women's Studies Association conference. Minneapolis, June 1988.

———. "Weaving the Delicate Web: The Origins of Women's International Networks, 1820–1880." Paper presented at the Berkshire Conference on the History of Women. New Brunswick, NJ, June 1990.

Mohanty, Chandra Talpade. "Under Western Eyes: Feminist Scholarship and Colonial Discourses." Mohanty, Russo, and Torres 51–80.

Mohanty, Chandra Talpade, Ann Russo, and Lourdes Torres, eds. *Third World Women and the Politics of Feminism*. Bloomington: Indiana UP, 1991.

Neverdon-Morton, Cynthia. *Afro-American Woman of the South and the Advancement of the Race. 1895–1925*. Knoxville: U of Tennessee P, 1989.

Ramusack, Barbara. "Cultural Missionaries, Maternal Imperialists, Feminist Allies: British Women Activists in India, 1865–1945." Chaudhuri and Strobel 309–21.

Reddi, Muthulakshmi. "Creative Citizenship." *Our Common Cause — Civilization: Report of the International Congress of Women*. New York: National Council of Women of the U.S., 1933. 178–80.

Reinalda, Bob, and Natascha Verhaaren. *Vrouwenbeweging en Internationale Organisaties, 1868–1986*. Nijmegen, Neth.: Ariadne, 1989.

Rupp, Leila J. "Constructing Internationalism: The Case of Transnational Women's Organizations, 1888–1945." *American Historical Review* 99 (1994):1571–1600.

———. "Zur Organisationsgeschichte der internationalen Frauenbewegung vor dem Zweiten Weltkrieg." *Feministische Studien* 12 (1994):53–65.

Said, Edward. *Orientalism*. New York: Vintage, 1974.

Shaarawi, Huda. *Harem Years: The Memoirs of an Egyptian Feminist*. Trans. Margot Badran. New York: Feminist P, 1987.

Sinha, Mrinalini. "Reading Mother India: Empire, Nation, and the Female Voice." *Journal of Women's History* 6 (1994):6–44.

Tyrrell, Ian. *Woman's World, Woman's Empire: The Woman's Christian Temperance Union in International Perspective, 1880–1930*. Chapel Hill: U of North Carolina P. 1991.

Vellacott, Jo. "Feminist Consciousness and the First World War." *History Workshop: A Journal of Socialist and Feminist Historians* 23 (1987):81–101.

———. "A Place for Pacifism and Transnationalism in Feminist Theory: The Early Work of the Women's International League for Peace and Freedom." *Women's History Review* 2 (1993):23–56.

Wallerstein, Immanuel. *The Modern World-System*. 3 vols. New York: Academic P, 1974, 1980, 1989.

Whittick, Arnold. *Woman into Citizen*. London: Athenaeum with Frederick Muller, 1976.

Wikander, Ulla. "International Women's Congresses, 1878–1914: The Controversy over Equality and Special Labour Legislation." *Rethinking Change: Current Swedish Feminist Research*. Ed. Maud L. Eduards et al. Uppsala: Humanistisk-samhällsvetenskapliga forskningsradet, 1992. 11–36.

Wiltsher, Anne. *Most Dangerous Women: Feminist Peace Campaigners of the Great War*. London: Routledge, 1985.

———. *Women in a Changing World: The Dynamic Story of the International Council of Women since 1888*. London: Routledge, 1966.

Zonana, Joyce. "The Sultan and the Slave: Feminist Orientalism and the Structure of Jane Eyre." *Signs* 18 (1993):592–617.

Chapter Twenty-seven

Organizing International Women's Day in the Niagara Peninsula

June Corman

In many countries, International Women's Day (I.W.D.) is recognized by celebrations and protests in the form of marches, fairs, demonstrations, conferences, parties, and dances. These gatherings range from being heterogeneous to very homogeneous. Such events are made possible only when a group of volunteer activists sustain the enthusiasm to make the event happen. A major hurdle confronting the organizing committees for I.W.D. is resolving divisions among activists based on social group characteristics.[1] As Ryan (1989) has argued, the varied life experiences and different aspirations that activists bring to their organizations often result in conflict.

Using a contextually situated analysis of an International Women's Day Committee, I explore the utility of feminist organizing with identity politics and coalition politics. This analysis is informed by my location as a volunteer for the last five I.W.D. events in the Niagara Peninsula and also by my position at the local university as a professor of women's studies and sociology.

Niagara Region International Women's Day

The Niagara Region International Women's Day Committee formed in 1990 to organize the first public, free International Women's Day event in the Niagara Region of Ontario, Canada. This 1991 regionwide event and all subsequent events were held in St. Catharines, Ontario, a city of 130,000 people. In the morning, there is music and either a keynote speaker or a panel discussion. In the afternoon, smaller workshops are held on specific issues. Groups set up displays, people sell crafts and art. Entertainment has included plays, songs, stories, poetry readings, dance troupes, comedy, and a dance for women. Women politicians bring greetings. Free day care is provided, and events are wheelchair accessible. About two hundred people attend each year, and in 1995, 1996, and 1997 many also attended the opening of the affiliated art show of one hundred exhibits at the Art Gallery in Niagara Falls, Ontario.

Organizing an event of this magnitude involves issues common to any voluntary effort: a catalyst, volunteers, and financing.[2] The feminist character of International Women's Day raises additional organizational challenges, such as an emphasis on incorporating diversity and feminist process.[3] The Niagara committee has been explicitly committed to holding an inclusive event, that is, to encouraging and ensuring involvement from women of diverse backgrounds and experiences, with representation from various social classes, race and ethnic groups, generations, sexual orientations, and women with different abilities. Reaching out to diverse women has posed a challenge not faced by most single-issue groups: building a program for women with differing ideologies and goals.

Competing Visions

During the 1980s in the Niagara Peninsula, small in-house I.W.D. events were organized by special-interest groups to focus on particular issues. At the end of this decade, Deborah Toth, a newcomer to town, initiated a regionwide I.W.D. celebration to pull women together in a shared experience. She had previously been associated with the Women's Centre in the city of Hamilton, which formed the nucleus behind a Hamilton-wide I.W.D. event.

Deborah was committed to making the day relevant to all women and therefore worked to incorporate women from diverse backgrounds and from across the region. She issued one hundred invitations to individuals and representatives of woman-oriented associations. Some were multi-issue groups, for example, the Local Council of Women, and some single-issue groups, for example, pro-choice. Some groups were overtly feminist, for example, the Rape Crisis Centre; others, such as the Teacher's Federation, were not. Some supported gay issues, for example, the Gay and Lesbian Club; others, such as the Catholic Women's League, did not. Some groups represented businesses and professionals, for example, the Business and Professional Women's Association; some women were critical of capitalism. Overtures were also sent to the three main political parties: Liberal, Conservative, and New Democratic.

The first meeting was well attended: thirty-seven women representing a wide range of organizations.[4] Everyone was aware that the goal was to organize a public International Women's Day event. Every other decision had yet to be made: content of the event, location, fund-raising, program, role of men, organizational structure and process, division of labor, how to publicize the event, and types of constituencies to attract.

The success in the first year of involving women from diverse religious and political orientations generated problems: the goals of these women were mutually antagonistic, and they brought different stakes to the table. Trying to formulate an event that incorporated diverse women produced clashes stemming from contending ideologies, lifestyles, past experiences, and future visions of emancipated women. Dissension arose over such issues as profiling lesbian lifestyles, including men in the event, addressing difference, and feminist process. Meeting the challenge of incorporating diversity raised the challenge of addressing particular interests.[5]

Profiling Lesbian Lifestyles

One of the most contentious issues faced by the first organizing committee was the extent that lesbian lifestyles would be profiled in the event.[6] Some lesbian and heterosexual women wanted to profile and to celebrate lesbian lifestyles and to close the day with a women-only dance. Some of the women, with jobs in the establishment, violently opposed the women-only dance, arguing it would seriously disturb the community. The committee resolved to embrace diversity and not to discriminate against people based on sexual orientation.

This resolution, however, came after much dissension and emerged only after some people left the committee.[7] Some women were uncomfortable with publicly associating themselves with a lesbian lifestyle, and some lesbians reacted with anger to these antigay sentiments and withdrew from the committee. The dance was held as planned. The struggle over format and program epitomized sharp differences over visions of emancipation.

Through time, many lesbians have come to embrace the I.W.D. celebrations. Some have sat on the organizing committees and others have run workshops on lesbian issues. A lesbian who became president of the Teachers Association joined the committee. An invitation to the organizing committee of year five to attend a women-only party closed the chapter on alienation for many people. This reconciliation was possible because each committee deliberately included lesbian issues in the event even when there were no lesbians on the committee. The distaste was so strong among other lesbians, though, that even six years later they did not attend the event despite the fact that the dissenters had left the committee. In 1997, one of the original disenchanted lesbians told an organizer, who is herself lesbian, "I.W.D. is controlled by a reactionary bunch of establishment types."

On the other side, concern about the inclusion of lesbian-focused activities has meant that some women, who identify themselves as feminist, have distanced themselves and their companies from association with the event. Based on the initial program, an owner of a private school criticized the event as being "too extreme and not respectable." Did she assume that she had too much to lose by associating her school's reputation with what she saw as a lesbian-friendly event? The irony is that in the first year the keynote speaker had been a white heterosexual vice president of the local university.

Although these women shared concerns with the patriarchal status quo, each differed in the way she envisioned emancipated lives: in heterosexual relationships supported by jobs in the establishment; in lesbian relationships, advocating alternative arrangements. These different visions led to a pattern of factionalism in which, as Ryan (1989) has pointed out, women did not want to associate with competing visions. In this case, achieving a workable consensus resulted in losing representation.

A Role for Men

Just as there was division of opinion regarding the inclusion of lesbian issues, so too was there dissension over the role men might play in the event.[8] Liberal-minded women who thought inequality was due to misguided men who had been socialized to consider women inferior, and women who located oppression as endemic to the capitalist mode of production advocated reeducating men at the event. These women suggested canvasing men's groups for donations as a token of support. In contrast, women who associated oppression directly with men did not want men to be part of the event.

The moderate position taken by the group in the first year reconciled the conflict: speakers would be women and financial donations would be solicited only from women's groups, but men would be invited to the event. The Niagara committee unanimously believed that the event should be organized by women. In subsequent years, the committee has affirmed these principles. In response to a man who wanted to join the organizing committee in 1994, and again in 1995, the committee suggested that he continue his promotional work instead. At the same time, a male chiropractor was refused permission to set up a display table because the group decided that men should not profit from an event organized by women to promote women. An organizer who ran a martial arts studio volunteered some of her male students to help with security. Continuing through 1997, men's involvement was limited to staffing information tables, publicizing the event, security, and sitting in the audience.

Building Inclusivity

The third issue that shook the committee was an accusation that the event was dominated by white middle-class women. The homogeneity of speakers in the third year sparked this criticism. The primary event was a panel discussion with practitioners of traditional and alternative forms of medicine: a touch therapist, a midwife, and two medical doctors. In keeping with the goal of involving native women, the group had tried to get a native healer, but this attempt was unsuccessful. The workshops in the afternoon were also all moderated by white women. This lack of diversity was a departure from both previous years. In 1991, three First Nations women had moderated a workshop; in 1992, a First Nations woman and four refugee women were profiled.

After the 1993 event, the committee received a formal letter containing the following: "This committee and the event literally scream white middle class, a power-over position that needs to be removed to be inclusionary and representative of all women." The committee interpreted the criticism as faulting the composition of the committee, not apprehending at that time that the writer could also be referring to the speakers at the event. Organizers were hurt and angry. Committee members wondered: "Is it our fault if most of us are white? Membership on the committee was open to anyone. Why should we be criticized if others don't volunteer their time? If it wasn't for us, there wouldn't even be an event."

Initially, some people felt like packing up their papers, going home, and not bothering to donate time the following year. Instead, everyone engaged in long discussions over ways to increase representation.[9] The committee renewed efforts to be inclusive relative to the two elements it controlled: content of the day and type of displays. In 1996, the plenary session was devoted to a First Nations woman and a union representative. In 1997, a First Nations woman opened and closed the festivities, and the panel included a fugitive slave's great-granddaughter who is the president of the Black History Association, a Catholic Sister who works with refugees, a Paralympic athlete and medal winner, a president of a union representing five-thousand airline workers, and the founder of the I.W.D. committee, who operates a martial arts center. The committee also supported diversity by inviting First Nations women, lesbians, and social/labor activists to be workshop facilitators.

In keeping with the 1992 mandate to incorporate diversity, the committee ensured that display tables included groups concerned with racism and Third World issues.[10] Feminist organizations were encouraged to publicize lesbian issues. The Local Labour Council and other unions were invited to publicize labor issues. The goal was to encourage diverse participation in the event so people would become informed about the types of issues confronting women other than themselves.[11] After these renewed attempts at building inclusivity into the panel, the workshops, and display tables, the committee did not receive any more complaints on its evaluation forms, in letters, or during face-to-face interactions.

The committee was still left with two other areas over which it had less control: the social composition of the committee and the profile of the public who attend the event. Over the years, close to fifty people have sat on the organizing committee, with about nine people doing the work in any one year. The membership of the annual committees has fluctuated, but five people, all white, provided continuity for the first five years. First Nations and South American women have also sat on the committee. These women did not claim to speak for their communities nor did they wish to contribute solely to that single issue. Another First Nations woman and a Sudanese woman joined the 1998 committee. The committee, regardless of its composition, focuses on making the program inclusive and responsive to the needs of the various groups in the Niagara Peninsula.

In keeping with the population of St. Catharines, the audience is largely white, although the recognizable social characteristics of the crowd vary, reflective of the program. Focusing on inclusivity in the program and display tables has contributed to a more mixed crowd. In 1996, moving the location to the Canadian Autoworkers Hall and profiling both a First Nations activist and a labor activist as keynote speakers attracted members of the First Nations community and trade unionists.[12]

Getting the word out about the event and motivating a diverse group of people to attend is much more difficult than putting together a meaningful, inclusive program. The temptation of many committee members has been to focus on the program as the pièce de résistance rather than putting the necessary energy into building a sizeable and diverse audience.

A Catalyst for Change

Prior to the first International Women's Day event in the Niagara Peninsula, groups and individuals that were devoted to progressive social change around issues associated with gender, racism, labor, and poverty had little opportunity to come together to learn from one another and to help one another advance their goals.[13] For seven years, the public I.W.D. event has provided a forum for activists associated with many issues to come together. These connections among women of different backgrounds and institutional affiliations manifest themselves in two ways: single-issue groups are expanding their membership through access to a recruitment pool at the I.W.D. event; umbrella groups, formed through I.W.D. connections, are sponsoring events that challenge the status quo.

A Recruitment Pool

The region is dotted with many single-issue social change organizations. First Nations women associated with the Friendship Centres work to keep their children in school. Black women struggle to provide opportunities for black youth by bringing alive the important contributions of fugitive slaves to our region. Immigrant women devote themselves to improving the plight of Latin American refugees who seek refuge at our border with the United States. Academics focus on building gender equity into the university curriculum. The list goes on.

The I.W.D. event has given single-issue groups opportunities to educate members of the community and to recruit new supporters by being guest speakers, running workshops, or having a display table. These opportunities are pursed by antiracism action groups, Third World education groups, AIDS activists, feminist publications, health awareness groups, and self-employed feminists who attract clients by having a display table or buying advertisements in the I.W.D. brochure.

Collective Strategies

In Canada, politicians are reacting to the globalization of capital and economic restructuring by cutting programs such as education, health, housing, and other services associated with the welfare state. The burden falls on women. Resistance by individuals or single-issue groups to the systematic efforts by business and government to limit general social rights appears increasingly futile. Only a mass movement built on a coalition of interests will be large enough to command attention. The encompassing character of I.W.D. events provides the catalyst enabling the kind of coalition politics needed to win these struggles.

The Niagara event makes this kind of coalition building possible by bringing together an assortment of people who otherwise would not have an occasion to meet. Concerned activists, who staff more than thirty information tables, have opportunities to network. Scores of other people visit the tables, meeting the activists on a first-name basis and familiarizing themselves with their specific concerns.

Networking has resulted in the formation of social action groups such as the "1996 On to Ottawa Protest" against cuts in social programs and the newly formed Niagara Feminist Network, which is an outreach initiative by labor activists. On a smaller scale, contacts have resulted in linkages between unions, First Nations women, university women, and feminist activist groups. These contacts made it possible for the Women's Committee of the Canadian Autoworkers to invite a representative of the Women's Studies Program and a First Nations woman to give an address at a rally to protest violence against women. Similarly, contacts from the event have facilitated invitations for community activists to speak at the university.

Moving Ahead

Groups that adhere to identity politics are in a strong position to mobilize people in a similar situation. Under "liberal" political regimes, applying continuous pinpoint pressure on the system can produce dents in the armor. Similarly, single-issue groups that garner support from a multitude of diverse activists can win specific goals, such as abortion rights, women's shelters, and school lunch programs. But, pinpoint pressure applied by atomized groups is woefully insufficient in a conservative fiscal climate. As well, the premises of identity politics—that only people who experience oppression can understand and mobilize against it—limit the involvement of many potential supporters.[14] Only massive actions, taken by many groups in concert, can stay the avalanche of cutbacks and advance the cause of progressive change.

NOTES

Special thanks for commenting on this paper to members of Niagara Region International Women's Day Committee: Deborah Toth, Glenna Janzen, Leila Lustig, and Jane Helleiner. Ester Reiter, Daiva Stasiulis, Ingrid Makus, Murray Smith, Liza McCoy, and Meg Luxton each contributed a piece of the puzzle.

   1. For an analysis of the issues faced by the Toronto, Ontario, I.W.D. committee, see Egan (1987); Egan, Gardner, and Persad (1988); Adamson, Briskin, and McPhail (1988); and Agnew (1996). Metropolitan Toronto is a multiethnic city of more than two million people.

   2. For a review of the literature on citizen participation and voluntary organizations, see Florin and Wandersman (1990). See Freeman (1995:397) for a discussion of these issues in regard to the women's movement. She argues that movements are inherently unstable when they are dependent on volunteer energy.

3. For a discussion of these issues, see Adamson, Briskin, and McPhail (1988); Agnew (1996); Backhouse and Flaherty (1992); Connelly and Armstrong (1992); Burt, Code, and Dorney (1993); Wine and Ristock (1991). And for the United States, see Deckard (1983); Katzenstein and Muller (1987); Ryan (1992); Ferree and Hess (1994); and Ferree and Martin (1995).

4. Some of these included Brock University, Women's Teachers Association, Y.W.C.A., Big Sisters, churches, unions, women's shelters, Family and Children Services, Council of Women, and a representative from a member of the Provincial Legislature.

5. Agnew (1996:66) argues that the goal of representing interests of all women equally is embedded in difficulties because all women do not have equal skills and expertise.

6. See Ryan (1989) and Ferree and Hess (1994) for an analysis of the divisiveness of this issue in the United States. Ryan (1989) argues that many women considered the women's movement irrelevant because they associated it with a lesbian orientation.

7. These disagreements culminated in a 1991 statement of principles that included recognition of diversity of experience and of diverse racial and class backgrounds and sexual orientations.

8. For a discussion of the controversy over the role of men by members of the Toronto I.W.D. committee, see Egan (1987) and for the American women's movement, see Ryan (1989).

9. Backhouse and Flaherty (1992) contains examples of responses by women's groups to criticism of white privilege, unintentional racism, and inclusiveness. Mukherjee (1992) and Simms (1992) argue that white women have to be less ethnocentric and appreciate that white middle class is not the norm.

10. A 1992 mission statement read: "The main purpose of celebrating International Women's Day is to inform and educate the people of the Niagara Region on the services available to women and their families and the issues that are important to them and to join in with others around the world in recognition of women."

11. This strategy is in keeping with Rhode's (1990) observation that strategies to build inclusivity are most fruitful when the focus is on inequalities that flow as a consequence of difference rather than on difference per se.

12. University students, other than those from women's studies, and other young people are also notably absent.

13. The Take Back the Night March organized by the Sexual Assault Counselling Centre is the only other public gathering of activists in St. Catharines.

14. Problems with this position for achieving human emancipation from exploitative relations have been eloquently stated by Smith (1994); Wood (1995); Hobsbawm (1996); and Briskin (1992). Smith (1994) argued that because forms of oppression often crisscross, liberation has the best chance to succeed if it is supported by a broad-based coalition of people who understand one another's particular forms of oppression. Briskin (1992:270) is critical of the politics of identity because it hides interconnections, promotes individualism, and suggests a hierarchy of competitive oppressions.

REFERENCES

Adamson, Nancy, Linda Briskin, and Margaret McPhail. 1988. *Feminist Organizing for Change: The Contemporary Women's Movement in Canada.* Toronto: Oxford University Press.

Agnew, Vivay. 1996. *Resisting Discrimination: Women from Asia, Africa, and the Caribbean and the Women's Movement in Canada.* Toronto: University of Toronto Press.

Backhouse, Constance, and David H. Flaherty, eds. 1992. *Challenging Times: The Women's Movement in Canada and the United States.* Montreal and Kingston: McGill-Queen's University Press.

Briskin, Linda. 1992. "Socialist Feminism: From the Standpoint of Practice." In M. Patricia Connelly and Pat Armstrong, eds. *Feminism in Action: Studies in Political Economy.* Toronto: Canadian Scholars Press.

Burt, Sandra, Lorraine Code, and Lindsay Dorney, eds. 1993. *Changing Patterns: Women in Canada.* Toronto: McClelland and Stewart.

Connelly, M. Patricia, and Pat Armstrong, eds. 1992. *Feminism in Action: Studies in Political Economy.* Toronto: Canadian Scholars Press.

Deckard, Barbara Sinclair. 1983. *The Women's Movement: Political, Socioeconomic and Psychological Issues.* New York: Harper and Row.

Egan, Carolyn. 1987. "Toronto's International Women's Day Committee: Socialist Feminist Politics." In Heather Jon Maroney and Meg Luxton, eds. *Feminism and Political Economy: Women's Work, Women's Struggles.* Toronto: Methuen.

Egan, Carolyn, Linda Lee Gardner, and Judy Vashti Persad. 1988. "The Politics of Transformation: Struggles with Race, Class, and Sexuality in the March 8th Coalition." In Frank Cunningham, Sue Findlay, Marlene Kadaar, Alan Lennon, and Ed Silva, eds. *Social Movements, Social Change: The Politics and Practices of Organizing.* Toronto: Between the Lines.

Ferree, Myra Marx, and Beth Hess. 1994. *Controversy and Coalition: The New Feminist Movement.* New York: Macmillan.

Ferree Myra Marx, and Patricia Yancey Martin, eds. 1995. *Feminist Organizations: Harvest of the New Women's Movement.* Philadelphia: Temple University Press.

Florin, Paul, and Abraham Wandersman. 1990. "An Introduction to Citizen Participation. Voluntary Organizations. and Community Development: Insights for Empowerment Through Research." *American Journal of Community Psychology* 13, no. 1: 41–51.

Freeman, Jo. 1995. "From Seed to Harvest: Transformations of Feminist Organizations and Scholarship." In Myra Marx Ferree and Patricia Yancey Martin, eds. *Feminist Organizations: Harvest of the New Women's Movement,* Philadelphia: Temple University Press.

Hobsbawm, Eric. 1996. "Identity Politics and the Left." *New Left Review,* no. 217: 38–47.

Katzenstein, Mary Fainsod, and Carol McClurg Muller, eds. 1987. *The Women's Movements of the United States and Western Europe.* Philadelphia: Temple University Press.

Mukherjee, Arun. 1992. "A House Divided: Women of Colour and American Feminist Theory." In Constance-Backhouse and David H. Flaherty, eds, *Challenging Times: The Women's Movement in Canada and the United States,* Montreal and Kingston: McGill-Queen's University Press.

Rhode, Deborah L., ed. 1990. *Theoretical Perspectives on Sexual Difference.* New Haven: Yale University Press.

Ryan, Barbara. 1989. "Ideological Purity and Feminism." *Gender & Society* 3 no. 2: 239–257.

Ryan, Barbara. 1992. *Feminism and the Women's Movement: Dynamics of Change in Social Movement Ideology and Activism.* New York: Routledge.

Simms, Glenda. 1992. "Beyond the White Veil." In Constance Backhouse and David H. Flaherty, eds. *Challenging Times: The Women's Movement in Canada and the United States.* Montreal and Kingston: McGill-Queen's University Press.

Smith, Sharon. 1994. "Mistaken Identity—or Can Identity Politics Liberate the Oppressed?" *International Socialism*, no. 62: 3–50.

Wine, Jeri Dawn, and Janice Ristock. 1991. *Women and Social Change: Feminist Activism in Canada*. Toronto: James Lorimer.

Wood, Ellen Meikins. 1995. *Democracy against Capitalism: Renewing Historical Materialism*. Cambridge: Cambridge University Press.

Chapter Twenty-eight

Sharing Power
A Latina in NOW

Rosa María Pegueros

In 1994, Patricia Ireland, president of the National Organization for Women (NOW), was recommended by the University of Rhode Island Honorary Degree Committee to be the 1994 Commencement Day Speaker, but President Robert Carothers vetoed the idea because, he said, she was too controversial. I am not sure what in particular he found controversial: the mere fact that she is the leader of the largest and most effective feminist organization in the country with more than a quarter million members, or the fact that virtually every newspaper and magazine article about her makes a point of mentioning that she is married yet has a woman lover. Since I am known as a feminist, many of my colleagues were quick to express to me their chagrin at the president's decision. Although I agreed with them that it was sad that the president chose to be cautious rather than daring, what they didn't know was that I have a bitter history with Patricia Ireland that made my feelings about her visit to URI ambivalent at best.

I spent eleven years as a NOW activist. There was a time when I wore my NOW pin on the lapel of every jacket and my NOW wristwatch with pride, and spent every dollar and hour I could spare on NOW activism. I started with NOW while I was still nursing my daughter, fitting meetings into my life between the "mommy and me" activities, gardening, and canning that dominated my life at the time. It was not my first experience with activism; as a teenager, I had worked with the United Farm Workers union (UFW) and on Bobby Kennedy's campaign, even though I wasn't old enough to vote for him. As a college student, I was involved in other types of activism, as many of the sixties generation were, but NOW gave me an unprecedented opportunity to learn, to develop my leadership skills, and to grow as a human being. During my NOW career, I was a chapter president; head of the fund-raising committee for the California NOW; a state action coordinator (the equivalent of a vice president in charge of actions—the state coordinator and I developed a plan that put the state organization back in the black after years of not only operating with a deficit but also running afoul of the IRS, and I coordinated a national boycott of Sunkist products). Eventually, I helped to found and became president of the California NOW Foundation, the educational affiliate of the political organization. I also created a plan to integrate California NOW, which has made it the most integrated state NOW organization in the country.

By the time that I joined the Committee to Combat Racism at the national level in 1986, Molly Yard was president and Patricia Ireland was the executive vice president of NOW. The national board had a few women of color token members and I continued to be the only woman of color on the California NOW board, though I was by that time, working on my plan to integrate the board. I am embarrassed to admit that I really thought that NOW could change, would change. Yard and Ireland expressed their sincere desire to work with women of color but asserted that they could get only a few to join. They picked us to be the keynote speakers at the state and national conferences, and trotted us out whenever they had the chance.

The staff position in NOW that was in charge of issues of racism was a revolving door. Black women would take the job (for some reason—as long as I was in NOW, only black women) and after a few months of trying to get board support and to get NOW to cough up money for one project or another, they would quit in disgust, reinforcing the public perception that it was, indeed, a white women's organization. *What took me a very long time to realize was that, at an organizational level, unless resources back up rhetoric, it is, as Shakespeare would say, "sound and fury, signifying nothing."*

By the time that Patricia Ireland came to California to tell me to "get in line," she was already thoroughly annoyed with me because I kept pushing NOW to fulfil its promise, to put resources behind its rhetoric about women of color, about combating racism; the staff person begged me not to leave NOW—she needed me, she said, to "watch her back." I wrote a controversial paper called "Our Sister's Keepers," that I presented to a conference of NOW state coordinators in Nashville. Ireland had expected me to be grateful for the opportunity to address the group and was furious when I pointed out the racial imbalances in the organization.

I must say that this tenacious bellicosity is not really my nature. In my family and among my friends, I am known to be the negotiator, the one who will talk until the cows come home in order to avoid a fight. But I had invested many years in the women's movement, and after checking out other feminist organizations, I felt that NOW was the most effective one. It was also clear to me, however, that it had unwritten policies that applied only to women of color. In short, so long as we followed the program, we were welcome. When we demanded a change in priorities, our favored status was withdrawn.

Ireland and I did not actually get into a confrontation over an issue of race but over one of class. National NOW decided to sponsor a lesbian conference in San Diego. As California action coordinator, I was asked to help find speakers for the workshops. The immediate dispute was that the national leadership expected the speakers to pay their way to the conference as well as pay the registration fee. A few of the women I was dealing with were glad to speak at the conference but could not afford the fee. NOW wouldn't waive it. I waited until I was calm and then wrote the leadership a serious and rational letter questioning the wisdom of this policy and pointing out how it discriminated against women who were not well-off. Ireland and the action coordinator, Sherry O'Dell, were miffed that I would take them to task over this issue. A few weeks later, when names were placed in nomination to head the committees, and mine was put forward to head the Committee to Combat Racism, I was rejected, even though every other woman on the committee supported me and expected me to be the next chair. The leadership then asked a new member of the national board, a Cuban woman who had never served on the committee, to serve as chair. She called me from the meeting to ask if I wasn't in line for the chair. She told me she'd been asked by Patricia to serve and asked me what should she do. I told her to follow her conscience. She declined to serve. Ireland then appealed to the retiring chair to change her mind, even though she had stated, quite clearly, that she was too overworked to continue. Some promises were made, and she finally accepted. Having hit the glass ceiling, I did what I probably should have done years earlier—I quit. It was not the only alternative: I could have run against Patricia Ireland in the next election, but without going into the arcane politics of NOW, suffice it to say that it would have been about as effective as taking on old Mayor Daley in Chicago. Like many other organizations, NOW has two dominant groups, and I as a woman of color, having different priorities, would have been a third-party candidate. Besides, by that time, I was in graduate school and didn't have the time or energy to fight back.

(Epilogue: A few years later, I wrote a letter to *Ms.* about a profile of Patricia Ireland in which she trumpeted the role of women of color in NOW. I described NOW's "glass ceiling" and I wrote that NOW treated its women of color the way that men treat women. *Ms.* printed the letter but edited out those passages, demonstrating to me that women may be entitled to be angry, but women of color better watch their mouths.)

I relate this story to you because even though, as any sociologist will be quick to point out, a sample of one is not a sample, my experience as a woman of color in NOW was unique only in two respects: that I stayed so long and that I got so far. (I should mention that my experience was similar in the American Civil Liberties Union (ACLU) and in the Democratic Socialists of America (DSA), although the difference between NOW and those groups was in getting the men in the organization to take note of women's issues.) Moreover, while one can theorize about feminism, the life of movements is in its activists.

As you can imagine, the experience left me with a bitter aftertaste. My involvement in NOW had absorbed eleven years of my life. When I finally left, it was like leaving a bad marriage: Even though there were many good reasons to leave, it left an unbearable hollowness. I had to *think* about my feminism and what it meant to me. For even though I had lived with it, argued for it before state senate committees, city council meetings, and attorney general hearings, I was no longer with NOW, but I am a feminist to the marrow of my bones.

In retrospect, I understand how marginal I was. Because I always spoke on behalf of women of color, represented NOW in welfare rights coalitions, and brought issues like immigrants' rights and women farm workers to the board, I was nicknamed the "Marxist on the Board." My friends who are real Marxists (and, I should add, not NOW members) had a good laugh over that one, for much as my politics have always been rather vaguely left, I have never even read Marx and would not presume to call myself a Marxist. The nickname indicates to me how essentially apolitical they were, that those issues that dealt with working-class women were recognized as being the province of the capital "L" Left, and I, as the one who brought them to their attention was good-naturedly red-baited. I say good-naturedly because they were almost always nice to me, putting up with me and my issues when they did not endure a *white* woman who tried to push them more to the left.

What does it mean to call yourself a feminist when within the organized movement, you are a second-class citizen? I looked for a while to the idea of *womanism,* but not being an African American, I doubted that that would be the answer; I had experienced marginalization in my encounters with Black women as well. Being Latina, I bring a certain set of experiences that differs from that of either of the larger groups. Most of the Latinas I know are barely one generation from the border crossing or the sweatshop; many are immigrants themselves. Moreover, many have memories of horror of their own: they arrived in the United States but their siblings did not survive the revolution in their countries. Some had members of their immediate families "disappeared." I grew up the daughter of a Salvadoran immigrant who left El Salvador after the troubles there during the 1930s and went with her family to Guatemala—out of the frying pan, into the fire. Guatemala was in a state of unrest from 1944 to 1954, and she left there to come to the United States in 1948. Even after she came here, the terror in Guatemala followed her. Her brother was once mistaken for a subversive because he had a similar name, and so was "disappeared" and tortured while we in San Francisco and his mother and other brothers in Guatemala waited in anguish for a word from him. Two weeks later, naked and half-dead, he was dumped by his captors on his mother's doorstep; realizing they had the wrong man, they didn't kill him. Another uncle was playing soccer with his son and some friends in a field near the airport when he came upon a human skull. I asked him what he did when he found it. In the relative safety of my home, my first thought would have been to run to the police. He told me that he dug a hole with his fingers and covered it up. Why not tell the police? If you lived in a country that Amnesty International says has the worst human rights records in the world, would *YOU* tell the police?

Once, when I was leading a pro-choice march on the state capitol in Sacramento, I was asked by an Argentine woman who had joined the march to translate for her. She expressed her solidarity with us and then told us a horrific story about being tortured by the Argentine military, complete with rape and the use of rats. As a historian who has read accounts of the teaching of torture techniques by the CIA to the military in various countries in Latin America, I cannot begin to describe the complexity of emotions that I felt as I translated for her. One of my students, Ana, was the daughter of a minister in Allende's government who was kidnapped. After the family had assumed he was dead, he showed up one night with guards, who escorted him and the terrified family to the airport, where they were sent to New York with only the clothes on their backs. Ana was only three when they arrived here; so traumatized was she by the whole experience that she stopped speaking and eating. They had to feed her intravenously—getting her to talk took much longer. She never did understand why her father was released or why they were sent to the United States. My sister-in-law is the daughter of the former bursar of the University of El Salvador; her father got them out of El Salvador when the university was violently shut down in 1975. I could tell you stories . . . But my point is that our experience as Latinas is significantly different from that of either white or African American women, and because of this, we approach feminism from a different perspective.

As a Latina who has seen the destruction of families through civil war and state terrorism, I have a deep understanding of the devotion to family that characterizes Latino culture, and I am mystified by the sometimes casual dismissal of family on the part of many feminists from the United States. As a woman from a culture that has witnessed the wholesale slaughter of our menfolk, I cannot entertain the underlying hostility toward men that characterizes much of American feminism. Even though I am in agreement with the determination to ensure that women have the same professional and political opportunities that men have, I must confess a repugnance at the idea of demanding equal rights for women in the military; to me, the American military has been hand in glove with the CIA in its covert and overt domination of Latin America, as well as being its coconspirator in state-sponsored terror. When women march for equal access to military training, I stay home. To me, there is but one way to be in relation to the American military: against it.

May I say that I am NOT saying that American feminists hate men or the family, only that we have different attitudes based on very different experiences. It is supremely ironic to me that one of the chief complaints of feminism against men is that women are construed as "the other" when we—working-class and/or women of color—are clearly "the other" to mainstream feminism. Even though the language of American feminism is inclusive, the movement seems to have as little sense of how to deal with the racial and ethnic divisions of our society as the country does in general. Only numbers have made a difference in our society: The needs of African Americans or Chinese Americans or Latinos are recognized only when there are too many of us to ignore. That's when ballots and street signs in Spanish or Chinese are printed, and then only under protest from the English Only organization and its sympathizers.

Worse yet is capitalism's approach to the problem, the commercial co-optation of identity. What can we sell to the Hispanic market? Let's produce little brown Cabbage Patch dolls and brown Barbie dolls. If they were really like us, the Latina Barbie dolls would not only be browner but rounder! In Los Angeles, the Vons supermarket introduced its *Tianguis* markets that sold traditional Latino foods, displayed the fruits and vegetables as you would see them displayed in a marketplace in Mexico, and featured mariachis strolling and singing in the aisles on Saturday afternoons. *Tianguis* put many of the small, local, ethnic markets out of business because its prices, subsidized by the volume prices at which the chain can purchase goods were much lower than the little mom-and-pop stores in Los Angeles could get from wholesalers.

This commercial response to ethnic diversity does not create a greater acceptance of foreign cultures in our midst; it merely takes advantage of the dollars that can be elicited from an ethnically and racially diverse population. In the same way, the language of political correctness has not improved our lot in feminism. The divisions I see in NOW appear everywhere in the movement: in the National Women's Studies Association, the Berkshire Conference on Women's History, the Women's Rights Committee of the American Civil Liberties Union, the Women in the Law Conferences, the Democratic Socialists of America, and *Ms.* magazine. I see the same phenomenon with numbing regularity: A handful of women of color, trying to work in those groups and then giving up on organized feminism and returning to their own ethnic or racial groups, or giving up on activism while they figure "it" out.

Today, we have a very fragmented movement. It seems that women have agreed that working in coalition is more effective than as a unified whole. We would do well to remember the standard rule of organizing: Broad coalitions are possible with narrow issues. A broadly stated platform of issues will find only a narrow coalition.

When I left NOW, I had a few choices. I was being courted by the retiring executive director of Amnesty International in Southern California to take his place. CARECEN, the Salvadorean refugee organization in Los Angeles asked me to apply for the position of executive director there. I struggled with my desire to continue to do activism and decided to go instead to graduate school. I see my teaching as an opportunity to influence young people in a positive and feminist way, so that they can someday find the answers that we lack. As the old bumper sticker says, "Frustrate the conservatives: Educate their children."

Am I a feminist? Yes, still and always. I believe that women have the right to the same political, economic, and personal options that men have; that we have the right to physical autonomy and are in all ways the equals of men. I believe that multiculturalism—in the university, in the women's movement, and in American society—is the central struggle of our time. Unless we can embrace multiculturalism, we will continue to have turf wars—jealousies between various Latino groups, between African Americans and Latinos, and among women from various ethnic and racial groups in the women's movement. There must be compromise. Priorities cannot be set by the majority group that then expects compliance from the less powerful groups. Power may concede nothing, but we are *one* movement.

Chapter Twenty-nine

A Writing Spider Tries Again
From Separatist to Coalitional Identity Politics

Diane L. Fowlkes

Often when I sit down to write about the political and philosophical significance of feminist identity politics, I get tangled in a web of thoughts and find myself going off on tangents that turn out to be related twists and moves.[1] I have been writing and rewriting a political philosophical treatise for the past five years. I guess I have been trying to remake my own web of identity. Sometimes I tell myself to let go, take up another topic, and get on with things. But something draws me back to remaking my web. I have to give it yet another try. The essay that follows reconnects some earlier moments with my present in an effort to understand parts of a process that I and no doubt others undergo in creating and re-creating feminist identities. Such identities position us for possible coalitions in women's movement, a claim I have developed elsewhere.[2]

At this point in my own journey from the margins of the civil rights movement of the early 1960s to formal study in the discipline of political science during the early 1970s and from there, since the mid-1970s, through women's movement and women's studies to feminist theory and identity politics, I have come to think of myself metaphorically as a writing spider. I have long been entranced with the appearance and behavior of these large, strikingly colored creatures. As far back as my childhood in the 1940s, my mother introduced me to them when they appeared in the flower gardens that she nurtured. The black-with-yellow-striped spiders build their webs behind and between bushes or tall flowers. They write their signatures of zigzag heavy white webbing across the gossamer main webs. As insects fly into and tear the webs, the spiders wrap the insects in more webbing before dining on them. The spiders then remake their webs in preparation for the next engagement.

The image of the writing spider continually remaking her web feeds my political stance as well. The web stands for my identity through attachment to place—where I live and work in academia within the larger community, whether that has been in a political science department or in some evolving women's studies program, in one or another federally funded project to integrate women's studies in order to transform curriculum, and in one or another research project to read and write feminist theory for self-transformation and for societal change. My engagements with writers and other actors who challenge some aspect of my self-construction cause me to digest what they teach me and to restructure myself and my web in preparation for another engagement.

Through this process, I have become increasingly conscious of how I myself along with my place of living and working have been and continue to be shaped by structures of gender, race, and class. I have come to believe that patriarchy and compulsory heterosexuality, white/Aryan supremacy, and capitalism continue to privilege some at the expense of most others. I have reached a position of feminist materialist intersubjectivity (Fowlkes 1997), which means that I have become conscious of how the interdependence of my position with those of others requires that I attend to the lives and works of those others, as they to mine, if "we"[3] are to have any chance of accomplishing even some of what we are attempting. I know better why I need to struggle (cf. Combahee River Collective 1983)

with other white women and men about and against forms of white-skin privilege and racism in which we participate,

with other heterosexual women and men about and against forms of heterosexual privilege and homophobia in which we participate,

with other middle-class women and men about and against forms of middle-class privilege in which we participate,

with all women about and against forms of sexual oppression we experience,

and with myself about the need to keep on struggling in these ways, no matter my own tiredness and no matter the feelings of distrust and anger that get stirred up among and within us when we engage in identity politics.

It is this last awareness that brought to me the image of the writing spider, again and again remaking her web. She keeps on struggling and writing and enduring until she dies. I also have no doubt that reading Gloria Anzaldúa's (1987) evocation of the great serpent goddess touched off in me this spiritual connection with the spider, another figure associated with the ancient goddess. In any case, I owe my awareness of these sites of struggle to those authors I have already acknowledged and to others about whom I shall write in this essay, though they are not the only ones to whom I owe appreciation—and sometimes chagrin—for causing me to remake my web again and again.

From Questions of Origin to Questions of Intent

"Identity politics" is a concept that refers to a group's practice of organizing to combat its own oppression, however defined. But who can say where or when the concept, much less the practice, of identity politics originated? Having reread recently Sara Evans's *Personal Politics: The Roots of Women's Liberation in the Civil Rights Movement and the New Left* (1980), I was struck by how strongly she plays the theme of identity politics throughout the book without making the concept an explicit organizing device and without placing the term in her index. From reading Evans, I concluded that *identity politics* may be a contemporary term for what has long been a political theoretical practice.

I next concluded that the roots of identity politics as some understand it today in the contemporary United States women's movement could be traced to the commencement of identity politics in the Black liberation movement of the mid-1960s. Evans recounts that in the Student Nonviolent Coordinating Committee, "black power advocates . . . stated that each oppressed group should organize itself first and flatly rejected as paternalistic racism any wish of young whites to engage in civil rights work" (Evans 1980, 173). Identity politics then developed as separatist Black Power politics. The white civil rights workers who departed from SNCC went on to join Students for a Democratic Society, one of the main organizations of the New Left. Following the lead of SNCC, SDS began to organize consciously around its members' identity as oppressed students, the "new working class," on campuses that they saw as deeply enmeshed in research for the military-industrial complex and in preparing managers for corporate America (Evans 1980, 174). Some of the women of SDS, increasingly alienated by sexual exploitation from men of the New Left, then broke away to create separate women's groups that organized the women's liberation movement (Evans 1980, 174). Women's liberation, which became associated in the minds of many with predominantly white women, in turn was slow to incorporate "out" Lesbian feminists, some of whom then split off into Lesbian separatist groups, such as The Furies (Bunch 1987).

Movements for justice thus appear to have multiplied through the 1960s and 1970s more often than not by splitting into singularly identified collectivities, which then seemed to many of their members to work at cross-purposes. In the face of what later came to be recognized as creating a hierarchy of oppressions and engaging in horizontal hostility (Lorde 1984b, 47–48), people argued over whether white supremacy or capitalism or patriarchy or compulsory heterosexuality was "the root" oppression and, therefore, whether race or class or gender or sexual preference was "the" dimension of identity around which they should organize.

I well remember my own practice of separatist identity politics during this period. My lover-to-become-husband, a white political scientist, and I left Memphis for Atlanta in 1968. We moved from civil rights and antiwar politics within and against the Democratic Party to leftist antiracist community politics. He was now teaching at Atlanta University, a historically Black institution. I completed a master's degree in political science at Georgia State University, where I also worked as a secretary, then earned a doctoral degree at Emory University, and while finishing my dissertation was able to take a position as a tenure-track assistant professor of political science at Georgia State.

During this time, women's movement began to emerge as yet another source of change—first the creation of the National Organization for Women (NOW), modeled on the National Association for the Advancement of Colored People (NAACP) and designed to work for anti-sex-discrimination law enforcement, followed shortly by the mushrooming of the radical women's liberation groups (Freeman 1975) out of the New Left. Having finished my dissertation, trying to recuperate from what I came to consider the dehumanizing experience of graduate school, naively ignorant of the even worse experiences of tenure and promotion that lay ahead of me, I began to read literature from women's movements in England, France, and the United States.

Soon I was in the grips of another round of consciousness-raising, this time around sexism and the rise of powerful sisterhood. I became aware of sexist treatment in my political science department as most of the men either ignored me or commented on my mode of dress; hardly anyone, except for the one other woman, who thankfully was a feminist, seemed to be interested in my ideas. The demands on my time and energy were escalating to the point that I could not physically and emotionally stay involved in leftist and antiracist work along with women's liberation and academic work. I remember screwing up my courage and declaring that I could no longer go to my husband's meetings and that he and his comrades should be on notice that women's liberation was as revolutionary if not more revolutionary than Marxist liberation struggle. We both continued our efforts to integrate antiracist perspectives into our teaching and research. Antiracism, however, was not the main factor in the feminist work that now consumed my energies. Operating on the separatist model of identity politics, I compartmentalized my feminist from my antiracist work and gave precedence to feminism over antiracism.

Before describing the emergence of a different form of identity politics, I want to return briefly to the question with which I began this section: Who can say where or when identity politics originated? While reading histories of feminism in an attempt to understand the concepts "first-," "second-," and "third-wave" feminisms, I discovered Elizabeth Sarah's (1982) review of *Feminism in Europe: Liberal and Socialist Strategies, 1789–1919,* by Kumari Jaywardena and Maria Mies, in which Sarah critiques what she calls a masculinist framework of liberal and socialist movements as determinants of feminist movements. Such a framework, for example, cannot explain, according to Sarah, "how a 'daughter' of socialism like Suzanne Voilquin . . . was able to argue that women had to fight for their own freedom and that men could not do it for them" (Sarah 1982, 703). Here again, embedded in Sarah's argument against explaining feminist movements as derivative of other movements, is an implicit reference to identity politics. I expect that additional examples of early identity politics could be found in feminist, socialist, Afrocentric, and other thinkers and movements. This discovery casts a different light, then, on my project of seeking the origins of identity politics because historical roots seem always traceable to still earlier interactive phenomena. The question, therefore, becomes for me not so much one of *origins* as of *uses* and possible *consequences* of identity politics.

Using Feminist Identity Politics for Coalition Building

I stated earlier that identity politics were used as a separatist strategy by some in the Black liberation, New Left, women's liberation, and Lesbian feminist movements of the 1960s and 1970s. But some Women of Color[4] during this same period were preparing the way for another use of identity politics: coalition building. As far as I know, the "Statement" of the Combahee River Collective (1983) is the original source for the idea of identity politics as a strategy for coalition building among feminists.[5] Certain Black women in the Black liberation movement had been agitating against the sexism within that movement as well as societal racism (Cade 1970; Evans 1980). But when the Black Lesbian feminists of the Combahee River Collective took identity politics in a new direction by proclaiming their own *simultaneous* oppressions of racism and sexism and heterosexism and class exploitation, they changed the dynamic of identity politics from separatist to coalitionist by changing the terms of identity from *unidimensional to multidimensional*.

In their "Statement" the Combahee River Collective named their oppressions as "racial, sexual, heterosexual, and class oppression" and claimed "as our particular task the development of integrated analysis and practice based upon the fact that the major systems of oppression are interlocking" (1983, 272). They professed further: "We believe that sexual politics under patriarchy is as pervasive in Black women's lives as are the politics of class and race. We also often find it difficult to separate race from class from sex oppression because in our lives they are most often experienced simultaneously" (275). Because of the simultaneous and interlocking character of their oppressions, their strategy became that of seeking alliances through struggle with the groups that enjoyed certain privileges at their expense through this interlocked system.

For those same reasons, they explicitly rejected the use of identity politics for separation. Thus, they reasoned,

> Although we are feminists and Lesbians, we feel solidarity with progressive Black men and do not advocate the fractionalization that white women who are separatists demand. . . . We struggle together with Black men against racism, while we also struggle with Black men about sexism. . . . As Black feminists we are made constantly and painfully aware of how little effort white women have made to understand and combat their racism, which requires among other things that they have a more than superficial comprehension of race, color, and Black history and culture. Eliminating racism in the white women's movement is by definition work for white women to do, but we will continue to speak to and demand accountability of this issue. (275, 281)

Because they were organizing around their own oppressions, however, they were not leaving the larger feminist movement. They reminded everyone that "Black, other Third World, and working women have been involved in the feminist movement from its start, but both outside reactionary forces and racism and elitism within the movement itself have served to obscure our participation" (273). It was their experiences in the Black liberation as well as feminist movements "that led to the need to develop a politics that was anti-racist, unlike those of white women, and anti-sexist, unlike those of Black and white men" (273).

Reading the Combahee River Collective "Statement" in the context of the movements I myself had experienced and also read about, I think I understood how these Black Lesbian feminists were positioning themselves and in the process were mapping out a reordering of priorities that would transform the hierarchy of oppressions that so many of us, myself included, had been competing within. Their statement and example were loud and clear—to Black men and to white women and to all heterosexuals: because they suffer simultaneous oppressions, they have to wage the struggle on simultaneous fronts; and because Black men and white women are privileged differently by sex or sexual preference or race, but all at Black Lesbians' expense, they challenge Black men and white women to join in a struggle against racism and sexism and heterosexism, including both the oppressions and the privileges that affect everyone systemically in one way or another. They defined "identity politics" as a way to fight against their own multiple and interlocked oppressions, which were different in form from those of all others for whom they had also been fighting. They also presented their redefinition of identity politics as a basis for the coalition politics that Bernice Johnson Reagon (1983) would call for and as a basis for making powerful connections across differences that Audre Lorde (1984a, 112) would call for.

I might not have thought that what these Black Lesbian feminists were calling for was possible, however, if I had not also been reading certain works of bell hooks and Angela Davis while experiencing the possibilities of working closely with certain Black feminists in Atlanta. Having read and used bell hooks's *Ain't I a Woman: Black Women and Feminism* (1981) as a course text, I distinctly remember discussing my use of this book with a white feminist colleague from southern California at a political science meeting. She said she would have a difficult time using this book as a text because it seemed rather raw in its critique of white feminists and she was not sure how her students would take the book. I said I had found using the book as a text a good experience. The significance of the book for me was that hooks did not stop with critiquing what white men have done through what she called institutionalized sexism and racial imperialism but went on to critique Black men for their participation in patriarchy and white women for our participation in racial imperialism. She also challenged Black women to remember a tradition of Black feminism that dates from at least the nineteenth century onward. The effect of her book for me was to point toward a form of analysis that could take the position and critical perspective of one group of women, in her case, Black women, while envisioning a "struggle for liberation" not only with an oppressor group, white men, but also with other self-defined oppressed groups, Black men and white women. This multidimensional struggle "takes place within a feminist movement that has as its fundamental goal the liberation of all people" (hooks 1981, 13).

I believe bell hooks helped me begin to see a way to remake my web by breaking down compartments in my thinking and in my work. At Georgia State University, a number of women faculty who felt as isolated in their departments as I did in mine (my feminist colleague left to go to Israel) began to meet regularly in the mid-1970s as the Women's Studies Group. We designed and introduced courses on women in our various departments, despite some outspoken and often mean-spirited negativity toward such courses. And we sought and received federal funding to organize a scholarly conference on "gender-balancing" for the purposes of curriculum transformation.[6] One of the key features of the whole project for me was that, since very few Black faculty, women or men, had been hired to teach at Georgia State University, we were fortunate to be able to link up with Black women teaching at Atlanta University and other colleges in the Atlanta University Center (Spelman, Morehouse, Clark, Morris Brown Colleges and Gammon Interdenominational Theological Seminary) to bring Black and white women's perspectives to the design and presentation of the conference. The vestiges of slavery in the Old South had come forward through the hardly desegregated institutions of higher education in the New South, and it was perceived needs of faculty at Georgia State to reach out and willingness of faculty at the Atlanta University Center to respond in cooperation that made it possible to give the "gender-balancing" conference some degree of racial integration. Still, there was an institutional separation between white women and Black women that remained to be bridged, if not actually integrated.

Added to this racial interinstitutional separation, for me personally and for others at Georgia State as well, was a division that I was coming to experience as a split between the disciplines of the liberal arts and sciences, organized rigidly by departments, and the growing interdisciplinary field of women's studies. This gender-based intrainstitutional separation, manifested by feminist perspectives in women's studies and predominantly masculinist perspectives in the disciplines, seemed to me as wrong as racial separation. I understood women's studies as intersecting all the disciplines. Many in each of those disciplines, on the other hand, saw women's studies as something that took a faculty member's loyalty and energy away from the "home" discipline and department. I would struggle to close this split for approximately twenty years before leaving my department of political science for the Women's Studies Institute, which the Women's Studies Group finally was able to bring to fruition in 1994 (but that is another story).

Besides hook's *Ain't I a Woman*, another book that helped me make sense of my attempts to weave antiracist work with political science and women's studies during the early 1980s was Angela Davis's *Women, Race, and Class* (1983). I found this book particularly significant not only for its critique of the racial expediency of certain white women suffragists and contemporary white feminists but also for its excavation of a submerged history of some Black and white women working in common struggles for education and for abolition of slavery. As a Black Marxist philosopher and revolutionary honed in the liberation movements of the 1960s, Angela Davis showed that one could critically reveal the racism of white women, among others, while also critically revealing the coalitional possibilities for the present and future, based on the actualities of the past. If some white women and Black women could work together then for common ends, though starting from different positions in "the Master's house" (Lorde 1984a), then it was possible for some of us to find a way now to work together.

A personal gut-wrenching experience, which came during a conference at Spelman College, "Black Women and Public Policy in the 1980s," burned the ideas from these readings as well as my feelings about the insufficiencies of the gender-balancing project into my very psyche. I had by now become friends with my husband's Black feminist political science colleague, and she invited me to the conference because she thought I would appreciate what was going to be said and done. She had become a key player in Georgia State's gender-balancing project. I knew a couple of other women who were speaking at the conference in addition to her. Gloria Watkins was also at the conference, and I was excited to meet bell hooks of *Ain't I a Woman* and to get her autograph in my copy of her book. Otherwise I was one of a handful of white women amidst a large number of Black women, most of whom, Black or white, I did not know.

Little did my friend or I know what I would experience during that conference. As I listened to the speakers state how much courage it took for them to speak out as Black women, detailing the economic and health consequences for Black women in the United States at that time, and this after all the energy and blood that so many had spent from the 1950s onward for racial and sexual and economic justice, I began to feel shame and guilt and self-disgust well up in me. By the break for dinner, I had developed an acute migraine headache, accompanied by nausea, brought on by the intense internal conflicts I was feeling. I spent most of the dinner period in the bathroom, sitting in a stall, trying to hold myself together, but also trying to throw up and get on through the headache. But, significantly, I could not vomit it out. That would have been too easy. I had to work within myself through all the mixed feelings of personal guilt and sadness about and anger toward what white supremacy had wrought and was continuing to wreak.

Despite the strong critique of state and society, including white women's movement, made by speakers at this conference, I did not in any way feel attacked personally by the Black women at the conference. In fact, I agreed with their critique. I think all those facts about Black women's lives presented in person and passionately—not something I had read or heard presented by Black men, as so much was in those days—finally got through to me on more than an intellectual level. I did make it home, where I eventually regained my physical equilibrium. But emotionally and politically I was stripped and changed in a way that set me solidly on the path to working with white women and with Black women against racism and sexism in the ways I could—mainly in my teaching, continuing to assign readings by Black feminists as a part of my ongoing "homework" to learn the histories and present practices and thoughts of people of African descent.

By 1985 I had finished my work on the "gender-balancing" project and was already well into a new research project on "white political women" that I had begun on my own in 1981. Through writing the book (Fowlkes 1992) that would result from this research was the way that I would yet again remake my web (and that is also another story), I want to revisit another group project that flew into my web, calling on me to integrate the consequences of that experience and the work of two additional writers, Minnie Bruce Pratt and Adrienne Rich, into another web. The project—I chaired the Task Force on Women and American Government for the American Political Science Association—was federally funded to develop texts with which to integrate the newly emerging subfield of women and politics into courses on "American" (meaning United States) government and politics.[7]

The APSA project would cause me much conflict—within myself and with other white women. The task force was constituted to represent the various subfields of political science in relation to United States government and politics. As we assembled, however, it was abundantly clear that we were not otherwise representative: We were a group of white, predominantly heterosexual women, and we decided that the task force should be made more racially diverse. The project director then named one Black woman to the task force, but her workload did not allow her to participate. I suggested that my Atlanta University friend and colleague be invited to join us on the basis of her presentation at the Spelman conference; the group agreed, and she agreed to join our ongoing work. Still this strategy produced a feeling of tokenism, not only because the original group had already met and engaged in vigorous theoretical discussions about how to frame and implement the texts we were to write but also because we added several other women to collaborate with task force authors and yet she remained the sole Black woman in the group. The larger issue of *why* Women of Color were not asked to participate should have been raised but was not.

As we proceeded over the next few years to complete the project, another issue of inclusion arose over Lesbian visibility in a text on constitutional law in which the author discussed cases involving Lesbian parenting and custody. By this time, I was working with a subgroup composed of the project director and two public law scholars. The other members of this subgroup argued on what they considered to be substantive grounds that the content of the module was not correct. I disagreed and suggested we ask an outside reviewer for an opinion. We did, and her evaluation was positive; but resistance to the text continued. In fact, this text was never finally produced, and I concluded that the real but submerged reason was its attention to Lesbian issues.

Looking back, I remember both how excited I was to be asked to chair the task force and yet how dismayed I and others became as we realized we had agreed to participate in a federally funded national project that would reproduce the very exclusions by race and class and sexuality of which we were slowly and painfully becoming aware in political science in the mid-1980s. At the time, however, the conflicts among us were experienced as personally hurtful, especially since we barely addressed the issues of systemic racism and homophobia; and class issues remained submerged entirely. We maintained a veneer of professionalism, rendering unsaid too many things that should have been said, perhaps out of fear of discrediting the project in the eyes of the larger organization and also of retarding career advancement for some. We should have discussed why it was important to center Black feminist liberationist and Lesbian feminist perspectives among others when addressing women, citizenship, and change. At least, that is my assessment, and I hold myself along with others responsible for not being willing to work openly through the conflicts.

What I did learn was how bitter I could feel once I stepped into the minefield that Adrienne Rich (1979) describes as "disloyalty to civilization." Why could I not raise issues of racism and homophobia, both institutional and personal, and why could others not respond to them as legitimate problems in white women's work? I believe that we white heterosexual women were backing into territory we did not know had been previously entered by some intrepid foremothers whose history we had not learned and whose own, no doubt, painful experiences and lessons had not been institutionally passed on to us. We still had, and have yet, a lot of homework to do on learning about our resisting white heterosexual and Lesbian foremothers, whose history of disloyalty to civilization is still being written (e.g., Lerner 1971; Faderman 1981; Karcher 1994).

During this period, I also caught in my web the work of Minnie Bruce Pratt (1984) and of Adrienne Rich (1979, 1986a), which proved to be particularly nourishing for a newly emerging idea: to specify the political realities, in all their variety, of white women. Just as the idea of singular identity was being shown by the Black Lesbian feminists of the Combahee River Collective to be ineffective in organizing heterogeneous groups, so too the idea of monolithic experience of any particular group was being shown by other radical Women of Color (Moraga and Anzaldúa 1983) to be out of touch with reality in everyday life. Simply put, women are not all alike. White women, like any other group of women one could define, are not all alike. And yet the ideas of Pratt, a white Lesbian of southern Christian upbringing, and of Rich, a white Jewish lesbian of southern Christian upbringing,[8] resonated forcefully with me. There are some similarities among us: we all three are white southerners raised as Christians, though Rich also later claimed her Jewish identity. Both Pratt and Rich, however, are Lesbians, in contrast to me, a heterosexual woman. I believe a resonance for me with them sprang from their and my attempts to struggle through our racism and antiracism. As I understood that similarity between them and me, it also helped me begin to work through my own homophobia.

From reading Rich, I also received reinforcement for my epiphany at the Spelman conference. Just as she said that too often we try to " 'grasp' " racism "as an intellectual or theoretical concept" and thus "lose touch with the feelings black women are trying to describe to us, their lived experience *as women*" (Rich 1979, 281), so I knew from my own experience at the conference that it was the very telling by those women of their pain and anger that had broken through my intellectual armor and made my head pound and my stomach churn in both sympathy and empathy. I agreed with Rich that it was a task for white women to account for our guilt in and ignorance of "the real lives of black women" and to begin "lasting and meaningful feminist action" (Rich 1979, 281), which for me in this instance meant writing more self-consciously from a white feminist perspective that acknowledged and sought to understand respectfully the many differences among all women.

From reading Pratt, I received greater understanding of what white heterosexual women may feel as their racial and sexual privileges are challenged, even threatened. Pratt described the emptiness she felt as she consciously unwrapped each layer of privilege, which appeared to her as shrouding. The shrouding was her upbringing in the same racially and heterosexually privileged southern culture in which I had been raised. It was as if she feared she would find that her core self was nothing—that she had been shrouded while still living but had died in the process. In the end, she found herself buried alive; but contrasting herself to the buried woman in Edgar Allen Poe's story, she was able not only to emerge and break apart the constraints of society but also to live to fight and tell about it.

Pratt's account of her painful but eventually empowering emptiness reminded me of the emptiness I had felt during the Spelman conference. No doubt many other white women with whom I worked, including those on the APSA task force, when confronted with challenges to their racism and homophobia, felt the same threatening emptiness and filled it, as I had, with physical nausea and emotional guilt, sadness, anger, defensiveness, but were not sure what to do beyond that. Many Black women, as oppressed as they were, had knowledge of their foremothers' resistance and survival transmitted orally, or in writing, once Black and African-American and Africana studies began the excavations of history and literature that surfaced such knowledge. But most white women knew mainly the critiques of racist white women or the many histories of "women" that did not sufficiently problematize colonialism, capitalism, white supremacy, or compulsory heterosexuality. So the suggestions of both Pratt and Rich could be valuable in pointing white women toward role models of our own: that we might learn more of our white foremothers who resisted structures that constrained them and divided them from others differently oppressed and privileged. I believe many more engagements among white women, heterosexual and Lesbian, of different classes, can move us along in this project.

For now, I pause to reflect on what I have learned about the uses of feminist identity politics for coalition building. I learned early from my mother that writing spiders are insufficient unto themselves. They need nourishment from others, and they need continuously to rebuild their webs in places that nourish them. Speaking metaphorically, I as a feminist am similarly insufficient. I need to restructure my identity continually in the process of learning more of how I have been privileged and oppressed and how I can work against unjust systems. I learn these things through working with others, reading, and writing about their work.

But here the writing spider metaphor itself becomes insufficient, because writing spiders live and work in isolation from one another. If I engage in identity politics only for the purpose of identity reconstruction, I risk simply appropriating the work of others without giving something of myself back to those who nourish me with their ideas and actions. To give back I have to leave my web. Actually, I have to shuttle back and forth between my web—my place of identity reconstruction, and the garden—the places of my coalition seeking. Recognizing that for me the processes of creating identity and coalition are closely interlaced, I cannot continue the struggle without seeking others with whom to weave together ever-changing definitions of problems and strategies to carry forward women's movement.

NOTES

Heartfelt thanks to my writers group—Charlene Ball, Linda Bell, Valerie Fennell, and Elizabeth Knowlton—for listening and offering constructive criticism to the many drafts that became this essay.

1. I am uncomfortable with the term "the women's movement" because too often it has been understood, by those speaking of it and those hearing it spoken of, as a monolithic

unified movement focused predominantly, and unconsciously, on white heterosexual middle-class women's issues. Although I do not agree entirely with this perception, a historical and deconstructive analysis of the concept "the women's movement" is beyond the scope of my essay. I instead use the term "women's movement" and believe that "the women's movement," to the extent that it *does* privilege white heterosexual middle-class women's issues, *necessitates* identity politics among all those "advocating feminism." (hooks 1984)

2. More specifically, I have made a case elsewhere (Fowlkes 1997), drawing from political philosophical works of Latina feminists, that feminist identity politics, through the telling of complex identity narratives, entails a feminist materialist standpoint of intersubjectivity. There is not space here for the details of that argument, but what I recount in this writing-spider essay started me on the way to that argument.

3. I recognize that "we" and "us" cannot simply be assumed but must be struggled for in a never-ending politics of identity and coalition building.

4. The term "Women of Color" was created by a coalition of Black, Latina, Asian Pacific, and Native American women at the National Women's Conference in Houston, Texas, in 1977, according to Loretta Ross, in a presentation at Georgia State University in February 1991. Black women developed a plank for the conference document to replace a plank for "minority women," drafted by conference organizers, and were joined by other women who wanted to include their neglected concerns as well. The group finally coined the term "Women of Color" to cover the multiracial and multiethnic nature of their coalition, and the group was successful in persuading the conference to accept its plank in place of the "minority women's plank." Chela Sandoval (1990) recounts how Women of Color at the 1981 National Women's Studies Association came to use that name for themselves. See, also, Moraga and Anzaldúa (1983).

5. Interestingly, the Combahee River Collective was writing about its practice of identity politics in the mid-1970s, during the same period that Sara Evans must have been conducting the research for *Personal Politics,* in which she described separatist identity politics without using the term.

6. We received a three-year grant from the Women's Educational Equity Act Program of the U.S. Department of Health, Education and Welfare. The conference, " 'A Fabric of Our Own Making': Southern Scholars on Women," also served as the annual meeting of the 1981 Southeastern Women's Studies Association. An edited book describing the conference process and including selected papers was published following the conference (Fowlkes and McClure 1984).

7. The project was supported by a grant from the Fund to Improve Post-Secondary Education of the U.S. Department of Education. The five texts finally produced were Cook et al. (1988), Gelb and Klein (1988), Hedblom (1988), Sapiro (1988), and Shanley with Lewis (1988). The project was introduced in Fowlkes (1987).

8. Rich treats the contradiction of being born of a Jewish father and Gentile mother and raised in a Christian setting in "Split at the Root" (1986b), and in "Notes Toward a Politics of Location" (1986a, 216). She claims her identity as "North American Jew."

REFERENCES

Anzaldúa, Gloria. 1987. *Borderlands/La Frontera: The new mestiza.* San Francisco: Spinsters/Aunt Lute.

Bunch, Charlotte. 1987. *Passionate politics: Feminist theory in action.* New York: St. Martin's Press.

Cade, Toni. 1970. *The black woman: An anthology.* New York: New American Library.

Combahee River Collective. 1983. Statement. In Barbara Smith, ed. *Home girls: A Black feminist anthology,* 272–282. New York: Kitchen Table: Women of Color Press.

Cook, Beverly B., Leslie F. Goldstein, Karen O'Connor, and Susette M. Talarico. 1988. *Women in the judicial process.* Washington, D.C.: American Political Science Association.

Davis, Angela Y. 1983. *Women, race, and class.* New York: Vintage Books.

Evans, Sara. 1980. *Personal politics: The roots of women's liberation in the civil rights movement and the new left.* New York: Vintage Books.

Faderman, Lillian. 1981. *Surpassing the love of men: Romantic friendship and love between women from the Renaissance to the present.* New York: William Morrow and Company.

Fowlkes, Diane L. 1987. "Feminist theory—reconstructing research and teaching about American politics and government." *News for teachers of political science,* no. 52 (Winter): 6–9.

———. 1992. *White political women: Paths from privilege to empowerment.* Knoxville: University of Tennessee Press.

———. 1997. "Moving from feminist identity politics to coalition politics through a feminist materialist standpoint of intersubjectivity in Gloria Anzaldúa's *Borderlands/La Frontera: The new mestiza.*" *Hypatia* 12(2): 105–24.

Fowlkes, Diane L., and Charlotte S. McClure, eds. 1984. *Feminist visions: Toward a transformation of the liberal arts curriculum.* University, AL: University of Alabama Press.

Freeman, Jo. 1975. *The politics of women's liberation: A case study of an emerging social movement and its relation to the policy process.* New York: David McKay Company.

Gelb, Joyce, and Ethel Klein. 1988. *Women's movements: Organizing for change.* Washington, D.C.: American Political Science Association.

Hedblom, Milda K. 1988. *Women and power in American politics.* Washington, D.C.: American Political Science Association.

hooks, bell. 1981. *Ain't I a woman: Black women and feminism.* Boston: South End Press.

———. 1984. *Feminist theory from margin to center.* Boston: South End Press.

Karcher, Carolyn L. 1994. *The first women in the republic: A cultural biography of Lydia Maria Child.* Durham: Duke University Press.

Lerner, Gerda. 1971. *The Grimké sisters from South Carolina: Pioneers for woman's rights and abolition.* New York: Schocken Books.

Lorde, Audre. 1984a. The master's tools will never dismantle the master's house. In *Sister outsider: Essays and speeches,* 110–113. Trumansburg, NY: Crossing Press.

———. 1984b. Scratching the surface: Some notes on barriers to women and loving. In *Sister outsider: Essays and speeches,* 45–52. Trumansburg, NY: Crossing Press.

Moraga, Cherríe, and Gloria Anzaldúa, eds. 1983. *This bridge called my back: Writings by radical women of color.* New York: Kitchen Table: Women of Color Press.

Pratt, Minnie Bruce. 1984. Identity: Skin blood heart. In Elly Bulkin, Minnie Bruce Pratt, and Barbara Smith, *Yours in struggle: Three feminist perspectives on anti-Semitism and racism,* 11–63. Brooklyn: Long Haul Press.

Reagon, Bernice Johnson. 1983. Coalition politics: Turning the century. In Barbara Smith, ed. *Home girls: A Black feminist anthology,* 356–368. New York: Kitchen Table: Women of Color Press.

Rich, Adrienne. 1979. Disloyal to civilization: Feminism, racism, gynephobia. In *On lies, secrets, and silence: Selected prose, 1966–1978,* 275–310. New York: W. W. Norton and Company.

————. 1986a. Notes toward a politics of location. In *Blood, bread, and poetry: Selected prose, 1979–1985,* 210–31. New York: W. W. Norton and Company.

————. 1986b. Split at the root: An essay on Jewish identity. In *Blood, bread, and poetry: Selected prose, 1979–1985,* 100–23. New York: W. W. Norton and Company.

Sandoval, Chela. 1990. Feminism and racism: A report on the 1981 National Women's Studies Association conference. In Gloria Anzaldúa, ed., *Making face, making soul=haciendo caras: Creative and critical perspectives by women of color,* 55–71. San Francisco: Aunt Lute Foundation.

Sapiro, Virginia. 1988. *Women, political action, and political participation.* Washington, D.C.: American Political Science Association.

Sarah, Elizabeth. 1982. Finding a feminist historical framework: A review of *Feminism in Europe, liberal and socialist strategies, 1789–1919. Women's studies international forum* 5(6): 701–706.

Shanley, Mary Lyndon, with an introduction and epilogue by Shelby Lewis. 1988. *Women's rights, feminism, and politics in the United States.* Washington, D.C.: American Political Science Association.

Chapter Thirty

"Look at the World through Women's Eyes"
On Empathy and International Civil Society

Liza Grandia

As the twentieth century draws to a close, we find ourselves in a critical moment of history. The forces of economic globalization are seriously undermining the power and legitimacy of democratic nation-states. Who or what will fill this power vacuum in the coming years—religious fundamentalists? multinational corporations? military dictators? or, performative postmodern subjects? In support of the last, many postmodern theorists delight in describing the discursive "deaths" of "Man, "History," and "Metaphysics." Yet, they rarely mention the real deaths of people around the world that are the consequences of rising political repression, ethnic hatred, economic misery, environmental destruction, and other forces that threaten democracy. Postmodern critics embrace language that celebrates the multiplicity of identities with fluid boundaries/borders—yet they fail to acknowledge that real border crossings (such as those of multinational corporations) can be harmful and dangerous to powerless people like women factory workers. The postmodern critics merrily deconstruct texts, with seemingly little concern that wars are "deconstructing"/ripping apart communities around the world.

This is not to suggest, however, that all current academic theory is inherently unproductive—far from it. Rather, as the conditions of our planet continue to deteriorate, we desperately need critical theories that, in the words of Seyla Benhabib, can help reassert "democratic control over runaway megastructures of modern capital and technology."[1] In other words, we, in our increasing complex and troubled world, need theorists to help us imagine a new normative ethics that would be able to address difference and identity without reverting to the relativist claims of many postmodern theorists. Seyla Benhabib's *Situating the Self* attempts to do just that through an impressive discursive project that brings theories of postmodernism, feminism, and communitarianism into conversation with each other. At the intersections of these realms of thought, Benhabib develops a concept of "interactive universalism," which offers a vision of how we might strengthen democracy in a postmodern world.

In this chapter, I will explore Benhabib's theory of "interactive universalism" to (a) challenge certain tenets of postmodern theory on identity and discourse and (b) describe how we might begin to build an international civil society based on community, dialogue, and an ethics of empathetic understanding. In the latter part of the chapter, I will discuss how Benhabib's theory might be applied to the real world by illustrating how the 1995 NGO Forum of the Fourth World Conference on Women beautifully embodied her idea of "interactive universalism" and helps us imagine new forms of feminist and democratic global governance.

On Postmodern Identity Theory

Because Judith Butler's writings have been so influential in the formation of feminist, postmodern theory, I begin this essay with a critique of her ideas on identity in *Gender Trouble*. In this seminal book, Butler strongly encourages feminists to abandon their attention on the "doer," who Nietzche says is "merely a fiction added to the deed—the deed is everything." She continues to argue, "There is no gender identity behind the expressions of gender; that identity is performatively constituted by the very 'expressions' that are said to be its results."[2] Although Butler's arguments are quite compelling within the framework of (timeless) Western philosophical thought, they are weakened when contextualized within the historical moment in which we live. Marginalized peoples (women, people of color, gays and lesbians, et al.) have begun to claim in large numbers their identities as "doers"/subjects. It seems ironic that at the same time, postmodern theorists like Butler have begun to announce the "death" of the subject—thereby effectively undermining these claims to subjecthood.[3] Rosi Braidotti insightfully writes, "The truth of the matter is: one cannot de-sexualize a sexuality one has never had; in order to deconstruct the subject one must first have access to a place of enunciation."[4] Hence I ask, as women, can we afford to give up subjecthood so easily? Is not one of the primary goals of the feminist movement to help women build their sense of agency, empowerment, and self-esteem? Benhabib shares these concerns, writing, "Given how fragile and tenuous women's sense of self-hood is in many cases, how much of a hit-and-miss affair their struggles for autonomy are, this reduction of female agency to 'doing without a doer' at best appears to me making virtue out of necessity."[5]

The other criticism I would offer about Butler's abandonment of subjects/doers concerns the implicit *intentionality* required of the "subject site" (i.e., person) who is performing acts/deeds of gender expression that are meant to disrupt/subvert discourse. What role does *community* play in supporting the development of individuals for these subversive acts of identity expression? If the subversive acts are performed by a "person in a subject site" who has no coherent identity other than that which is "performatively constituted," then exactly who is accountable for these acts? Is accountability even possible in Butler's postmodern world? If not, how serious can these disruptive acts be? Benhabib expresses similar concerns:

> What is baffling though is the lightheartedness with which postmodernists simply assume or even posit those hyper-universalist and superliberal values of diversity,

heterogeneity, eccentricity, and otherness. In doing so, they rely on the very norms of autonomy of subjects and the rationality of democratic procedures which otherwise they seem to so blithely dismiss.

In other words, the playfulness of postmodern identities and acts of subversion assumes that we are all working within democratic structures. Yet, not everyone has equal opportunity to express postmodern playfulness. As Benhabib points out, only those who have already enjoyed "the privileges of the modern" can afford to enjoy the fluidity of identity.[6]

All in all, I would argue that postmodern identity theory—as illustrated by Butler's idea of performative "subject sites" that work to disrupt/subvert discourse— will not necessarily be liberating for women. After deconstruction and disruption, what next? This is the fundamental question that Benhabib seeks to address in her return to discourse about normative ethics and community.

On Empathy

It requires something more than personal experience to gain a philosophy or point of view from any specific event. It is the quality of our response to the event and the capacity to enter into the lives of others that help us to make their lives and experiences our own.

—Emma Goldman

Atticus was right. One time he said you never really know a man until you stand in his shoes and walk around in them. Just standing on the Radley porch was enough.
—Scout, in *To Kill A Mockingbird*, by Harper Lee[7]

To begin, I would like to give a philosophical background on Benhabib's ideas about ethics, identity, and community. Like many postmodernists, Benhabib seeks to challenge Enlightenment conceptions of hegemonic "truth" and "justice," but she is not willing to abandon the need for certain universal (what many postmodernists would consider "essentialist") concepts and the possibility of developing normative ethics for them. After all, as feminists, we hold fundamental beliefs about the equality of women. To work toward these and other normative goals, Benhabib proposes her theory of "interactive universalism" or empathetic discourse. For her, the *process* of dialogue—in other words, the moral conversation—is more important than the results per se. Consensus is not a requisite outcome of the dialogue because she recognizes that not everyone will agree. In order to keep the dialogue going amongst diverse peoples, Benhabib argues that the two following principles are necessary: universal moral respect ("the right of all beings capable of speech and action to be participants in the moral conversation") and egalitarian reciprocity (the right of everyone to "various speech acts, to initiate new topics, to ask for reflection about presuppositions of the conversation, etc.").[8] She proposes a type of theoretical "table" or constantly shifting public spaces that are formed wherever people engage in dialogue about political and ethical norms. One of Benhabib's central concerns is how to enable more people to participate in these public spaces. She recognizes that we must first create an egalitarian social and economic order so that everyone has the capacity to come to discursive "tables" to speak.

To summarize Benhabib's theory, an ideal situation of ethical discourse might be the following: All those affected (directly and indirectly) by the subject of discourse would be present at a "table" and could present their ideas and life narratives in a manner that would be coherent and understandable to those listening. All participants would have an equal chance to do this. Moreover, everyone at the "table" would have a healthy respect for all participants as *generalized others,* which "requires us to view each and every individual as a rational being entitled to the same rights and duties we would want to ascribe to ourselves" (that is, the Golden Rule: "Do unto others as you would have them do unto you").[9] Without this respect for equality and reciprocity, she argues, we would revert to relativism and find it impossible to define a moral point of view.[10] At the same time, everyone at the "table" would need to view his or her fellow participants as *concrete others,* that is, as radically contextualized beings with full life narratives.

Thus, to be participants in discourse, we must have some kind of coherent identities—in other words, we must be able to re-present ourselves as "concrete others." In the construction of this discursive identity, Benhabib argues that "the Self is both the teller of tales and that about whom tales are told." A person with a coherent identity (which does not mean a homogenous or fixed identity) is able to integrate those tales into a "meaningful life history." She writes,

> Neither the concreteness or the otherness of the "concrete other" can be known in the absence of the *voice* of the other. The viewpoint of the concrete other emerges as a distinct one only as a result of self-definition. It is the other who makes us aware both of her concreteness and her otherness. Without engagement, confrontation, dialogue . . . we tend to constitute the otherness of the other by projection and fantasy or ignore it in difference.[11]

Hence, what is unique about Benhabib's theory is that she accepts the need for postmodern specificity/historicity in the construction of identity but does so without rejecting the possibility of meaningful discourse and the negotiation of universal norms amongst peoples.

Yet, there are problems with this ideal situation of ethical discourse. In real life, not everyone can make it to a "table"—because of geographical, educational, emotional, economic, and other constraints. Also, in real life, not everyone who manages to join discursive "tables" necessarily has equal negotiating power. Moreover, not everyone will be able to negotiate for him/herself, and so, many people may rely on a group or community to represent them. Certainly, it is more difficult to reach mutual understanding between complex communities than between individuals.

These and other representational problems become magnified when the discursive "tables" become internationalized. As economic globalization continues to link peoples around the world, we desperately need to broaden our discursive "tables" to include geographically distant (though economically close) people. I wonder, is it possible at all to develop international, moral communities based on empathetic understanding? Indeed, in my darkest moments, I despair, "How can anyone in the U.S. really understand poverty in the Third World without experiencing it personally?"[12] Realistically, I recognize that very few people would leave the comfort of their lives in the United States to live in a one-room thatched hut for six months with no running water and electricity with a family of six in order to understand subsistence poverty. (I did this and thought it was wonderful, but as my friends always remind me, I am a little "unusual.") How else can privileged citizens of developed countries, then, understand the extreme poverty found in developing countries? They certainly could not develop this empathetic understanding of poverty from the media. Practically the only images of the Third World the media gives us are of crisis situations—wars, famines, natural disasters, and the like. News images are usually so objectifying and repetitive that even the most compassionate people become numbed to the pain and suffering they witness on television.

For these and other reasons, perfect international understanding may be virtually impossible to achieve. Yet, I am not willing to abandon the concept of cross-cultural empathy altogether. I am not sure if we need complete empathy, anyway. There is so much injustice today both in the United States and abroad that even minimal, empathetic understanding could be sufficient for political organizing (for example, I may not know the full life-narratives of Ken Saro-Wiwa and the eight other environmental activists who were executed in Nigeria in November of 1996, but I know enough of the circumstances behind their wrongful deaths to help organize demonstrations in front of Shell gasoline stations to protest the company's involvement in these political murders). Thus, in the rest of this paper, I want to focus on the roles of international activists as generators of cross-cultural empathy for the purposes of political organizing.

On the NGO Forum and Four Methods of Catalyzing International, Empathetic Discourse

Look at the World through Women's Eyes
—Motto of the 1995 NGO Forum on Women

In this section, I want to write about the 1995 NGO Forum of the Fourth World Conference on Women held outside Beijing (August 30–September 8) as a gathering of *translators* committed to international dialogue on women's issues. Indeed, this NGO Forum demonstrated that more than thirty thousand women from upwards of 180 countries could have meaningful dialogue and international cooperation.[13] The forum served to highlight the many cultural, economic, and political differences among women around the world, but an underlying purpose was also to give women an opportunity to identify and share their common experiences. In other words, a guiding parameter of the forum might have been expressed this way: "Let's not assume that we all agree just because we are women. Instead, let's try to recognize our differences and appreciate our commonalties, too." Certainly, some thirty thousand women from around the world would not have traveled all the way to China without a basic belief in commonalties among women—in other words, a belief in the possibility of empathetic understanding and what Benhabib calls "interactive universalism."

Benhabib emphasizes that everyone at discursive "tables" will not be like-minded. Thus, the point of discourse is not necessarily to reach consensus but to experience an empathetic process of discussion or "reflexivity" as Benhabib calls it. Certainly, not everyone in Beijing agreed. In fact, many conservative and/or fundamentalist women came to the conference, and some held counterdemonstrations. Yet, there was an incredible sense of commitment by the participants to try to enter the imagined spaces of other women's lives—including the conservative women. Indeed, the objectives of most workshops at the forum were for women from different countries to have the opportunity to describe their organizing experiences to diverse audiences. Some examples of the workshop titles were "Guatemala and the Participation of Women in the Peace Process," "Constraints and Difficulties Facing Muslim Women in Europe," "Sexual Harassment, Dignity, Shame—What Has Been Done in the Nordic Countries," "Sudanese Women in Income Generating Family Programmes," and so on. In such workshops, women carefully represented their life narratives and work, thus performatively constituting themselves as "concrete others." Hence, if someone asked me to summarize in one sentence what happened at the forum, I would say: Women listened empathetically to the testimonies of other women from around the world.[14]

How did they do this? In the sections that follow, I will explain four methods that translators, that is people committed to facilitating the development of an international civil society, can employ to catalyze cross-cultural empathetic understanding: (1) strengthening representational politics, (2) drawing analogies across oppressions, (3) building coalitions, and (4) empowering new discursive participants. With each method, I will try to highlight in italics the aspects of the NGO Forum that embodied these methods. These memories of the forum are extracted from a series of speeches and presentations I made upon returning from China in an effort to share what I had the privilege to have experienced with those who could not go.

(1) On Strengthening Representational Politics

Although postmodernists have inculcated us with the idea that representation always involves slippages and distortions, it is nevertheless a necessary organizing tool in today's world. Due to geographical, economic, educational, emotional, and other constraints, "concrete others" may not always be able to join discursive "tables" in person in order to present their life narratives. They must send proxies, representatives, spokespeople (in other words, translators). Unfortunately, the representatives may not always be entirely accountable to the people on whose behalf they speak. Plus, as Benhabib notes, any dialogue will have communication problems: "Certainly, language always says much more than what we mean and what we say."[15] Yet, despite these problems, we must have faith in representation if we are to believe in collective rights. If not, we remain stuck with postmodern individualism, which would require individuals to re-present themselves constantly through endless performances. Marginalized people, then, would find themselves wasting their time trying to educate their oppressors on an individual basis. In her writing, Audre Lorde condemns this representational/educational burden placed on marginalized groups:

> Women of today are still being called upon to stretch across the gap of male ignorance, and to educate men as to our existence and our needs. This is an old and primary tool of all oppressors to keep the oppressed occupied with the master's concerns. Now we hear that it is the task of black and third world women to educate white women, in the face of tremendous resistance, as to our existence, our differences, our relative roles in our joint survival. This is a diversion of energies and a tragic repetition of racist patriarchal thought.[16]

To avoid placing this burden on marginalized peoples, translator figures can strive to be thoughtful educators and accountable representatives of "concrete others" who cannot attend discursive "tables." Although these "concrete others" may not be physically present in international gatherings like the Fourth World Conference on Women (FWCW), such meetings can nevertheless bring legitimacy to their work. Again and again, women at the NGO Forum of the FWCW stressed the importance of international documents such as the Platform for Action in helping them to pressure their own governments to pass more progressive legislation for women. They also stressed the importance of making international contacts for their organizations at the NGO Forum, sometimes stating explicitly that these international ties may help protect them from government repression and even death.

Perhaps the greatest challenge of representational politics is the time and energy required to enable as many people as possible to attend themselves or be represented by others at discursive "tables." Certainly the extraordinary, three-year preparatory process for the FWCW is a good example of this.

All told, it has been the largest, most inclusive, and most participatory process for any of the global conferences that the UN has held in the last decade. In addition to three global preparatory meetings held in New York by the Commission on the Status of Women in 1993, 1994, and 1995, the UN sponsored five regional preparatory meetings between July and November of 1994. Each of these regional gatherings had a government meeting plus a parallel NGO meeting—and in each region more than three times the number of women expected showed up! In addition to these officially sponsored meetings, women organized innumerable preparatory meetings in their homes, villages, communities, offices, universities, and so on.

Despite the amazing preparatory process, not everyone could go to Beijing, of course. Yet, many groups worked hard to provide scholarships for economically disadvantaged women who otherwise would not have been able to travel to China. Then, at the forum, there was widespread remembrance of the women who were unable to attend. Of course, representation of others can never be perfect or complete, but the participants at the forum nevertheless made a concerted effort to be accountable to the women from their home countries by speaking on behalf of them in public discussions. Many women attending the conference had brought pages of documents with them that their fellow countrywomen had sent, including position statements, group declarations, detailed amendments to propose to the Platform for Action, and so on. Technology certainly facilitated the representation of women who could not attend the forum in person. Videotapes, satellite hook-ups, e-mail communication, and the like all served to bring women's voices—if not their bodies—to the forum events. What was so impressive about all this was the interest women at the forum gave to listening to the voices of women who were not present.

(2) On Drawing Analogies across Oppressions

In our increasingly interconnected world, we can no longer afford to remain trapped within rigid identity politics; we must cease to allow ourselves as activists to be "divided and conquered." To do this, we must learn to appreciate the commonalities of our struggles by understanding one another's oppressions through analogy and empathy. To elaborate on this point, I would like to quote Cherríe Moraga at length, because she reaches some very insightful conclusions on the subject:

> When I finally lifted the lid to my lesbianism, a profound connection with my mother reawakened in me. It wasn't until I acknowledged and confronted my own lesbianism in the flesh, that my heartfelt identification and empathy for my mother's oppression—due to being poor, uneducated, and Chicana—was realized. My lesbianism is the avenue through which I have learned the most about silence and oppression, and it continues to be the most tactile reminder to me that we are not free human beings. . . .

> What I am saying is that the joys of looking like a white girl ain't so great since I realized I could be beaten on the street for being a dyke. If my sister's being beaten because she's Black, it's pretty much the same principle. We're both getting beaten any way you look at it. . . .

> In this country, lesbianism is a poverty—as is being brown, as is being a woman, as is being just plain poor. The danger lies in ranking the oppressions. The danger lies in failing to acknowledge the specificity of the oppression. The danger lies in attempting to deal with oppression purely from a theoretical base. Without an emotional, heartfelt grappling with the source of our own oppression, without naming the enemy within ourselves and outside of us, no authentic, non-hierarchical connection among oppressed groups can take place.

> When the going gets rough, will we abandon our so-called comrade in a flurry of racist/heterosexist/what-have-you panic? To whose camp, then, should the lesbian of color retreat? Her very presence violates the ranking and abstraction of oppression. Do we merely live hand to mouth? Do we merely struggle with the "ism" on top of our own heads?

> The answer is: yes, I think first we do; and we must do so thoroughly and deeply. But to fail to move out from there will only isolate us in our own oppression—will only insulate rather than radicalize us.[17]

By seeing analogies between oppressions and by remembering their own hurt, even the most privileged members of our society can identify empathetically with concrete others. For example, as a feminist I begin my analysis of oppression through the lens of gender. Yet, once I begin to deconstruct the binary opposition of men/women, I discover that I must deconstruct other dualisms that shape Western thought: culture/nature, rationality/madness, order/disorder, light/dark, good/evil, rich/poor, and so on. As I begin to see how systems of gender-race-class-sexuality oppression overlap and reinforce one another, I learn that I cannot rank oppressions. I cannot believe that women are more oppressed than people of color—because I would not be able to fit the category of "women of color" into such a false hierarchy. Moreover, in practical terms, I know that multinational corporations and totalitarian dictators take advantage of anyone they can in order to reap their profits; they happily exploit people across many systems of oppression.[18] Thankfully, however, the participants at the NGO Forum were able to move beyond identity politics to strategize and work together on how to address the condition of women in our increasingly globalized world.

At the NGO Forum women from around the world held incredibly rich discussions about the impacts of structural-adjustment programs and multinational corporations on different groups in their home countries. I attended many workshops about economic globalization—which were always filled beyond the room capacity. These workshops transcended the strong identity politics that shaped the NGO Forum overall. The forum site was organized around numerous regional and diversity tents that largely had their own activities and lobbying agendas. The regional tents included (1) Latin America and the Caribbean, (2) Europe and North America, (3) Africa, (4) Western Asia, and (5) Asia and the Pacific. Diversity tents were designated for the following groups/themes: indigenous women, older women, lesbians, women with disabilities, grassroots women, science and technology, refugees, youth, health, and peace.

What was impressive about the forum was the significant yet humble participation of men, as well as the cross-fertilization among the "identity" tents. Through empathetic understanding, the men at the forum were witnesses to the testimonies of women. Rarely have I attended feminist conferences in which a small minority of men did not try to dominate the gathering, but somehow in Beijing this did not seem to happen. Nor did women from industrialized countries dominate the forum. Indeed, I was struck by the fact that the regional tent for Europe and North America was virtually empty; it had none of the vivid decorations and presentations that the other regional tents had organized. Instead, women from this economically privileged region dedicated their time and energy to listening to other women's stories.

(3) On Building Coalitions

Once there is a recognition of the similarities of systems of oppression, the next logical step is to organize coalitions. The process of building coalitions is not an easy one; it requires constant sensitivity and internal reevaluation by the members.

Despite the difficulties of coalition building, it is an extremely worthwhile endeavor and a very effective political tool. Moraga challenges us to build coalitions, saying, "If it takes head-on collisions, let's do it: this polite timidity is killing us."[19] Once we begin to build coalitions across identity groups, the "Master" can no longer "divide and conquer" us. Coalitions can be much more powerful and cohesive than the kinds of collaborative organizing to which we are accustomed and in which political infighting is common. As Benedict Anderson so brilliantly argues in *Imagined Communities* (1983), the seemingly all-powerful nation-state is but a construction of the modern world. In other words, the nation-state has been a highly powerful coalition (or "imagined community") of diverse peoples held together by symbols and ideologies. We can surely imagine equally powerful political coalitions among women.

Coalitions are important because social movements need a broad range of people working together—ranging from those who write theory, to those who work within "the system," to those who lobby professionally outside "the system," to the radicals who tie themselves to trees (for example, our women's history lessons show us that the radical suffragists of the National Women's Party who picketed the White House demanding major reforms made the suffragists from NAWSA who lobbied Congress for the passage of the Nineteenth Amendment seem much more moderate). Indeed, Seyla Benhabib argues that we need a "plurality and variety of goodnesses" with which to live: "Whether the good life is to be fulfilled as an African famine relief fighter, a Warsaw ghetto resistant, a Mother Theresa or a Rosa Luxemburg, ethical theory cannot prejudge."[20]

I certainly witnessed a "plurality and variety of goodnesses" in coalitions throughout the NGO Forum of the FWCW in Beijing.

While some of the more conservative and/or fundamentalist women who attended the NGO Forum unkindly argued that radical feminists and lesbians made the women's movement "look bad," by and large, there was a general sentiment of cooperation among many different groups—especially in lobbying government delegations on the official document of the conference, which was called the Platform for Action. Bella Abzug and her organization, the Women's Environment and Development Organization (WEDO), played a key leadership role in building a strong coalition of NGOs for lobbying on the document. Abzug began her international coalition work a few years ago at the 1992 UN Conference on Environment and Development (UNCED) in Rio de Janeiro. As a result of the work of her famous "Women's Caucus" there, the document that was produced at the end of the conference devoted an entire chapter to women's roles in sustainable development and also included one hundred twenty other references related to women throughout the document. Inspired by their success at UNCED, Abzug and others organized very strong and effective Women's Caucuses at the UN's other thematic conferences of this decade on human rights, in Vienna; population and development, in Cairo; small island nations, in Barbados; and social development, in Copenhagen. Women's organizations from around the world attended these conferences in record numbers and strongly influenced the language in the final documents.

Of course, it would have been somewhat redundant to organize a "Women's Caucus" in Beijing because almost all thirty thousand of us were women! Instead, Abzug organized a "Linkage Caucus" that focused on advancing gains made by women at prior UN conferences because the Platform for Action was very weak at the beginning of the preparatory process and many feared that governments might retreat from language already adopted at other conferences. So, the Linkage Caucus brought together representatives from many smaller caucus groups and produced a comprehensive lobbying document. Much of the language in this document was eventually incorporated into the official government document—oftentimes word for word!

Interestingly, the Lesbian Caucus contributed a lot to the language about women's sexuality in the Linkage Caucus document. They found that governments rejected their ideas when they lobbied as a (radical) "Lesbian Caucus," but that governments accepted the same ideas when (more moderate) members of the Linkage Caucus lobbied for them!

(4) On Empowering New Discursive Participants

Although we must have faith in representation, we nevertheless should try to empower as many people as possible to participate in decentralized discursive "tables." UN conferences, after all, are extraordinary events. Important dialogue occurs in millions of different discursive, public spaces around the world every day. Therefore, our challenge is not to bring all the women of the world together for one conference at one time in one place but, rather, to create a social order in which everyone has the capacity and the motivation to participate in discursive "tables" wherever they may live and work. In doing so, we must begin to think about the rights of communities (and not just individuals). Moreover, capacity building should not be limited to political empowerment of individuals and groups but should include economic, spiritual, and other kinds of empowerment. I would particularly emphasize economic empowerment because the global feminization of poverty increasingly precludes women and their children from participating in discursive "tables."

As activists, too often we talk only among ourselves. Yet, as translator figures, we need to be more willing to engage in dialogue with people who disagree with us, for it is only through such difficult conversations that we can raise awareness and empathy about important international issues. We must engage in such dialogue not only during extraordinary world conferences but in our daily lives—in our classrooms, places of work, neighborhoods, recreational areas, churches, and so on. Outreach must become a way of life! As we do this, we will create more public spaces of discourse that can empower more people—because public space is not a limited, distributive good. Newly empowered people, in turn, will create more public spaces of discourse to contest oppressive institutions that have been protected by a veil of "privacy." This is certainly what happened at the Forum.

Benhabib would have loved the Forum because, in short, the participants were in dialogue everywhere. Hundreds of workshops, plenaries, panels, and performances were scheduled every day; these constituted the "official" public spaces. Yet, even these overwhelmingly diverse activities did not fully satisfy the participants; the women wanted to create more public spaces. In fact, the NGO Forum planning committee was overwhelmed at the conference with dozens of additional proposals each day for new workshops (which were accommodated as best as possible, given the limited facilities of the site). The participants established "public spaces" in every possible meeting place on the forum site: in hotel rooms, on street corners, in bathrooms, in classrooms, in tents, and so on.

Admittedly, the overwhelming number of interacting public spaces created a general sense of chaos at the site. Consequently, many of the workshops were canceled at the last moment. Yet, women were not dissuaded from dialogue. For instance, one of the best workshops I attended was supposed to have focused on small credit programs for women. Unfortunately, the organizers of the workshop did not show up, but those of us who had come decided to hold a discussion anyway among ourselves because we obviously had similar interests. In the next two hours I witnessed the most intensive networking I have ever seen among women! Hugs, smiles, and business cards were warmly exchanged at the end—ensuring that the public dialogue would continue over time and long distances. Indeed, the participants of the NGO Forum demonstrated well that public discourse need not be limited by geography. E-mail, fax, and telephone networks are becoming increasingly important for women's global dialogue.[21]

Conclusions

The NGO Forum on Women was an event unprecedented in history. Never before have so many women from around the world gathered together to discuss their lives as women. By facilitating dialogue committed to what Benhabib calls "interactive universalism," the forum catalyzed the most unlikely encounters of women from different life situations. It is hoped that the dialogue will continue over time and retain the spirit of exuberant diversity that pervaded the forum in Beijing. In closing, I would like to invoke the official theme of the conference, "Look at the World Through Women's Eyes." As a witness to the incredible ways in which women empathetically fulfilled this challenge, my life is forever changed. No longer will I reconcile myself to the postmodern idea that all feminists can do is to disrupt discourse. I say, deconstruction is not enough! In Beijing, I saw—through other women's eyes—the possibility of building a global community for/by women in the reconstruction of a better world.

NOTES

1. Seyla Benhabib, *Situating the Self: Gender, Community, and Postmodernism in Contemporary Ethics* (New York: Routledge, 1992), 25.

2. Judith Butler, *Gender Trouble: Feminism and the Subversion of Identity* (New York: Routledge 1990), 25.

3. I would add that we can see a similar pattern in discourse about nationalism in the Third World. Just at the historical moment that developing countries have begun to assert economic independence in opposition to the invasions of multinational corporations, economists from the developed world have begun to espouse the inevitability of economic globalization. By supporting the emergence of "free trade networks" (for example, NAFTA), these Western economists effectively undermine the attempts of some developing countries to develop a degree of economic self-sufficiency.

Moreover, I find it dangerous to abandon entirely the notion of subjecthood at this particular historical moment in which members of late-capitalist economies have been transformed in the media from individual "citizens" to faceless "consumers." In short, according to media representation, we no longer have "lives," but, rather, "lifestyles." We are no longer "doers" who participate in democratic processes but, rather, consumers who are defined by our economic needs. It occurs to me that we are perhaps witnessing the emergence of new categories of capitalist exploitation of consumer identity. The "proletariat" is being increasingly exploited not only in its productive role but in its consumptive role as well. We are told by the economists that if the economy is to keep growing that consumers must purchase ever more products at the encouragement/brainwashing of increasingly sophisticated advertising.

4. Benhabib, footnote 39, 237.

5. Ibid., 215.

6. Ibid., 16.

7. Harper Lee, *To Kill a Mockingbird* (New York: J. B. Lippincott Company, 1960), 294.

8. Benhabib, 29.

9. Ibid., 158.

10. Ibid., 164.

11. Ibid., 14.

12. Although in this paragraph I discuss wealth and poverty in terms of the "First World" and the "Third World," respectively, I recognize that economic inequalities are more complex than this dualism. Within the United States, the "richest country in the world," extreme poverty exists. Likewise, even the most economically depressed developing countries have a rich elite. In fact, several of the world's newest millionaires and billionaires are in developing countries.

13. I should clarify that in this paper, I am focusing on the NGO Forum held in Huairou and not the official government conference held in Beijing proper.

14. Of course, the forum was not without its problems. Much of the dialogue could have greatly benefited from the insights of feminist theory, but unfortunately feminist theorists were conspicuously absent from the conference. I must say that I am completely baffled (and disappointed) as to why well-known women's studies scholars did not participate in the forum. I would like to ask women in academia why they did not go to China. Was it for political reasons? economic constraints? scheduling conflicts? or, a simple lack of interest? Because of the lack of formal gender analysis in the dialogue, at times, the conference often seemed like a "women's world fair" rather than a feminist gathering. I heard many presentations and speeches that were decidedly "essentialist" because they lacked a consciousness of gender as being different from sex.

15. Benhabib, 216.

16. Audre Lorde, "The Master's Tools Will Never Dismantle the Master's House," in *This Bridge Called My Back,* ed. Cherríe Moraga and Gloria Anzaldúa (New York: Kitchen Table, Women of Color Press, 1981), 100.

17. Cherríe Moraga, "La Guerra," in *This Bridge Called My Back: Writings by Radical Women of Color,* ed. Cherríe Moraga and Gloria Anzaldúa (New York: Kitchen Table, Women of Color Press, 1981), 28–30.

18. Pastor Martin Niemoller, a victim of the Nazis, summarized this quite eloquently when he wrote, "First they came for the Jews and I did not speak out—because I was not a Jew. Then they came for the communists and I did not speak out—because I was not a communist. Then they came for the trade unionists and I did not speak out—because I was not a trade unionist. Then they came for me, and there was no one left to speak out for me."

19. Moraga, 34.

20. Benhabib, 75.

21. A very exciting aspect of the forum to me was the computer training for women. Apple had donated millions of dollars' worth of computers, and the APC network (which provides Internet access for many nonprofit organizations) gave free, temporary e-mail accounts to anyone who attended the conference. This technology greatly facilitated information exchange with those who could not attend the conference but were nevertheless monitoring the events on-line. I was impressed by the commitment of the participants to take the time to write home after a long day's lobbying work in order to get feedback from their fellow countrywomen about the upcoming amendments to the Platform for Action.

Part VII

Building a Movement for the Twenty-First Century

The problems of identity politics and the need for it have been illuminated in the previous chapters. Failures and successes have been discussed. What of the future? Where do feminist activists go from here to confront these issues within their own organizations and to think about women in other circumstances, including countries where the difficulties may be deeper and of a different nature from what may have been addressed before? The articles that follow attempt to reconcile some of the dichotomies raised and to reach into another realm—the future and the unknown dilemmas that will emerge.

In the first article in this section Shane Phelan writes of her efforts to rethink identity politics in line with what might be feminist political strategies. She notes the cost of focusing on identities has been a divergence from crucial societal battles over homophobia, racism, poverty, and violence against women. Perhaps, she suggests, it is time to consider entry rather than withdrawal (or revolt) as the more radical tactic to achieve mutual goals, even as this may mean working on reformist rather than revolutionary strategies. One advantage to this is the allowance for diversity in people's lives; all that matters is adherence to a cause. Second, the ability to work with others who are different is not only politically effective but may increase one's sense of personal efficacy. Deconstructing the words themselves, Phelan (1989:170) notes that "identity politics must be based not only on identity but on an appreciation for politics as the art of living together."

Audre Lorde takes us into the realm of learning difference, a learned fear perceived as deviant rather than different from the self. It is those who have been outside mythical norms who have had the responsibility of explaining to others why their actions have been harmful and what needs to be done in the future to prevent those kinds of interactions again. What we have not been taught is the way to use difference for creative change in our own lives, and "to use each other's difference to enrich our visions and our joint struggles" (Lorde 1984).

Who is to tell us which identity we should privilege and which we should ignore? How are we to work together if we are looking only for people who have experienced the same constraints that we have? What small communities we would have if everyone had to fit our own identity configuration. In the next article I consider the difference between interacting with those people we like and feel most comfortable with, and working for social change with those who support the same issues we do. Coalition work can be done without compromising one's identity or ideological positions. Or, most important, people can decide to become active with any group(s) they wish; the crucial ingredient is to get involved in any way one can.

Adrienne Rich relates her efforts to involve herself with women's issues and Jewish issues. Both parts are crucial to her identity, and both are interwoven in her life. She believes that no single group can survive when it is for only itself, and thus, her identities call for working with others who care about these two groups as well as all denigrated groups. She asks: How can I favor one and ignore the other? How can I see myself and not others?

This section closes with an article by Priscilla Sears on the Beijing conference, the 1995 UN Conference on Women. Much has been written about this conference and the impact it had on participants and on future organizing by women on a global level. What did these thousands of women from nearly every country in the world have in common? Violence against women, inequality, discrimination, oppression. They had their gender commonality, the one that has less power in decision making on all levels and in every society. And yes, there were also differences. Some participants were elite, some poor, there were princesses and nuns, prime ministers and prostitutes. Read her report and feel a part of the gathering, the stories women told one another, the touching events, the moving exchanges. Read it and begin to believe the message she uses for the title of her paper: What Is difficult May Be Done at Once. What Is Impossible Takes a Little Longer.

REFERENCES

Lorde, Audre. 1984. *Sister Outsider*. Watsonville, CA: Crossing Press.
Phelan, Shane. 1989. *Identity Politics: Lesbian Feminism and the Limits of Community*. Philadelphia: Temple University Press.

Chapter Thirty-one

Rethinking Identity Politics

Shane Phelan

How can we think past the old dichotomies and categories? How can we maintain the will and conviction to act for change without sliding into essentialism? I believe that the single best source of experience and thinking on this problem today is the writing of women of color and those white women who have seriously addressed the fact of their race and social location. Repeatedly we have seen how easy it is for white, middle-class women in white society to ignore other differences in favor of the common bond between women. Women of color have been in the uncomfortable position of knowing that white feminism is ignoring them and yet also needing and wanting much that has been formulated by white feminists. This is compounded for lesbians who live within overtly homophobic cultures to which they remain committed. Unable to ignore economic reality, unable to form separatist communities with the ease of bourgeois white women, women of color have had to stay and fight with all those who want to foster and support only some *part* of them. This experience has given rise to a complexity and depth of analysis unmatched in any other contemporary literature, feminist or not. These are the voices, within us and among us, to which we must listen.

Cheryl Clarke has vividly described the homophobia of the black community. She cites a flyer distributed at the First National Plenary Conference on Self-Determination that stated that "revolutionary nationalists and genuine communists cannot uphold homosexuality in the leadership of the Black Liberation Movement nor uphold it as a correct practice. Homosexuality is a genocidal practice." She points out that this homophobia is shared by the dominant white culture, and states that "if I were a 'revolutionary nationalist' or even a 'genuine communist,' I would be concerned if my political vision in any way supported the designs of my oppressors."[1] This problem goes beyond revolutionary black men to include many black feminists, who are so concerned to maintain alliance with black men that they ignore or silence black lesbians. "Like her black male counterpart, the black woman intellectual is afraid to relinquish heterosexual privilege. So little else is guaranteed black people."[2]

Nonetheless, Clarke is frustrated with "the accusations of homophobia hurled at the black community by many gay men and lesbians, as if the whole black community were more homophobic than the heterosexist culture we live in. . . . It is not accurate to attribute homophobia to the mass of black people." Citing examples from her life and from black history, Clarke argues that the "poor and working-class black community," more than bourgeois blacks, "has often tolerated an individual's lifestyle prerogatives, even when that lifestyle was disparaged by the prevailing culture."[3] She thus suggests that class is somehow historically relevant to tolerance; a thesis that Foucault explored repeatedly, most especially in the *History of Sexuality*. If the white bourgeoisie enslaved itself first, then those emulating it may well be next. She does not, however, dismiss the black bourgeoisie as enemies, to be disposed of; such a luxury is not open to her.

One of the first, and most cogent, statements of black feminism was the "Combahee River Collective Statement." While the Collective writes in advocacy of the concept of identity politics, the idea does not take on quite the extensive form that it has among some white lesbian feminists. Stating that "the most profound and potentially most radical politics come directly out of our own identity, as opposed to working to end somebody else's oppression,"[4] they point out that this is revolutionary for black women, trained always to give priority to some other, be it white men and women or black men.

While noting that they "often find it difficult to separate race from class from sex oppression because in our lives they are most often experienced simultaneously," they know that "there is such a thing as racial-sexual oppression which is neither solely racial nor solely sexual." In this they reject both blacks who argue that sexual oppression either does not exist or is a product of racism, and white feminists who argue that racism in the women's movement does not exist or is a product of sexism. As socialists, they believe that "the liberation of all oppressed peoples necessitates the destruction of the political-economic systems of capitalism and imperialism as well as patriarchy." They are not certain, however, "that a socialist revolution that is not also a feminist and anti-racist revolution will guarantee our liberation."[5]

While they support the idea that the personal is political, that does not lead the collective to some of the positions that earlier lesbian feminists took (and still take). Lesbian separatism is not only economically difficult,

> it leaves out far too much and far too many people, particularly Black men, women, and children. We have a great deal of criticism and loathing for what men have been socialized to be in this society: what they support, how they act, and how they oppress. But we do not have the misguided notion that it is their maleness, per se—i.e., their biological maleness—that makes them what they are. As Black women we find any type of biological determinism a particularly dangerous and reactionary basis upon which to build a politic. We must also question whether Lesbian separatism is an adequate and progressive political analysis and strategy, even for those who practice it, since it so completely denies any but the sexual sources of women's oppression, negating the facts of class and race.[6]

We can see from this statement that the members of the Collective by 1974 had rejected the limiting features of lesbian separatism as both "mistaken" and, more importantly, as politically dangerous. Biological arguments have too often been used against feminism and against nonwhite peoples for these women to be comfortable with it. Further, such a position entails the abandonment of political coalition with the men of the community, and this is something that black women cannot afford.

The problem of racism within the women's movement is also challenged in the statement. This racism, unlike earlier ones, consists in the privileging of sexual oppression and the denial of significant differences among women, with the consequent charge of false consciousness or male identification for those who question this. In a letter to Mary Daly, Audre Lorde illustrated this process. While she did not question Daly's "good faith toward all women," she was bothered by her exclusive use of "white, western european, judeo-christian" goddess images in a book that amply documented black women's victimization and participation in their sisters' oppression. This imbalance reinforces the idea that nonwhite women have no strong cultural traditions, that salvation will come only from western feminism and the abandonment of their heritage. Within this book, with its extensive documentation and research, Lorde was the only black woman cited. Her reaction was strong: "To me, this feels like another instance of the knowledge, crone-ology and work of women of Color being ghettoized by a white women dealing only out of a patriarchal western European frame of reference."[7]

Lorde notes that the feminist community suffers from racism just as does the rest of the United States. And one major way in which that racism is manifest is in the denial of difference. "The oppression of women knows no ethnic nor racial boundaries, true, but that does not mean it is identical within those differences.[8]

She extends her analysis of difference among women in her comments at the Second Sex conference in 1979. The problem is as follows:

> As women, we have been taught either to ignore our differences, or to view them as causes for separation and suspicion rather than as forces for change. Without community there is no liberation, only the most vulnerable and temporary armistice between an individual and her oppression. But community must not mean a shedding of our differences, nor the pathetic pretense that these differences do not exist.[9]

This is not a danger only for whites: "Those of us who are Black must see that the reality of our lives and our struggle does not make us immune to the errors of ignoring and misnaming difference. . . . The need for unity is often misnamed as a need for homogeneity."[10]

This problem is also noted by Asian-American, Hispanic, and Native American women. One lesbian says that "I no longer believe that feminism is a tool which can eliminate racism—or even promote better understanding between different races and kinds of women. I have felt less understanding between different races and from many lesbian women than I do from some straight people. At least their heterosexual indifference allows me more freedom to be myself."[11] Mitsuye Yamada states that "Asian Pacific American women will not speak out to say what we have on our minds until we feel secure within ourselves that this is our home too: and until our white sisters indicate by their actions that they want to join us in our struggle because it is theirs also."[12]

Perhaps the most difficult place in which to celebrate difference is the academy. The nature of theory has been to make connections, to tell grand stories that tie threads together. This has been evident at least since Plato's *Republic*, in which every animal, every person, manifests the degree of order and harmony that rules the polis. Until the advent of postmodernism, the aim of theoretical work was to smooth and connect, not to disrupt or disorient us. But people who are left out of the story know the price of such simple smoothing. We cannot progress by hiding out and building a safe world where problems such as racism cannot intrude; this will be simply to ignore them, and such ignorance serves only to perpetuate them. The failure of lesbian feminism to deal with sexual differences is not the same as, but is related to, its failure to deal with racial and cultural ones. Many Third World women have expressed the sense that fights about sadomasochism are white women's fights, the fights of people who have no real occupation or struggle. While perhaps overstated at times, the charge carries some weight. The price of developing a cultural feminism with its own standards and identities has too often been the divergence of our attention from more immediate battles in our lives: the resurgence of homophobia, of racism, of violence against women, of poverty. Addressing these issues requires that we all resist the impulse for total separatism[13] and for purity in our allies in favor of workable coalitions and porous but meaningful communities.

Political Strategies

What exactly does this mean for our political action? What will the new configuration of feminist politics look like? I do not exactly know. I do know that the inclusion (not assimilation) of other people will of necessity change the old configuration, not because women or nonwhites or workers are inherently virtuous, but simply because they are different. The suggestion that assimilation will be total reflects either a lack of confidence in the strength of marginal peoples, or an ahistorical belief in the capitalist, male-dominated modern world. Without sounding facile, I want to suggest that strategies of entry are, at this point, more directly radical than strategies of withdrawal or revolt.[14] The creation and support of nonhegemonic cultural resources and community are encouraging, stimulating developments. They will be more so as they decline to classify and discipline their participants.

What exactly does this mean for lesbians? Lesbians, as members of one of the primary "deviant" classes in society, have attempted to counter the prevailing stereotypes of their lives by a variety of strategies. In the lesbian feminist strategy, the priority is on the creation of a community and a history that will offer the lesbian a sense of belonging rather than exclusion, positive identity through membership in a group that has a culture of its own—a culture, in fact, superior to that denied them. On the other hand a "reformist" strategy has focused on the elimination of institutional and legal barriers to membership in the larger society and on the development of a sense of pride, not as lesbians per se, but as persons who are lesbian.

The second path has been characterized by lesbian feminists and others as mere assimilation, the denial of one's true self in order to participate. The two strategies, in fact, reflect the conflict that is endemic to modernity: given the current fact of otherness within the self, given the consensus among theorists that contemporary societies exact a high price for stability and order, we are faced, as Connolly has noted, with the choice between a vision "in which the goal is to integrate otherness into more perfect forms of identification with the will of a rational community" and one that suggests that "we should strive to create more institutional space to allow otherness to be."[15] What I hope to have demonstrated, through examination of lesbian feminism as a communitarian project, is that the first option is not available to us as we are presently constituted: that otherness is a constant, harassing presence that will not vanish under any political or discursive regime in modernity, and that acceptance of this fact must be the base for any future politics—for lesbians, for women, for heterosexual white men.

This in turn suggests that the politics of reform has several advantages. First, it does not require one to define and to subjectify one's difference in order to claim rights. Within the lesbian feminist community, membership is based on standards no less restrictive than in the larger society, and these standards have so far not shown themselves to be sufficiently unproblematic that their restrictiveness should be overlooked. If anything, this community is under more pressure to justify its standards, because it is less diffuse and more intimate than the heterosexual culture surrounding it. The comparison to medieval society is apt in this regard. Excommunication was not simply a matter of losing one's political rights or one's job; it involved the loss of the structure of one's life—friends, church, family, God. To the extent that lesbians form an insular community, members face similar risks in challenging common beliefs. In contrast, broader-based reform movements may work without insisting that participants adhere to a particular way of life, thus leaving issues of other differences open to discussion at a less volatile level.

A second advantage is that, while reform movements may appear to gain less in terms of direct identity support than community strategies, they in fact may achieve more. Specifically, mainstream efforts may provide their actors with a strong personal identity that is more resilient than that offered by alternative communities, because it is broader based. A lesbian may indeed find herself capable of alliance and friendship—even community—with straight women, as well as with men of all sorts, that will prove more personally durable as well as politically effective. The community of lesbian feminists, to the extent that it ignores the society surrounding it, runs the continual risk of reaction and oppression by that society. It is inconceivable that an attitude of hostility and separation will engender anything other than itself; few of us are in a position to make that worthwhile. This is not a caution against any agitation. It is, rather, a suggestion that such action must be conducted in a spirit of goodwill and hope for common action rather than one that suspects even potential allies. This is increasingly being recognized by lesbian feminists who are broadening their politics to encompass both the needs of community and the need for a politics that operates beyond community boundaries.

One such activist is Bernice Johnson Reagon. In a talk in 1981, she described the politics that she sees as essential. Beginning in the civil rights movement of the 1960s, Reagon has worked for more than twenty years to build a world she can live in. However, Reagon's aim is not to build a world that she can be comfortable in. She suggests that in doing coalition work, "most of the time you feel threatened to the core and if you don't, you're not really doing no coalescing. . . . You don't go into coalition because you just *like* it. The only reason you would consider trying to team up with somebody who could possibly kill you, is because that's the only way you figure you can stay alive."[16]

Using the metaphor of a barred room, she describes the world and the impulse that leads many to separatism. While recognizing the appeal, she rejects it. She suggests that separatist communities will always feel pressure to open up, whether the pressure be racial, class, sexual, or whatever; and when that pressure is eased by including more people, then the community doesn't feel as safe as it once did. There is simply no way short of exclusion to keep a community from feeling threatened; and the premise of contemporary feminism is the sisterhood, thus non-exclusion, of women.

Political work, then, must always be a flow from the safe, nurturing point to the dangerous point of coalition and back. She says that in coalition work "you shouldn't look for comfort"; that "you don't get fed a lot in a coalition. In a coalition you have to give, and it is different from your home. You can't stay there all the time."[17]

If coalition work is so hard and painful, why do it? Simply because "the barred rooms will not be allowed to exist. They will all be wiped out."[18] The forces against people of color, against women, against gays and lesbians, against others, do not celebrate difference either; and they have never, will never, make us welcome without our pressure. None of us, then, can do without the others, not because our fights are the same, but because we can support each other's fights while waging our own.

Biddy Martin and Chandra Talpade Mohanty have produced a reading of "Identity: Skin Blood Heart," the work of a white Christian lesbian, Minnie Bruce Pratt, that addresses the motifs of home, identity, and community among feminists. Citing Reagon's work, they argue that her challenge to the simple appeal of "home" is vital and that Pratt's piece is an example of the "questioning of the all-too-common conflation of experience, identity, and political perspective."[19] Stating that "unity through incorporation has too often been the white middle-class feminist's mode of adding on difference without leaving the comfort of home," they treat Pratt's work as an exploration of "the exclusions and repressions which support the seeming homogeneity, stability, and self-evidence of 'white identity,' which is derived from and dependent on the marginalization of differences within as well as 'without.' "[20] Women of color are not to be taken simply as the voices of diversity breaking in upon the uniform consciousness of white women, but as writers who remind all of us of the tentative, constructed, but historically real and particular nature of our identities.

Lesbian feminism derived its theoretical force from the assimilation of apparently diverse relations into a single-system framework. Not every lesbian feminist is or was a separatist; some have done coalition work throughout their lives. The structure of the theory, however, makes this coalition work incoherent. Men cannot be worked with, if we take the theory seriously. Women of color can be invited into the community, but only on the condition that their race or culture be seen as secondary, unimportant among lesbians. Straight women can only be worked with if they condemn men. The fact that any of us have engaged in coalitions is testimony to the richness of life beyond theory; but we must strive to make our theory cohere more closely with our lives. Identity politics does mean building our public action on who we are and how that identity fits into and does not fit into our society. This is and must be the basis for political action that addresses nonjuridical, nonstate-centered power. However, if we transform it into a requirement for purity at every level of our lives, we deny the lives we began fighting for. If we are to be free, we must learn to embrace paradox and confusion; in short, we must embrace politics. Identity politics must be based, not only on identity, but on an appreciation for politics as the art of living together. Politics that ignores our identities, that makes them "private," is useless; but nonnegotiable identities will enslave us whether they are imposed from within or without.

NOTES

1. Cheryl Clarke, "The Failure to Transform: Homophobia in the Black Community," in *Home Girls: A Black Feminist Anthology,* ed. Barbara Smith (New York: Kitchen Table Press, 1983), pp. 197–98.

2. Ibid., p. 205.

3. Ibid., p. 206.

4. Combahee River Collective, "The Combahee River Collective Statement" in Smith, ed., *Home Girls,* p. 275.

5. Ibid., pp. 275–76.

6. Combahee River Collective, "A Black Feminist Statement," in *Feminist Frameworks: Alternative Theoretical Accounts of the Relations Between Men and Women,* ed. Alison Jaggar and Paula S. Rothenberg (New York: McGraw-Hill, 1984), p. 206.

7. Audre Lorde, "An Open Letter to Mary Daly," in *This Bridge Called My Back: Writings by Radical Women of Color,* ed. Cherríe Moraga and Gloria Anzaldúa (New York: Kitchen Table Press, 1983), pp. 95–96.

8. Ibid., p. 97.

9. Audre Lorde, "The Master's Tools Will Never Dismantle the Master's House," in *Sister Outsider: Essays and Speeches* (Trumansburg, N.Y.: Crossing Press, 1984), p. 112.

10. Lorde, "Age, Race, Class, and Sex," in *Sister Outsider,* p. 119.

11. Chrystos, "I Don't Understand Those Who Have Turned Away From Me," in *This Bridge Called My Back,* ed. Moraga and Anzaldúa, p. 69.

12. Mitsuye Yamada, "Asian Pacific American Women and Feminism," in *This Bridge Called My Back,* ed. Moraga and Anzaldúa, p. 75.

13. Again, I do not mean to attack any need for closed, supportive communities; my concern is with those that do not feed us in our more public work, but remove us from it.

14. For a discussion on the differences between revolt and revolution, and the relation of liberation to freedom, see Hannah Arendt, *On Revolution* (New York: Penguin Books, 1977), chap. 1.

15. William Connolly, "Taylor, Foucault, and Otherness," *Political Theory* 13, no. 3 (Aug. 1985), p. 375.

16. Bernice Johnson Reagon, "Coalition Politics: Turning the Century," in *Home Girls*, ed. Smith, pp. 356–57.

17. Ibid., p. 359.

18. Ibid., p. 362.

19. Biddy Martin and Chandra Talpade Mohanty, "Feminist Politics: What's Home Got to Do with It?" in *Feminist Studies/Critical Studies*, ed. Teresa de Lauretis (Bloomington: University of Indiana Press, 1986), p. 192.

20. Ibid., p. 193.

Chapter Thirty-two

Our Difference Is Our Strength

Audre Lorde

As a 49-year-old, black, lesbian, feminist, socialist mother of two, including one boy, and a member of an interracial couple, I usually find myself a part of some group defined as other, deviant, inferior, or just plain wrong. Traditionally, in American society, it is the members of oppressed, objectified groups who are expected to stretch out and bridge the gap between the actualities of our lives and the consciousness of our oppressor. For, in order to survive, those of us for whom oppression is as American as apple pie have always had to be watchers, to become familiar with the language and manners of the oppressor, sometimes even adopting them for some illusion of protection. Whenever the need for some pretense of communication arises, those who profit from our oppression call upon us to share our knowledge of them. In other words, it is the responsibility of the oppressed to teach the oppressors their mistakes. I am responsible for educating teachers who dismiss my children's culture in school. Black and Third World people are expected to educate white people as to our humanity. Women are expected to educate men. Lesbians and gay men are expected to educate the heterosexual world. The oppressors maintain their position and evade responsibility for their own actions. There is a constant drain of energy, which might be better used in redefining ourselves and devising realistic scenarios for altering the present and constructing the future.

Institutionalized rejection of difference is an absolute necessity in a profit economy that needs outsiders as surplus people. As members of such an economy, we have *all* been programmed to respond to the human differences between us with fear and loathing and to handle those differences in one of three ways: ignore them, and if that is not possible, copy them if we think they are dominant, or destroy them if we think they are subordinate. But we have no patterns for relating across our human differences as equals. As a result, those differences have been misnamed and misused in the service of separation and confusion.

Certainly there are very real differences between us, of race, age, and sex. But it is not those differences that are separating us. It is rather our refusal to recognize those differences, and to examine the distortions that result from our misnaming them and their effects upon human behavior and expectation.

Racism, the belief in the inherent superiority of one race over all others and thereby the right to dominance. Sexism, the belief in the inherent superiority of one sex over the other and thereby the right to dominance. Ageism. Heterosexism. Elitism. Classism.

It is a lifetime pursuit for each of us to extract these distortions from our living at the same time that we recognize, reclaim, and define those differences upon which they are imposed. For we have all been raised in a society where those distortions were endemic within our living. Too often, we pour the energy needed for recognizing and exploring difference into pretending those differences are insurmountable barriers, or that they do not exist at all. This results in voluntary isolation, or false and treacherous connections. Either way, we do not develop tools for using human difference as a springboard for creative change within our lives. We speak not of human difference, but of human deviance.

Somewhere, on the edge of consciousness, there is what I call a *mythical norm*, and each of us within our hearts knows "that is not me." In America, this norm is usually defined as *white, thin, male, young, heterosexual, Christian, and financially secure.* It is with this mythical norm that the trappings of power reside within this society. Those of us who stand outside that power often identify one way in which we are different, and we assume it to be the primary cause of all oppression, forgetting other distortions around difference, some of which we ourselves may be practicing. By and large within the women's movement today, white women focus upon their oppression as women and ignore differences of race, sexual preference, class, and age. There is a pretense to a homogeneity of experience covered by the word *sisterhood* that does not in fact exist.

Unacknowledged class differences rob women of each other's energy and creative insight. Recently a women's magazine collective made the decision for one issue to print only prose, saying poetry was a less "rigorous" or "serious" art form. Yet even the form our creativity takes is often a class issue. Of all the art forms, poetry is the most economical. It is the one that is the most secret, that requires the least physical labor, the least material, and one that can be done between shifts, in the hospital pantry, on the subway, and on scraps of surplus paper. Over the last few years, writing a novel on tight finances, I came to appreciate the enormous differences in the material demands between poetry and prose. As we reclaim our literature, poetry has been the major voice of poor, working-class, and colored women. A room of one's own may be a necessity for writing prose, but so are reams of paper, a typewriter, and plenty of time. The actual requirements to produce the visual arts also help determine, along class lines, whose art is whose. In this day of inflated prices for materials, who are our sculptors, our painters, our photographers? When we speak of a broadly based women's culture, we need to be aware of the effect of class and economic differences on the supplies available for producing art.

As we move toward creating a society within which we can each flourish, ageism is another distortion of relationship that interferes with our vision. By ignoring the past, we are encouraged to repeat its mistakes. If the younger members of a community view the older members as contemptible or suspect or excess, they will never be able to join hands and examine the living memories of the community, nor ask the all-important question "Why?" This gives rise to a historical amnesia that keeps us working to invent the wheel every time we have to go to the store for bread.

We find ourselves having to repeat and relearn the same old lessons that our mothers did, because we do not pass on what we have learned, or because we are unable to listen. For instance, how many times has this all been said before? For another, who would have believed that once again our daughters are allowing their bodies to be hampered and put in purgatory by girdles and high heels and hobble skirts?

Ignoring the differences of race between women and the implications of those differences presents the most serious threat to the mobilization of women's joint power.

As white women ignore their built-in privilege of whiteness and define *woman* in terms of their experience alone, then women of color become "other," the outsider whose experience and tradition is too "alien" to comprehend.

Refusing to recognize difference makes it impossible to see the different problems and pitfalls facing us as women.

Thus, in a patriarchal power system where white-skin privilege is a major prop, the entrapments used to neutralize black women and white women are not the same. For example, it is easy for black women to be used by the power structure against black men, not because they are men, but because they are black. Therefore, for black women, it is necessary at all times to separate the needs of the oppressor from our own legitimate conflicts within our communities. This same problem does not exist for white women. Black women and men have shared racist oppression and still share it, although in different ways. Out of that shared oppression we have developed joint defenses and joint vulnerabilities to each other that are rarely duplicated in the white community.

On the other hand, white women face the pitfall of being seduced into joining the oppressor under the pretense of sharing power. This possibility does not exist in the same way for women of color. The tokenism that is sometimes extended to us is not an invitation to join power; our racial "otherness" is a visible reality that makes that quite clear. For white women there is a wider range of pretended choices and rewards for identifying with patriarchal power and its tools.

Today, with the defeat of the Equal Rights Amendment, the tightening economy, and increased conservatism, it is easier once again for white women to believe the dangerous fantasy that if you are good enough, pretty enough, sweet enough, quiet enough, teach the children to behave, hate the right people, and marry the right man, then you will be allowed to coexist with patriarchy in relative peace, at least until a man needs your job or the neighborhood rapist happens along. And true, unless one lives and loves in the trenches it is difficult to remember that the war against dehumanization is ceaseless.

But black women and our children know that the fabric of our lives is stitched with violence and with hatred, that there is no rest. For us, increasingly, violence weaves through the daily tissues of our living—in the supermarket, in the classroom, in the elevator, in the clinic and the school yard, from the plumber, the baker, the saleswoman, the bus driver, the bank teller, the waitress who does not serve us.

Some problems we share as women, some we do not. You fear your children will grow up to join the patriarchy and testify against you; we fear our children will be dragged from a car and shot down in the street, and you will turn your backs upon the reasons they are dying.

The threat of difference has been no less blinding to people of color. Those of us who are black must see that the reality of our lives and our struggle does not make us immune to the errors of ignoring and misnaming difference. Within black communities, where racism is a living reality, differences among us often seem dangerous and suspect. The need for unity is often misnamed as a need for homogeneity, and black feminist vision is often mistaken for betrayal of our common interests as a people. Because of the continuous battle against racial erasure that black women and black men share, some black women still refuse to recognize that we are also oppressed as women, and that sexual hostility against black women is practiced not only by the white racist society, but within our black communities as well. It is a disease striking the heart of black nationhood, and silence will not make it disappear. Exacerbated by racism and the pressures of powerlessness, violence against black women and children often becomes a standard within our communities, one by which manliness can be measured. But these woman-hating acts are rarely discussed as crimes against black women.

Differences between ourselves as black women are also being misnamed and used to separate us from one another. As a black lesbian feminist comfortable with the many different ingredients of my identity, and as a woman committed to racial and sexual freedom from oppression, I find I am constantly being encouraged to pluck out some one aspect of myself and present this as a meaningful whole, eclipsing or denying the other parts of self. But this is a destructive and fragmenting way to live. My fullest concentration of energy is available to me only when I integrate all the parts of who I am, openly, allowing power from particular sources of my living to flow back and forth freely through all my different selves, without the restrictions of externally imposed definition. Only then can I bring myself and my energies as a whole to the service of those struggles that I embrace as part of my living.

A fear of lesbians, or of being accused of being a lesbian, has led many black women into testifying against themselves. It has led some of us into destructive alliances, and others into despair and isolation. In the white women's communities, heterosexism is sometimes a result of identifying with the white patriarchy. Sometimes it reflects a die-hard belief in the protective coloration of heterosexual relationships, sometimes a self-hate, which all women have to fight against, taught us from birth.

Although elements of these attitudes exist for all women, there are particular resonances of heterosexism and homophobia among black women. Despite the fact that woman-bonding has a long and honorable history in the African and African American communities, and despite the knowledge and accomplishments of many strong and creative women-identified black women in the political, social, and cultural fields, heterosexual black women often tend to ignore or discount the existence and work of black lesbians. Part of this attitude has come from an understandable terror of black male attack within the close confines of black society, where the punishment for any female self-assertion is still to be accused of being a lesbian and therefore to be unworthy of the attention or support of the scarce black male. But part of this need to *misname and ignore black lesbians comes from a very real fear that openly women-identified black women who are no longer dependent upon men for their self-definition may well reorder our whole concept of social relationships.*

As a tool of *social control,* women have been encouraged to recognize only one area of human difference as legitimate, those differences that exist between women and men. And we have learned to deal across those differences with the urgency of all oppressed subordinates. All of us have had to learn to live or work or coexist with men, from our fathers on. We recognized and negotiated these differences, even when this recognition only continued the old dominant/subordinate mode of human relationship, where the oppressed must recognize the masters' difference in order to survive.

But our future survival is predicated upon our ability to relate within equality. As women, we must root out internalized patterns of oppression within ourselves if we are to move beyond the most superficial aspects of social change. Now we must recognize differences among women who are our equals, neither inferior nor superior, and devise ways to use each other's difference to enrich our visions and our joint struggles.

The future of our earth may depend upon the ability of all women to identify and develop new definitions of power and new patterns of relating across difference. The old definitions have not served us, or the earth that supports us. The patterns, no matter how cleverly rearranged to imitate progress, still condemn us to cosmetically altered repetitions of the same old exchanges, the same old guilt, hatred, recrimination, lamentation, and suspicion.

For we have built into all of us old blueprints of expectation and response, old structures of oppression, and these must be altered at the same time we alter the living conditions that are a result of those structures. For the master's tools will never dismantle the master's house.

As Paulo Freire shows so well in *The Pedagogy of the Oppressed,* the true focus of revolutionary change is never merely the oppressive situations that we seek to escape, but that piece of the oppressor that is planted deep within each of us, and that knows only the oppressors' tactics, the oppressors' relationships.

Change means growth, and growth can be painful. But we sharpen self-definition by exposing the self in work and struggle together with those whom we define as different from ourselves, although sharing the same goals. For black and white, old and young, lesbian and heterosexual women alike, this can mean new paths to survival.

Chapter Thirty-three

Having It All
The Search for Identity and Community

Barbara Ryan

The women's movement has been cited as a "New Social Movement," a designation that is given even though the movement has a long history and does not fit many of the characteristics claimed for new social movements (Roseneil 1995). Particularly problematic in new social movement theory is the built-in assumption of unity within groups—women, people of color, gays and lesbians—when, in fact, these social movements are not without divisions themselves as multiple identities interact and compete in the search for common goals.

Contemporary social movements appear to draw participants who are interested in establishing a sense of community; however, theorists find this search to be more troublesome than those of the past do. For instance, Alberto Melucci argues that complex societies are made up of large-scale organizations, which "increasingly attempt to regulate and control every aspect of the lives of individuals," and that increasing control from above stimulates the growth of social movements organized around questions of personal identity (1989:7). Alain Touraine places identity at the center of his analysis of social change in postmodern societies. Thus, he is particularly interested in explaining the appeals in recent years to "specificity, difference, nationalism, and all forms of identity which are based on biology, heredity, or any unconscious factor," appeals to that which he considers least social in collective organizing (Touraine 1988:77–78).

The concern of these theorists is that the impetus for social movement involvement in late-twentieth-century European and North American societies is coming from identity politics rather than class relations or ideological commitment—that it is reactionary rather than liberatory, exclusive rather than inclusive, and concerned with personal rather than social change. But, whatever concerns theorists may have, the fact is, identity politics are here. Identity issues, both within and outside social movements, are of importance because they affect how people define themselves, and that self-definition affects the part they will play in movements for change. It behooves us all to pay attention to the voices that are claiming a politics of identity.

My interest is in the challenges raised for the women's movement, where identity politics has played such an important part in new definitions of that movement.

Through discursive analysis, this paper looks at identity politics in the contemporary U.S. women's movement from the early 1980s through the late 1990s.[1] The consequences of movement divisions based on social characteristics, such as sexual practice and race/ethnicity, are examined by looking at both the meaning of complex identities and their associative effects on the women's movement. This work is primarily a discussion of the different sides to this debate and my efforts to present them objectively. It is meant to enlighten—a searching for meaning rather than solutions.

The Politics of Identity in the Women's Movement

Identity politics refers to discourses and social activism focused on racial, religious, sexual, ethnic, gender, or national identity. These groups are usually involved in power bids, particularly in making demands on the state, although some are more expressive than political in nature (Moghadam 1994). There are mixed opinions about the value of a social movement's organizing around lifestyle and personal identity characteristics. On the one hand, it is seen as something new (and, therefore, problematic); on the other hand, we could define identity politics broadly enough to include all social movements. It is safe to say that it is a complex, and in many ways, a contradictory topic. Beyond that is contested territory.

In the case of the contemporary women's movement, this discussion needs, first, to be grounded in the recognition that the question of identity politics in the women's movement did not arise when feminist groups organized on the basis of gender. Even though theorists who have not studied the women's movement think of it as typifying identity politics (that is, that it is a unified movement of women), activists and students of feminism know that there have always been contentious ideological divisions (Ryan 1989), and that the current politics of identity actually emerged out of challenges to the movement raised by the women who felt left out. Identity politics is an issue because divisions among women have led to separate group formations and because there have been charges of racism and classism in the women's movement. In *Inessential Woman*, Elizabeth Spelman (1988) points out that the "problem of difference" is not really one of looking at commonalities and differences among women, it is one of looking at the differences of women outside the norm of "woman." Feminist discourse about diversity, pluralism, multiculturalism, and identity politics is really a discourse about women who are the other "Other"—that is, *other than* white heterosexual middle-class women.[2]

The two identity divisions within the U.S. women's movement that generate the most heated challenges are those raised by lesbian feminists, particularly in what is sometimes called the women's culture; and the womanist organizing of women of color.[3] Both of these "gender-plus" identities contest the primacy of comparing women with men and, at their base, challenge the concept of "universal sisterhood" (A. Davis 1981; Dill 1983; hooks 1981; Moraga and Anzaldúa 1983; Smith 1982).

Historically, the women's movement has focused on gender equality; a position based on similarities between the sexes. This emphasis can be traced to the beginning of the organized woman's movement in the mid-1800s, and can also be found in the Equal Rights Amendment (ERA) campaign of more recent times.[4] However, alongside the "similarity" argument has run a "difference" argument. In this view, advocates call for changed social relations premised on women's particular needs and special values, a position found in one sector of the women's suffrage movement and in a new (much more radicalized) form in the women's culture of contemporary times.[5] The framework, however, for both similarity and difference arguments has been the relations *between* women and men, an emphasis that has always failed to address differences *among* women (see Ryan 1992 for a fuller discussion). This, then, is the fault line from which identity politics originates. And it is identity politics, more than previous concepts, that has created a shift in focus in the women's movement.

Lesbianism as Identity

In the organizing period of the contemporary women's movement, activists posited the need for social space that allowed members of an oppressed group to develop a sense of worth in contrast to the inferior status of their received definition (Evans 1979). Developing a positive female identity became a precondition for further activism. Following this line of thinking, lesbian feminists utilized the concept "woman-identified woman," and chose an alignment with the women's movement rather than the gay liberation movement. In various ways, the women's groups that emerged were all dedicated to creating spaces for women apart from men. But since that time, the terms *separate space* and *oppressed group* have become more narrowly and particularly defined, to the point where women are often excluded from other women. For instance, in the early years, the issue of lesbianism created virulent divisions that led to a separatist women's culture as a distinct strand of the movement by the mid-1970s.[6]

Studies on lesbian feminist communities reveal the positive aspects of redefining a maligned identity into one of value, of finding acceptance and emotional support where it is lacking in the outside world (Krieger 1982, 1983; Taylor and Whittler 1992). The identity affirmation found in the lesbian feminist culture is strongly focused on separatism, essentialism, female values, and the primacy of women's relationships. It is also overwhelmingly white and middle-class. Radical lesbian feminists are forthright in proclaiming the superiority of women's values over men's, and it is this notion of superior and universal female values that "sits uneasily with the recognition of differences among women" (Taylor and Rupp 1993:41).

Not only does an essentialist, radical feminist, separatist ideology create distance from men, it also creates distance from heterosexual women, racial/ethnic women, and even other lesbians.[7] In the case of the latter, sadomasochism created polarization to the extent that some lesbian feminists who had been active in the movement for many years found themselves labeled antifeminists (K. Davis 1981). Engaging in identity politics in other than social movement interactions has frequently resulted in negative consequences (Taylor and Raeburn 1995). Equally or more disconcerting can be the divisions and affronts that alienate group members from one another.[8] As one participant in a lesbian community says, "I often don't respect what people choose to do with feelings and find the expression and communication self-indulgent, immature, (and) offensive. . . . I'm afraid of personal attacks in the group" (Paz 1994:10).

What can it mean when people are afraid to speak for fear of being attacked from members of their self-selected identity-enhancing group? Shane Phelan (1989) considers this question in *Identity Politics: Lesbian Feminism and the Limits of Community* and concludes that lesbian feminists have valorized and reified lesbianism to the extent that they have forfeited the plurality of lesbian lives. Within the lesbian feminist community, she found there is a socially acceptable way to love women and it does not include the behavior of bar lesbians, butch/femme roles, s/m practices, "queer" lesbians who align with gay men, or the "bad girl" style of heavy makeup, black leather, and sexually explicit behavior (Phelan 1989; also see Franzen 1993). Indeed, in reaction to what is often perceived as a suffocating conformity in the women's community, Vera Whisman claims that "today's 'bad girls' rebel as much against their feminist predecessors as against male power" (1993:48).

Womanist Women of Color

Women of color see separatism from men as a racist stance, since this divides them from their racial group. Living in a largely segregated society, women of color feel a bonding with men of color that they do not usually feel with white women. For most African American women, race loyalty overshadows gender issues (Dill 1983), expressing itself as a felt need to empower both women and men of their racial community (Collins 1990). But something else has been occurring among activist women of color. Since the mid-1980s, "hyphenated" women have been self-defining themselves and declaring their solidarity in a united front (Bell-Scott 1994). White women are not included in this sisterhood because a "common" gender politics is seen as the excuse privileged women use "to ignore the differences between their social status and the status of masses of women" (hooks 1984:5). Even for African American women, well aware of the sexist treatment they receive from men of their own race, it is not missed that a policy of women's separatism feigns ignorance among white women of the historical reality that "their race had always consigned black women to a category other than female" (Fleming 1993:72).

For women of color, race solidarity has been a source of joy and nurturance in a hostile world (A. Davis 1993); but like the lesbian community, women of color have divisions and conflicts. Class differences have created a widening gap among all ethnic/racial groups; and among African Americans, the politic of skin color has long existed within their own ranks (Fleming 1993; Giddings 1988; Russell, Wilson, and Hall 1992; Scales-Trent 1995). And, women of color know that racial/ethnic movements have never considered women's claims to be as important or as valid as those of "the people"—which usually turns out to mean raising the position of men first (Garcia 1989; Hernton 1985; King 1988; Morris 1984; Moraga 1993).

A recent incident where race/gender issues collided within the African American community was the hearings in the confirmation process of Clarence Thomas for Supreme Court justice. Thomas, a black man, was accused by Anita Hill, a black woman law professor, of sexual harassment. White feminists rushed to applaud Hill; black feminists paused to consider the "politics of raising voice or remaining silent" (McKay 1993:278). That nonseeing of how the issue of gender was connected to the issue of race, and the complexities of the situation for black women, represents the often-felt irreconcilable division between black and white women. As Nellie McKay argues, in spite of her feeling that Thomas's nomination was an insult to black people and that she saw Hill as her sister, she had mixed feelings about Hill's "breaking the conspiracy of silence" black women have held "to protect them from white racists and (to) keep peace with their Black brothers" (1993:269–270).

When more than one hundred African American women took out a full-page ad in the *New York Times* supporting Hill, they received negative reactions from established black groups, all headed by men. Ad signers were dismayed, but not surprised, to find this act interpreted as black women's commitment to gender superseding racial solidarity (see Chrisman and Allen 1992; Morrison 1992). As a result, black feminists organized a group called African American Women in Defense of Ourselves to give black women their own forum to work toward gender and racial equality (Simmons 1993).

Another incident of being "left out" occurred when black women were asked to stay home rather than participate in the Million Man March organized by Louis Farrakhan. Although by far the response by black women was one of support for the "men-only" march, there were women leaders, such as Myrlie Evers-Williams, Mary Frances Berry, and Angela Davis, who protested their exclusion. Objectors pointed out that African American women share all too equally in racist attitudes and practices; yet, this march was an indication of the refusal on the part of Farrakhan (and perhaps black men in general) to support or accept "black women's partnership and leadership" (Belton 1995).

Within the women's movement, there was a notably different context to the separate organizing that emerged out of a racial schism in the National Women's Studies Association (NWSA). Members of the Women of Color Caucus and the Lesbian Caucus walked out of the 1990 conference after charging NWSA with racist practices.[9] NWSA canceled the meeting for 1991 and reorganized the following year with a new director, a woman of color. But the Women of Color Caucus held a separate conference to found the National Womanist/Feminist Women of Color Association, later called Sisters of Color International (SOCI). Sisters of Color International advertises that it is open to all women of color and identifies itself as an activist organization that brings together women of color in sisterhood (cad 1991; Footnotes 1994; Women of Color Association 1991).

In this case, there was less emphasis on creating a space for women of color than one of separating from white feminists. But what are the effects of charging other feminists with racism and homophobia, and why the rush to factional politics? Is it true, as Alice Kessler-Harris (1992:800–801) argues, that these types of actions have led to a "widespread and unspoken consensus that we are eating each other alive"?

Critical Discourse on Identity Politics

Social movements and social movement theories are reflections of social environments and, as discussed earlier, there has been a change in the social environment.[10] One change is what could be called the rise of a racial-ethnic cult, or at least a cultlike ambiance. For instance, African American scholar Ann duCille is discovering written texts and spoken words from the 1980s and 1990s that have led her to think of herself "as a kind of sacred text" (1994:592).

DuCille labels this phenomenon "the commodification of Otherness." In this conception, racial-ethnic groups are the spice—something new—a romantic vision that is really a figment of the imagination. She argues that this preoccupation with black women is an objectification and idealization imbedded in the present multicultural moment when racial-ethnic groups have become "politically correct, intellectually popular, and commercially precious sites of literary and historical inquiry" (duCille 1994:594). Paradoxically she finds herself both resenting white scholars for invading her research area and pleased by the sense that the black womanhood she has championed is part of the recognition now taking place. What is most interesting about her analysis is her probing look at the socially constructed rise of the primacy of black women in women's studies and the women's movement.

Others have also considered the implications of a socially constructed "pedestal" and found it problematic. Michelle Wallace points to "opportunistic Sapphires (and Kingfishes) on the lecture-circuit gravy train" (1995:8). Wallace is referring to the excesses she finds in the work of bell hooks, whom she is hesitant to criticize because black feminists (herself included) worry that exposing the "guilt mongering" of a prominent black woman scholar could "kill the goose that laid the golden egg" or (translated) "call into question the intentions of all other black feminists, and with it the precious hard-won academic appointments, anthologies, conferences, grants and travel budgets."

In another vein, James and Busia (1993) challenge the concept of a socially constructed black woman, African American identity, or as Patricia Hill Collins (1990) calls it, "black feminist thought." They argue that these socially constructed notions are based on the flawed assumption that there is a united community or a unitary perspective. Instead, they point out that there are black identities and that there is no more one black feminism than there is one feminism.

Similarly, the new emphasis in the gay and lesbian community on queer theory is another look at the social construction of group categories. Queer theory is a rebellion from separatism because it calls into question all categories upon which conventional notions of identity rely. It is opposed to identity politics "as a form of expressive pluralism where identity is reified—that is, understood to be represented in a self-evident and authentic way through one's body—and collectivity is reduced to group affiliation defined according to the standard of authentic embodiment" (Hennessy 1993:964).

Identity politics assumes a conforming identity, and queer theory explicitly critiques normativity, monolithic identities, and assimilationist policies (see Stein 1993). Instead, "queer" is used to signify diverse inclusive politics within the gay and lesbian community.[11] For example, when members of the Philadelphia Lesbian and Gay Community gathered to discuss the question "Who is a member of our group?" panel members represented Female Trouble, a s/m leather group; Transsexual Support, a group for male-to-female transsexuals; Invisible Queers, a group for female-to-male transsexuals; and Bi-Unity, an organization of bisexuals. The panel concluded that anyone who identifies as a sexual minority belongs to the Philadelphia Lesbian and Gay Community (Cwiek 1994).

More Discourse — The Ambivalence of Identity Politics

Arguments in favor of social movements' organizing around identity politics fall into two categories: (1) the value to the participants in life enhancement, pleasure, comfort, intellectual stimulation, and increasing self-esteem through association with others who have received similar treatment because of their skin color, sexual orientation, or ethnic origin; and (2) their resistance to associating with those whom they feel have contributed to their social denigration, isolation, and self-alienation.

The desire to join together with others like oneself, a form of affinity politics, has strong appeal. Of course, there are a number of problems and omissions in advocating this type of collective response. One of the most obvious is the knowledge that people have more than one social group characteristic. Women of color, for instance, have to fight both sexism within their racial/ethnic group, and race/class/ethnicity within white women's feminist groups. They are working from competing and intersecting identities, although the idea of living with "multiple identities" (as if you were a person with multiple personalities) is someone else's construct — it is lived, as Cherríe Moraga says, as "one identity; we're just made to think of it as multiple" (Moraga interview in Brandt 1993:30).

Yet, if all our various identities merge to become "the self," how do we choose which collective to join when each of our identity components has been subcontracted out into separate and exclusive groups? Either we broaden the category, in which case some of our identities might feel diminished, or we narrow the category and deny connectedness with others. In the case of the latter, we could make the group so particular that it encompasses all our identities, at least as we currently recognize and experience them, but our group might be very small and short lived.

And what about class — where is class situated in a "plurality of social identities and special oppressions" (Wood 1994:28)? What is a person to do, as Dorothy Allison (1993) asks, when she addresses all her identities — lesbian, incest victim, feminist, activist, sadomasochist — only to discover that being born into a condition of poverty has been the central fact of her life, and that class differences are not being adequately addressed in either the feminist or lesbian movements?

At its base, identity politics calls for organizing around your own oppression, a tendency that works to reduce coalition building and debate among diverse peoples. In the end, it operates to keep out new and challenging ideas (Willis 1994). There is even the possibility that participants can become so entrenched within their groups "that they may perpetuate the very outsider identity and status that they were originally protesting and seeking to overcome" (Gitlin 1993:176).

Ellen Willis (1992) cogently argues for ideological beliefs and shared principles as the basis for creating a political community. An ideological foundation is seen as necessary to lessen the tendency of diverting political struggles into efforts for self-transformation or to promote individual solutions to social problems (Kauffman 1990; Touraine 1988). Opposition to identity politics centers on depoliticalization theories and the loss of socialism as a forum for reorganizing human relations. It contends that once the concept of capitalism is replaced by a plurality of social identities, socialism as the antithesis to capitalism loses all meaning. As Ellen Meiksins Wood (1994:28) says, we can celebrate differences of race, culture, gender, life style—but how can we think of celebrating class differences? And what does that tell us about identity politics and structural analysis?

It is ironic that at the same time middle-class white progressives are advocating a mutually respectful and interactive multicultural society, racial ethnic groups are moving toward separatist policies where subgroup identity becomes the basis for legitimating one's politics (Willis 1992). Long-term social movement activists see this occurrence tied to a post-Marxist, postmodernist attempt to disaggregate people into separate identities, which disarms opposition to the existing order (Kauffman 1990; Wood 1994).

Identity politics is a social construct, just as social movements are socially constructed. Likewise, group identities and a collective conscience are socially derived. This means they can be reformulated. It can also mean, if we stretch the possibilities, that the self is, at least in some ways, the "architect of [its own] social reality (Swann 1985:100).[12] This is not to say that identity is solely a matter of choice; for instance, even though race is a social construct, it is imposed to create inferiority and to affirm a racial hierarchy. Still, if we are to recognize that we have many identities to choose from, all of which impact our life, then we have to acknowledge that identity politics is the process of privileging one over others. Further, we have to think about why we are privileging one (or a selective combination of more than one), and about the effect of doing so on the overall goals of social movement(s) we say we support. In discussing the consequences of privileging, Aldon Morris (1992:359) argues that "class consciousness, race consciousness, gender consciousness, and the like cannot be understood comprehensively or properly assessed as independent entities." But we are talking about identity *politics* and politics is about power. Thus, privileging and exclusion in identity-focused groups are also practices of power.

The Search for Community(ies)

The search for community is deeper and more widespread than any particular group. Yet, as deep and widespread as the search is, there is no community in most people's lives, including those involved in social movements.[13] Although this is a sad commentary on the state of our collective "communities," the importance of identity in the social movement organizing of the 1990s is also a reflection of a sociological and feminist success: a heightened social consciousness in peoples' lives.

The women's movement is a good example of social movement change, most notably through the effort to achieve a collective identity premised solely on gender connectedness, that is, the recognition of belonging to a group called women. That was what it was *before* identity politics declared an end to the hegemony of a gender bond that looked very much like a white, middle-class, heterosexual bond. For some time now, organized groups in the women's movement have been making a serious effort to create a more inclusive social movement, an effort that demands practices and theories that incorporate an analytic view of interrelated systems of domination. But let us not forget in the rush to be inclusive, how those movements that have historically claimed to be representative of "all the people," have not represented every group equally well. And it is their failures that led to the supposed crisis of identity politics we find ourselves in today.

I use the term *supposed crisis* because I am not sure if it is or is not. I am critical of identity politics because I believe that the movement and activists involved would benefit from united multicultural organizing efforts. Yet, I know separate organizing focused on particular social group characteristics is an important source of self-affirmation. And that racism, sexism, homophobia, classism, and ethnocentrism are forces that lead people to seek association with people the most like themselves. Ideally, prejudice and discrimination would not exist in social movements or society in general. But they do, and given that reality, who is to say what is best for any group of people except those people themselves? Organizations that think of themselves as feminist must be representative of and actively work for all women. And, if that happens, there is more likelihood of diversity in women's groups, coalition work, and the continuation of identity politics that work—that is, that draw women into activism for self-affirmation and for issues that reflect the many varied manifestations of their interests.

Lessons can be taken from opponents of identity politics who point out that politics in a multicultural society is alliance making, and thus "we ought to be building bridges" (Gitlin 1995:114). Differences among women do not mean there is no basis for unity. For progressive activists today, building bridges is the work of creating a dynamic society, one that is free of dominance relations. With that foundation, the crucial question may not be whether groups are inclusive or exclusive, whether they work in separatist arenas or participate in coalition politics. Instead (if those bridges get built), it is time for Charlotte Perkins Gilman's call to just get in the game.[14] And, borrowing from postmodern theory, perhaps the goal is not to find the answer but to keep the conversation going.

NOTES

For their suggestions and comments, I would like to thank Jill Brystydziensleu, Sondra Farganis, Hank Johnston, Alicja Muszynski, Janet Rosenberg, and Bruce Arrigo.

1. Sections of this paper were presented at the International Institute of Sociology, Trieste, Italy, 1995, and the American Sociological Association, Washington, DC, 1995. A longer and more theoretically oriented version of this paper can be found in Ryan 1997.

2. A twist on de Beavoir's concept of woman compared to man: "defined and differentiated with reference to man and not he with reference to her; she is the incidental, the inessential as opposed to the essential. He is the Subject, he is the Absolute—she is the Other" (de Beauvoir 1952:xix).

3. *Womanist,* rather than *feminist,* is the preferred term for some African American women.

4. For sex similarity arguments of the early movement, see Buhle and Buhle 1978; Cott 1987; DuBois 1978, 1981; Flexner 1975. More information on ERA campaigns can be found in Buechler 1990; Hoff-Wilson 1986; Mansbridge 1986; Rupp and Taylor 1987; Ryan 1992.

5. The social feminist position of the late-nineteenth and early-twentieth centuries can be found in Addams 1917; Lemons 1973; Gusfield 1970; Papachristou 1976. For a lesbian feminist essentialist position, see Daly 1978; Echols 1989; Johnson 1989; Johnston 1973.

6. Questions of race, ethnicity, and class also arose in the early years of the contemporary movement, and there were both separate racial-ethnic groups that formed and integrative efforts on the part of white-dominated groups. However, at that time, these divisions occupied a peripheral role in movement priorities. Later, in the 1980s, this emphasis changed, leaving race, ethnicity, and class (particularly race) as a major focus as well as a dividing issue within the movement.

7. Some lesbian separatists resist spending time with straight women because the latter give their energy to men. At all-women events, such as the Michigan Womyn's Music Festival, males are not allowed, including boy children over the age of three, and male-to-female transsexuals. Women of color find separatist strategies disregard their need to work with their racial-ethnic group.

8. Personal attacks on members of one's own group, known as trashing, were excessively practiced in the early years of the contemporary women's movement. The most extreme cases occurred in the radical feminist sector, particularly over sexual-orientation issues. Many of these groups self-destructed, yet the creation of a separatist culture did not eliminate personal attacks (see Echols 1989 and Ryan 1989 for more developed descriptions of trashing in the women's liberation movement).

9. For NWSA officers, such charges seemed unfounded in light of their expressed concern about issues of race and lesbianism, including organizational policies to address these issues. In particular, they point to the extra delegate seats designated for women of color and lesbians, which allowed them to have disproportionate representation on decision-making bodies (see Leidner 1991). In my discussion of this conflict, I am not interested in the "truth" of the charges. My interest is in the manner in which the issue was raised and the meaning underlying the actions that took place.

10. For instance, Vaclav Havel in his Fourth of July speech in Philadelphia upon accepting the Freedom and Liberty Prize spoke of how "the world of our experiences seems chaotic, disconnected, confusing" (quoted in Raspberry 1994:A22). His remedy was a return to religion. This prescription might make sense coming from someone living in a country where

religion had been banned for over half a century, but in the United States, religion is often the very essence of control over private life that people are joining social movements to overcome.

11. Of course, although it is inclusive for some, it is exclusive in other than gay, lesbian, bisexual, transsexual, and transgendered classifications. Moreover, there are gays and lesbians who do not wish to engage with this group, and who find the use of the word *queer* offensive.

12. For an example of the process of reformulating a collective gender consciousness, see Mueller 1987.

13. See, for instance, Claudia Card's challenge to the conception of a lesbian community (1995).

14. Quoted in Tax 1980, originally published in Charlotte Perkins Gilman, *The Forerunner,* vol. 1 (October 1910):25.

REFERENCES

Addams, Jane. 1917. "Why Women Should Vote." Pp. 110–129 in *The Blue Book, Woman Suffrage: History, Arguments and Results,* edited by F. Bjorhmand and A. Porritt. New York: National Woman Suffrage Publishing.

Allison, Dorothy. 1993. "A Question of Class." Pp. 46–60 in *Sisters, Sexperts, Queers: Beyond the Lesbian Nation,* edited by Arlene Stein. New York: Plume Books.

Bell-Scott, Patricia, ed. 1994. *Life Notes: Personal Writings by Contemporary Black Women.* New York: Norton.

Belton, Don. 1995. "No March Is Needed to Find 'Manhood.' " *The Philadelphia Inquirer* (16 October):A9.

Brandt, Kate. 1993. "Cherríe Moraga: A Question of Identity." Interview in *Happy Endings: Lesbian Writers Talk about Their Lives and Work,* by Kate Brandt. Tallahassee: Naiad Press.

Buechler, Steven M. 1990. *Women's Movements in the United States: Woman Suffrage, Equal Rights and Beyond.* New Brunswick: Rutgers University Press.

Buhle, Marijo, and Paul Buhle, eds. 1978. *The Concise History of Woman Suffrage: Selections from the Classic Work of Stanton, Anthony, Gage and Harper.* Urbana: University of Illinois Press.

cad. 1991. "NWSA Staff Resigns." *off our backs* 21 (Jan.):6.

Card, Claudia. 1995. *Lesbian Choices.* New York: Columbia University Press.

Chrisman, Robert, and Robert L. Allen, eds. 1992. *Court of Appeal: The Black Community Speaks Out on the Racial and Sexual Politics of Clarence Thomas vs. Anita Hill.* New York: Ballantine Books.

Collins, Patricia Hill. 1990. *Black Feminist Thought: Knowledge, Consciousness, and the Politics of Empowerment.* Boston: Unwin Hyman.

Cott, Nancy. 1987. *The Grounding of Modern Feminism.* New Haven: Yale University Press.

Cwiek, Timothy. 1994. "Who Is a Member of Our Community?" *Philadelphia Gay News* 18 (July 8–14):4.

Daly, Mary. 1978. *GynEcology: The Metaethics of Radical Feminism.* Boston: Beacon Press.

Davis, Angela. 1981. *Women, Race and Class.* New York: Random House.

Davis, Angela. 1993. "Black Nationalism: The Sixties and the Nineties." In *Black Popular Culture,* edited by Gina Dent. Seattle: Bay Press.

Davis, Katherine. 1981. "Introduction: What We Fear We Try to Keep Contained." Pp. 7–13 in *Coming to Power,* edited by SAMOIS. Boston: Alyson Publications.

de Beauvoir, Simone. 1952. *The Second Sex.* New York: Vintage Books.

Dill, Bonnie Thornton. 1983. "Race, Class and Gender: Prospects for an All-Inclusive Sisterhood." *Feminist Studies* 9:131–150.

DuBois, Ellen. 1978. *Feminism and Suffrage: The Emergence of an Independent Women's Movement in America, 1848–1869.* Ithaca: Cornell University Press.

DuBois, Ellen. 1981. *Elizabeth Cady Stanton, Susan B. Anthony: Correspondence, Writings, Speeches.* New York: Schocken Books.

duCille, Ann. 1994. "The Occult of True Black Womanhood: Critical Demeanor and Black Feminist Studies." *Signs: Journal of Women in Culture and Society* 19:591–629.

Echols, Alice. 1989. *Daring to Be Bad: Radical Feminism in America, 1967–1975.* Minneapolis: University of Minnesota Press.

Evans, Sara. 1979. *Personal Politics: The Roots of Women's Liberation in the Civil Rights Movement and the New Left.* New York: Vintage Books.

Fleming, Cynthia Griggs. 1993. "Black Women Activists and the Student Nonviolent Coordinating Committee: The Case of Ruby Doris Smith Robinson." *Journal of Women's History* 4:64–82.

Flexner, Eleanor. 1975 [1959]. *Century of Struggle: The Woman's Rights Movement in the United States.* Rev. ed. Cambridge: Belknap Press of Harvard University Press.

Footnotes. 1994. Organizational Notices. *American Sociological Association* 22 (May):14.

Franzen, Trisha. 1993. "Differences and Identities: Feminism and the Albuquerque Lesbian Community." *Signs: Journal of Women in Culture and Society* 18:891–906.

Garcia, Alma. 1989. "The Development of Chicana Feminist Discourse, 1970–1980." *Gender & Society* 3:217–238.

Giddings, Paula. 1988. *In Search of Sisterhood: Delta Sigma Theta and the Challenge of the Black Sorority Movement.* New York: Morrow.

Gitlin, Todd. 1993. "The Rise of 'Identity Politics': An Examination and a Critique." *Dissent* (Spring):172–177.

Gitlin, Todd. 1995. *The Twilight of Common Dreams: Why America Is Wracked by Culture Wars.* New York: Henry Holt.

Gusfield, Joseph R. 1970. *Symbolic Crusade: Status Politics and the American Temperance Movement.* Chicago: University of Illinois Press.

Hennessy, Rosemary. 1993. "Queer Theory: A Review of the *Differences* Special Issue and Wittig's *The Straight Mind*." *Signs: Journal of Women in Culture and Society* 18:964–973.

Hernton, Calvin. 1985. "The Sexual Mountain and Black Women Writers." *Black Scholar* 16:2–11.

Hoff-Wilson, Joan, ed. 1986. *Rights of Passage: The Past and Future of the ERA.* Bloomington: Indiana University Press.

hooks, bell. 1981. *Ain't I a Woman: Black Women and Feminism.* Boston: South End Press.

hooks, bell. 1984. *Feminist Theory from Margin to Center.* Boston: South End Press.

James, Stanlie M., and Abena P. Busia, eds. 1993. *Theorizing Black Feminisms: The Visionary Pragmatism of Black Women.* New York: Routledge.

Johnson, Sonia. 1989. *Wildfire: Igniting the She/Volution.* Albuquerque: Wildfire Books.

Johnston, Jill. 1973. *Lesbian Nation: The Feminist Solution.* New York: Simon & Schuster.

Kauffman, L. A. 1990 "The Anti-Politics of Identity." *Socialist Review* 90:67–80.

Kessler-Harris, Alice. 1992. "The View from Women's Studies." *Signs: Journal of Women in Culture and Society* 17:794–805.

King, Deborah K. 1988. "Multiple Jeopardy, Multiple Consciousness: The Context of a Black Feminist Ideology." *Signs: Journal of Women in Culture and Society* 14:42–72.

Krieger, Susan. 1982. "Lesbian Identity and Community: Recent Social Science Literature." *Signs: Journal of Women in Culture and Society* 8:91–108.

Krieger, Susan. 1983. *The Mirror Dance: Identity in a Women's Community*. Philadelphia: Temple University Press.

Leidner, Robin. 1991. "Stretching the Boundaries of Liberalism: Democratic Innovation in a Feminist Organization." *Signs: Journal of Women in Culture and Society* 16:263–289.

Lemons, J. Stanley. 1973. *The Woman Citizen: Social Feminism in the 1920s*. Chicago: University of Illinois Press.

Mansbridge, Jane J. 1986. *Why We Lost the ERA*. Chicago: University of Chicago Press.

McKay, Nellie Y. 1993. "Acknowledging Differences: Can Women Find Unity through Diversity?" Pp. 267–282 in *Theorizing Black Feminisms: The Visionary Pragmatism of Black Women,* edited by Stanlie M. James and Abena P. Busia. New York: Routledge.

Melucci, Alberto. 1989. *Nomads of the Present: Social Movements and Individual Needs in Contemporary Society*. Philadelphia: Temple University Press.

Moghadam, Valentine M., ed. 1994. *Identity Politics and Women: Cultural Reassertions and Feminisms in International Perspective*. Boulder: Westview Press.

Moraga, Cherríe. 1993. *The Last Generation: Prose and Poetry*. Boston: South End Press.

Moraga, Cherríe, and Gloria Anzaldúa, eds. 1983. *This Bridge Called My Back: Writings by Radical Women of Color*. 2d ed. New York: Kitchen Table, Women of Color Press.

Morris, Aldon D. 1984. *The Origins of the Civil Rights Movement: Black Communities Organizing for Change*. New York: Free Press.

Morris, Aldon D. 1992. "Political Consciousness and Collective Action." Pp. 351–373 in *Frontiers in Social Movement Theory,* edited by Aldon D. Morris and Carol McClurg Mueller. New Haven: Yale University Press.

Morrison, Toni, ed. 1992. *Race-ing Justice, En-gendering Power: Essays on Anita Hill, Clarence Thomas, and the Construction of Social Reality*. New York: Pantheon.

Mueller, Carol McClurg. 1987. "Collective Consciousness, Identity Transformation, and the Rise of Women in Public Office in the United States." In *The Women's Movements of the United States and Western Europe: Consciousness, Political Opportunity, and Public Policy,* edited by Mary Fainsod Katzenstein and Carol McClurg Mueller. Philadelphia: Temple University Press.

Papachristou, Judith. 1976. *Women Together*. New York: Alfred A. Knopf.

Paz, Juana Maria Gonzalez. 1994. "Commentary: Psychological Warfare." *off our backs* 14 (May):10.

Phelan, Shane. 1989. *Identity Politics: Lesbian Feminism and the Limits of Community*. Philadelphia: Temple University Press.

Raspberry, William. 1994. "Vaclav Havel on Freedom." *The Philadelphia Inquirer* (4 July): A22.

Roseneil, Sasha. 1995. *Disarming Patriarchy: Feminism and Political Action at Greenham*. Buckingham, UK: Open University Press.

Rupp, Leila J., and Verta Taylor. 1987. *Survival in the Doldrums: The American Women's Rights Movement, 1945–1960*. New York: Oxford University Press.

Russell, Kathy, Midge Wilson, and Ronald Hall. 1992. *The Color Complex*. New York: Harcourt Brace Jovanovich.

Ryan, Barbara. 1989. "Ideological Purity and Feminism: The U.S. Women's Movement from 1966 to 1975." *Gender & Society* 3:239–257.

Ryan, Barbara. 1992. *Feminism and the Women's Movement: Dynamics of Change in Social Movement Ideology and Activism.* New York: Routledge.

Ryan, Barbara. 1997. "How Much Can I Divide Thee, Let Me Count the Ways: Identity Politics in the Women's Movement." *Humanity and Society* 21, no. 1 (February):67–83.

Scales-Trent, Judy. 1995. *Notes of a White Black Woman: Race, Color, Community.* University Park: Pennsylvania State University Press.

Simmons, Rose. 1993. "Black Women in Shadows of Black Men, White Women." *The Philadelphia Inquirer* (31 January): E1, E6.

Smith, Barbara. 1982. Review of *Ain't I a Woman: Black Women and Feminism* by bell hooks. *The New Women's Times Feminist Review* 9:24.

Spelman, Elizabeth. 1988. *Inessential Woman: Problems of Exclusion in Feminist Thought.* Boston: Beacon Press.

Stein, Arlene, ed. 1993. *Sisters, Sexperts, Queers: Beyond the Lesbian Nation.* New York: Plume Books.

Swann, W. B. 1985. "The Self as Architect of Social Reality." In *The Self and Social Life,* edited by B. R. Schlenker. New York: McGraw-Hill.

Taylor, Verta, and Nicole C. Raeburn. 1995. "Identity Politics as High-Risk Activism: Career Consequences for Lesbian, Gay, and Bisexual Sociologists." *Social Problems* 42 (May): 252–270.

Taylor, Verta, and Leila J. Rupp. 1993. "Women's Culture and Lesbian Feminist Activism: A Reconsideration of Cultural Feminism." *Signs: Journal of Women in Culture and Society* 19:33–61.

Taylor, Verta, and Nancy Whittier. 1992. "Collective Identity in Social Movement Communities: Lesbian Feminist Mobilization." Pp. 104–129 in *Frontiers in Social Movement Theory,* edited by Aldon Morris and Carol McClurg Mueller. New Haven: Yale University Press.

Tax, Meredith. 1980. "The United Front of Women." *Monthly Review* 32:30–48.

Touraine, Alain. 1988. *Return of the Actor: Social Theory in Postindustrial Society.* Minneapolis: University of Minnesota Press.

Wallace, Michelle. 1995. "Art for Whose Sake?" Review of *Art on My Mind: Visual Politics,* by bell hooks. In *The Women's Review of Books* 13 (October):8.

Whisman, Vera. 1993. "Identity Crises: Who Is a Lesbian, Anyway?" Pp. 47–60 in *Sisters, Sexperts, Queers: Beyond the Lesbian Nation,* edited by Arlene Stein. New York: Penguin Books.

Willis, Ellen. 1992. *No More Nice Girls: Countercultural Essays.* Hanover, NH: University Press of New England.

Willis, Ellen. 1994. "Great Expectations: When Feminists Review Feminists." *Women's Review of Books* 11 (May):14–15.

Women of Color Association. 1991. "Speaking for Ourselves from the Women of Color Association." *Women's Review of Books* 8 (Fall):27–29.

Wood, Ellen Meiksins. 1994. "Identity Crisis." *In These Times* (13 June): 28–29.

Chapter Thirty-four

If Not with Others, How?

Adrienne Rich

I have been reflecting on what feels so familiar about all this; to identify actively as a woman and ask what that means; to identify actively as a Jew and ask what that means. It is feminist politics—the efforts of women trying to work together as women across sexual, class, racial, ethnic, and other lines—that have pushed me to look at the starved Jew in myself; finally, to seek a path to that Jewishness still unsatisfied, still trying to define its true homeland, still untamed and unsuburbanized, still wandering in the wilderness. Over and over, the work of Jewish feminists has inspired and challenged me to educate myself, culturally and politically and spiritually, from Jewish sources, to cast myself into the ancient and turbulent river of disputation which is Jewish culture.

Jews, like women, exist everywhere, our existence often veiled by history; we have been "the Jewish question" or "the woman question" at the margins of Leftist politics, while Right Wing repressions have always zeroed in on us. We have—women and Jews—been the targets of biological determinism and persistent physical violence. We have been stereotyped both viciously and sentimentally by others and have often taken these stereotypes into ourselves. Of course, the two groups interface: women are Jews, and Jews are women; but what this means for the Jewish vision, we are only beginning to ask. We exist everywhere under laws we did not make; speaking a multitude of languages; excluded by law and custom from certain spaces, functions, resources associated with power; often accused of wielding too much power, of wielding dark and devious powers. Like Black and other dark-skinned people, Jews and women have haunted white Western thought as Other, as fantasy, as projected obsession.

My hope is that the movement we are building can further the conscious work of turning Otherness into a keen lens of empathy, that we can bring into being a politics based on concrete, heartfelt understanding of what it means to be Other. We are women and men, *Mischlings* (of mixed parentage) and the sons and daughters of rabbis, Holocaust survivors, freedom fighters, teachers, middle- and working-class Jews. We are gay and straight and bisexual, older and younger, differently

Reprinted by permission of the author and W. W. Norton & Company, Inc., from *Blood, Bread, and Poetry: Selected Prose 1979–1985* by Adrienne Rich. New York: Norton, 1986. Copyright © 1986 by Adrienne Rich.

able and temporarily able-bodied; and we share an unquenched hope for the survival and sanity of the human community. Believing that no single people can survive being only for itself, we want a base from which to act on our hope.

I feel proud to be identified as a Jew among Jews, not simply a progressive among progressives, a feminist among feminists. And I ask myself, What does that mean? What is this pride in tribe, family, culture, heritage? Is it a feeling of being better than those outside the tribe? The medieval philosopher Judah ha-Levi claimed a hierarchy of all species, places on earth, races, families, and even languages. In this hierarchy, the land, language, and people of Israel are naturally superior to all others. As a woman, I reject all such hierarchies.

Then is pride merely a cloak I pull around me in the face of anti-Semitism, in the face of the contempt and suspicion of others? Do I invoke pride as a shield against my enemies, or do I find its sources deeper in my being, where I define myself for myself?

Difficult questions for any people who for centuries have met with derogation of identity. Pride is often born in the place where we refuse to be victims, where we experience our own humanity under pressure, where we understand that we are not the hateful projections of others but intrinsically ourselves. Where does this take us? It helps us fight for survival, first of all, because we know, from somewhere, we deserve to survive. "I am not an inferior life form" becomes "There is sacred life, energy, plenitude in me and in those like me you are trying to destroy." And if, in the example of others like me, I learn not only survival but the plenitude of life, if I feel linked by a texture of values, history, words, passions to people long dead or whom I have never met, if I celebrate these linkages, is this what I mean by pride? Or am I really talking about love?

Pride is a tricky, glorious, double-edged feeling. I don't feel proud of everything Jews have done or thought, nor of everything women have done or thought. The poet Irena Klepfisz has confronted in her long poem "Bashert" the question of sorting out a legacy without spurning any of it, a legacy that includes both courage and ardor, and the shrinking of the soul under oppression, the damages suffered. In any one like me, I have to see mirrored my own shrinkings of soul, my own damages.

Yet I must make my choices, take my positions according to my conscience and vision now. To separate from parts of a legacy in a conscious, loving, and responsible way in order to say "This is frayed and needs repair; that no longer serves us; this is still vital and usable" is not to spurn tradition, but to take it very seriously. Those who refuse to make these distinctions—and making distinctions has been a very Jewish preoccupation—those who suppress criticism of the Jewish legacy suppress further creation.

As an American Jew, I fear the extent to which both Americans and Israelis, in their national consciousness, are captives of denial. Denial, first, of the existence of the peoples who, in the creation of both nations, have been swept aside, their communities destroyed, pushed into reservations and camps, traumatized by superior might calling itself destiny. I fear that this denial, this unaccountability for acts which are still continuing, is a deep infection in the collective life and conscience of both nations.

America wants to forget the past, and the past in the present; and one result of that was Bitburg. Israeli denial is different. Years ago, I remember seeing, with great emotion, on the old Jerusalem—Tel Aviv road, rusted tanks left from the 1948 war, on one of which was painted "If I forget thee, O Jerusalem . . ." But Palestinian memory has been violently obliterated. I fear for the kind of "moral autism" (Amos Oz's phrase) out of which both the United States and Israel, in their respective capacities of power, have made decisions leading to physical carnage and to acute internal disequilibrium and suffering.

I say this here, knowing my words will be understood or at least not heard as anti-Semitism. But many of us have experienced a censorship in American Jewish communities, where dissent from official Israeli policies and actions is rebuked and Jewish critical introspection is silenced. "The armored and concluded mind" (Muriel Rukeyser's phrase[1] is not what the Jewish mind has been overall. Torah itself is not a closed system; we have been a people unafraid of argument, a people of many opinions. Our forebears were instructed to commit suicide rather than idolatry; yet Israel has become a kind of idol for many American Jews. Israel is not seen and cared about as an unfinished human effort, harrowed and flawed and full of gashes between dreams and realities, but as an untouchable construct: The Place Where Jews Can Be Safe. I think that the taboo on dissent among American Jews damages all Jews who, in the wake of the Holocaust and the birth of a Jewish state, are trying to imagine a Jewish future and a Jewish consciousness that does not stop with Hillel's first question.[2]

The word *safe* has two distinct connotations: one, of a place in which we can draw breath, rest from persecution or harassment, bear witness, lick our wounds, feel compassion and love around us rather than hostility or indifference. The safety of the mother's lap for the bullied child, of the battered-women's shelter, the door opened to us when we need a refuge. Safety in this sense implies a place to gather our forces, a place to move from, not a destination. But there is also the safety of the "armored and concluded mind," the safety of the barricaded door which will not open for the beleaguered Stranger, the psychotic safety of the underground nuclear-bomb shelter, the walled and guarded crime-proof condominium, the safety bought with guns and money at no matter what cost, the safety bought and sold at the cost of shutting up. And this safety becomes a dead end in the mind and in the mapping of a life or a collective vision. I want to say that though the longing for safety has been kept awake in us by centuries of danger, mere safety has not been the central obsession of the Jewish people. It has not been an ultimate destination. How to live in compassion, pursue justice, create a society in which "what is hateful to you, do not do to your neighbor," how to think, praise, celebrate life—these have been fundamental to Jewish vision. Even if strayed from, given lip service, even if in this vision Jewish women have remained Other, even if many Jews have acted on this vision as social reformists and radicals without realizing how Jewish— though not exclusively Jewish—a vision it is. And I don't believe that the Jewish genius has completed itself on this earth: I think it may be on the verge of a new, if often painful and disorienting, renascence.

All of us here live in two dissonant worlds. There is the world of this community and others like it in America: Jewish and gentile, men and women, Black and brown and red and yellow and white, old and young, educated in books and educated in what Tillie Olsen has named "the college of work," in poverty or in privilege—the communities of those who are trying to "turn the century," in Black activist musician Bernice Reagon's words.[3] In this world of vision and struggle, there is still myopia, division, anti-Semitism, racism, sexism, heterosexism. But there is also passion, and persistence, and memory, and the determination to build what we need, and the refusal to buy safety or comfort by shutting up. We affirm the diversity out of which we come, the clashes and pain we experience in trying to work together, the unglamorous ongoing labors of love and necessity.

And there is that other world, that America whose history is Disneyland, whose only legitimized passion is white male violence, whose people are starving for literal food and also for intangible sustenance they cannot always name, whose opiate is denial. As progressives, we live in this America, too, and it affects us. Even as we try to change it, it affects us. This America that has never mourned or desisted in or even acknowledged the original, deliberate, continuing genocide of the indigenous American people now called the Indians. This America that has never acknowledged or mourned or desisted in the ordinary, banal murderousness of its racism—murderous of the individuals and groups targeted by skin color, and murderous of the spiritual integrity of all of us.

As Jews, we have tried to comprehend the losses encompassed by the Holocaust, not just in terms of numbers or communities or families or individuals, but in terms of unknown potentialities—voices, visions, spiritual and ethical—of which we and the world are irreparably deprived. As American Jews, our losses are not from the Holocaust alone. We are citizens of a country deprived of the effective moral, ethical, and aesthetic visions of those whom white racism has tried to quench in both subtle and violent ways; whose capacity, nonetheless, to insist on their humanity, to persevere and resist, to educate their fellow citizens in political reality, to carry their "message for the world," as W. E. B. Du Bois called it, should be supported and celebrated by Jews everywhere.

For progressive American Jews, racism as it exists here in America, around and also within us, in the air we breathe, has both an ethical and a pragmatic urgency. We cannot continue to oppose the racism of Kahane and his like or of South African apartheid and take less oppositional stands on the malignancy of racism here where we live. The depth of the work we do depends on its rootedness—in our knowledge of who we are and also of where we are—a country which has used skin color as the prime motive for persecution and genocide, as Europe historically used religion. As Elly Bulkin indicates in a mind-stretching essay, "Hard Ground": "In terms of anti-Semitism and racism, a central problem is how to acknowledge their differences without contributing to the argument that one is important and the other is not, one is worthy of serious attention and the other is not."[4] It is difficult to move beyond these polarizations, but we are learning to do so and will, I believe, continue to help each other learn.

We must continue to insist that the concepts of Jewish survival and "what is good for the Jews" have an expanding, not a constricting, potential. I long to see the widest range of progressive issues defined as Jewish issues everywhere in this country. I long to see the breaking of encrustations of fear and caution, habits of thought engrained by centuries of endangerment and by the spiritual sterility of white mainstream America. I long to see Jewish energy, resources, passion, our capacity to celebrate life pouring into a gathering of thousands of American Jews toward "turning the century." I believe the potential is there; I long to see it stirred into glowing life. I believe we may be at the watershed for such a movement. And I would like to end by reading Hillel's three questions, which can never really be separated, and by adding a fourth, which is implicit in what we are doing:

> If I am not for myself, who will be for me?
> If I am only for myself, what am I?
> If not now, when?
>
> If not with others, how?

NOTES

1. *The Collected Poems of Muriel Rukeyser* (New York: McGraw-Hill, 1978), 102.

2. "If I am not for myself, who will be for me?" See *Sayings of the Fathers, or Pirke Aboth, the Hebrew Text, with a New English Translation and a Commentary by the Very Rev. Dr. Joseph H. Hertz* (New York: Behrman House, 1945), 25.

3. Bernice Reagon, "Coalition Politics: Turning the Century," in *Home Girls: A Black Feminist Anthology,* ed. Barbara Smith (New York: Kitchen Table/Women of Color Press, 1983), 356–68.

4. Elly Bulkin, "Hard Ground: Jewish Identity, Racism, and Anti-Semitism," in Elly Bulkin, M. B. Pratt, and B. Smith, *Yours in Struggle: Three Feminist Perspectives on Anti-Semitism and Racism* (Brooklyn, N.Y.: Long Haul, 1984; distributed by Firebrand Books, Ithaca, N.Y.).

Chapter Thirty-five

What Is Difficult Can Be Done at Once. What Is Impossible Takes a Little Longer
The Beijing Conference

Priscilla Sears

"China Braces for Feminist Streakers and Others." The Louisville *Times* ran this headline about the Third UN Conference on Women, the largest gathering of women in the history of the world. Thirty to fifty thousand women from all but three countries in the world met to discuss peace, equality, and sustainable development, yet media coverage often focused on trivia such as the report that the Chinese police had stocked up on sheets to cover the streakers, nude women being a fearsome sight likely to foment disturbances.

The Chinese police wasted their money. I saw women in robes and veils and gowns and habits and saris and dashikis and Mao uniforms, but none nude, unless the Buddhist nuns with shaved heads counted. Another newspaper characterized the meeting as a "Middle Class Coffee Klatch," another as "Bitches Bitching." On National Public Radio the correspondent to Beijing from the *Manchester Guardian*, who was also a guest editor at NPR, said that he couldn't see what First and Third World women had in common. After all, he said, First World women's notion of oppression is the continued publication of *Playboy*.

Yes, it is true that the middle class was well represented, but 400 women from Africa and 600 from India had received grants from the "Send a Sister to Beijing" program and other funding agencies. An estimated 200 women paid for their trips by selling goods at the meeting. The agenda, furthermore, was not dominated by middle class concerns.

The know-nothing from the *Manchester Guardian* should have had his mouth washed out with soap and his press pass revoked. What did we women have in common? Rape, domestic violence, unequal rights, discrimination in the workplace, inequitable opportunity, second class education, oppression by the patriarchy? We have in common the "reality" of the equation: difference—threat or danger or competition or war. Audre Lorde, whose spirit was in Beijing, has said:

Reprinted by permission from *NWSA JOURNAL* 8, no. 1 (Spring 1986): 174–85. Copyright © Indiana University Press.

I am a lesbian woman of color whose children eat regularly because I work in a university. If their full bellies make me fail to recognize my commonality with a woman of color whose children do not eat regularly because she cannot find work, who has no children because her insides are rotted from home abortions and sterilization, if I fail to recognize the lesbian who chooses not to have children, the woman who remains closeted because her homophobic community is her only life support, the woman who chooses silence instead of another death, if I fail to recognize them as other faces of myself, then I am contributing not only to each of their oppressions but also to my own, and the anger which stands between us must be used for clarity and mutual empowerment, not for evasion by guilt or for further separation. I am not free while any woman is unfree, even when her shackles are very different from my own. And I am not free as long as one person of Color remains chained. Nor is any one of you. (Lorde 72)

There were many women with many differences in Huairou and Beijing. (This really requires a sprawling epic poem, but I can only manage a Whitmanesque list.) Princesses, queenmothers from Africa, members of the German parliament, actor Sally Field, the vice presidents of Vietnam and Uganda, aboriginal Australians, Buddhist nuns, actor and activist Jane Fonda, Navajos, the president of Iceland, the prime minister of Pakistan, refugees from Bosnia, communist party officials, women from Chernobyl, Muslim women, Yoga nuns in fluorescent orange robes, members of the Israeli parliament, Sweet Honey in the Rock, Wangari Matthai, Winnie Mandella, Bahai women, prostitutes from Bangkok and LA, women sweeping the streets with stick brooms wearing Mao dingies and baseball caps that said "West Point." Japanese women in shoes that make then shuffle. Bella Abzug (she told reporters that she had two colds—one from Beijing and one from Huairou and announced that we women were making modest demands: "We want 50 percent of everything."). Betty Friedan was there. And Tibetan women marching down a wide boulevard singing "We Shall Overcome." The woman standing next to me on the sidewalk, a stranger, began to cry and I, too, and then she embraced me. She told me later she was a member of the Israeli Parliament. The whole wide boulevard designed for tanks and the People's Parades, was full of women singing and crying. Women from Chernobyl revealed the truth about the health effects of the accident—the incidence of leukemia was up about 70 percent, and birth defects had increased exponentially. The contaminated food from Chernobyl had been sent to Uganda and Lebanon and probably elsewhere. There were women from Fiji, from Peru, from the North Pole. From ghettos. From refugee camps. Mother Teresa couldn't come at the last moment, but she sent a message. Hillary Clinton. While much of the media was characterizing the meeting as a sort of mud-wrestling event, "we"—with all the antecedents I've mentioned—were talking about peace and human security, education, health, the girl child, human rights, the environment, religion, technology, medicine, art, culture, race—talking about "the world through women's eyes."

And yes, as the media suggested, it was not a Sunday school picnic. It rained. It was muddy. Some people got their visas late. Some human rights activists were denied visas. Some Tibetan exiles were issued visas, but they were afraid the Chinese would detain them. The American Embassy escorted them to their planes and put them aboard. Some of the accommodations were not up to North American standards. I had a concrete cubicle furnished with a board disguised as a bed, a pillow stuffed with peas, a communal toilet that flushed sometimes, a mirror, four coat hangers, an overhead light. A sign warned against drinking the tap water, and I brushed my teeth with orange soda. The food wasn't familiar: breakfast consisted of cold French fries, soup, greens, steamed buns, and tea. (For the first few days, only tea was available. When the enterprising Chinese discovered coffee was wanted, coffee stands sprang up like mushrooms.)

And yes, there was pushing and shoving among the four thousand or so women who were left out in the rain outside of the auditorium where Hillary Clinton spoke. (The venue was changed from an outdoor theater to an auditorium because of the weather.) She had been delayed, and the speech took place at 11:00 instead of 9:30. But at 10:00 a semi-miracle happened. A black gospel singer from Anchorage Alaska, Shirley Springer, got up on the stage and said she knew that people were cold and wet and tired—and mad. She said, "I'd be mad. Plenty mad. But I guarantee you that in fifteen minutes you'll feel better. If you don't, I've decided on my own that you will get your money back."

Then Shirley began to sing in this voice that hit you in your solar plexus. She sang the theme song of the meeting. The refrain was:

> We're moving forward
> We're moving forward
> We're moving forward
> And we're never turning back

We all sang. We invented different verses:

> North and South together—We are moving forward
> We are all sisters—We are moving forward
> We shall not be denied—We are moving forward
> Let us thank our mothers—We are moving forward
> East and West together—We are moving forward

And soon everyone was not only singing but standing—Muslim women in black robes, women in shorts, Chinese women, Australian women, Polish women, holding one another's hands above their heads—standing and singing, sometimes humming if they didn't know the words. There was so much transformative energy, I think we could have levitated the Pentagon. And nobody got their money back.

This was a very hard act to follow. Before Hillary Clinton appeared, the audience chanted "We Want Shirley." But once Hillary did appear, dry, unlike Donna Shalala and the Secret Service who were soaked, the crowd gave her a standing ovation.

And yes, as the press reported, there were many sessions devoted to problems more prevalent among the middle class. But to those who think that Western middle class women dominated the meeting and met Third World women with noblesse oblige, let me tell you about the Grameen bank in Bangladesh that serves some of the poorest women in the world and serves as a powerful example for the West. The Grameen Bank in Bangladesh specializes in lending small amounts of money, often ten to twenty dollars, to women in need. The bank agent comes round on his/her bicycle, distributes the money, and returns weekly for payments, often given in pennies. These women borrow so they can buy a milk cow or chickens or a sewing machine with which they can help support their families, their communities, and their countries. Here is development that is local, ecologically minded, rural, agricultural, for everyday people, and based on cooperation. Their repayment rate is 97 percent. They often repay within one year, and they invest their money well. In Uganda the money is lent to groups of five women. Part of the interest they pay is put into a collective savings account. As the women pay interest, they accumulate capital.

Hillary Clinton announced that the Clinton Administration is following this Third World model both by implementing micro-economic enterprises within the US and by grants and loans to Third World banks.

And yes, it is also true that some parts of the media didn't report much of anything about this conference. No news. Silence. Even though every day in Huairou the "fomenters of disturbance" and the "agents of confusion" as some of the Chinese press called us, had 320 lectures, workshops, discussions, and panels. Every night, while I was passed out on my board in the bunker, sweating and dreaming about a brave world and about refrigeration, entertainment was provided by different countries and regions—everything from high wire balancing acts (wonderful symbolic reverberations) to Indian dancing.

I saw only one bumper sticker. (In fact there were only a few bumpers.) The sticker said "Feminism or Death." That was the conclusion that many of these sessions suggested. We know from Cairo that overpopulation is the primary cause of ecologic failure, and we learned that the only consistently successful means of reducing overpopulation is the education of women. We know that ecofeminism is crucial to establishing a sustainable world. Recent studies by Riane Eisler suggest that the countries in which the status of women is higher the quality of life for all tends to be higher. The measures for the quality of life included: level of health care, life span, quality of schools, the economy, political and human rights, and environmental protection. Eisler and David Loye at the Center for Partnership Studies say that the US ranks high in the areas of social equality for women, life expectancy, and human rights, but it is among the lowest for infant and maternal mortality and in participation by women in government—5.3 percent in contrast to 34.4 percent in Norway and 33.9 percent in Cuba.

When Hillary Clinton came to Huairou, she talked about the importance of the non-governmental agencies in improving the quality of life for all. She said to the 1,500 people in the auditorium: "You will be the key players in determining whether or not this conference goes beyond rhetoric and actually does something to improve the lives of women and children. The faces of the women who are here mirror the faces of the millions who are not. It is our responsibility, those of us who have been able to attend this Conference and the NGO Forum, to make sure that the voices that go unheard will be heard. . . . We know that much of what we do, we are doing not for ourselves but we are doing for our daughters, our nieces, our granddaughters. We are doing it because we hope that the changes we work for will take root and flower in their lives."

I agree that those of us at grass roots level are key players. I myself have made or remade commitments to my teaching in women's studies, in lectures about this meeting to small groups to helping with an effort to introduce a foreign study program in women's studies at my college, and to contributing in any way I can to giving what Adrienne Rich says is the greatest gift one woman can give another, the gift of extending her sense of possibility.

Many women at this conference gave me the gift of increasing my sense of individual possibility. These women were sometimes in the front of the room giving a paper, beside me on the bus, across from me at the dinner table, at the next stall in the ladies' room, or singing with me at the workshops given by Sweet Honey in the Rock. These singers inspired all of us with their power, their beauty, their political activism, their dignity. At the final concert they sang a freedom song, "By the River of Babylon":

> By the river of Babylon
> Where we sat down,
> And where we wept
> As we remembered Zion.
>
> The wicked carried us away
> And required of us a song.
> But how could we sing our song
> In a strange land?
>
> May the words of my mouth
> And the meditations of my heart
> Be acceptable in thy sight
> Oh my sisters.

I'd like to mention just two of the many women, the sisters, at this conference who increased my sense of possibility. Anabell Watson, an English woman from an organization called Hazelwood House, a small philanthropic agency, received in 1993 an invitation from a Bosnian women's organization to a Peace Conference of Women of the World. She and four other English women went. They ranged in age from 25 to 72, and one woman had had two hip replacements. They were able to drive most of the way, but in order to get into Sarajevo they had to walk through a small, one way tunnel, about five feet and four inches high. The woman with two hip replacements thought she might not make it. The rest reassured her that they would carry her. When they came out of the tunnel, many Bosnian soldiers were waiting to pass through. They gave the women a great cheer and shouted "Welcome to Hell." As they walked onward toward the city they came under bombardment and sniper fire. The next day the First Peace Conference of Women of the World was attended by five women from England and thirty-six from the former Yugoslavia. The meeting was held in the beautiful National Theater, despite the fact that half of the roof was missing. (I got wind of this here, but I couldn't find anyone who knew anything about it. Many women suggested that we'll be able to keep one another informed and by-pass the media through the Internet.) Anabell Watson, one of the English women, said "What we took in was food, medical supplies, information, and ourselves—we were wonderfully focused by danger and humbled by what we met."

A Bosnian refugee in Huairou described the horrors that this group of women from England had heard about in Sarajevo: sons forced to try to rape their mothers in the presence of the family; soldiers raping young girls, the family forced to watch, children tortured with their parents present, unable to intervene.

"What we took out," Anabell continued, "was a few refugees, messages, a strengthened resolve to continue and expand the work of this group. And to bring something unexpected that many women had asked for: music." As they left Sarajevo, they saw a sign for them. It said, "Don't forget us."

They didn't forget. Last year 75 women attended the conference in Sarajevo, women from the United States, England, Germany, Italy, France. They met with politicians, military leaders, and medical authorities. They redoubled their efforts. "We did," Anabelle said, "what we do best; we made it work." They didn't forget.

The second example of the gift of possibility took place at a meditation meeting attended by witches, Muslims, Christians, Jews, Buddhists and others. We were in a small, crowded, concrete room that was part of a middle school complex. The purpose was to to rest and recover. (The temperature on average was 95 degrees and the humidity was, by my temperate zone calculation, also 95 percent.) We sang "Kali Ma," a Hindu chant. We sat quietly, speaking names or phrases into silence if we wanted, and then the leader asked us to choose a partner and tell her anything we wanted for five minutes and she would do the same. Neither of the listening partners was to make any response. A woman from South Africa in an orange and gold dashiki and I became partners. At first she told me the things you would tell a stranger: she lived in the green hills among beautiful lakes. She had three children. After a long pause she said, "My daughter died of poisoning in a police station; my son was shot after a demonstration." She began to cry. I began to cry. At the end we exchanged addresses. I kissed her goodbye. She said, "Don't forget me."

I won't forget.

I hope you will not forget that what is difficult may be done at once; what is impossible may take a little longer. I hope you won't forget that difference needn't mean division or competition or war. I hope you won't forget that between the points of difference, a creative spark may surge, and that this requires willingness to meet and to speak. As Audre Lorde says, "The fact that we are here [we in

Huairou, we in Beijing, and we in NWSA], and that I speak these words is an attempt to break the silence and bridge some of the differences between us, for it is not difference which immobilizes us, but silence. And there are so many silences to be broken" (Lorde 42).

REFERENCE

Lorde, Audre. *Sister Outsider*. Trumansburg, New York, Crossings Press, 1984.

Contributors

Bernice McNair Barnett is Assistant Professor of Sociology and Educational Policy Studies at the University of Illinois at Urbana-Champaign and a Faculty Affiliate in the Afro-American Studies and Research Program, and Women's Studies General Counsel. She has presented papers and published articles in a variety of sociological and women's studies conferences and journals.

Julie Bettie is Assistant Professor of Sociology and an affiliate of Women's Studies at the University of California, Santa Cruz, where she teaches courses in feminist theory and cultural studies. She is the author of *Women without Class: Race, Identity, and Performance among White and Mexican-American Youth* (forthcoming). She has also published on class as a cultural identity among working-class white and Mexican American high school girls in *Signs* (2000) and *Social Text* (1995).

Eileen Bresnahan has been a radical feminist activist for more than a decade. She was formerly a collective member, editor, and writer of *Big Mama Rag Feminist Newsjournal;* a collective member, editor, writer, and reader of "Women Everywhere" Feminist Radio Collective; and a founding member of the Denver Feminist Organizing Committee. She was also a founding member of the Board of Directors of the University of South Florida Women's Center, in Tampa, where she was born. She has been employed as a postal worker, a printing press operator, a taxi driver, and a hospital worker. She earned her Ph.D. in political science from Yale University and is Assistant Professor and Director of Women's Studies at Colorado College in Colorado Springs with her partner, Kate Sharp, and five disagreeable cats.

Hazel V. Carby is Chair of the Department of African American Studies and Professor of American Studies at Yale University where she has taught since 1989. She has published articles in a number of journals, and her books include *Reconstructing Womanhood* (1987); *Race Men* (1998); and *Cultures in Babylon* (1999). She is currently writing a history of radical black women in the 1930s and '40s.

The Combahee River Collective is a collective of Black feminists who began meeting in 1974. They have been involved in the process of defining and clarifying their politics, while at the same time doing political work within their own group and in coalition with other progressive organizations and movements. The most general statement of their politics is that they are committed to struggling against interlocking racial, sexual, heterosexual, and class oppressions.

June Corman is Associate Professor of Sociology and Past Director of the Women's Studies Program at Brock University in St. Catharines, Ontario, Canada. She has volunteered on the Niagara Region International Women's Day Committee since 1992.

Ann duCille is Chair of the African American Studies Program and Director of the Center for African American Studies at Wesleyan University. She is author of *The Coupling Convention: Sex, Text, and Tradition in Black Women's Fiction* (1993) and *Skin Trade* (1996). Her current research focuses on the black middle class and on representations of race in popular culture.

Diane L. Fowlkes is Professor of Political Science and Director of the Women's Studies Institute at Georgia State University. Her next projects include an examination of the meanings of interdisciplinarity in women's studies and a critical reconstruction of women's movements in the United States through an examination of 1960s and 1970s writings by white women and women of color.

Trisha Franzen is Director of the Anna Howard Shaw Center for Women's Studies and co-chairs the Center for the Interdisciplinary Study of Ethnicity, Gender and Global Issues at Albion College. She received her M.A. and Ph.D. from the University of New Mexico. Her book *Spinsters and Lesbians: Independent Womanhood in the United States* was published by New York University Press in 1996. She is currently researching Anna Howard Shaw. She serves on the Albion Board of Education.

Marilyn Frye teaches Philosophy and Women's Studies at Michigan State University. She is author of *The Politics of Reality: Essays in Feminist Theory* (1983); *Willful Virgin: Essays in Feminism* (1992); *Feminist Interpretations of Mary Daly* (edited with Sarah Lucia Hoagland; 2000), and many articles. She is co-owner/manager of Bare Bone Studios for Women's Art in Lansing, Michigan.

Joshua Gamson is Associate Professor of Sociology at Yale University, author of *Freaks Talk Back: Tabloid Talk Shows and Sexual Nonconformity* one of the Voice Literary Supplement's twenty-five favorite books of 1998, and winner of the Society for Cinema Studies Kovacs Award and the ASA Sociology of Culture Book Award. His research and teaching focus on the sociology of culture, social movements, participant-observation methodology and techniques, and the history, theory, and sociology of sexuality. Recent published work can be found in *Gender & Society, Sociological Forum, Social Problems,* the *Nation,* the *American Prospect, Tikkun,* and the *Utne Reader.*

Todd Gitlin is one of America's best known cultural critics and the author of widely admired books, including *The Sixties: Years of Hope, Days of Rage* (praised by the *New York Times* as "required reading for anyone who wants to grasp the youthful spirit of the time") and *The Twilight of Common Dreams: Why Amer-*

ica Is Wracked by Cultural Wars. He is a professor in the departments of Culture and Communication, Journalism, and Sociology at New York University, as well as a novelist (*Sacrifice*), a contributor to many periodicals, and a lecturer in the United States and abroad.

Liza Grandia is a graduate student in Anthropology at the University of California-Berkeley. She graduated from Yale University with a B.A. and honors in Women's Studies. Her prize-winning senior thesis "From Dawn 'Til Dawn: Valuing Women's Work in the Peten, Guatemala" focused on the role of women in sustainable development in the changing global economy. She has worked with Conservation International in a Guatemala program and was awarded a Fulbright to return to the Peten to research the socioeconomic and cultural factors that influence women's fertility decisions. She was a leader of the international youth caucus at the U.N.'s Fourth World Conference on Women in Beijing.

June Jordan is a professor at the University of California, Berkeley and a renowned poet and speaker. She has authored five children's books, a novel, three plays, four books of political essays, and five books of poetry, the most recent titled *Poetry for the People: A Blueprint for the Revolution.* Her honors include a Rockefeller Foundation Grant, the National Association of Black Journalists Award, and fellowships from the Massachusetts Council on the Arts, the National Endowment for the Arts, and the New York Foundation for the Arts.

L. A. Kauffman is writing *Direct Action: Radicalism in Our Time,* a history of U.S. activism since 1970. A longtime radical journalist and organizer, she is active in a number of New York City direct action campaigns, and is founder/author of *Free Radical: A Chronicle of the New Unrest,* a free cyber column (www.free-radical/org). Her work has appeared in the *Village Voice,* the *Nation,* the *Progressive, Spin, Mother Jones, Salon.com,* and numerous other publications.

Bonnie Sherr Klein is a successful feminist filmmaker who's most-known works include *Not a Love Story: A Film About Pornography* and *Speaking Our Peace* (both produced through the National Film Board of Canada). She lost much of her mobility when she was struck down in her mid-40s by a catastrophic brain-stem stroke. *Mile Zero,* a documentary about four teenagers organizing against nuclear arms, was finished after she became disabled.

Robin Leidner is Associate Professor of Sociology at the University of Pennsylvania. She is the author of *Fast Food, Fast Talk: Service Work and the Routinization of Everyday Life* (University of California Press 1993) and of several articles on feminist organizations, work, and gender. She is currently researching parents' responses to advice and information on child rearing.

Audre Lorde, who passed away in 1992 after a long battle with breast cancer, grew up in the West Indian community of Harlem in the 1930s, the daughter of immigrants from Grenada. She attended Hunter College (later becoming Professor of English there), ventured to the American expatriate community in Mexico, and participated in the Greenwich Village scene of the early 1950s. She is a major figure in the lesbian and feminist movements. Among her works are *Sister Outsider; Zami: A New Spelling of My Name; Uses of the Erotic; Chosen Poems Old and New; The Black Unicorn,* and *From a Land Where Other People Live.*

Daphne Patai is Professor of Women's Studies and of Portuguese at the University of Massachusetts at Amherst. She is author and editor of numerous books, including those on Brazilian women, British women writers, Edward Bellamy's *Looking Backward,* and the George Orwell mystique of male ideology. She is coeditor with Sherna Berger Gluck of *Women's Words: The Feminist Practice of Oral History* (1991), and coauthor with Noretta Koertge of *Professing Feminism: Cautionary Tales from the Strange World of Women's Studies* (1994).

Rosa María Pegueros has a long record of activism with the women's movement, as well as with other peace and justice movements. She has served as the Action Coordinator for California NOW Foundation; a member of the National NOW Committee to Combat Racism; the West Coast organizer for the Great Peace March, and the State President of Californians for a Fair Share. She was the first coordinator of Programs for the Homeless for the City of West Hollywood. She holds a J.D. from the People's College of Law, as well as M.A. and Ph.D. degrees in Latin American History from UCLA. Currently, she is a professor of Latin American history and Women's Studies at the University of Rhode Island and continues her activism with the American Association of University Professors.

Ruth Perry is Professor of Literature and Women's Studies at MIT. She is the founder of the Women's Studies Program and has been actively involved with it since 1984. Her research focuses on eighteenth-century English literature and culture, and the influence of gender on the production of art. She is the author of four books and dozens of articles, has written on canonical figures such as Pope, Sterne, Richardson, Austen, and Hawthorne, as well as contemporary women writers such as Grace Paley and Mary Gordon.

Shane Phelan is Director of Women Studies and Associate Professor of Political Science at the University of New Mexico. She is the author of several books, including *Identity Politics: Lesbian Feminism and the Limits of Community,* and the forthcoming *Sexual Strangers: Lesbians, Gays, and Citizenship.* She is the editor of the Queer Politics, Queer Theories series at Temple University Press, and a sought-out speaker for women's studies conferences.

Minnie Bruce Pratt was educated at the University of Alabama, Tuscaloosa and the University of North Carolina, Chapel Hill, but feels her real education was gained through her grassroots organizing with women in the army-base town of Fayetteville, North Carolina, and through teaching at historically Black universities. She has written three volumes of poetry, *The Sound of One Fork, We Say We Love Each Other,* and *Crime against Nature,* which won the 1989 Lamont Poetry Prize, the 1991 American Library Association Gay and Lesbian Book Award for Literature, and was nominated for a Pulitzer Prize in poetry. She is a former member of the editorial collective of *Feminary: A Feminist Journal for the South, Emphasizing Lesbian Visions,* the coauthor with Elly Bulkin and Barbara Smith, of *Yours in Struggle: Three Feminist Perspectives on Anti-Semitism and Racism.* She has been granted a creative writing fellowship in poetry by the National Endowment for the Arts.

Carol Queen has been featured in articles on the new bisexuality, sex-positive feminism, and lesbian sex in *Elle, Vogue, Ms., Penthouse, Hustler,* and other magazines. She is a regular columnist for the East Bay Express. She is the author of *The Leather Daddy and the Femme* (1998), *Real Live Nude Girl: The Chronicles of Sex-Positive Culture* (1997), and *Exhibitionism for the Shy* (1995). She lives in San Francisco, is a worker/owner at Good Vibrations, and recently received a doctorate in sexology.

rubina ramji is a part-time professor in the Department of Classics and Religious Studies at the University of Ottawa, where she is currently completing her doctorate. Her research focuses on the portrayal of religion, specifically women in Islam, within the mass media. She is cochair of the Religion, Film and Visual Culture Group for the American Academy of Religion. Her publications include "Building Community Word by Word: Religion in the Virtual World," in *God in the Details: American Religion in Everyday Life;* and "Executive Decision: Just Another Hijacking Thriller?" in *Islam in America.*

Adrienne Rich has, since the selection of her first volume by W. H. Auden for the Yale Series of Younger Poets in 1951, continually broken new ground, moving from closed forms to a feminist poetics. She has written seven books of poetry and has had many other books and articles published. Her most famous works include *Of Woman Born: Motherhood as Experience and Institution; On Lies, Secrets and Silence; Blood, Bread, and Poetry; and What Is Found There: Notebooks on Poetry and Politics.* Her work has received many awards, including the Ruth Lilly Prize, the Los Angeles Times Book Award, the Lambda Literary Award, the Poets' Prize, the Lenore Marshall/Nation Award, a MacArthur Fellowship, and the Dorothea Tanning Prize.

Leila J. Rupp teaches women's history, world history, and the history of same-sex sexuality at Ohio State University. She is author of *Mobilizing Women for War: German and American Propaganda, 1939–1945* (1978), *Worlds of Women: The Making of an International Women's Movement* (1997), and *A Desired Past: A Short History of Same-Sex Love in America* (1999); and coauthor with Verta Taylor of *Survival in the Doldrums: The American Women's Rights Movement, 1945 to the 1960s* (1987). She is also the editor of the *Journal of Women's History.*

Barbara Ryan is Professor of Sociology and Director of Women's Studies at Widener University. She has published in various journals and presented papers at numerous international conferences. She is author of two books, *Feminism and the Women's Movement: Dynamics of Change in Social Movement Ideology and*

Activism (1992) and *The Women's Movement: References and Resources* (1996). In 1998 she was a Fulbright Scholar in India, and in 2000 she was a presenter at a symposium in Havana, Cuba, "The State of Social and Economic Thought: Marxist, Third World, and Feminist Perspectives." She is currently working on a biography of Alice Paul.

Priscilla Sears has taught at Dartmouth for twenty-three years in the English Department and for Women's Studies. She has two books, *A Pillar of Fire to Follow: American Indian Dramas* and *Unheard Of: A Collection of Essays* (edited). In addition she has published poems, short stories, and professional papers; and has won a teaching award as Woman Scholar of the Year from Delta Kappa Gamma Society International. For the past four years she has been working for women's organizations in Bosnia, and has previously given lecture tours in Poland, Lithuania, Estonia, and the People's Republic of China.

kristin severson graduated with an M.A. in Women's Studies and Liberal Arts with a concentration in feminist ethics from George Washington University in 1997. She was a collective member of *off our backs: a feminist newsjournal* from 1997 to 1998. She is currently a doctoral student in the Philosophy Department at Duquesne University. Her interests include postmodern ethics, psychoanalysis, and contemporary French feminist theory. Her master's thesis was titled *Feminist Postmodern Moral Authority: A Lesbian Mormon Case Study.*

Sonia Shah is an editor at South End Press and the daughter of immigrants from India. She has cofounded a South Asian women's group in Boston, and her writings have appeared in *Sojourner; In These Times; Gay Community News,* and other anthologies. She was formerly managing editor of *Nuclear Times* magazine.

Barbara Smith is an author and independent scholar who has played a groundbreaking role in opening up a national cultural and political dialogue about the interactions of race, class, sexuality, and gender. She has edited three major collections about Black women, including *All the Women Are White, All the Blacks Are Men, but Some of Us Are Brave: Black Women's Studies,* with Gloria T. Hull and Patricia Bell Scott (1982), and *Home Girls: A Black Feminist Anthology* (1983, re-released 2000). She is a coauthor of *Yours in Struggle: Three Feminist Perspectives on Anti-Semitism and Racism* (1984) and general editor of *The Reader's Companion to U.S. Women's History* (1998). Her newest book is *The Truth That Never Hurts: Writings on Race, Gender, and Freedom* (1998).

victoria stanhope graduated with an M.A. in Women's Studies and Public Policy from George Washington University in 1993. She has been a collective member of *off our backs: a feminist newsjournal* since 1996 and has written extensively on political and cultural issues. She has also been an advocate in the area of mental health and education policy, and is currently pursuing a master's degree in Social Work at the University of Pittsburgh. Her publications include *Pathways* to Tolerance: Student Diversity and Behavioral Interventions *and* Creating a Safe School Environment.

Arlene Stein is Associate Professor of Sociology at Rutgers University. She is interested in intersections between cultural politics, gender, and sexuality. Her publications include *Sex and Sensibility: Stories of a Lesbian Generation* (1997) and an edited book, *Sisters, Sexperts, Queers: Beyond the Lesbian Nation* (1989). Her most recent book is *The Stranger Next Door: The Story of a Small Community's Battle over Sex, Faith, and Civil Rights* (2001).

Rebecca Walker has written for or been featured in stories in the *New York Times,* the *Chicago Times, Harper's Bazaar, Elle, Esquire,* and *U.S. News & World Report.* She has appeared on CNN, MTV, and Charlie Rose, among others. She is founder of Third Wave Direct Action Foundation, a national nonprofit organization devoted to cultivating young women's leadership and activism.

Index